YOUTH VIOLENCE, CRIME, AND GANGS
CHILDREN AT RISK

ISSN 1548-8020

YOUTH VIOLENCE, CRIME, AND GANGS

CHILDREN AT RISK

Kathleen Edgar

INFORMATION PLUS® REFERENCE SERIES
Formerly published by Information Plus, Wylie, Texas

THOMSON
GALE

Detroit • New York • San Francisco • San Diego • New Haven, Conn. • Waterville, Maine • London • Munich

Youth Violence, Crime, and Gangs: Children at Risk

Kathleen Edgar

Project Editor
Ellice Engdahl

Editorial
Beverly Baer, Paula Cutcher-Jackson, Pamela A. Dear, Debra Kirby, Prindle LaBarge, Elizabeth

Manar, Kathleen Meek, Charles B. Montney, Heather Price

Permissions
Margaret Abendroth, William Sampson, Sheila Spencer

Composition and Electronic Prepress
Evi Seoud

Manufacturing
Keith Helmling

LIBRARY OF CONGRESS CATALOGING-IN-PUBLICATION DATA

ISBN 0-7876-5103-6 (set)
ISBN 0-7876-9106-2
ISSN 1548-8020

Printed in the United States of America
10 9 8 7 6 5 4 3 2 1

TABLE OF CONTENTS

CHAPTER 1

Youth violence and crime have a long history in the United States. This chapter introduces readers to the subject and provides various examples of youthful offenders from the nineteenth century to the present. Included are discussions of Billy the Kid, Willie Bosket, Charles Starkweather, Caril Ann Fugate, and Michael Carneal, among others. The chapter also delves into violence at school, including a look at violence during desegregation, anti-war protests, and the more recent spree of school shootings.

CHAPTER 2

Although certain conditions increase the risk of a youth turning to violence and/or crime, the factors can differ considerably between individuals. To help the reader gain perspective on the plethora of issues facing today's youth, this chapter provides a brief overview of general statistics, including population trends, living arrangements, child care, poverty, abuse and neglect, education, health, attitudes toward drugs and alcohol, and teen pregnancy.

CHAPTER 3

Youth violence and crime have declined since the mid-1990s but are still committed in large numbers. This chapter presents information based on the Federal Bureau of Investigation's Uniform Crime Reports and the Bureau of Justice Statistics' National Crime Victimization Survey. Historical trends are discussed leading up to the most recent reports pertaining to homicide, suicide, rape, assault, robbery, burglary, larceny-theft, and motor vehicle theft perpetrated by and against youth. Also included are sections devoted to youth committing bank robberies, sniper attacks, and bombings as well as those involved in killing law enforcement officers and those engaged in computer hacking.

CHAPTER 4

Are students safe at school? This chapter focuses on a variety of issues pertaining to violence and crime at school, including homicides, suicides, and physical attacks and threats aimed at students, and in some cases, teachers. The time of day when most crimes occur is also discussed as is the fear and avoidance some students experience. The prevalence of drugs and weapons at schools is revealed, including a detailed section on the Columbine High School shooting in 1999. School safety issues are featured, including the No Child Left Behind Act's notion of "persistently dangerous schools" and how it may impact the number of crimes reported to authorities.

CHAPTER 5

From the evolution of youth gangs to the consequences of being involved in gang activity, this chapter presents information on the characteristics of gang members and gangs in general. Included are statistics from the National Youth Gang Survey as well as sections devoted to the gender, age, race, and stereotypes associated with gang membership. Also featured are segments on gang slang, graffiti, colors, hand signs, and initiations. In addition, gang-related activities in school are discussed.

CHAPTER 6

Charting the rise of the juvenile justice system in the United States, this chapter continues on to cover the growing trend of sentencing juvenile perpetrators of serious crimes as adults. Arrest trends are presented based on age groups, gender, and race, followed by information on the disposition of those being detained. Also included are statistics on the number of youthful offenders in prison or jail, and those on death row as a result of crimes committed when they were juveniles. The topics of residential placement as well as overcrowding of those being confined are also discussed.

CHAPTER 7

Topics receiving significant national attention are presented in this chapter, including hate crimes, bullies and bullying, hazing, youth and guns, and juveniles and the death penalty. Sections address hate at school, hate crime perpetrators, arson, hate as terrorism, the characteristics of both bullies and their victims, the effects of being victimized, cyber-bullying, anti-bullying programs being tried at schools, and hazings that turn violent. Also presented is information on gun-related suicides, homicides, and crimes, as well as a history of juveniles and the death penalty.

CHAPTER 8

The problem of youth violence and crime has led to the creation of numerous programs aimed at reducing such occurrences. This chapter discusses various methods, including school, police, community, and religious programs designed to help youth. Also discussed is peer and adult mentoring as well as the idea of holding parents responsible for their children's crimes and the role that curfews play in curbing youth crime.

PREFACE

Youth Violence, Crime, and Gangs: Children at Risk is one of the latest volumes in the Information Plus Reference Series. The purpose of each volume of the series is to present the latest facts on a topic of pressing concern in modern American life. These topics include today's most controversial and most studied social issues: abortion, capital punishment, care for the elderly, crime, health care, the environment, immigration, minorities, social welfare, women, youth, and many more. Although written especially for the high school and undergraduate student, this series is an excellent resource for anyone in need of factual information on current affairs.

By presenting the facts, it is Thomson Gale's intention to provide its readers with everything they need to reach an informed opinion on current issues. To that end, there is a particular emphasis in this series on the presentation of scientific studies, surveys, and statistics. These data are generally presented in the form of tables, charts, and other graphics placed within the text of each book. Every graphic is directly referred to and carefully explained in the text. The source of each graphic is presented within the graphic itself. The data used in these graphics are drawn from the most reputable and reliable sources, in particular from the various branches of the U.S. government and from major independent polling organizations. Every effort has been made to secure the most recent information available. The reader should bear in mind that many major studies take years to conduct, and that additional years often pass before the data from these studies are made available to the public. Therefore, in many cases the most recent information available in 2004 dated from 2001 or 2002. Older statistics are sometimes presented as well if they are of particular interest and no more recent information exists.

Although statistics are a major focus of the Information Plus Reference Series, they are by no means its only content. Each book also presents the widely held positions and important ideas that shape how the book's subject is discussed in the United States. These positions are explained in detail and, where possible, in the words of their proponents. Some of the other material to be found in these books includes: historical background; descriptions of major events related to the subject; relevant laws and court cases; and examples of how these issues play out in American life. Some books also feature primary documents or have pro and con debate sections giving the words and opinions of prominent Americans on both sides of a controversial topic. All material is presented in an even-handed and unbiased manner; the reader will never be encouraged to accept one view of an issue over another.

HOW TO USE THIS BOOK

The issues of youth violence, crime, and gangs are of major concern to politicians, law enforcement, and citizens alike. Although the level of youth crime and violence has decreased significantly since the late 1980s/early 1990s, such crimes still occur in great numbers and have a major impact not only on the victims but on the youthful perpetrators as well. Such incidents have also affected U.S. schools, prompting administrators, parents, and even students themselves to find ways to improve safety. So how prevalent is youth crime and violence in the United States today? What types of crimes are youth most likely to commit? What impact do crime and violence have on school safety and on the students themselves? Do students feel safe at school or traveling to and from school? Are school shootings as widespread as one might think based on media reports? What is the nature of gangs in America? What are tagging, "flying the colors," and "clicking in"? What message does gang-related graffiti carry? How many youths are arrested, in prison, and even on death row? And what programs are being tried and tested to reduce youth- and gang-related crime and violence? These and other basic questions are discussed in this volume.

Youth Violence, Crime, and Gangs: Children at Risk consists of eight chapters and three appendices. Each of the chapters is devoted to a particular aspect of youth crime in the United States. For a summary of the information covered in each chapter, please see the synopses provided in the Table of Contents at the front of the book. Chapters generally begin with an overview of the basic facts and background information on the chapter's topic, then proceed to examine subtopics of particular interest. For example, Chapter 7, A Culture of Violence?: Current Topics of Special Interest, begins with a discussion of the types of crimes that have received a lot of attention in recent years. It begins by focusing on hate crimes, including information about the perpetrators of hate as well as hate at school. Then the chapter explores bullies and bullying, including the common traits of those who bully and their victims. It also delves into the concept of cyberbullying, which includes harassment via cell phones and the Internet. A discussion of hazing follows, then a look at guns and youth. The chapter concludes with a section on juveniles and the death penalty, including the controversy surrounding whether youth should be tried as adults and sentenced to death row. Readers can find their way through a chapter by looking for the section and subsection headings, which are clearly set off from the text. They can also refer to the book's extensive index if they already know what they are looking for.

Statistical Information

The tables and figures featured throughout *Youth Violence, Crime, and Gangs: Children at Risk* will be of particular use to the reader in learning about this issue. These tables and figures represent an extensive collection of the most recent and important statistics on youth crime and related issues—for example, graphics in the book cover the percentage of students (12–18) who report being afraid or bullied at school; the number of victimizations, arrests, homicides, and nonfatal crimes perpetrated by youth, including attacks or threats made against teachers; and arsons and school shootings committed by young offenders. Thomson Gale believes that making this information available to the reader is the most important way in which we fulfill the goal of this book: to help readers to understand the issues and controversies surrounding youth violence, crime, and gangs in the United States and to reach their own conclusions.

Each table or figure has a unique identifier appearing above it for ease of identification and reference. Titles for the tables and figures explain their purpose. At the end of each table or figure, the original source of the data is provided.

In order to help readers understand these often complicated statistics, all tables and figures are explained in the text. References in the text direct the reader to the relevant statistics. Furthermore, the contents of all tables and figures are fully indexed. Please see the opening section of the index at the back of this volume for a description of how to find tables and figures within it.

Appendices

In addition to the main body text and images, *Youth Violence, Crime, and Gangs: Children at Risk* has three appendices. The first is the Important Names and Addresses directory. Here the reader will find contact information for a number of government and private organizations that can provide further information on youth crime in the United States. The second appendix is the Resources section, which can also assist the reader in conducting his or her own research. In this section, the author and editors of *Youth Violence, Crime, and Gangs: Children at Risk* describe some of the sources that were most useful during the compilation of this book. The final appendix is the detailed Index, which facilitates reader access to specific topics in this book.

ADVISORY BOARD CONTRIBUTIONS

The staff of Information Plus would like to extend their heartfelt appreciation to the Information Plus Advisory Board. This dedicated group of media professionals provides feedback on the series on an ongoing basis. Their comments allow the editorial staff who work on the project to make the series better and more user-friendly. Our top priority is to produce the highest-quality and most useful books possible, and the Advisory Board's contributions to this process are invaluable.

The members of the Information Plus Advisory Board are:

- Kathleen R. Bonn, Librarian, Newbury Park High School, Newbury Park, California
- Madelyn Garner, Librarian, San Jacinto College—North Campus, Houston, Texas
- Anne Oxenrider, Media Specialist, Dundee High School, Dundee, Michigan
- Charles R. Rodgers, Director of Libraries, Pasco-Hernando Community College, Dade City, Florida
- James N. Zitzelsberger, Library Media Department Chairman, Oshkosh West High School, Oshkosh, Wisconsin

COMMENTS AND SUGGESTIONS

The editors of the Information Plus Reference Series welcome your feedback on *Youth Violence, Crime, and Gangs: Children at Risk*. Please direct all correspondence to:

Editors
Information Plus Reference Series
27500 Drake Rd.
Farmington Hills, MI 48331-3535

ACKNOWLEDGMENTS

The editors wish to thank the copyright holders of material included in this volume and the permissions managers of many book and magazine publishing companies for assisting us in securing reproduction rights. We are also grateful to the staffs of the Detroit Public Library, the Library of Congress, the University of Detroit Mercy Library, Wayne State University Purdy/Kresge Library Complex, and the University of Michigan Libraries for making these sources available to us.

Following is a list of the copyright holders who have granted us permission to reproduce material in Youth Violence, Crime, and Gangs: Children at Risk. *Every effort has been made to trace copyright, but if omissions have been made, please let us know.*

For more detailed source citations, please see the sources listed under each individual table and figure.

Bureau of Alcohol, Tobacco, and Firearms: Table 3.17, Figure 7.4

Centers for Disease Control and Prevention: Table 2.19, Table 2.20, Table 2.21, Table 2.24, Table 3.8, Table 4.4, Table 4.6

Centers for Disease Control and Prevention, National Center for Health Statistics, National Vital Statistics System: Table 3.2, Table 3.3

Child Trends, Inc.: Figure 2.7, Table 2.22, Table 2.23

Executive Office of the President, Office of National Drug Control Policy: Table 3.19, Table 4.9

Federal Bureau of Investigation: Table 3.1, Table 3.4, Table 3.5, Table 3.7, Table 3.13, Table 3.14, Table 3.15, Table 3.16, Table 3.18, Table 6.1, Table 6.2, Table 6.3, Table 6.4, Table 6.5, Table 7.1, Table 7.2, Table 7.3, Table 7.4, Table 7.5

Federal Interagency Forum on Child and Family Statistics: Figure 2.2, Table 2.1, Table 2.2, Table 2.3, Table 2.4, Table 2.5, Table 2.6, Table 2.7, Table 2.9

Gale Group: Table 4.13, Figure 6.2, Table 7.7

National Church Arson Task Force: Figure 7.2

National Institute on Drug Abuse: Figure 2.5, Figure 2.6, Table 2.17, Table 2.18

U.S. Department of Agriculture, Center for Nutrition Policy and Promotion: Table 2.8

U.S. Department of Education, Institute of Education Sciences, National Center for Education Statistics: Figure 2.1, Table 2.10, Table 2.11, Table 2.12, Table 2.13, Table 2.14, Table 2.15, Table 2.16, Figure 4.4, Figure 4.5, Table 4.14, Table 4.15, Table 5.3, Figure 7.3

U.S. Department of Education, Institute of Education Sciences, National Center for Education Statistics, and U.S. Department of Justice, Office of Justice Programs, Bureau of Justice Statistics: Figure 2.3, Figure 2.4, Figure 4.1, Figure 4.2, Figure 4.3, Figure 4.6, Figure 4.7, Figure 4.8, Figure 4.9, Table 4.1, Table 4.2, Table 4.3, Table 4.5, Table 4.7, Table 4.8, Table 4.10, Table 4.12, Figure 5.3, Figure 7.1, Table 7.6, Table 7.8

U.S. Department of Health and Human Services, Administration for Children and Families, Administration on Children, Youth and Families, Children's Bureau: Figure 3.8

U.S. Department of Health and Human Services, Office of the Surgeon General: Table 3.21

U.S. Department of Justice, Office of Justice Programs, Bureau of Justice Assistance: Table 6.8

U.S. Department of Justice, Office of Justice Programs, Bureau of Justice Statistics: Figure 3.4, Figure 3.5, Table 3.9, Table 3.10, Table 3.11, Table 3.12, Table 3.20, Figure 6.1, Table 6.6, Table 6.7, Table 6.9, Table 6.10, Table 6.11, Table 6.12, Table 7.10

U.S. Department of Justice, Office of Justice Programs, National Institute of Justice: Table 4.11

U.S. Department of Justice, Office of Justice Programs, Office of Juvenile Justice and Delinquency Prevention: Figure 3.1, Figure 3.2, Figure 3.3, Figure 3.6, Figure 3.7, Table 3.6, Figure 5.1, Figure 5.2, Table 5.1, Table 5.2, Table 6.13, Table 6.14, Table 6.15

Victor L. Streib, Ohio Northern University, Claude W. Pettit College of Law: Table 7.9

CHAPTER 1

YOUTH CRIME AND VIOLENCE:
PAST, PRESENT, AND FUTURE

In the early 2000s newspapers and newscasts throughout the country told gruesome stories of violent acts committed by youth in the United States. Such violence is common throughout the country, whether in large metropolitan cities, in the suburbs, or in rural areas. For some youth, violence is a way of life—a way to survive life on the streets. For others, it is a rite of passage, whether it is done to prove one's alleged worthiness for gang membership, to show one's so-called strength or toughness, or to humiliate a newer student through a brutal hazing. For still others, it is said to be an act of self-defense, for years of being bullied, teased, or harassed. And for some, it appears to be random—a way to take out one's frustrations in life or to see what it feels like to hurt someone else. Whatever the reasons, violence among America's youth is of great concern to both politicians and citizens alike.

While violent crime in general has decreased substantially since the mid-1990s, such actions by youthful offenders still occur in great numbers. The prevalence of such crimes is the subject of numerous studies by government entities, nonprofit agencies, police organizations, religious groups, and even school students themselves. As such groups study the problem of youth violence, they are constantly provided with new cases. And as new examples occur, the media quickly rush to the scene to investigate and report the details.

All of the coverage devoted to youth violence makes some people wonder if the attention is contributing to further acts of aggression. For example, after two students at Columbine High School in Littleton, Colorado, went on a shooting rampage in April 1999 and killed 12 students and one teacher before killing themselves, a rash of violent incidents erupted at schools throughout the country. Were these other incidents attempts to copycat the violence so other student offenders could make a name for themselves? Or does the problem of youth violence go

deeper than that? Researchers are still trying to answer such questions.

Researchers are constantly involved in studies looking at factors that might push juveniles and older youths toward violence, crime, and membership in gangs. (For the purposes of this book, a youth is defined as someone under age 20, whereas a juvenile is someone under age 18. Some studies extend the youth range, however, to age 24.) They study the impact of sociological factors, such as home environment (living conditions, parents' income and education levels, how many parents/grandparents/siblings are present in the home); highest education level attained (dropouts, those still in school, graduates); geographic location; school environment/conditions; health. Ultimately, by understanding what factors create youthful criminals, citizens may help the troubled youth avoid lives of crime.

In addition to violent crime, youth also commit significant amounts of larceny-theft, vandalism, and arson. Many continue to be arrested on drug abuse and alcohol-related charges. (Statistics for such crimes are explained in greater detail later in this book.) According to the Federal Bureau of Investigation (FBI), in 2002 juveniles represented 16.5 percent of all arrests nationwide. However, juvenile arrests dropped 3 percent from 2001 to 2002.

Some citizens believe that tougher legislation is responsible for the decline in violent crime and the overall drop in arrests. In response to a surge of youth violence in the early 1990s, many states adopted legislation that allowed more juveniles to be tried as adults for serious crimes. As such, potential young criminals might face life in jail if tried as adults. Other citizens laud the efforts of law enforcement officers for working with youth, especially in schools and community-oriented programs, and helping them build lives free of crime.

Although the 1,393,752 arrests of juveniles in 2002 represents a 10.9 percent decrease since 1993, according to FBI statistics, the problem of youth violence, crime, and gangs continues to draw much concern and debate. The issue, however, is not new to the United States. The country has a long history of violent and troubled youth. At the same time, it also has a fascination with such youths, as evidenced in the amount of attention and press devoted to them.

Among the reasons that the public follows stories of violent youth is that people in general have a hard time believing that seemingly innocent children can resort to such acts of brutality. For each of the crimes receiving widespread media attention, hundreds do not receive much, if any, press. Still, a review of cases making national news can provide insight into the nature of youth crimes and violence as well as how such acts have evolved over time. The section that follows takes a look at some selected examples of violent youth from the late nineteenth century through today.

VIOLENT YOUTH: SELECTED EXAMPLES IN U.S. HISTORY

Jesse Pomeroy (aka "The Boston Boy-fiend")

During the nineteenth century, most people never imagined that juveniles were capable of becoming serial killers. The case of Jesse Pomeroy in 1870s' Boston, however, proved it could happen. Pomeroy's violence remained unchecked for several years as he sexually tortured and mutilated other young boys. Signs of Pomeroy's propensity for violence surfaced early in his youth when he began to torture animals. He then turned his attention toward other children, beginning when he was about 11 or 12 years of age.

A boy with a physically deformed eye, Pomeroy came from a poor family and had been abused himself. His reign of terror ended briefly in 1874 when he was arrested for murder at age 14. His deeds, considered by the public to be unthinkable from a boy so young, earned him the nickname "The Boston Boy-fiend." During that era, politicians and the media often used such nicknames to grab the public's attention. (Such monikers continue even today although they are usually less sensational.)

In Pomeroy's time, people generally believed that juveniles could be rehabilitated, thus the youth was sent to reform school. After a little more than a year, Pomeroy convinced authorities that he had reformed and his release was granted. But Pomeroy's violent tendencies soon resurfaced and he killed a young girl shortly after his release. He was not caught initially and went on to kill a young boy. When questioned by police about the murders, Pomeroy seemed indifferent. Ultimately, he was sentenced to death, but the public demanded that a boy so young not be killed. Instead, Pomeroy was sent to prison for life and placed into solitary confinement. He remained in the prison system until he died in 1932.

William H. Bonney Jr. (aka "Billy the Kid")

One of the most notorious outlaws of the Old West, William H. Bonney Jr. (aka "Billy the Kid") was actually born in New York City around 1859. After moving west with his family, young Bonney began a life of lawlessness and earned a reputation as a hardened killer. Although the exact number of murders he committed is unknown, it is believed he killed between 20 and 30 men during his short life.

While living in New Mexico and other places in the American Southwest, Bonney often rode with gangs. He was frequently hunted by lawmen, including Sheriff Pat Garrett. The subject of books and debate then and today, Bonney's exploits included a famous jailbreak in April 1881. At that time, he was being held in the Lincoln County Courthouse jail in New Mexico territory, awaiting death by hanging for murder. Rather than wait to be hanged, he plotted an escape. As he attempted to flee, he shot and killed one deputy. As a second deputy ran to warn others of the pending escape, Billy shot him as well.

Bonney was just 21 years old when Sheriff Pat Garrett caught up with him in Fort Sumner, New Mexico, in July of that year and killed him. Today, the West contains many references to the gunfighter in museums and historical markers. To some, Billy was a hero because some of his deeds were against men out to monopolize business dealings in the West. To others, he was a cold-blooded killer who deserved his fate.

His demise, however, remains the subject of debate. Bonney was known to have been friends with Garrett earlier in his life. Some say that Billy the Kid's death was faked and he actually lived a long life. Even today, researchers are still investigating the life of one of America's most violent youths. As of early 2004 efforts were being considered to exhume the body of Bonney's mother to check her DNA against a man who claimed he was Billy the Kid when he died in 1950.

Leopold and Loeb

They wanted to plan and commit "the perfect crime," but teenagers Nathan Leopold and Richard Loeb did not succeed in their quest in 1924. The deeds of the two Chicago youth, both from prominent families, were described as a "thrill kill" because the pair picked a child at random to use in the commission of their crime.

After rehearsing their plan to kidnap a child for ransom and then kill their victim, Leopold and Loeb nabbed Bobby Franks, a 14-year-old cousin of Loeb. Since the would-be killers were familiar to Franks, he agreed to go with them and was subsequently murdered. The youths then mutilated the body so that police would have difficulty identifying the boy. However, Leopold inadvertently left a clue behind for police when he dropped his glasses near the scene of the crime.

Before long Leopold and Loeb both confessed to the murder. At the trial, they were represented by famous attorney Clarence Darrow. In the end, they both were sentenced to life in prison, even though their murder was clearly premeditated. Loeb never made it out of prison—he was killed by another inmate in the 1930s. However, Leopold gained his freedom in 1958 and relocated to Puerto Rico. He died in 1971 of natural causes.

Charles Starkweather and Caril Ann Fugate

Starkweather, 19, and Fugate, 14, were young lovers who shocked the nation when they embarked on a killing spree in Nebraska and Wyoming in January 1958. Modeling himself to look like rebel actor James Dean, Starkweather lived in Lincoln, Nebraska, where the killing spree began. Starkweather had fallen on hard times after losing his job as a garbage collector and being locked out of his home by his landlord for failing to pay rent. He and Fugate were also feeling the stress of their parents' disapproval regarding their relationship.

After killing a gas station attendant who refused to let him purchase a stuffed animal for Fugate on credit, Starkweather went to his girlfriend's house. With Fugate present, he killed her parents and baby stepsister. They then concealed Fugate's mother in the outhouse and then hid her stepfather and stepsister as well. After the murders, the couple relaxed and watched television. They managed to remain in the house for nearly a week, telling lies to anyone who inquired concerning the whereabouts of the family. When it appeared that the police would be coming to investigate, they fled by car.

The killing spree continued after Starkweather and Fugate left town. After murdering a family friend, they stole a car and killed the driver and passenger. Eventually, the duo returned to Lincoln and went to the home of an industrialist. Starkweather demanded that the businessman's wife cook him a meal—he was said to enjoy having the rich woman cook for him, her former garbage man. In the end, they murdered the industrialist, his wife, and the maid. After fleeing to Wyoming, the last killing occurred. When police unexpectedly arrived at the scene, Fugate ran to them claiming that Starkweather had been holding her against her will. Starkweather took off by car and a police chase began, sometimes exceeding speeds of more than 100 miles per hour.

Both offenders were charged with first-degree murder. Starkweather received the death sentence and was electrocuted in June of 1959. Due to her age, Fugate received life in prison. However, she was paroled in 1996. Like Billy the Kid, Starkweather also became a folk hero to some—a rebel who bucked the system. For many others, Starkweather's violent murder spree was anything but heroic. The story of Fugate and Starkweather has been fictionalized on film several times since the murders, most notably in *Badlands,* directed by Terence Malik, and *Natural Born Killers,* directed by Oliver Stone.

Willie Bosket

The deeds and attitudes of some criminals are considered so offensive that lawmakers create new legislation aimed at protecting society from similar actions and individuals. Young New Yorker Willie Bosket was one such criminal. The grandson of a convicted armed robber and the son of a convicted murderer, Bosket learned early in life that by being tough, he was given the respect he felt he deserved. By age 15, Bosket claimed he had committed more than 2,000 crimes. Although most of Bosket's crimes went undiscovered, his lawless behavior brought him to Family Court on occasion, beginning at age 9. Over the years, he had learned that if found guilty, he would be put in reform school and released after a short period of time.

In 1978 Bosket's behavior turned increasingly violent. He had bragged to others that he would become a murderer like his father, who had been locked away in prison since before Bosket's birth. (He had never met his father.) Soon Bosket found himself involved in a series of subway robberies and several murders. Eventually apprehended by police, Bosket believed that his young age was a factor in his favor. He showed no remorse and displayed arrogance in the court because he knew he could only be held until age 21 if convicted.

Bosket's demeanor angered the governor, other politicians, and the public. The end result was a new law permitting juveniles to be tried as adults beginning at age 13. Acknowledging the young criminal's role in creating the new legislation, it was nicknamed "the Willie Bosket Law." Bosket continued to commit acts of violence and eventually ended up in prison, where he later attacked several guards, nearly killing one. Such violence landed him in a special cell and with the reputation of being "the most violent criminal offender in New York State history, Hannibal Lecter some call him," according to David Gergen of *U.S. News & World Report.*

Michael Skakel

Sometimes crimes committed by juveniles go unpunished for many years. When this occurs and the accused has reached adulthood before he or she is apprehended, a decision must be made whether to try that individual as a juvenile or as an adult. Such is the case of Michael Skakel, a cousin of the prominent Kennedy family, who was arrested in 2000 for the 1975 murder of 15-year-old Martha Moxley. At the time of his arraignment, Skakel was 39 and stood accused of committing the murder when he was 15. A judge ruled that Skakel would be tried as an adult.

The Moxley murder occurred in a wealthy neighborhood in Greenwich, Connecticut, and had remained unsolved for more than 24 years. Skakel and his brother Thomas were suspects in the case, but no arrests were made until after the publication of several books about the case many years later. (Dominic Dunne, an author whose daughter was stalked and murdered by her ex-boyfriend, wrote one of those books; another was compiled by Mark Furman, an ex-Los Angeles Police Department detective who gained notoriety during the O.J. Simpson murder trial.)

Moxley's body was found bludgeoned to death with a golf club that was later matched to other clubs owned by the Skakel family. Besides the Skakels, others were investigated. For a time, the Skakel family cooperated with authorities. In later years, the Skakels hired private investigators to prove the brothers' innocence, but they ultimately found the brothers had told inconsistent stories about the night of the murder.

Debate has flourished about why it took police so long to arrest Skakel for the murder. Some critics believe the police were trying to cover up the murder because the suspect was from an important East Coast family. Others believe police in that area were unaccustomed to investigating such violent acts and mishandled the case. Still others, including Skakel himself, maintain his innocence. On June 7, 2002, Skakel was convicted of the murder. He received a prison sentence of 20 years to life. Still claiming Skakel's innocence, his attorneys were seeking an appeal as of early 2004.

Brenda Ann Spencer

Contrary to popular belief, teen violence is not limited to males, although boys account for the vast number of arrests for violent behavior. The case of Brenda Ann Spencer is proof that juvenile girls are capable of extreme violence as well. On January 29, 1979, 16-year-old Spencer opened fire from her family's house onto the Cleveland Elementary School playground across the street. She began shooting in the morning when some students were walking across the playground to the school, located near San Diego, California.

During the incident, Spencer killed the principal and a janitor and wounded eight students and one policeman before surrendering. Spencer held off police for more than six hours as they attempted to negotiate with her. Law enforcement personnel were able to cut off her line of fire by placing a truck between the Spencer house and the school. Authorities discovered that she was using a rifle that was given to her as a gift. When talking to a reporter during the incident, she was asked what prompted her violent rampage. Spencer responded with: "I don't like Mondays. This livens up the day." She was also reported to have said the incident was "like shooting ducks in a pond."

Spencer received a sentence of 25 years to life in prison after pleading guilty. She later claimed that various authorities conspired against her and tricked her into pleading guilty. The lack of remorse displayed in her words formed the basis of the song "I Don't Like Mondays" by the band The Boomtown Rats. Since that time, other bands have written songs about student violence, among them Pearl Jam with the song "Jeremy."

Erik and Lyle Menendez

One of the most highly publicized cases of young killers in the last half of the twentieth century concerned brothers Erik and Lyle Menendez, who were 18 and 21 respectively during the commission of their crimes. On August 20, 1989, the pair conspired and murdered their wealthy parents, Jose and Mary Louise "Kitty" Menendez, with a shotgun. Attempting to draw suspicion away from themselves when police arrived on the scene, the brothers cried and acted emotional. They were eventually arrested in March of 1990 and ordered to stand trial.

When tried initially, the cases of both brothers ended with mistrials in 1994 when each of their juries could not reach consensus. In court, the brothers had claimed that their parents abused them physically and psychologically, and that they killed their parents in self-defense. They alleged that such treatment left them emotionally scarred. Prosecutors, however, asserted that the brothers ended their parents' lives over monetary issues. Jose Menendez, they said, had planned to alter his will, disinheriting his sons, shortly before the murder.

When retried together, the brothers were eventually convicted of first-degree murder "with special circumstances" in 1996. Upon the jury's recommendation, the brothers were sentenced to life in prison without the possibility of parole. The prosecution had asked for the death sentence to be imposed. It was the brothers' young age that, according to some observers, kept the pair off death row for the murders. When discussing the sentencing, Prosecutor David Conn told reporters that the jury was unable to sentence the brothers to death due to their age.

The case of the Menendez brothers drew considerable attention because the people involved were very wealthy. The brothers lived with their parents in Beverly Hills, California, a location known for its affluent lifestyle. Jose, an entertainment executive, and Kitty lived in a mansion valued at more than $13 million. Many people imagine that the rich have everything they need, or at least have the money to buy the necessities in life.

Melissa Drexler

Teen violence manifests itself in many different ways. Sometimes teens who have not exhibited violent tendencies panic in stressful situations and do something uncharacteristically harmful. The case of Melissa Drexler falls under this category. In 1997 Drexler, a New Jersey high school student, hid her pregnancy from her parents and boyfriend and found herself in labor at her senior prom. She gave birth to a baby boy in a bathroom toilet stall.

Still hoping to keep the pregnancy secret, Drexler put her baby in a garbage bag, placed the baby in the trash, rejoined the dance, and ate a salad with her boyfriend. Her son eventually died of asphyxiation before being discovered by the banquet hall's maintenance staff.

Nicknamed "the Prom Mom" by the media, Drexler pled guilty to aggravated manslaughter charges. In court, she read a prepared statement acknowledging her crime, but did not explain it. She was given up to 15 years in prison for her act of infanticide.

Jessica Holtmeyer, Aaron Straw, and the Runaway Gang

Incidents of juvenile violence cause great distress in the communities where they occur. Lawmakers, police, and concerned citizens seek to understand what makes youth resort to violent crime. In some cases, young offenders can offer no reason for doing what they did. Sixteen-year-old Jessica Holtmeyer was one such teen. Holtmeyer, along with several other individuals, engaged in a brutal act of violence against Kimberly Jo Dotts, a 15-year-old learning-disabled acquaintance of theirs, in Clearfield, Pennsylvania, on May 10, 1998.

Holtmeyer was part of a group of teenagers who wanted to travel to Florida. Dubbed the "Runaway Gang," the youth had asked Dotts to accompany them. Dotts was eager to make new friends and joined the group as they waited for a ride to Florida later that day. However, the situation became tense when Holtmeyer and some of the others began to worry that Dotts might turn them in and ruin their plans. Holtmeyer and her then-fiancé, Aaron Straw, put a noose, constructed from a stolen clothesline, around Dotts' neck. The victim agreed, thinking it was part of an initiation into the group. Holtmeyer and Straw then hanged Dotts from a tree. The pair pulled on the rope more than once, but Dotts did not die immediately. As Dotts lay on the ground, Holtmeyer picked up a large rock and crushed the victim's skull. Other members of the group helped hide the body with brush, which remained undiscovered for more than a week.

Ultimately, 7 individuals, ranging in age from 14 to 24, were arrested for the crime. Four members of the gang were placed in juvenile detention facilities. The 24-year-old on the scene, who happened to be Dotts' cousin, received a sentence of 5 to 20 years. Holtmeyer, the first to be tried, was convicted of murder and other charges after less than three hours of deliberation. She was sentenced to life in prison without the possibility of parole. Straw was also convicted of murder and other charges after just 75 minutes of deliberation.

Lionel Tate

Is it fair and just to sentence a boy to life in prison without the possibility of parole for killing a family friend when he was just 12? That was the main controversy surrounding the case of Lionel Tate, a Florida youth, who claimed that he accidentally killed six-year-old Tiffany Eunick in 1999 while imitating some wrestling moves he saw on television. Tate, who weighed 166 pounds, was more than three times the size of Eunick (48 pounds) when the death occurred. The boy's lawyers argued that their client thought he could reenact wrestling moves and that no one would be hurt. Among the injuries Eunick sustained were broken ribs, a crushed skull, a lacerated liver, and other internal injuries.

Despite Tate's claims that the death was accidental, he was tried and convicted as an adult for first-degree murder. When sentenced in 2001, he was given life without parole, making him the youngest person to get such a sentence in Florida. Since that time, Florida's harsh laws regarding violent juvenile offenders have come under fire. Among the people stating that the Tate sentencing was too harsh were the deceased girl's mother and the prosecutor of the case.

In December 2003 an appeals court threw out Tate's conviction and ordered a new trial. The court called into question Tate's mental competency at the time of the trial. Earlier, following his conviction, Tate claimed that he did not take a plea agreement because he did not understand what the consequences would be if he was not acquitted in the case. According to Tate's lawyer, the boy was too young and immature to comprehend what was transpiring.

Fishtown Murder

Jason Sweeney's dreams of becoming a Navy Seal ended on May 30, 2003, when he was murdered allegedly by four of his friends and acquaintances. Sweeney, a 16-year-old from the Fishtown neighborhood of Philadelphia, Pennsylvania, had just cashed his paycheck before he headed out for a date with 15-year-old Justina Morley—a youth that he regarded as his girlfriend. According to confessions from two of the alleged killers, Morley was to lure Sweeney to a vacant field with the promise of sex. Once there, Morley's three accomplices, one of whom was Sweeney's best friend, would beat him and take the money.

Edward Batzig Jr., 16, Dominic Coia, 18, and Dominic's brother Nicholas Coia, 16, stand accused of helping Morley carry out the plan. As the boys, sporting latex gloves, repeatedly beat Sweeney with a hatchet, hammer, and brick, Morley watched Sweeney beg for his life. After beating in their victim's skull, according to participants' statements, the four took a moment for a group hug. Dominic Coia, as noted in newspaper reports, reportedly told police that after the gang took Sweeney's money, they "partied beyond redemption." They used Sweeney's $500 pay to purchase drugs.

Calling the crime "something out of the Dark Ages," Judge Seamus P. McCaffery ordered the teens to stand trial. As of January 2004, Dominic Coia awaited trial as an adult; he faces the death penalty if convicted. Sweeney's best friend Batzig and Nicholas Coia also face trial for murder and other charges, but prosecutors will not seek the death sentence. Since Morley, now dubbed the "Fishtown Femme Fatale," was only 15 at the time of the murder, prosecutors are unable to ask for the death penalty in her case per Pennsylvania law. Still, she will go to trial for murder, among other charges.

In their clients' defense, attorneys for the young offenders say that the teens listened to the Beatles' song "Helter Skelter" 42 times while planning the murder/robbery. The song was also said to have inspired Charles Manson's followers to commit murder in the late 1960s. Morley is said to be on a suicide watch at the facility where she is being held.

OTHER VIOLENT YOUTH

History is full of violent acts committed by juveniles throughout the world. The United Kingdom's Mary Flora Bell is one such example. At 11 years old she was found guilty of manslaughter in the deaths of two young boys in 1968. Nearly 30 years later, British nanny Louise Woodward, a teenager, was prosecuted for shaking a baby in her care so hard that his skull fractured and he died. In Colombia girls as young as 13 are trained for service in the Armed Revolutionary Forces group.

Newspaper headlines are full of tales of youth violence throughout the world. Whether in times of war, in a desperate quest to escape poverty, or just because they are bored, youth continue to commit acts of violence at high rates.

VIOLENCE AT SCHOOL

Violence has long been present at school. It has taken many forms—the nerdy kid being shoved against a locker for his lunch money; the awkward girl being bullied in gym class by the popular girls; the freshmen being humiliated by older students in hazing rituals; or kids deciding to meet behind the school after class to settle some score with a fistfight. Although school violence became increasingly more deadly in the 1990s due to school shootings, several prior incidents involving violence at school stand out in American history.

School Desegregation

Violence accompanied the desegregation of schools in the South during the 1950s and 1960s. Under segregation, whites and blacks could not legally attend the same schools. In the mid-1950s the U.S. Supreme Court ruled that such segregation was illegal and had to end. As integration of public schools began, the desegregation effort was often met with violence by parents, students, and other citizens who did not want African Americans attending school with white children.

In late September 1957 Little Rock Central High School in Arkansas was desegregated. Nine African American students, referred to as the "Little Rock 9," were slated to join the student body. It took them several tries to attend class at the school but they finally succeeded. During one of their attempts, they never made it into the school. They had arrived at the facility to find an angry mob waiting for them. As the crowd threw rocks, the Arkansas National Guard sent the new students away. On their next attempt, the nine entered the building without being noticed. When the crowd outside found out, violence ensued. The students were again sent home. But they persevered and returned the next day, under the protection of the U.S. Army. Ultimately, the teens braved racial slurs, death threats, and acts of violence to attend the formerly all-white school.

Similar hostility awaited six-year-old Ruby Bridges as she prepared to be the first African American to attend William Frantz Elementary School in New Orleans, Louisiana. As depicted in Norman Rockwell's painting "The Problem We All Live With," Bridges was escorted by four U.S. Marshals when she headed for class on November 14, 1960. Bridges admits that she did not recognize the extent of the rage being directed at her by the angry mob that formed outside the school. When the child entered the building, parents pulled their kids out of class. Because of the turmoil at the school, Bridges was not able to attend class until the next day. One teacher agreed to instruct Bridges. Thus, the teacher and student met together in an otherwise empty classroom. The boycott of the school lasted more than one year.

Student Protests—Kent State

Student protests at college and university campuses in the 1960s and 1970s about the Vietnam War also led to violence. The confrontation between student activists and the National Guard at Kent State University in May 1970 ended in the death of four students and the injury of nine others. Seeking an immediate end to the war, Kent State students staged a series of protests. However, over the course of several days, groups of students became more aggressive and rowdy in their activism. Some caused trouble in the town itself and were dispersed by police. On campus, the situation grew more intense after the school's Reserve Officers' Training Corps (ROTC) building was set on fire.

Ultimately the National Guard was brought in to restore order. They arrived with tanks, guns, and live ammunition. The Guard's presence, however, only fueled the students' aggression. Some of the students taunted the guardsmen and even hurled rocks and dirt in their direction. At the school, all demonstrations were banned and the Guard was to enforce a curfew. Tensions continued to mount and eventually a standoff occurred between the Guard and the students.

When a large group of students gathered in the Commons area, the Guard demanded that they disperse. When the students refused to leave, the Guard lobbed tear gas in their direction. Some of the students picked up the canisters and threw them back at the soldiers. Amid the chaos, a shot was heard and the Guard began firing into the crowd. The volley lasted 13 seconds but its effects had far-reaching consequences. In all, 28 guardsmen had fired. Some of the soldiers claimed that they feared for their lives because the students were becoming increasingly violent. The students asserted that they were unaware that the Guard had live ammunition. They claimed the Guard panicked, overreacted, and began shooting. When the smoke cleared, the dead and injured were taken away and the students sent home for the remainder of the semester. Eight soldiers were singled out for prosecution but were never tried due to a lack of evidence. A letter of regret was signed by the Guard members who fired into the crowd.

School Shootings

Violence in schools today is much different than in years past. Beginning in the 1990s, many students became apprehensive about attending class in the wake of a series of shootings at schools throughout the country. Parents also worried, "If my child isn't safe in school, where can he/she be safe?" They sought to understand why students were bringing guns to school and firing rounds at classmates. Although no one reason can explain why school shootings occur, politicians, government officials, parents, health professionals, and even the students themselves have looked to uncover the reasons why students resort to violence.

The reasons uncovered thus far include, but are not limited to, the following:

- The shooter was being bullied, picked on, or harassed
- The shooter lacked confidence and self-esteem
- The shooter believed she/he did not fit in
- The shooter wanted to feel the thrill of killing someone
- The shooter really wanted to harm herself/himself but took out his/her aggression on others instead
- The shooter sought revenge for some alleged wrongdoing
- The shooter was bored and needed excitement
- The shooter did not see any other way out of a stressful situation
- The shooter wanted to teach others a lesson
- The shooter hoped to gain notoriety and respect

School shootings have brought the problem of youth violence closer to the surface. Parents and educators now have a better idea of what kinds of aggressive behaviors are occurring in schools and how some children resort to violence when repeatedly victimized by it. They have also developed checklists to help others recognize the warning signs of potential violent behavior. In the wake of school violence, some students plot copycat crimes. Most never happen, thanks in large part to the vigilance of police, parents, teachers, and other students who spend countless hours working to end the cycle of violence.

West Paducah, Kentucky

One of the most publicized school shootings occurred in Kentucky in 1997. Even today, the effects of this incident are still felt. The incident was just one of a rash of school shootings in the 1990s. It involved 14-year-old Michael Carneal, who took a gun to Heath High School in West Paducah, Kentucky, and went on a shooting spree. After Carneal opened fire in a crowded lobby on December 1, 1997, three students were dead and five others injured. Carneal had taken aim at a group of students who arrived at school early for a prayer meeting.

As detectives sorted through the details of Carneal's life, they learned that the shooter harbored hostility for popular students, whom he called "preps." He had also harassed the student prayer group earlier. According to various media reports, the youth was picked on all his life and one day just exploded in anger. Before the incident, he had once worn a picture to school of one of his future victims accompanied by the words "Preps suck." Carneal reportedly told various classmates that he was planning "something big." Some were even warned to avoid the prayer circle. Carneal had taken guns to school in the past and showed them to other students.

In court Carneal entered a guilty plea but claimed mental illness; he was sentenced to life in prison. But the proceedings against Carneal did not stop there. The parents of the three slain girls sued Carneal. In 2000 the families' lawyer announced that a $42 million settlement had been reached. The case is considered largely symbolic—an effort to send a message that school violence will not be tolerated—as Carneal does not have the resources to pay the restitution.

Bloody Anniversary Planned

In early 2004 two students in Louisiana were arrested for allegedly plotting to recreate the school shooting spree that occurred at Columbine High School in Littleton, Colorado, in April 1999. At Columbine, two armed students shot and killed 12 students and 1 teacher and injured 23 others before turning the guns on themselves. The Louisiana teens, ages 17 and 19, were arrested and charged with one count of terrorizing. Their plot was uncovered after someone made an anonymous call to Dutchtown High School and warned that violence was being planned to coincide with the five-year anniversary of the Columbine shootings.

According to newspaper reports, police found articles and information about the Columbine killers in the possession of the alleged suspects along with drawings depicting violence at school. News of this reputed plot is just one of many to have surfaced since the Columbine tragedy and earlier school shootings. Due to the extent of the murders and injuries as well as the length of time the gunmen roamed the school looking for victims, the Columbine tragedy has become the school shooting most often cited and used when making comparisons of youth violence trends.

YOUTHFUL CRIMINALS

Although violence and murder are considered by many to be the worst crimes committed by youth, there are growing concerns about youths robbing banks and convenience stores, burglarizing homes and businesses, and holding up people at automated teller machines (ATMs) or on the street. Also of rising concern are computer crimes by youth.

Computer Hacking

As more juveniles become knowledgeable about computer technology, sometimes more knowledgeable than their parents, the potential for computer hacking grows. The first reported cases of juveniles hacking into computer systems date to the 1980s. Various governmental organizations—including the National Aeronautics and Space Administration (NASA), the U.S. Senate, and the White House—have been targeted by juvenile hackers. A few examples follow.

On December 6, 2000, 18-year-old Robert Russell Sanford pled guilty to six felony charges for breach of computer security and one felony charge of aggravated theft in connection with cyber attacks on U.S. Postal Service computers. Sanford, a Canadian, was placed on five years probation, although he could have been sentenced up to 20 years in prison. Sanford was also ordered to pay more than $45,000 in restitution fines for the cyber attacks.

On September 21, 2000, a 16-year-old from Miami entered a guilty plea and was sentenced to six months detention for illegally intercepting electronic communications on military computer networks. The juvenile admitted that he was responsible for computer intrusions in August and October of 1999 into a military computer network used by the Defense Threat Reduction Agency (DTRA), an arm of the Department of Defense. The DTRA is responsible for reducing the threat against the United States from nuclear, biological, chemical, and conventional and special weapons.

CHAPTER 2
GENERAL YOUTH STATISTICS

When studying youth violence, crime, and gangs, researchers seek to discover what elements might lead a juvenile or young adult to engage in violent activities. They have found that no one factor stands out as the leading contributor; instead, a combination of elements increases an individual's risk of developing violent behaviors. While some criminal youth share common traits, such as poverty, idleness, and unemployment, the factors leading to violence and crime can differ considerably between people. To illuminate the situation facing today's youth, this chapter covers a broad range of issues, from living arrangements and education to teen parenthood and health.

CHILD POPULATION FIGURES

The years following World War II (1939–45) showed a dramatic change from previous decades in the number of children born in the United States. During the period from 1946 to 1964 the nation recorded its highest-ever number of births. This phenomenon, known as the "baby boom," showed a significant increase in the nation's birthrate. The country had 17.2 million more children by 1960 than it had in 1950. (See Table 2.1.) In 1960 Amer-

ica's children comprised 36 percent of the population. (See Table 2.2.)

As the last of the baby boomers, born in the early 1960s, reached eighteen, the number of children in America decreased slightly through the 1970s and 1980s. The United States had a small "baby boomlet" in the late 1980s and early 1990s, as baby boomers started families. This reversed the long, steady decline, and the number of children in the nation has risen slowly since 1980, though in the decade between 1990 and 2000, there was an increase of 8.1 million children as opposed to the 17.2 million increase between 1950 and 1960. (See Table 2.1.) Despite this increase, the percentage of Americans younger than 18 remained steady from 1990 to 2000 at approximately 26 percent. (See Table 2.2.)

In 2001 there were 72.6 million individuals under the age of 18, dropping their percentage as part of the population slightly, to 25 percent. Despite projected increases in the number of children through 2020 (up to 80.3 million), American children are projected to make up only 24 percent of the population as the baby boomers—by far the biggest generation in the nation's history—continue to get older. (See Table 2.1 and Table 2.2.)

TABLE 2.1

Number of children under age 18 by age, selected years 1950–2001 and projected 2001–20

Number (in millions)

Age group	Estimates											Projected	
	1950	1960	1970	1980	1990	1995	1997	1998	1999	2000	2001	2010	2020
All children	47.3	64.5	69.8	63.7	64.2	69.5	70.9	71.4	71.9	72.3	72.6	74.4	80.3
Age group													
Ages 0-5	19.1	24.3	20.9	19.6	22.5	23.7	23.3	23.2	23.1	23.1	23.3	25.6	27.5
Ages 6-11	15.3	21.8	24.6	20.8	21.6	23.0	24.0	24.5	24.8	25.0	24.8	24.4	26.9
Ages 12-17	12.9	18.4	24.3	23.3	20.1	22.7	23.5	23.8	24.0	24.2	24.5	24.4	26.0

SOURCE: "Table POP1. Child population: Number of children under age 18 in the United States by age, selected years 1950–2001 and projected 2001–2020," in *America's Children: Key National Indicators of Well-Being 2003,* Federal Interagency Forum on Child and Family Statistics, Washington, DC, July 2003

TABLE 2.2

Persons in selected age groups as a percentage of the total population, and children under age 18 as a percentage of the dependent population, selected years 1950–2001 and projected 2002–20

Age group	Estimates											Projected	
	1950	1960	1970	1980	1990	1995	1997	1998	1999	2000	2001	2010	2020
Percentage of total population													
Ages 0-17	31	36	34	28	26	26	26	26	26	26	25	24	24
Ages 18-64	61	55	56	61	62	61	61	62	62	62	62	63	60
Ages 65+	8	9	10	11	13	13	13	13	13	12	12	13	16
Children under age 18 as a percentage of the dependent population*													
Ages 0-17	79	79	78	71	67	67	67	67	67	67	67	65	60

*The dependent population includes all persons ages 17 and under, and 65 and over.

SOURCE: "Table POP2. Children as a proportion of the population: Persons in selected age groups as a percentage of the total U.S. population, and children under age 18 as a percentage of the dependent population, selected years 1950–2001 and projected 2002–2020," in *America's Children: Key National Indicators of Well-Being 2003*, Federal Interagency Forum on Child and Family Statistics, Washington, DC, July 2003

TABLE 2.3

Percent of children under age 18 by race and Hispanic origin, selected years 1980–2000 and projected 2001–20

Race and Hispanic origin	Estimates									Projected	
	1980	1985	1990	1995	1996	1997	1998	1999	2000	2010	2020
White, non-Hispanic	74	72	69	67	66	66	65	65	64	59	55
Black, non-Hispanic	15	15	15	15	15	15	15	15	15	14	14
Hispanic[1]	9	10	12	14	14	15	15	16	16	21	23
Asian/Pacific Islander[2]	2	3	3	4	4	4	4	4	4	5	6
American Indian/ Alaska Native[2]	1	1	1	1	1	1	1	1	1	1	1

[1] Persons of Hispanic origin may be of any race.
[2] Excludes persons in this race group who are of Hispanic origin.

SOURCE: "Table POP3. Racial and ethnic composition: Percentage of U.S. children under age 18 by race and Hispanic origin, selected years 1980–2000 and projected 2001–2020," in *America's Children: Key National Indicators of Well-Being 2003*, Federal Interagency Forum on Child and Family Statistics, Washington, DC, July 2003

Diversity among American Youth

Non-Hispanic white children made up 74 percent of all minors in the United States in 1980, gradually decreasing to 64 percent by 2000. This level is projected to decrease further to 55 percent by 2020. (See Table 2.3.) The non-Hispanic black minor population has held steady at 15 percent from 1980 to 2000, and it is estimated to lessen to 14 percent of the minor population in 2020. Hispanic minors have experienced the largest increase in relative population since 1980, from 9 percent to 16 percent in 2000. The percentage of Hispanic children is expected to reach 23 percent of all American minors by 2020. Asian/Pacific Islanders made up 2 percent of children in 1980; their percentage doubled by 2000 and is expected to be 6 percent in 2020. The percentage of American Indian/Alaskan Native children remained at 1 percent for the two decades between 1980 and 2000 and is projected to remain at that level until 2020.

BIRTHRATES

According to the Centers for Disease Control and Prevention (CDC) report *Births: Final Data for 2002* (December 17, 2003), there were 4,021,726 live births in the United States in 2002, essentially unchanged from 2001 (4,025,933). Although the overall number of births did not change dramatically, changes were noticed among different ethnic groups. Births to non-Hispanic white and non-Hispanic black women fell 1 to 2 percent, while births among Hispanic women rose 3 percent. Asian/Pacific Islander births rose 5 percent and American Indian/Alaskan Native births rose 1 percent.

In 2002 the birthrate—the number of live births per 1,000 women in the population, regardless of their age—dropped to its lowest recorded rate since 1909 (when such data were first recorded), to 13.9 per 1,000. This rate has declined 17 percent since 1990. Despite this decrease, birthrates for women in the 35–39 age group (41.4 births per 1,000 women) and 40–44 age group (8.3 per 1,000) rose to their highest levels in three decades.

However, the birthrate among teenagers decreased 5 percent in 2002, bringing the teen level to a record low. For those 15–19, the birthrate was 43 births per 1,000

TABLE 2.4

Births to unmarried women, selected years, 1980–2001

(Live births to unmarried women per 1,000 in specific age group)

Age of mother	1980	1985	1990	1995	1996	1997	1998	1999	2000	2001
Total ages 15–44	29.4	32.8	43.8	44.3	43.8	42.9	43.3	43.3	44.0	43.8
Age group										
Ages 15–17	20.6	22.4	29.6	30.1	28.5	27.7	26.5	25.0	23.9	22.0
Ages 18–19	39.0	45.9	60.7	66.5	64.9	63.9	63.7	62.4	62.2	60.6
Ages 20–24	40.9	46.5	65.1	68.7	68.9	68.9	70.4	70.7	72.1	71.2
Ages 25–29	34.0	39.9	56.0	54.3	54.5	53.4	55.4	56.8	58.5	59.5
Ages 30–34	21.1	25.2	37.6	38.9	40.1	37.9	38.1	38.1	39.3	40.4
Ages 35–39	9.7	11.6	17.3	19.3	19.9	18.7	18.7	19.0	19.7	20.4
Ages 40–44	2.6	2.5	3.6	4.7	4.8	4.6	4.6	4.6	5.0	5.3

(Percentage of all births that are to unmarried women)

Age of mother	1980	1985	1990	1995	1996	1997	1998	1999	2000	2001
All ages	18.4	22.0	28.0	32.2	32.4	32.4	32.8	33.0	33.2	33.5
Age group										
Under age 15	88.7	91.8	91.6	93.5	93.8	95.7	96.6	96.5	96.5	96.3
Ages 15–17	61.5	70.9	77.7	83.7	84.4	86.7	87.5	87.7	87.7	87.8
Ages 18–19	39.8	50.7	61.3	69.8	70.8	72.5	73.6	74.0	74.3	74.6
Ages 20–24	19.3	26.3	36.9	44.7	45.6	46.6	47.7	48.5	49.5	50.4
Ages 25–29	9.0	12.7	18.0	21.5	22.0	22.0	22.5	22.9	23.5	24.4
Ages 30–34	7.4	9.7	13.3	14.7	14.8	14.1	14.0	14.0	14.0	14.3
Ages 35–39	9.4	11.2	13.9	15.7	15.7	14.6	14.4	14.4	14.3	14.4
Ages 40 and older	12.1	14.0	17.0	18.1	18.4	17.1	16.7	16.5	16.8	17.1

SOURCE: "Table POP7.A. Births to unmarried women: Birth rates for unmarried women by age of mother, selected years, 1980–2001" and "Table POP7.B. Births to unmarried women: Percentage of all births that are to unmarried women by age of mother, selected years 1980–2001," in *America's Children: Key National Indicators of Well-Being 2003,* Federal Interagency Forum on Child and Family Statistics, Washington, DC, July 2003

females. According to the CDC, "Rates declined for teenagers of all ages; the rate for the youngest teenagers, 10–14 years, declined to 0.7 per 1,000, exactly half the rate reported for 1994. Rates for teenagers 15–17 and 18–19 years attained record lows for the Nation; the rate for ages 15–17 years was 23.2 per 1,000, 40 percent below the 1991 level; the rate for ages 18–19 years was 72.8, down 23 percent since 1991."

The CDC also reported that the birthrate among teenaged mothers was down for all racial groups. Among those 15–19, Hispanic teens experienced the highest birthrates of any racial group in 2002, 83.4 per 1,000, a significant decrease from the 1991 rate of 104.6. For other racial groups, the birthrates among teens (15–19) were: 68.3 per 1,000 for non-Hispanic blacks, down from 118.2 in 1991; 53.8 per 1,000 for American Indians, down from 84.1 in 1991; 28.5 per 1,000 for non-Hispanic whites, down from 43.4 in 1991; and 18.3 per 1,000 for Asian/Pacific Islanders, down from 27.3 in 1991.

UNMARRIED PARENTS

Another trend in American households is that more children are being born to unmarried women. Unmarried women gave birth to 18.4 percent of all children in 1980; by 2001 that rate rose to 33.5 percent. (See Table 2.4.) According to the CDC, in 2002, unmarried women gave birth to 1,365,966 children, a 1 percent increase over 2001 (1,349,249), and the highest recorded number in the 6

decades that data have been collected. Although the numbers have increased, the rate has remained fairly stable since 1995. (This can occur because the number of unmarried women of childbearing age has risen). Yet since 1980, the rate has sharply increased. In 1980 for every 1,000 unmarried women between 15 and 44, there were 29.4 babies born to unmarried mothers. The rate rose to 43.7 for every 1,000 unmarried women by 2002, although this was a small decrease from 2001 (43.8).

According to the CDC, in 2002 birthrates for unmarried women in their early twenties were higher than those in other age groups (70.5 births per 1,000). Rates for women ages 25–29 (61.5) were somewhat lower and rates for all other age groups were significantly lower. Birthrates for unmarried teens 15–19 continued to decrease, reflecting a drop of 23 percent since 1994. The CDC notes in its *National Vital Statistics Reports* (December 17, 2003) that "declines for younger teenagers were more than double the declines for older teenagers (34 compared with 15 percent). Among population subgroups, rates for unmarried black teenagers have fallen most steeply. The rate for unmarried black teenagers 15–17 has fallen by half since 1991, from 79.9 to 39.9 per 1,000, and the rate for older black teenagers declined by 29 percent, to 104.1." The report further notes that "Since the mid-1990s rates for unmarried non-Hispanic white teenagers have declined as well, by 36 percent for ages 15–17 and 14 percent for ages 18–19 years, whereas the

TABLE 2.5

Percent of children under age 18 by presence of married parents in household, race, and Hispanic origin, selected years 1980–2002

Race, Hispanic origin, and family type	1980	1985	1990	1995	1996	1997	1998	1999	2000	2001	2002
Total											
Two married parents[1]	77	74	73	69	68	68	68	68	69	69	69
Mother only[2]	18	21	22	23	24	24	23	23	22	22	23
Father only[2]	2	2	3	4	4	4	4	4	4	4	5
No parent	4	3	3	4	4	4	4	4	4	4	4
White, non-Hispanic											
Two married parents[1]	–	–	81	78	77	77	76	77	77	78	77
Mother only[2]	–	–	15	16	16	17	16	16	16	16	16
Father only[2]	–	–	3	3	4	4	5	4	4	4	4
No parent	–	–	2	3	3	3	3	3	3	2	3
Black											
Two married parents[1]	42	39	38	33	33	35	36	35	38	38	38
Mother only[2]	44	51	51	52	53	52	51	52	49	48	48
Father only[2]	2	3	4	4	4	5	4	4	4	5	5
No parent	12	7	8	11	9	8	9	10	9	10	8
Hispanic[3]											
Two married parents[1]	75	68	67	63	62	64	64	63	65	65	65
Mother only[2]	20	27	27	28	29	27	27	27	25	25	25
Father only[2]	2	2	3	4	4	4	4	5	4	5	5
No parent	3	3	3	4	5	5	5	5	5	6	5

– = not available

[1] Excludes families where parents are not living as a married couple.

[2] Because of data limitations, includes some families where both parents are present in the household but living as unmarried partners.

[3] Persons of Hispanic origin may be of any race.

Note: Family structure refers to the presence of biological, adoptive, and stepparents in the child's household. Thus, a child with a biological mother and stepfather living in the household is said to have two married parents.

Two married parents family:

Children live in a two-parent family if they are living with a parent who is married with his or her spouse present. This is not an indicator of the biological relationship between the child and the parents. The parent who is identified could be a biological, step, or adoptive parent. If a second parent is present and not married to the first parent, then the child is identified as living with a single parent.

Single parent family:

A "single" parent is defined as a parent who is not currently living with a spouse. Single parents may be married and not living with their spouse, they may be divorced, widowed, or never married. As with the identification of two-parents described above, if a second parent is present and not married to the first, then the child is identified as living with a single parent.

SOURCE: "Table POP6. Family structure and children's living arrangements: Percentage of children under age 18 by presence of married parents in household, race, and Hispanic origin, selected years 1980–2002," in *America's Children: Key National Indicators of Well-Being 2003*, Federal Interagency Forum on Child and Family Statistics, Washington, DC, July 2003

rates for unmarried Hispanic teenagers have declined more slowly."

In 2002 the birthrate for men ages 15–54 years was 48.4 per 1,000 men of that age group. According to the CDC, this is the lowest rate on record. Among males 15–19 the birthrate was 17.4, representing a 6 percent decrease from the 2001 level of 18.5. The 2002 rate also reflected a 29 percent decline from 1994. However, the age of the father was missing on 13 percent of birth certificates issued in 2002.

LIVING ARRANGEMENTS

One of the more significant social changes to occur during the last decades of the 20th century was a shift away from what is commonly referred to as the "traditional" family structure—a married couple with their own child or children. The U.S. Census Bureau divides households into two major categories: family households (defined as groups of two or more people living together related by birth, marriage, or adoption) and nonfamily households (consisting of a person living alone or an indi-

vidual living with others to whom he or she is not related). The number of children under 18 in traditional living arrangements has decreased significantly, falling from 77 percent in 1980 to 69 percent in 2002. (See Table 2.5.) During that period, children in mother-only households rose from 18 percent overall to 23 percent, and children in father-only households increased from 2 to 5 percent.

In 2002 some 77 percent of non-Hispanic white children lived in married parents households, down from 81 percent in 1990. (See Table 2.5.) In Hispanic families, 65 percent of children lived with married parents in 2002, down from 75 percent in 1980. In black families, 38 percent of children lived with married parents in 2002, down from 42 percent in 1980. In 2002 black children were 2.7 times more likely to live with neither parent than non-Hispanic white children and 1.6 times more likely than Hispanic children to live with neither parent. Black children (at a rate of 48 percent) were significantly more likely to live in mother-only households than non-Hispanic white children (16 percent) and Hispanic children (25 percent.) (See Table 2.5.)

The rise in nonfamily households is the result of many factors, some of the most prominent being:

- People are postponing marriage until later in life and are thus living alone or with nonrelatives for a longer period of time.
- A rising divorce rate translates into more people living alone or with nonrelatives.
- A rise in the number of people who cohabit before or instead of marriage results in higher numbers of nonfamily households.

Family households, although a smaller percentage of all households in 2002 than in 1980, are still the majority of households. They are broken into three categories: (1) married couples with their own children, (2) married couples without children, and (3) other family households. The last category includes single-parent households and households made up of relatives (e.g., siblings) who live together or grandparents who live with grandchildren without members of the middle generation being present.

Multigenerational Families

Census 2000 recorded 3.9 million American households, or 3.7 percent of all households, composed of three or more generations living together. Since 1990, the number of multigenerational families increased approximately 60 percent. In 2000 there were 2.6 million multigenerational families that included the householder, his or her children, and his or her grandchildren. Nearly 1.3 million multigenerational families included the householder, his or her children, and his or her parents. Another 78,000 households, about 2 percent of all multigenerational family households, consisted of four generations.

The Census Bureau reported that multigenerational families may be most common in areas where recent immigrants live with relatives, housing shortages or high costs force families to share living space, and teenage birthrates are high. As older adults live longer, the need for family caregiving also creates multigenerational households.

GRANDPARENTS. On occasion grandparents provide housing for their own children and grandchildren, or provide housing only for their grandchildren, or reside in the homes of their children and grandchildren. The Census Bureau report *Grandparents Living with Grandchildren: 2001* (October 2003) states that in 2000 there were 5.8 million grandparents who lived in households with a grandchild under 18. Of these, 1.7 million children lived with their mothers and grandparents; 220,000 lived with their fathers and grandparents; and nearly 1.4 million lived with grandparents only (no parents present). The Census Bureau reports that in 2000 some 2.4 million grandparents (42 percent of those with whom grandchildren lived) were responsible for most of the basic needs (food, shelter, clothing) of one or more of the grandchildren living with

them. Native Hawaiian and Pacific Islander grandparents were most likely to be primary caregivers for their grandchildren (10 percent of all people age 30 and over living with grandchildren). Blacks (8.2 percent) and those of Hispanic origin (8.4 percent) were more likely to be primary caregivers to their grandchildren than were non-Hispanic whites (2.2 percent) in 2000.

Lesbian and Gay Parents

The Lambda Legal Defense and Education Fund, an advocacy organization supporting the civil rights of lesbians and gays, seeks to have same-sex couples included in the popular definition of family. The American Association of Single People estimates that 1.6 percent of households consist of same-sex partners. Census 2000 data reports 594,391 self-identified same-sex-partner households, representing 10.9 percent of unmarried-partner households and 0.6 percent of all households. (Reluctance on the part of many same-sex partners to self-identify may prevent accurate demographic analysis of families headed by lesbian and gay parents.) In a fact sheet created by the American Civil Liberties Union (http://archive.aclu.org/issues/gay/parent.html), researchers estimated that between 6 and 14 million children lived with at least one gay parent in 1999. Gay parents may have had children through previous marriages or relationships, while others may choose to have children through insemination, surrogacy, or adoption.

According to a 1999–2000 survey conducted by the Evan B. Donaldson Adoption Institute (David M. Brodzinsky, et al., *Adoption by Lesbians and Gays: A National Survey of Adoption Agency Policies, Practices, and Attitudes*, October 29, 2003), the number of gay couples becoming parents through adoption is increasing. Although adoption by same-sex couples is a controversial issue, 60 percent of the nation's adoption agencies accept applications from gays and lesbians, according to the report. Nearly 40 percent placed at least one child with a known gay/lesbian applicant (although the number is likely higher, as less than half of agencies asked applicants about their sexual orientation). About half of the agencies (47 percent) routinely informed birth parents when placing a child with a gay adoptive parent. About one-fourth of the agencies said some birth parents had objected to such a placement or specifically asked that their child not be placed in a gay household. In August 2003 the American Bar Association announced its position supporting state laws and decisions allowing unmarried couples of any sexual orientation to adopt children together.

ADOPTION

No comprehensive federal registry system is in place for adoptions. Adoptions can be arranged by government agencies, private agencies, governmental foster care systems, and through private arrangements between birth mothers and adoptive parents with the assistance of lawyers. The two types of adoptions tracked nationally are those of foreign-born infants and children and those arranged through the foster care system.

The U.S. Department of Health and Human Services (HHS), through the Adoption and Foster Care Analysis and Reporting System (AFCARS), in a preliminary report for 2001 (published in March 2003), stated that there were 126,000 children awaiting adoption on September 30, 2001; of these, 59,825 were females and 66,175 were males. The report estimated that 50,000 children were adopted from the public foster care system in 2001. Of these children, 25,117 were male and 24,883 were female. Foster parents accounted for 59 percent of adoptions, relatives other than parents for 23 percent, and nonrelatives for 17 percent.

More than two-thirds of children adopted through the foster care system were adopted by married couple families (67 percent). Single women adopted 30 percent of the children adopted through foster care in 2000; single men adopted 2 percent. The remaining 1 percent were adopted by unmarried couples.

In 1996 the federal government began to allow adoptive parents to take a $5,000 tax deduction; the deduction could be increased to $6,000 if the adopted child or children had special needs. Children with special needs, for purposes of this legislation, are defined as those with physical, mental, or emotional problems; those who wish to be adopted with their sibling(s); and/or children who are difficult to place because of age, race, or ethnicity. As of 2002, the tax deduction was increased to a maximum of $10,000, in general, for all adoptive parents. In 1997 Congress passed the Adoption and Safe Families Act (Public Law [PL] 105-200), designed to promote adoption of children waiting in foster care. The act also provided fiscal incentives to states to move children more quickly into adoptive families. States that increase the number of adoptions of foster children (in a given year over a base year) receive a standard payment of $4,000 per adopted child and $6,000 for the adoption of a special needs child.

FOSTER CARE

According to the American Public Welfare Association, substitute care includes foster care, group homes, emergency shelters, child-care facilities, hospitals, correctional institutions, college dormitories, and children living independently or in transitional settings. Foster care is the most common type of substitute care. Experts believe that substitute care is more common in the inner city, where many fathers have long been absent and many mothers are having to raise children in an environment in which drugs, violence, and acquired immunodeficiency syndrome (AIDS) are prevalent. Some of these children are "zero-par-

ent" children, living permanently with relatives or in foster homes or institutions. Others are shuttled about when a drug-abusing parent is unwilling or unable to care for them.

AFCARS estimates that as of September 30, 2001, some 542,000 children were in foster care. The average age of those in care was 10.6 years. Non-Hispanic blacks accounted for 38 percent of these children, non-Hispanic whites for 37 percent, Hispanics for 17 percent, American Indian/Alaskan Natives for 2 percent, and Asian/Pacific Islanders for 1 percent. The remaining 5 percent of children entering the foster care system in 2000 were not identified by race or ethnicity.

Children who lived in foster homes with no relative present made up 48 percent of those in foster care. Children who lived in foster homes with relatives accounted for 24 percent; pre-adoptive homes for 4 percent; institutions for 10 percent; group homes for 8 percent; and other placement types, 6 percent. In 2001 the parents of 75,000 children had their rights to their children terminated, making the children eligible for adoption.

It is becoming more difficult to place children in foster care. The number of potential foster care families is down, due in part to the fact that women, the primary givers of foster care, are entering the paid labor force in greater numbers.

CHILD CARE ARRANGEMENTS

Parents or other relatives cared for most American children under age 2 in 2001, with the parents (48 percent) or another relative (23 percent) providing exclusive care. For toddlers ages 3–6 who had not yet entered school, 26 percent were cared for by parents and 22 percent by other relatives. (See Table 2.6.)

In 2001 the percentage of children being cared for exclusively by their parents varied among racial groups. Among Hispanics, the rate was 53 percent; for non-Hispanic whites, 38 percent; and for blacks, 26 percent. Hispanic children (20 percent) were also less likely to be placed in center-based programs—including day care centers, nursery schools, and Head Start programs—than non-Hispanic whites (35 percent) and non-Hispanic blacks (41 percent). (See Table 2.6.)

Children living at or above the poverty line (63 percent), as well as those with mothers who graduated from college (69 percent) and those with mothers employed 35 hours or more per week (85 percent) were the most likely to have nonparental child care options. Children of mothers who are college graduates (42 percent) and those with mothers working 35 hours per week (42 percent) were the most likely to be in center-based programs. (See Table 2.6.)

Employment Status of Women

As women increasingly entered the workforce, more children were being cared for by other relatives or had

TABLE 2.6

Percent of children from birth through age 6, not yet in kindergarten, by type of care arrangement and child and family characteristics, 1995 and 2001

Characteristic	Parental care only		Total in nonparental care[2]		Care in a home[1] By a relative		Care in a home[1] By a nonrelative		Center-based program[3]	
	1995	2001	1995	2001	1995	2001	1995	2001	1995	2001
Total	40	39	60	61	21	23	18	16	31	34
Age/grade in school										
Ages 0–2	51	48	50	52	23	23	19	18	12	17
Ages 3–6, not yet in kindergarten	26	26	74	74	19	22	17	14	55	56
Race and ethnicity										
White, non-Hispanic	38	38	62	62	18	20	21	19	33	35
Black, non-Hispanic	34	26	66	75	31	34	12	14	33	41
Hispanic[4]	54	53	46	47	23	23	12	12	17	20
Other, non-Hispanic	42	35	58	65	25	23	13	15	28	37
Poverty status										
Below poverty	50	46	50	54	24	26	10	10	24	27
At or above poverty	36	37	64	63	20	22	21	18	33	35
Mother's highest level of education[5]										
Less than high school	62	56	38	44	20	21	7	9	16	21
High school graduate/GED	44	43	56	58	23	26	15	14	26	28
Vocational/technical or some college	34	37	66	64	24	25	19	16	34	36
College graduate	28	32	72	69	15	17	28	23	43	42
Mother's employment status[5]										
35 hours or more per week	12	15	88	85	33	33	32	26	39	42
Less than 35 hours per week	25	29	75	71	30	32	26	20	35	36
Looking for work	58	57	42	43	16	16	4	9	25	25
Not in the labor force	68	68	32	32	7	6	6	5	22	24

[1] Relative and nonrelative care can take place in either the child's own home or another home.

[2] Some children participate in more than one type of nonparental care arrangement. Thus, details do not sum to the total percentage of children in nonparental care.

[3] Center-based programs include day care centers, prekindergartens, nursery schools, Head Start programs, and other early childhood education programs.

[4] Persons of Hispanic origin may be of any race.

[5] Children without a mother in the home are excluded from estimates of mother's highest level of education and mother's employment status.

Note: Some children participate in more than one type of arrangement, so the sum of all arrangement types exceeds the total percentage in nonparental care. Center-based programs include day care centers, prekindergartens, nursery schools, Head Start programs, and other early childhood education programs. Relative and nonrelative care can take place in either the child's own home or another home.

SOURCE: "Table POP8.A. Child care: Percentage of children from birth through age 6, not yet in kindergarten, by type of care arrangement and child and family characteristics, 1995 and 2001," in *America's Children: Key National Indicators of Well-Being 2003*, Federal Interagency Forum on Child and Family Statistics, Washington, DC, July 2003

nonparental care. According to the U.S. Census Bureau report *Fertility of American Women: June 2002* (Barbara Downs, U.S. Census Bureau, Washington, DC, October 2003): "In June 2002, 2.1 million women who had infants were in the labor force: 1.9 million (91 percent) were employed at the time of the survey, while another 189,000 were unemployed." In 1976, 31 percent of all women, ages 15–44, who had a child in the previous year were in the labor force. This number rose steadily until 1998, when 58.7 percent of such mothers with infants were in the labor force. Since then, the number has dropped slightly, reaching 54.6 percent in 2002. One-third of mothers 15–44 who had a child in the past 12 months worked full-time (33.8 percent) in 2002; 15.7 percent worked part-time.

The number of mothers 15–44 in the workforce who no longer had an infant under 1 year old was significantly higher. In 2002, 72 percent were in the labor force, with 51.3 percent working full-time and 16.4 percent working part-time.

CHILDREN AND FAMILY INCOME

In 2001 the poverty line for the household income of a family of four was $18,104. Wealth is classified in relation to the poverty level. Children under 18 in extreme poverty (less than one-half of the poverty line) represented 6.6 percent of American children in 2001. Households earning between $9,052 and $18,103 had 9.1 percent of all American children. Low income ($18,104 to $36,207) households had 21.9 percent; medium income households ($36,208 to $72,415) had 33.2 percent; high income households ($72,416 to $108,624) had 29.2 percent; and 12.9 percent of children lived in households with income over $108,624. (See Table 2.7.)

THE COST OF RAISING CHILDREN

Table 2.8 provides a rough estimate of the costs associated with raising the younger child of a two-child family in a husband-wife family for the year 2002 (for an only child, the data should be multiplied by 1.24). Research

TABLE 2.7

Percent of related children under age 18 by family income relative to the poverty line, selected years 1980–2001

Poverty level	1980	1985	1990	1995	1996	1997	1998	1999	2000	2001
Extreme poverty	6.6	8.1	8.3	7.9	8.4	8.5	7.6	6.5	6.3	6.6
Below poverty, but above extreme poverty	11.3	12.0	11.6	12.2	11.4	10.8	10.7	10.1	9.4	9.1
Low income	24.0	22.8	21.8	22.5	22.7	21.4	21.2	21.9	21.3	21.9
Medium income	41.4	37.7	37.0	34.5	34.0	34.4	33.5	32.8	34.0	33.2
High income	16.8	19.4	21.3	22.8	23.5	25.0	27.0	28.7	29.0	29.2
Very high income	4.3	6.1	7.4	8.9	9.2	10.1	11.2	12.3	12.6	12.9

Note: Unless otherwise noted, estimates refer to children under age 18 who are related to the householder. The income classes are derived from the ratio of the family's income to the family's poverty threshold. Extreme poverty is less than 50 percent of the poverty threshold (i.e., $9,052 for a family of four in 2001). Poverty is between 50 and 99 percent of the poverty threshold (i.e., between $9,052 and $18,103 for a family of four in 2001). Low income is between 100 and 199 percent of the poverty threshold (i.e., between $18,104 and $36,207 for a family of four in 2001). Medium income is between 200 and 399 percent of the poverty threshold (i.e., between $36,208 and $72,415 for a family of four in 2001). High income is 400 percent of the poverty threshold or more (i.e., $72,416 or more for a family of four in 2001). Very high income is 600 percent of the poverty threshold and over (i.e., $108,624 or more for a family of four in 2001).

SOURCE: "Table ECON1.B. Income distribution: Percentage of related children under age 18 by family income relative to the poverty line, selected years 1980–2001," in *America's Children: Key National Indicators of Well-Being 2003,* Federal Interagency Forum on Child and Family Statistics, Washington, DC, July 2003

has found that spending on children varies with the pre-tax income of the parents. Parents with higher incomes provide more expensive housing, food, and health care, as well as spending more on entertainment and miscellaneous items. Costs for raising a child from birth to age 17 ranged from $127,080 for parents who earned less than $39,700 annually to $254,400 for parents who earned more than $66,900.

CHILD POVERTY

There were 72.6 million children in the United States in 2001. (See Table 2.1.) This means that more than 11 million children (using the 2001 poverty rate of 16 percent from Table 2.9) lived below the poverty line in 2001. Statistics from 2001 demonstrate that child poverty, while declining slightly overall (from 18 to 16 percent) in the United States from 1980 to 2001, still impacts many, especially black and Hispanic minors. (See Table 2.9.) Both black (30 percent) and Hispanic (27 percent) children are more than three times as likely to live below the poverty level than non-Hispanic white children (9 percent). Also black children (16 percent) are much more likely than non-Hispanic white children (3 percent) or Hispanic children (10 percent) to live in a household in extreme poverty. (See Table 2.9.)

Child Poverty and Female-Headed Families

Census 2000 data reveal that children in married-couple families are much less likely to live in poverty. Many children who live in single-parent households do not fare as well as children who live in two-parent families. This is especially true of female-headed—and particularly female-headed minority—families. Children who live in this type of family are likely to have greatly reduced economic, educational, and social opportunities. Single parents are more likely to have a low income and less education, and are more likely to be unemployed and to be renting a home or living in public housing.

In 2001, 8 percent of all children in married couple families lived below the poverty level. Those children in female-householder families with no husband present were almost five times as likely (39 percent) to live in poverty. This difference was consistent for blacks and non-Hispanic whites. While 10 percent of related black children of married couples lived below the poverty line, 47 percent of related black children lived in poverty in female-headed households with no husbands present. Similar statistics exist for non-Hispanic white children (jumping from 5 percent below poverty to 29 percent). Hispanic children were more likely to live below the poverty level in households with married parents (20 percent) than either non-Hispanic whites or blacks, thus nearly half of the related Hispanic children living in female-headed households with no husband present lived in poverty (49 percent). (See Table 2.9.)

Risks to Low-Income Children

Great wealth and extreme poverty coexist within U.S. society. Statistics show that 16 percent of American children live in poverty, and some in extreme poverty. (See Table 2.9.) The realities faced by impoverished children differ greatly from the day-to-day realities of children from wealthier families. The Children's Defense Fund (CDF), a child advocacy organization, discussed such issues in its 2002 report *The State of Children in America's Union: A 2002 Action Guide to Leave No Children Behind.* The document included summary charts in a report on American youths to explain the situation faced by many American children, who by accident of birth, face unique challenges within American society.

Most children in the United States never face the difficult circumstances encountered by those most at risk in

TABLE 2.8

Estimated annual expenditures on a child by husband-wife families, 2002

Age of child	Total	Housing	Food	Trans-portation	Clothing	Health care	Child care and education	Miscel-laneous[1]
Before-tax income: less than $39,700 (average = $24,800)								
0 - 2	$ 6,620	$ 2,550	$ 930	$ 770	$ 360	$ 480	$ 890	$ 640
3 - 5	6,780	2,520	1,030	750	350	460	1,010	660
6 - 8	6,860	2,440	1,330	870	390	530	600	700
9 - 11	6,850	2,200	1,590	950	440	580	360	730
12 - 14	7,670	2,450	1,670	1,060	730	590	250	920
15 - 17	7,580	1,980	1,810	1,430	650	620	420	670
Total	$127,080	$42,420	$25,080	$17,490	$ 8,760	$ 9,780	$10,590	$12,960
Before-tax income: $39,700 to $66,900 (average = $52,900)								
0 - 2	$ 9,230	$ 3,450	$ 1,110	$ 1,150	$ 420	$ 630	$ 1,470	$ 1,000
3 - 5	9,480	3,420	1,280	1,120	410	610	1,630	1,010
6 - 8	9,470	3,340	1,630	1,250	460	700	1,040	1,050
9 - 11	9,370	3,100	1,920	1,320	510	750	680	1,090
12 - 14	10,110	3,350	1,940	1,440	850	760	500	1,270
15 - 17	10,300	2,880	2,150	1,820	760	800	860	1,030
Total	$173,880	$58,620	$30,090	$24,300	$10,230	$12,750	$18,540	$19,350
Before-tax income: more than $66,900 (average = $100,100)								
0 - 2	$ 13,750	$ 5,490	$ 1,470	$ 1,610	$ 560	$ 730	$ 2,220	$ 1,670
3 - 5	14,050	5,460	1,660	1,580	540	700	2,420	1,690
6 - 8	13,860	5,370	2,000	1,710	600	800	1,660	1,720
9 - 11	13,670	5,130	2,330	1,780	650	860	1,160	1,760
12 - 14	14,520	5,390	2,450	1,900	1,080	870	890	1,940
15 - 17	14,950	4,910	2,580	2,300	980	920	1,560	1,700
Total	$254,400	$95,250	$37,470	$32,640	$13,230	$14,640	$29,730	$31,440

Note: Estimates are based on 1990–92 Consumer Expenditure Survey data updated to 2002 dollars using the Consumer Price Index. For each age category, the expense estimates represent average child-rearing expenditures for each age (e.g., the expense for the 3–5 age category, on average, applies to the 3-year-old, the 4-year-old, or the 5-year-old). The figures represent estimated expenses on the younger child in a two-child family. Estimates are about the same for the older child, so to calculate expenses for two children, figures should be summed for the appropriate age categories. To estimate expenses for an only child, multiply the total expense for the appropriate age category by 1.24. To estimate expenses for each child in a family with three or more children, multiply the total expense for each appropriate age category by 0.77. For expenses on all children in a family, these totals should be summed.

[1]Miscellaneous expenses include personal care items, entertainment, and reading materials.

SOURCE: Mark Lino, "Table 1. Estimated annual expenditures on a child by husband-wife families, overall United States, 2002," in *Expenditures on Children by Families, 2002,* Miscellaneous Publication no. 1528-2002, U.S. Department of Agriculture, Center for Nutrition Policy and Promotion, Alexandria, VA, May 2003

society, particularly members of racial minorities born into poverty. The CDF employs the image of a family with five children under three years old. Four receive excellent support, encouragement, food, and quality health care to best ensure success during these formative years. The fifth child often goes hungry, does not receive adequate health care, and later attends a dangerous and inferior school.

Children from low-income families face significantly higher risks for poor or inadequate medical care and less academic success than children from homes with higher levels of income. Children in poverty are much more likely to die in infancy, be born premature, have no regular source of health care, and go hungry. These children also have a much greater probability of repeating a grade, falling behind in math and reading at a young age, and dropping out of school. They are only half as likely to finish a four-year college degree, a major factor in determining earning potential, which may then put their children at risk.

INFANT AND CHILD MORTALITY

While many children in the United States face difficult life circumstances, American children do not face the same risk of infant and child mortality as children in most third-world countries. The infant mortality rate approximates the number of children who die each year within one year of birth per 1,000 children. The child mortality rate is the number of deaths in the 1–4 year age group per 1,000. The infant and child mortality rates for the United States are comparable to Canada, Australia, and most western European countries, as is the American life expectancy. The annual infant mortality rate in the United States from 2000–2005 is 7 per 1,000. The child mortality rate in 1998 was estimated for males at 0.4 per 1,000 and for females at 0.3 per 1,000. Most American male children born in the years from 2000–2005 can expect to live 74.3 years. Females can expect to live to almost 80.

ABUSE AND NEGLECT

According to the AFCARS report *Child Maltreatment 2001* (U.S. Department of Health and Human Services, Washington, DC, 2003), an estimated 903,000 children (about 12.4 per 1,000) were victims of abuse and neglect in 2001, a small increase from 2000 (12.2 per 1,000), but a significant drop from 1993 (15.3 per 1,000). Neglect (including medical neglect) was the most frequent type of

TABLE 2.9

Percent of related children[1] under age 18 living below selected poverty levels by age, family structure, race, and Hispanic origin, selected years 1980–2001

Characteristic	1980	1985	1990	1995	1996	1997	1998	1999	2000	2001
Under 100 percent of poverty										
Children in all families										
Related children	18	20	20	20	20	19	18	17	16	16
White, non-Hispanic	–	–	12	11	10	11	10	9	9	9
Black	42	43	44	42	40	37	36	33	31	30
Hispanic[2]	33	40	38	39	40	36	34	30	28	27
Related children under age 6	20	23	23	24	23	22	21	18	18	18
Related children ages 6-17	17	19	18	18	18	18	17	16	15	15
Children in married-couple families										
Related children	–	–	10	10	10	10	9	9	8	8
White, non-Hispanic	–	–	7	6	5	5	5	5	5	5
Black	–	–	18	13	14	13	12	11	9	10
Hispanic[2]	–	–	27	28	29	26	23	22	21	20
Related children under age 6	–	–	12	11	12	11	10	9	9	9
Related children ages 6–17	–	–	10	9	9	9	9	8	8	7
Children in female-householder families, no husband present										
Related children	51	54	53	50	49	49	46	42	40	39
White, non-Hispanic	–	–	40	34	35	37	33	29	28	29
Black	65	67	65	62	58	55	55	52	49	47
Hispanic[2]	65	72	68	66	67	63	60	52	50	49
Related children under age 6	65	66	66	62	59	59	55	51	50	49
Related children ages 6–17	46	48	47	45	45	45	42	39	36	35
All children[3]	18	21	21	21	21	20	19	17	16	16
Under 50 percent of poverty										
Children in all families										
Related children	7	8	8	8	8	8	8	6	6	7
White, non-Hispanic	–	–	4	3	4	4	4	3	3	3
Black	17	22	22	20	20	20	17	15	15	16
Hispanic[2]	–	–	14	16	14	16	13	11	9	10
Under 150 percent of poverty										
Children in all families										
Related children	29	32	31	32	31	30	29	28	26	27
White, non-Hispanic	–	–	21	19	19	19	18	17	16	17
Black	57	59	57	56	56	51	52	48	45	46
Hispanic[2]	–	–	55	59	57	56	52	49	47	46

– = not available

[1] A related child is a person under age 18 who is related to the householder by birth, marriage, or adoption, but is not the householder or the householder's spouse.
[2] Persons of Hispanic origin may be of any race.
[3] Includes children not related to the householder.
Note: Unless otherwise noted, estimates refer to children under age 18 who are related to the householder. The poverty level is based on money income and does not include noncash benefits, such as food stamps. Poverty thresholds reflect family size and composition.

SOURCE: "Table ECON1.A. Child poverty: Percentage of related children under age 18 living below selected poverty levels by age, family structure, race, and Hispanic origin, selected years 1980–2001," in *America's Children: Key National Indicators of Well-Being 2003*, Federal Interagency Forum on Child and Family Statistics, Washington, DC, July 2003

maltreatment (59.2 percent), followed by physical abuse (18.6 percent); "other," which included abandonment, threats of harm to the child, and congenital drug addiction (19.5 percent); sexual abuse (9.6 percent); and emotional or psychological maltreatment (6.8 percent).

The youngest children, from birth to age 3, had the highest rates of maltreatment, with this group representing 27.7 percent of children suffering victimization. As children got older, the rates declined. Males and females were almost equally as likely to be abused (except for sexual abuse); 48 percent of victims of abuse were male, and 51.5 percent of the victims were female. (The gender was unreported in 0.5 percent of the cases.) The majority of the victims of child abuse were white (50.2 percent of victims), with African American children (25 percent) and Hispanic children (14.5

percent) comprising most of the remainder. American Indians/Alaskan Natives accounted for 2 percent, while Asian/Pacific Islander children represented 1.3 percent.

In 2001 women (59.3 percent of all perpetrators) were more likely than men (40.7 percent) to commit some type of maltreatment of children, possibly because women are more likely to be caregivers for children and spend more time with children. Female perpetrators (42.3 percent) were more likely to be under age 30 than male perpetrators (31.9 percent). One or more parents were involved in 84 percent of child victimizations, with other relatives accounting for 6.8 percent.

Maltreatment Fatalities

The most severe types of maltreatment of children lead to fatalities, which are measured in rates per 100,000 children. In 2001 this number was 1.81 children of every 100,000 children in the population, translating to a total of 1,300 reported child deaths from abuse and neglect during the year. As with other types of maltreatment, younger children were more likely to suffer, with 84.5 percent of the deaths in the age range from birth to 6 years, and 40.9 percent of all deaths from maltreatment being perpetrated on those children under one year of age. Male children in all age groups were more likely to die from maltreatment than females, accounting for 56 percent and 44 percent of victims respectively.

Some 82.8 percent of child fatality victims were maltreated by a parent or both parents, with nearly a third (32.4 percent) of child fatalities attributed to the mother only. The majority of victims suffered from neglect (35.6 percent), with physical abuse alone causing 26.3 percent of deaths and a combination of physical abuse and neglect associated with 21.9 percent. Other causes included those unknown, physical abuse and other maltreatment, neglect and other maltreatment, and any type except physical abuse and neglect.

EDUCATION

Poverty and maltreatment, as well as other national issues, may affect the nation's children in terms of social adjustment and learning. During the 1980s the nation became increasingly aware of critical issues such as low academic performance, high dropout rates, and drug use and violence in the schools. Despite these problems, the United States remains one of the most educated countries in the world.

School Enrollment

Virtually all children 5 to 17 years old are enrolled in school. In 2001 more than 95 percent of all young people from 5 to 17 years old attended school. The enrollment of 3- and 4-year-olds has increased substantially since 1980, from 36.7 percent in that year to 52.4 percent in 2001. (See Table 2.10.)

The proportion of people enrolled in school drops sharply after age 18. By this age young people either graduate from or leave high school and may not immediately go on to any form of higher education. However, the proportion of older teens attending school has increased since 1980. In 2001 the proportion of 18- and 19-year-olds enrolled in school reached 61 percent, up from 46.4 percent in 1980. (See Table 2.10.)

ENROLLMENT NUMBERS CHANGE. The number of students enrolled in elementary and secondary schools is directly proportional to the birthrates of the previous two decades. Following the baby boom, school enrollment grew rapidly during the 1950s and 1960s as these babies matured to school age. Birthrates declined as the baby boom waned, and so did school enrollments in the 1970s.

Total enrollment peaked at 51.3 million in 1971, a number not attained again until 25 years later. An "echo effect" occurred in the 1980s, when those born during the baby boom started their own families. This increase in birthrates triggered an increase in school enrollment in the 1990s. In 1991 the enrollment of students in elementary and secondary schools was 47.3 million; it grew steadily until fall 2000, when it was at 53.2 million. (See Table 2.11.)

Elementary enrollment, which includes public prekindergarten–grade 8 and private kindergarten–grade 8, reached a record high of 36.7 million in 1969. From 1969 to the mid-1980s, elementary enrollment in public and private schools gradually declined. After leveling off in the late 1980s at around 33 million, elementary enrollment rose through the 1990s to 38.4 million in 2000. High school enrollment peaked at 15.7 million in 1976 and dropped until 1990 (12.5 million), then rose to 14.8 million in 2000. (See Table 2.11.)

Projections to 2012

The National Center for Education Statistics (NCES) estimates that the total public and private elementary and secondary enrollment will increase slightly from 53.5 million in 2001 to 53.9 million in 2006, and then begin to fall back to about 53.5 million in 2010, after which it is projected to begin to increase to 53.7 million in 2012. Enrollment in public and private kindergarten through eighth grade is projected to decrease slightly until 2008 and then rise slightly until 2012. Public high school enrollment, which began to decline in the late 1970s, started to increase again in the mid-1990s and is expected to continue to grow until 2007, and then to start to fall slightly. (See Table 2.11.)

PREPRIMARY GROWTH. In contrast to the declining elementary and secondary school enrollment during the 1970s and early 1980s, preprimary enrollment showed substantial growth. Between 1970 and 1980, preprimary enrollment rose from 4.1 million to 4.9 million preschool-age children. While the population of three- to five-year-olds grew 29 percent from 1980 to 1993, enrollment in preprimary programs rose about 35 percent, to 6.6 million. In 1994 new data collection methods indicated that 61 percent of the nation's 12.3 million three- to five-year-olds were enrolled in preprimary programs. These increases reflect the greater availability of and interest in preschool education. In 1965 only 27.1 percent of the 12.5 million children in this age group were enrolled in nursery school or kindergarten. By October 2001, 63.9 percent of the 11.9 million preschool-age children in the United States were enrolled in preprimary programs. Note that because of the change in data collection methods, figures prior to 1994 may not be comparable to later years. (See Table 2.12.)

As the proportion of working mothers has grown, the proportion of young children in full-day preprimary

TABLE 2.10

Percent of the population 3–34 years old enrolled in school, by race/ethnicity, sex, and age, October 1980–October 2001

	Total				Males				Females			
Year and age	Total	White, non-Hispanic	Black, non-Hispanic	Hispanic origin	Total	White, non-Hispanic	Black, non-Hispanic	Hispanic origin	Total	White, non-Hispanic	Black, non-Hispanic	Hispanic origin
1	2	3	4	5	6	7	8	9	10	11	12	13
1980												
Total, 3 to 34 years	49.7 (0.2)	48.8 (0.2)	54.0 (0.7)	49.8 (1.1)	50.9 (0.3)	50.0 (0.3)	56.2 (1.0)	49.9 (1.5)	48.5 (0.3)	47.7 (0.3)	52.1 (0.9)	49.8 (1.5)
3 and 4 years	36.7 (0.9)	37.4 (1.1)	38.2 (2.4)	28.5 (2.6)	37.8 (1.3)	39.2 (1.6)	36.4 (3.4)	30.1 (3.6)	35.5 (1.3)	35.5 (1.6)	40.0 (3.5)	26.6 (3.8)
5 and 6 years	95.7 (0.4)	95.9 (0.5)	95.5 (1.0)	94.5 (1.4)	95.0 (0.6)	95.4 (0.7)	94.1 (1.7)	94.0 (2.2)	96.4 (0.5)	96.5 (0.6)	97.0 (1.2)	94.9 (1.9)
7 to 9 years	99.1 (0.1)	99.1 (0.2)	99.4 (0.3)	98.4 (0.6)	99.0 (0.2)	99.0 (0.3)	99.5 (0.4)	97.7 (1.0)	99.2 (0.2)	99.2 (0.2)	99.3 (0.5)	99.0 (0.7)
10 to 13 years	99.4 (0.1)	99.4 (0.1)	99.4 (0.3)	99.7 (0.2)	99.4 (0.1)	99.4 (0.2)	99.4 (0.4)	99.4 (0.4)	99.4 (0.1)	99.3 (0.4)	99.3 (0.4)	99.0 (0.2)
14 and 15 years	98.2 (0.2)	98.7 (0.2)	97.9 (0.7)	94.3 (1.9)	98.7 (0.3)	98.9 (0.3)	98.4 (0.9)	96.7 (2.1)	97.7 (0.4)	98.5 (0.3)	97.3 (1.2)	92.1 (3.0)
16 and 17 years	89.0 (0.5)	89.2 (0.6)	90.7 (1.4)	81.8 (3.2)	89.1 (0.7)	89.4 (0.8)	90.7 (2.0)	81.5 (4.7)	88.8 (0.7)	89.0 (0.8)	90.6 (2.0)	82.2 (4.5)
18 and 19 years	46.4 (0.8)	47.0 (0.9)	45.8 (2.6)	37.8 (3.9)	47.0 (1.1)	48.5 (1.3)	42.9 (3.7)	36.9 (5.4)	45.8 (1.1)	45.7 (1.3)	48.3 (3.5)	38.8 (5.7)
20 and 21 years	31.0 (0.7)	33.0 (0.9)	23.3 (2.2)	19.5 (3.3)	32.6 (1.1)	34.8 (1.2)	22.8 (3.3)	21.4 (4.9)	29.5 (1.0)	31.3 (1.2)	23.7 (3.0)	17.6 (4.4)
22 to 24 years	16.3 (0.5)	16.8 (0.6)	13.6 (1.5)	11.7 (2.3)	17.8 (0.7)	18.7 (0.8)	13.4 (2.3)	10.7 (3.1)	14.9 (0.7)	15.0 (0.7)	13.7 (2.0)	12.6 (4.3)
25 to 29 years	9.3 (0.3)	9.4 (0.3)	8.8 (1.0)	6.9 (1.4)	9.8 (0.5)	9.8 (0.5)	10.6 (1.7)	6.8 (2.1)	8.8 (0.4)	9.1 (0.5)	7.5 (1.3)	6.9 (2.0)
30 to 34 years	6.4 (0.3)	6.4 (0.3)	6.9 (1.0)	5.1 (1.3)	5.9 (0.4)	5.6 (0.4)	7.2 (1.5)	6.2 (2.1)	7.0 (0.4)	7.2 (0.4)	6.6 (1.3)	4.1 (1.7)
1985												
Total, 3 to 34 years	48.3 (0.2)	47.8 (0.3)	50.8 (0.7)	47.7 (1.1)	49.2 (0.3)	48.7 (0.4)	52.6 (1.0)	47.5 (1.6)	47.4 (0.3)	46.9 (0.4)	49.2 (1.0)	47.9 (1.6)
3 and 4 years	38.9 (0.9)	40.3 (1.1)	42.8 (2.4)	27.0 (2.6)	36.7 (1.3)	39.1 (1.6)	34.6 (3.4)	26.4 (3.5)	41.2 (1.3)	41.6 (1.6)	50.3 (3.4)	27.7 (3.9)
5 and 6 years	96.1 (0.4)	96.6 (0.4)	95.7 (1.0)	94.5 (1.4)	95.3 (0.6)	95.6 (0.7)	94.5 (1.6)	95.3 (1.9)	97.0 (0.5)	97.6 (0.5)	97.1 (1.2)	93.7 (2.2)
7 to 9 years	99.1 (0.2)	99.4 (0.2)	98.6 (0.5)	98.4 (0.6)	99.0 (0.2)	99.3 (0.2)	98.4 (0.8)	98.9 (0.8)	99.2 (0.2)	99.4 (0.2)	98.9 (0.6)	98.0 (1.0)
10 to 13 years	99.3 (0.1)	99.3 (0.1)	99.5 (0.3)	99.4 (0.3)	99.2 (0.2)	99.2 (0.2)	99.1 (0.5)	99.1 (0.6)	99.4 (0.2)	99.3 (0.2)	99.9 (0.1)	99.7 (0.3)
14 and 15 years	98.1 (0.2)	98.3 (0.3)	98.1 (0.7)	96.1 (1.8)	98.3 (0.3)	98.4 (0.4)	98.5 (0.9)	96.2 (2.6)	97.9 (0.4)	98.1 (0.4)	97.6 (1.2)	96.0 (2.4)
16 and 17 years	91.7 (0.5)	92.5 (0.5)	91.8 (1.5)	84.5 (3.2)	92.4 (0.7)	92.9 (0.7)	92.0 (2.1)	88.9 (3.9)	90.9 (0.7)	92.2 (0.8)	91.6 (2.1)	80.0 (5.1)
18 and 19 years	51.6 (0.9)	53.7 (1.0)	43.5 (2.7)	41.8 (4.8)	52.2 (1.3)	53.4 (1.5)	49.4 (3.9)	38.6 (6.8)	51.0 (1.3)	54.0 (1.5)	37.8 (3.7)	44.7 (6.7)
20 and 21 years	35.3 (0.8)	37.2 (1.0)	27.7 (2.4)	24.0 (4.1)	36.5 (1.2)	38.8 (1.4)	29.9 (3.6)	20.3 (5.6)	34.1 (1.1)	35.7 (1.3)	25.8 (3.2)	27.4 (6.0)
22 to 24 years	16.9 (0.5)	17.5 (0.6)	13.8 (1.5)	11.6 (2.3)	18.8 (0.8)	19.8 (0.9)	13.5 (2.3)	12.6 (3.2)	15.1 (0.7)	15.4 (0.8)	14.0 (2.1)	10.4 (3.2)
25 to 29 years	9.2 (0.3)	9.6 (0.4)	7.4 (0.9)	6.6 (1.3)	9.4 (0.4)	9.7 (0.5)	5.8 (1.2)	8.2 (2.1)	9.1 (0.4)	9.4 (0.5)	8.7 (1.3)	4.9 (1.7)
30 to 34 years	6.1 (0.3)	6.2 (0.3)	5.2 (0.8)	5.7 (1.4)	5.4 (0.3)	5.6 (0.4)	3.9 (1.1)	4.0 (1.7)	6.8 (0.4)	6.9 (0.4)	6.2 (1.2)	7.5 (2.3)
1990												
Total, 3 to 34 years	50.2 (0.2)	49.8 (0.3)	52.2 (0.7)	47.2 (1.1)	50.9 (0.3)	50.4 (0.4)	54.3 (1.0)	46.8 (1.5)	49.5 (0.3)	49.2 (0.4)	50.3 (1.0)	47.7 (1.5)
3 and 4 years	44.4 (1.0)	47.2 (1.2)	41.8 (2.6)	30.7 (2.7)	43.9 (1.4)	47.9 (1.7)	38.1 (3.6)	28.0 (3.7)	44.9 (1.4)	46.6 (1.7)	45.5 (3.7)	33.6 (4.0)
5 and 6 years	96.5 (0.4)	96.7 (0.4)	96.5 (0.9)	94.9 (1.3)	96.5 (0.5)	96.8 (0.6)	96.2 (1.3)	95.8 (1.7)	96.4 (0.5)	96.7 (0.6)	96.9 (1.2)	93.9 (2.0)
7 to 9 years	99.7 (0.1)	99.7 (0.1)	99.8 (0.2)	99.5 (0.4)	99.7 (0.1)	99.7 (0.2)	99.9 (0.2)	99.5 (0.5)	99.6 (0.1)	99.7 (0.2)	99.8 (0.3)	99.4 (0.5)
10 to 13 years	99.6 (0.1)	99.7 (0.1)	99.9 (0.1)	99.1 (0.6)	99.6 (0.1)	99.6 (0.1)	99.9 (0.2)	99.0 (0.6)	99.7 (0.1)	99.7 (0.1)	99.8 (0.2)	99.1 (0.6)
14 and 15 years	99.0 (0.2)	99.0 (0.2)	99.4 (0.5)	99.0 (0.9)	99.1 (0.3)	99.2 (0.3)	99.7 (0.5)	99.1 (1.1)	98.9 (0.3)	98.9 (0.4)	99.1 (0.8)	98.8 (1.5)
16 and 17 years	92.5 (0.5)	93.5 (0.6)	91.7 (1.6)	85.4 (3.2)	92.6 (0.7)	93.4 (0.8)	93.0 (2.1)	85.5 (4.4)	92.4 (0.7)	93.7 (0.8)	90.5 (2.4)	85.3 (4.7)
18 and 19 years	57.2 (0.9)	59.1 (1.1)	55.0 (2.8)	44.0 (4.4)	58.2 (1.3)	59.7 (1.6)	60.4 (4.0)	40.7 (6.2)	56.3 (1.3)	58.5 (1.6)	49.8 (4.0)	47.2 (6.1)
20 and 21 years	39.7 (0.9)	43.1 (1.1)	28.3 (2.6)	27.2 (3.8)	40.3 (1.3)	44.2 (1.6)	31.0 (3.8)	21.7 (4.9)	39.2 (1.3)	42.0 (1.5)	25.8 (3.5)	33.1 (5.8)
22 to 24 years	21.0 (0.6)	21.9 (0.8)	19.7 (2.0)	9.9 (2.0)	22.3 (0.9)	23.7 (1.1)	19.3 (3.0)	11.2 (3.0)	19.9 (0.9)	20.3 (1.0)	20.0 (2.7)	8.4 (2.8)
25 to 29 years	9.7 (0.3)	10.4 (0.4)	6.1 (0.9)	6.3 (1.3)	9.2 (0.5)	10.0 (0.6)	4.7 (1.1)	4.6 (1.6)	10.2 (0.5)	10.7 (0.6)	7.3 (1.3)	8.1 (2.1)
30 to 34 years	5.8 (0.3)	6.2 (0.3)	4.5 (0.7)	3.6 (1.0)	4.8 (0.3)	5.0 (0.4)	2.3 (0.8)	4.0 (1.5)	6.9 (0.4)	7.4 (0.5)	6.3 (1.2)	3.1 (1.3)
1995												
Total, 3 to 34 years	53.7 (0.2)	53.8 (0.3)	56.3 (0.6)	49.7 (0.6)	54.3 (0.3)	54.2 (0.4)	58.6 (0.8)	49.1 (0.9)	53.2 (0.3)	53.4 (0.4)	54.1 (0.8)	50.3 (0.9)
3 and 4 years	48.7 (0.9)	52.2 (1.1)	47.8 (2.0)	36.9 (1.6)	49.4 (1.2)	51.1 (1.5)	52.4 (2.8)	40.8 (2.2)	48.1 (1.2)	53.5 (1.6)	43.4 (2.7)	32.7 (2.2)
5 and 6 years	96.0 (0.3)	96.6 (0.4)	95.4 (0.8)	93.9 (0.8)	95.3 (0.5)	95.9 (0.6)	94.6 (1.3)	93.6 (1.2)	96.3 (0.4)	97.4 (0.5)	96.3 (1.1)	94.3 (1.1)
7 to 9 years	98.7 (0.2)	98.9 (0.2)	97.7 (0.5)	98.5 (0.4)	98.9 (0.2)	99.0 (0.2)	98.1 (0.6)	98.8 (0.5)	98.5 (0.3)	98.9 (0.3)	97.2 (0.8)	98.2 (0.6)

TABLE 2.10

Percent of the population 3–34 years old enrolled in school, by race/ethnicity, sex, and age, October 1980–October 2001 [CONTINUED]

Year and age	Total				Males				Females			
	Total	White, non-Hispanic	Black, non-Hispanic	Hispanic origin	Total	White, non-Hispanic	Black, non-Hispanic	Hispanic origin	Total	White, non-Hispanic	Black, non-Hispanic	Hispanic origin
1	2	3	4	5	6	7	8	9	10	11	12	13
1995												
10 to 13 years	99.1 (0.1)	99.0 (0.2)	99.2 (0.3)	99.2 (0.2)	99.1 (0.2)	99.0 (0.2)	99.5 (0.3)	98.8 (0.4)	99.0 (0.2)	98.9 (0.2)	98.9 (0.4)	99.5 (0.3)
14 and 15 years	98.9 (0.2)	98.8 (0.2)	99.0 (0.5)	98.9 (0.6)	99.0 (0.2)	98.9 (0.3)	99.6 (0.4)	98.4 (0.9)	98.8 (0.3)	98.7 (0.3)	98.3 (0.8)	99.4 (0.6)
16 and 17 years	93.6 (0.4)	94.4 (0.5)	93.0 (1.2)	88.2 (1.8)	94.5 (0.5)	95.0 (0.6)	95.6 (1.3)	88.4 (2.6)	92.6 (0.6)	93.8 (0.7)	90.3 (1.9)	88.0 (2.6)
18 and 19 years	59.4 (0.9)	61.8 (1.0)	57.5 (2.4)	46.1 (2.6)	59.5 (1.2)	61.9 (1.4)	59.2 (3.5)	47.4 (3.6)	59.2 (1.2)	61.8 (1.5)	56.1 (3.3)	44.8 (3.8)
20 and 21 years	44.9 (0.9)	49.7 (1.1)	37.8 (2.5)	27.1 (2.4)	44.7 (1.3)	50.0 (1.6)	36.7 (3.7)	24.8 (3.3)	45.1 (1.3)	49.3 (1.5)	38.7 (3.3)	29.2 (3.4)
22 to 24 years	23.2 (0.6)	24.4 (0.7)	20.0 (1.6)	15.6 (1.5)	22.8 (0.8)	24.1 (1.0)	20.6 (2.4)	14.8 (2.0)	23.6 (0.8)	24.8 (1.0)	19.5 (2.2)	16.6 (2.3)
25 to 29 years	11.6 (0.3)	12.3 (0.4)	10.0 (0.9)	7.1 (0.9)	11.0 (0.5)	12.2 (0.6)	6.3 (1.2)	5.6 (1.1)	12.2 (0.5)	12.3 (0.6)	13.0 (1.4)	8.7 (1.4)
30 to 34 years	5.9 (0.2)	5.7 (0.3)	7.7 (0.8)	4.7 (0.7)	5.4 (0.3)	5.0 (0.4)	6.9 (1.1)	4.5 (0.9)	6.5 (0.3)	6.3 (0.4)	8.3 (1.1)	4.9 (1.0)
2000												
Total, 3 to 34 years	55.9 (0.2)	56.0 (0.3)	59.3 (0.6)	51.3 (0.6)	55.8 (0.3)	55.8 (0.4)	59.7 (0.9)	50.5 (0.9)	56.0 (0.3)	56.1 (0.4)	59.0 (0.8)	52.2 (0.9)
3 and 4 years	52.1 (0.9)	54.6 (1.2)	59.8 (2.2)	35.9 (1.6)	50.8 (1.3)	54.1 (1.7)	58.0 (3.0)	31.9 (2.2)	53.4 (1.3)	55.2 (1.7)	61.8 (3.1)	40.0 (2.3)
5 and 6 years	95.6 (0.4)	95.5 (0.5)	96.7 (0.8)	94.3 (0.8)	95.1 (0.6)	94.5 (0.8)	96.0 (1.2)	95.4 (0.9)	96.1 (0.5)	96.4 (0.6)	97.5 (1.0)	93.1 (1.2)
7 to 9 years	98.1 (0.2)	98.4 (0.2)	97.5 (0.5)	97.5 (0.4)	98.0 (0.3)	98.1 (0.4)	98.2 (0.6)	96.6 (0.7)	98.2 (0.3)	98.6 (0.3)	96.7 (0.9)	98.4 (0.5)
10 to 13 years	98.3 (0.2)	98.5 (0.2)	98.5 (0.4)	97.4 (0.4)	98.3 (0.2)	98.2 (0.3)	98.8 (0.4)	98.4 (0.4)	98.3 (0.2)	98.8 (0.2)	98.1 (0.6)	96.4 (0.7)
14 and 15 years	98.7 (0.2)	98.9 (0.2)	99.6 (0.3)	96.2 (1.0)	98.7 (0.3)	98.8 (0.3)	98.8 (0.4)	96.9 (1.3)	98.6 (0.3)	99.0 (0.3)	99.6 (0.4)	95.4 (1.5)
16 and 17 years	92.8 (0.4)	94.0 (0.5)	91.7 (1.3)	87.0 (1.8)	92.7 (0.6)	94.7 (0.7)	88.9 (2.1)	85.7 (2.6)	92.9 (0.6)	93.3 (0.8)	94.6 (1.5)	88.3 (2.4)
18 and 19 years	61.2 (0.8)	63.9 (1.0)	57.2 (2.3)	49.5 (2.5)	58.3 (1.2)	61.2 (1.5)	51.5 (3.5)	48.0 (3.4)	64.2 (1.2)	66.7 (1.4)	62.2 (3.1)	51.1 (3.6)
20 and 21 years	44.1 (0.9)	49.2 (1.1)	37.4 (2.4)	26.1 (2.2)	41.0 (1.2)	45.8 (1.5)	31.3 (3.4)	24.2 (3.0)	47.3 (1.3)	52.7 (1.6)	42.3 (3.3)	28.1 (3.3)
22 to 24 years	24.6 (0.6)	24.9 (0.8)	24.0 (1.8)	18.2 (1.6)	23.9 (0.9)	25.0 (1.1)	22.0 (2.5)	15.2 (2.1)	25.3 (0.9)	24.8 (1.1)	25.8 (2.5)	21.6 (2.6)
25 to 29 years	11.4 (0.4)	11.1 (0.5)	14.5 (1.2)	7.4 (0.9)	10.0 (0.5)	10.5 (0.6)	11.6 (1.6)	5.1 (1.1)	12.7 (0.5)	11.8 (0.7)	16.7 (1.7)	9.5 (1.4)
30 to 34 years	6.7 (0.3)	6.1 (0.3)	9.9 (1.0)	5.6 (0.7)	5.6 (0.4)	4.7 (0.4)	8.5 (1.3)	5.7 (1.1)	7.7 (0.4)	7.4 (0.5)	11.2 (1.4)	5.5 (1.0)
2001												
Total, 3 to 34 years	56.3 (0.2)	56.6 (0.3)	59.5 (0.6)	51.4 (0.6)	56.2 (0.3)	56.3 (0.4)	59.9 (0.9)	51.2 (0.9)	56.4 (0.3)	56.8 (0.4)	59.0 (0.8)	51.7 (0.9)
3 and 4 years	52.4 (0.9)	55.2 (1.2)	60.5 (2.1)	39.9 (1.6)	51.7 (1.3)	54.5 (1.7)	56.7 (3.1)	43.0 (2.3)	53.1 (1.3)	56.0 (1.7)	64.3 (3.0)	36.6 (2.3)
5 and 6 years	95.3 (0.4)	95.3 (0.5)	95.9 (0.9)	93.6 (0.8)	95.2 (0.6)	94.8 (0.7)	95.5 (1.3)	94.8 (1.0)	95.4 (0.6)	95.9 (0.7)	96.4 (1.2)	92.3 (1.2)
7 to 9 years	98.2 (0.2)	98.5 (0.2)	97.9 (0.5)	97.4 (0.4)	98.5 (0.3)	98.8 (0.3)	98.6 (0.6)	97.9 (0.6)	97.8 (0.3)	98.3 (0.4)	97.1 (0.8)	96.9 (0.7)
10 to 13 years	98.4 (0.2)	98.8 (0.2)	96.9 (0.5)	98.3 (0.3)	98.1 (0.2)	98.4 (0.3)	95.9 (0.8)	98.6 (0.4)	98.8 (0.2)	99.1 (0.2)	98.0 (0.6)	98.1 (0.5)
14 and 15 years	98.1 (0.2)	98.2 (0.3)	97.9 (0.7)	97.8 (0.7)	98.1 (0.3)	97.8 (0.4)	99.1 (0.6)	98.5 (0.9)	98.1 (0.3)	98.6 (0.4)	96.7 (1.2)	97.2 (1.2)
16 and 17 years	93.4 (0.4)	94.6 (0.5)	92.0 (1.3)	88.3 (1.7)	93.0 (0.6)	94.0 (0.7)	92.9 (1.7)	87.8 (2.4)	93.9 (0.6)	95.3 (0.6)	90.9 (1.9)	88.9 (2.5)
18 and 19 years	61.0 (0.8)	64.0 (1.0)	60.4 (2.3)	45.6 (2.4)	58.8 (1.2)	62.4 (1.4)	58.7 (3.2)	39.8 (3.3)	63.2 (1.2)	65.7 (1.5)	62.1 (3.1)	51.3 (3.3)
20 and 21 years	46.0 (0.9)	50.7 (1.1)	37.2 (2.3)	28.0 (2.3)	44.8 (1.2)	49.2 (1.5)	36.7 (3.6)	24.2 (3.1)	47.2 (1.2)	52.3 (1.5)	37.5 (3.1)	31.8 (3.3)
22 to 24 years	25.4 (0.6)	25.6 (0.8)	27.1 (1.9)	15.6 (1.5)	24.0 (0.9)	23.8 (1.1)	23.6 (2.6)	14.6 (2.0)	26.7 (0.9)	27.4 (1.1)	30.2 (2.7)	16.7 (2.2)
25 to 29 years	11.8 (0.4)	11.7 (0.5)	11.8 (1.1)	7.9 (0.9)	10.5 (0.5)	10.9 (0.6)	7.5 (1.3)	6.7 (1.2)	13.0 (0.5)	12.5 (0.7)	15.3 (1.6)	9.2 (1.4)
30 to 34 years	6.9 (0.3)	6.4 (0.3)	11.7 (1.1)	4.4 (0.7)	5.8 (0.4)	5.4 (0.4)	8.6 (1.4)	3.5 (0.8)	7.9 (0.4)	7.4 (0.5)	14.3 (1.5)	5.3 (1.0)

Note: Includes enrollment in any type of graded public, parochial, or other private schools. Includes nursery schools, kindergartens, elementary schools, high schools, colleges, universities, and professional schools. Attendance may be on either a full-time or part-time basis and during the day or night. Enrollments in "special" schools, such as trade schools, business colleges, or correspondence schools, are not included. Beginning in 1995, preprimary enrollment was collected using new procedures. May not be comparable to figures for earlier years. Total includes persons from other racial/ethnic groups not shown separately. Standard errors appear in parentheses.

SOURCE: Thomas D. Snyder and Charlene M. Hoffman, "Table 7.—Percent of the population 3 to 34 years old enrolled in school, by race/ethnicity, sex, and age: October 1980 to October 2001," in *Digest of Education Statistics, 2002*, NCES 2003-060, U.S. Department of Education, National Center for Education Statistics, Washington, DC, June 2003

TABLE 2.11

Enrollment in educational institutions, by level and control of institution, 1869–70 to fall 2012

[In thousands]

Year	Total enrollment, all levels	Elementary and secondary, total	Public elementary and secondary schools			Private elementary and secondary schools[1]			Degree-granting institutions[2]		
			Total	Pre-kindergarten through grade 8	Grades 9 through 12	Total	Kindergarten through grade 8	Grades 9 through 12	Total	Public	Private
1	2	3	4	5	6	7	8	9	10	11	12
1869–70	—	—	6,872	6,792	80	—	—	—	52	—	—
1879–80	—	—	9,868	9,757	110	—	—	—	116	—	—
1889–90	14,491	14,334	12,723	12,520	203	1,611	1,516	95	157	—	—
1899–1900	17,092	16,855	15,503	14,984	519	1,352	1,241	111	238	—	—
1909–10	19,728	19,372	17,814	16,899	915	1,558	1,441	117	355	—	—
1919–20	23,876	23,278	21,578	19,378	2,200	1,699	1,486	214	598	—	—
1929–30	29,430	28,329	25,678	21,279	4,399	2,651	2,310	341	1,101	—	—
1939–40	29,539	28,045	25,434	18,832	6,601	2,611	2,153	458	1,494	797	698
1949–50	31,151	28,492	25,111	19,387	5,725	3,380	2,708	672	2,659	1,355	1,304
Fall 1959	44,497	40,857	35,182	26,911	8,271	5,675	4,640	1,035	3,640	2,181	1,459
Fall 1969	59,055	51,050	45,550	32,513	13,037	[3]5,500	[3]4,200	[3]1,300	8,005	5,897	2,108
Fall 1970	59,838	51,257	45,894	32,558	13,336	5,363	4,052	1,311	8,581	6,428	2,153
Fall 1971	60,220	51,271	46,071	32,318	13,753	[3]5,200	[3]3,900	[3]1,300	8,949	6,804	2,144
Fall 1972	59,941	50,726	45,726	31,879	13,848	[3]5,000	[3]3,700	[3]1,300	9,215	7,071	2,144
Fall 1973	60,047	50,445	45,445	31,401	14,044	[3]5,000	[3]3,700	[3]1,300	9,602	7,420	2,183
Fall 1974	60,297	50,073	45,073	30,971	14,103	[3]5,000	[3]3,700	[3]1,300	10,224	7,989	2,235
Fall 1975	61,004	49,819	44,819	30,515	14,304	[3]5,000	[3]3,700	[3]1,300	11,185	8,835	2,350
Fall 1976	60,490	49,478	44,311	29,997	14,314	5,167	3,825	1,342	11,012	8,653	2,359
Fall 1977	60,003	48,717	43,577	29,375	14,203	5,140	3,797	1,343	11,286	8,847	2,439
Fall 1978	58,897	47,637	42,551	28,463	14,088	5,086	3,732	1,353	11,260	8,786	2,474
Fall 1979	58,221	46,651	41,651	28,034	13,616	[3]5,000	[3]3,700	[3]1,300	11,570	9,037	2,533
Fall 1980	58,305	46,208	40,877	27,647	13,231	5,331	3,992	1,339	12,097	9,457	2,640
Fall 1981	57,916	45,544	40,044	27,280	12,764	[3]5,500	[3]4,100	[3]1,400	12,372	9,647	2,725
Fall 1982	57,591	45,166	39,566	27,161	12,405	[3]5,600	[3]4,200	[3]1,400	12,426	9,696	2,730
Fall 1983	57,432	44,967	39,252	26,981	12,271	5,715	4,315	1,400	12,465	9,683	2,782
Fall 1984	57,150	44,908	39,208	26,905	12,304	[3]5,700	[3]4,300	[3]1,400	12,242	9,477	2,765
Fall 1985	57,226	44,979	39,422	27,034	12,388	5,557	4,195	1,362	12,247	9,479	2,768
Fall 1986	57,709	45,205	39,753	27,420	12,333	[3]5,452	[3]4,116	[3]1,336	12,504	9,714	2,790
Fall 1987	58,253	45,487	40,008	27,933	12,076	5,479	4,232	1,247	12,767	9,973	2,793
Fall 1988	58,485	45,430	40,189	28,501	11,687	[3]5,242	[3]4,036	[3]1,206	13,055	10,161	2,894
Fall 1989	59,279	45,741	40,543	29,152	11,390	[3]5,198	[3]4,035	[3]1,163	13,539	10,578	2,961
Fall 1990	60,269	46,451	41,217	29,878	11,338	5,234	4,084	1,150	13,819	10,845	2,974
Fall 1991	61,681	47,322	42,047	30,506	11,541	[3]5,275	[3]4,113	[3]1,162	14,359	11,310	3,049
Fall 1992	62,633	48,145	42,823	31,088	11,735	[3]5,322	[3]4,175	[3]1,147	14,487	11,385	3,103
Fall 1993	63,118	48,813	43,465	31,504	11,961	[3]5,348	[3]4,215	[3]1,132	14,305	11,189	3,116

programs has also increased. In 2001 more than one-half (51.8 percent) of children in preprimary programs attended school all day, compared to 31.8 percent in 1980 and 17 percent in 1970. (See Table 2.12.)

School Attendance

In 2000, according to the Council of Chief State School Officers, 34 states required 180 or more days per year of school, 9 states required between 175 and 179 days, and 7 states required a set number of hours rather than days, or had variation based on student grade level. Since 1998 Hawaii, Kansas, Mississippi, Oklahoma, and Texas have increased the number of days in the school year, ranging from 1 to 12 added days. The number of required hours per day ranged from 3 to 7, with 37 states requiring 5 or more hours per day.

Most industrialized Western nations require children to attend school for about 10 years. In 2000 nearly all U.S.

states required students to attend school starting between ages 5 and 8, and continuing through ages 16 to 18. Age 5 is the required age to start school in 7 states (14 percent); age 6 in 21 states (42 percent); age 7 in 18 states (36 percent); and age 8 in 2 states (4 percent). Two states (4 percent) did not report age data to the Council of Chief State School Officers. Students are required to attend school until age 16 in 28 states (56 percent), until age 17 in 7 states (14 percent), and until age 18 in 13 states (26 percent).

High School Graduation

In 1899–1900 only 6.4 percent of 17-year-olds had graduated from high school. By 1929–1930 this proportion had risen to 29 percent, and by 1949–1950, it had grown to 59 percent. The proportion peaked at about 77 percent in 1968–1969 and then dropped to around 71 percent from 1979–1980. The proportion fluctuated between 71 and 74 percent throughout much of the 1980s and the

TABLE 2.11

Enrollment in educational institutions, by level and control of institution, 1869–70 to fall 2012 [CONTINUED]

[In thousands]

Year	Total enrollment, all levels	Elementary and secondary, total	Public elementary and secondary schools			Private elementary and secondary schools[1]			Degree-granting institutions[2]		
			Total	Pre-kinder-garten through grade 8	Grades 9 through 12	Total	Kinder-garten through grade 8	Grades 9 through 12	Total	Public	Private
1	2	3	4	5	6	7	8	9	10	11	12
Fall 1994	63,888	49,609	44,111	31,898	12,213	[3]5,498	[3]4,335	[3]1,163	14,279	11,134	3,145
Fall 1995	64,764	50,502	44,840	32,341	12,500	5,662	4,465	1,197	14,262	11,092	3,169
Fall 1996	65,743	51,375	45,611	32,764	12,847	[3]5,764	[3]4,551	[3]1,213	14,368	11,120	3,247
Fall 1997	66,470	51,968	46,127	33,073	13,054	5,841	4,623	1,218	14,502	11,196	3,306
Fall 1998	66,983	52,476	46,539	33,346	13,193	[3]5,937	[3]4,702	[3]1,235	14,507	11,138	3,369
Fall 1999	67,666	52,875	46,857	33,488	13,369	6,018	4,765	1,254	14,791	11,309	3,482
Fall 2000	68,479	53,167	47,223	33,709	13,514	[3]5,944	[3]4,678	[3]1,266	15,312	11,753	3,560
Fall 2001[4]	68,962	53,520	47,576	33,854	13,722	5,944	4,668	1,276	15,442	11,864	3,578
Fall 2002[4]	69,174	53,566	47,613	33,756	13,857	5,953	4,660	1,292	15,608	11,986	3,622
Fall 2003[4]	69,456	53,700	47,746	33,677	14,069	5,954	4,644	1,310	15,756	12,101	3,655
Fall 2004[4]	69,747	53,800	47,846	33,500	14,346	5,954	4,620	1,334	15,947	12,247	3,699
Fall 2005[4]	70,001	53,866	47,912	33,315	14,597	5,954	4,603	1,351	16,135	12,388	3,746
Fall 2006[4]	70,183	53,862	47,912	33,174	14,739	5,950	4,592	1,358	16,321	12,528	3,793
Fall 2007[4]	70,292	53,789	47,847	33,078	14,768	5,942	4,588	1,355	16,503	12,665	3,839
Fall 2008[4]	70,390	53,652	47,719	33,069	14,649	5,933	4,592	1,341	16,738	12,842	3,896
Fall 2009[4]	70,516	53,538	47,607	33,122	14,485	5,931	4,604	1,327	16,978	13,023	3,955
Fall 2010[4]	70,683	53,498	47,561	33,244	14,317	5,937	4,625	1,313	17,185	13,179	4,007
Fall 2011[4]	70,956	53,538	47,586	33,389	14,197	5,952	4,649	1,303	17,418	13,351	4,068
Fall 2012[4]	71,365	53,692	47,715	33,578	14,137	5,977	4,680	1,297	17,673	13,537	4,136

—Not available.

[1]Beginning in fall 1980, data include estimates for an expanded universe of private schools. Therefore, direct comparisons with earlier years should be avoided.

[2]Data for 1869–70 through 1949–50 include resident degree-credit students enrolled at any time during the academic year. Beginning in 1959, data include all resident and extension students enrolled at the beginning of the fall term.

[3]Estimated.

[4]Projected.

Note: Elementary and secondary enrollment includes pupils in local public school systems and in most private schools (religiously affiliated and nonsectarian), but generally excludes pupils in subcollegiate departments of colleges, federal schools, and home-schooled children. Based on the National Household Education Survey, the home-schooled children numbered approximately 850,000 in the spring of 1999. Public elementary enrollment includes most preprimary school pupils. Private elementary enrollment includes some preprimary students. Public elementary and secondary enrollment for 2001 are state estimates. Higher education enrollment includes students in colleges, universities, professional schools, and 2-year colleges. Degree-granting institutions are 2-year and 4-year institutions that were eligible to participate in Title IV federal financial aid programs. Data for degree-granting institutions for 1999 are imputed using alternative procedures. Detail may not sum to totals due to rounding.

SOURCE: Thomas D. Snyder and Charlene M. Hoffman, "Table 3.—Enrollment in educational institutions, by level and control of institution: 1869–70 to fall 2012," in *Digest of Education Statistics, 2002,* NCES 2003-060, U.S. Department of Education, National Center for Education Statistics, Washington, DC, June 2003

early 1990s, and dropped to between 69 and 70 percent until 1998–1999. At the end of the 2001–2002 school year, 2.9 million students graduated from high school, representing 72.5 percent of all 17-year-olds. (See Table 2.13.) High school graduates are not the same as completers—students who finish their high school education through alternative programs, such as the General Educational Development (GED) program.

Dropping Out of High School

In general, high school dropout rates have declined since 1960. The total status dropout rate for persons 16 through 24 years of age was 27.2 percent in 1960, 14.1 percent in 1980, 12.1 percent in 1990, and 10.7 percent in 2001. (Status dropouts are persons who are not enrolled in school and who are not high school graduates or holders of General Educational Development [GED] diplomas.) (See Table 2.14.)

Historically, Hispanic students have had significantly higher dropout rates than either whites or African Americans. In 1980 non-Hispanic white students had a dropout rate of 11.4 percent; non-Hispanic black students, 19.1 percent; and Hispanic students, 35.2 percent. By 2001 the estimated non-Hispanic white rate was 7.3 percent, the non-Hispanic black rate was 10.9 percent, and the Hispanic rate was 27 percent. (See Table 2.14.)

THE COSTS OF DROPPING OUT. Young people who drop out before finishing high school usually pay a high price. Dropouts have a much harder time making the transition from school to work and economic independence. The employment rates of high school graduates and GED holders have consistently been higher than those of dropouts. In 2001 the proportion of females ages 16 to 24 who did not complete high school and were unemployed was 16.2 percent, compared to 10.6 percent of high school graduates and 4.9 percent of college graduates. For male

TABLE 2.12

Enrollment of 3–, 4–, and 5–year–old children in preprimary programs, by level and control of program and by attendance status, October 1965–October 2001

[In thousands]

Year and age	Total population, 3 to 5 years old	Enrollment by level and control						Enrollment by attendance		
		Total	Percent enrolled	Nursery school		Kindergarten		Full-day	Part-day	Percent full-day
				Public	Private	Public	Private			
1	2	3	4	5	6	7	8	9	10	11
Total, 3 to 5 years old										
1965	12,549	3,407 (87)	27.1 (0.7)	127	393	2,291	596	— (—)	—	— (—)
1970	10,949	4,104 (71)	37.5 (0.7)	332	762	2,498	511	698 (36)	3,405	17.0 (0.8)
1975	10,185	4,955 (71)	48.7 (0.7)	570	1,174	2,682	528	1,295 (47)	3,659	26.1 (0.9)
1980	9,284	4,878 (69)	52.5 (0.7)	628	1,353	2,438	459	1,551 (51)	3,327	31.8 (1.0)
1985	10,733	5,865 (78)	54.6 (0.7)	846	1,631	2,847	541	2,144 (62)	3,722	36.6 (0.9)
1986	10,866	5,971 (78)	55.0 (0.7)	829	1,715	2,859	567	2,241 (63)	3,730	37.5 (0.9)
1987	10,872	5,931 (78)	54.6 (0.7)	819	1,736	2,842	534	2,090 (62)	3,841	35.2 (0.9)
1988	10,993	5,978 (87)	54.4 (0.8)	851	1,770	2,875	481	2,044 (68)	3,935	34.2 (1.0)
1989	11,039	6,026 (87)	54.6 (0.8)	930	1,894	2,704	497	2,238 (70)	3,789	37.1 (1.0)
1990	11,207	6,659 (82)	59.4 (0.7)	1,199	2,180	2,772	509	2,577 (71)	4,082	38.7 (0.9)
1991	11,370	6,334 (84)	55.7 (0.7)	996	1,828	2,967	543	2,408 (69)	3,926	38.0 (1.0)
1992	11,545	6,402 (85)	55.5 (0.7)	1,073	1,783	2,995	550	2,410 (69)	3,992	37.6 (1.0)
1993	11,954	6,581 (86)	55.1 (0.7)	1,205	1,779	3,020	577	2,642 (72)	3,939	40.1 (1.0)
1994[1]	12,328	7,514 (86)	61.0 (0.7)	1,848	2,314	2,819	534	3,468 (80)	4,046	46.2 (0.9)
1995[1]	12,518	7,739 (87)	61.8 (0.7)	1,950	2,381	2,800	608	3,689 (81)	4,051	47.7 (0.9)
1996[1]	12,378	7,580 (90)	61.2 (0.7)	1,830	2,317	2,853	580	3,562 (84)	4,019	47.0 (0.9)
1997[1]	12,121	7,860 (87)	64.9 (0.7)	2,207	2,231	2,847	575	3,922 (85)	3,939	49.9 (0.9)
1998[1]	12,078	7,788 (87)	64.5 (0.7)	2,213	2,299	2,674	602	3,959 (85)	3,829	50.8 (0.9)
1999[1]	11,920	7,844 (86)	65.8 (0.7)	2,209	2,298	2,777	560	4,154 (86)	3,690	53.0 (0.9)
2000[1]	11,858	7,592 (86)	64.0 (0.7)	2,146	2,180	2,701	565	4,008 (85)	3,584	52.8 (0.9)
2001[1]	11,899	7,602 (87)	63.9 (0.7)	2,164	2,201	2,724	512	3,940 (85)	3,662	51.8 (0.9)
3 years old										
1965	4,149	203 (24)	4.9 (0.6)	41	153	5	4	— (—)	—	— (—)
1970	3,516	454 (28)	12.9 (0.8)	110	322	12	10	142 (16)	312	31.3 (3.1)
1975	3,177	683 (33)	21.5 (1.0)	179	474	11	18	259 (22)	423	37.9 (2.6)
1980	3,143	857 (36)	27.3 (1.1)	221	604	16	17	321 (24)	536	37.5 (2.4)
1985	3,594	1,035 (41)	28.8 (1.1)	278	679	52	26	350 (27)	685	33.8 (2.2)
1986	3,607	1,041 (41)	28.9 (1.1)	257	737	26	21	399 (28)	642	38.3 (2.3)
1987	3,569	1,022 (41)	28.6 (1.1)	264	703	24	31	378 (28)	644	37.0 (2.3)
1988	3,719	1,027 (45)	27.6 (1.2)	298	678	24	26	369 (30)	658	35.9 (2.5)
1989	3,713	1,005 (45)	27.1 (1.2)	277	707	3	18	390 (31)	615	38.8 (2.6)
1990	3,692	1,205 (45)	32.6 (1.2)	347	840	11	7	447 (31)	758	37.1 (2.2)
1991	3,811	1,074 (44)	28.2 (1.2)	313	702	38	22	388 (30)	687	36.1 (2.3)
1992	3,905	1,081 (44)	27.7 (1.1)	336	685	26	34	371 (29)	711	34.3 (2.3)
1993	4,053	1,097 (45)	27.1 (1.1)	369	687	20	20	426 (31)	670	38.9 (2.3)
1994[1]	4,081	1,385 (48)	33.9 (1.2)	469	887	19	9	670 (38)	715	48.4 (2.1)
1995[1]	4,148	1,489 (49)	35.9 (1.2)	511	947	15	17	754 (40)	736	50.6 (2.1)
1996[1]	4,045	1,506 (51)	37.2 (1.3)	511	947	22	26	657 (39)	848	43.7 (2.1)
1997[1]	3,947	1,528 (51)	38.7 (1.3)	643	843	25	18	754 (41)	774	49.4 (2.1)
1998[1]	3,989	1,498 (51)	37.6 (1.3)	587	869	27	14	735 (40)	763	49.1 (2.1)
1999[1]	3,862	1,505 (50)	39.0 (1.3)	621	859	13	12	773 (41)	732	51.3 (2.1)
2000[1]	3,929	1,541 (51)	39.2 (1.3)	644	854	27	16	761 (41)	779	49.4 (2.1)
2001[1]	3,985	1,538 (51)	38.6 (1.3)	599	901	14	23	715 (40)	823	46.5 (2.1)
4 years old										
1965	4,238	683 (42)	16.1 (1.0)	68	213	284	118	— (—)	—	— (—)
1970	3,620	1,007 (38)	27.8 (1.1)	176	395	318	117	230 (21)	776	22.8 (1.9)
1975	3,499	1,418 (41)	40.5 (1.2)	332	644	313	129	411 (27)	1,008	29.0 (1.7)
1980	3,072	1,423 (40)	46.3 (1.3)	363	701	239	120	467 (28)	956	32.8 (1.8)
1985	3,598	1,766 (45)	49.1 (1.3)	496	859	276	135	643 (35)	1,123	36.4 (1.7)
1986	3,616	1,772 (45)	49.0 (1.3)	498	903	257	115	622 (34)	1,150	35.1 (1.7)
1987	3,597	1,717 (45)	47.7 (1.3)	431	881	280	125	548 (32)	1,169	31.9 (1.7)
1988	3,598	1,768 (50)	49.1 (1.4)	481	922	261	104	519 (35)	1,249	29.4 (1.8)
1989	3,692	1,882 (51)	51.0 (1.4)	524	1,055	202	100	592 (37)	1,290	31.4 (1.8)
1990	3,723	2,087 (48)	56.1 (1.3)	695	1,144	157	91	716 (38)	1,371	34.3 (1.6)
1991	3,763	1,994 (48)	53.0 (1.3)	584	982	287	140	667 (37)	1,326	33.5 (1.7)
1992	3,807	1,982 (49)	52.1 (1.3)	602	971	282	126	632 (36)	1,350	31.9 (1.7)
1993	4,044	2,178 (50)	53.9 (1.2)	719	957	349	154	765 (39)	1,413	35.1 (1.6)
1994[1]	4,202	2,532 (51)	60.3 (1.2)	1,020	1,232	198	82	1,095 (45)	1,438	43.2 (1.6)
1995[1]	4,145	2,553 (50)	61.6 (1.2)	1,054	1,208	207	84	1,104 (45)	1,449	43.3 (1.6)
1996[1]	4,148	2,454 (52)	59.2 (1.3)	1,029	1,168	180	77	1,034 (46)	1,420	42.1 (1.6)

TABLE 2.12

Enrollment of 3–, 4–, and 5–year–old children in preprimary programs, by level and control of program and by attendance status, October 1965–October 2001 [CONTINUED]

[In thousands]

Year and age	Total population, 3 to 5 years old	Enrollment by level and control						Enrollment by attendance		
		Total	Percent enrolled	Nursery school		Kindergarten		Full-day	Part-day	Percent full-day
				Public	Private	Public	Private			
1	2	3	4	5	6	7	8	9	10	11
4 years old										
1997[1]	4,033	2,665 (50)	66.1 (1.2)	1,197	1,169	207	92	1,161 (47)	1,505	43.5 (1.6)
1998[1]	4,002	2,666 (49)	66.6 (1.2)	1,183	1,219	210	53	1,179 (48)	1,487	44.2 (1.6)
1999[1]	4,021	2,769 (48)	68.9 (1.2)	1,212	1,227	207	122	1,355 (49)	1,414	48.9 (1.6)
2000[1]	3,940	2,556 (49)	64.9 (1.3)	1,144	1,121	227	65	1,182 (48)	1,374	46.2 (1.6)
2001[1]	3,927	2,608 (49)	66.4 (1.2)	1,202	1,121	236	49	1,255 (48)	1,354	48.1 (1.6)
5 years old[2]										
1965	4,162	2,521 (55)	60.6 (1.3)	18	27	2,002	474	— (—)	—	— (—)
1970	3,814	2,643 (40)	69.3 (1.1)	45	45	2,168	384	326 (24)	2,317	12.3 (0.9)
1975	3,509	2,854 (33)	81.3 (0.9)	59	57	2,358	381	625 (32)	2,228	21.9 (1.1)
1980	3,069	2,598 (29)	84.7 (0.9)	44	48	2,183	322	763 (34)	1,835	29.4 (1.3)
1985	3,542	3,065 (31)	86.5 (0.9)	73	94	2,519	379	1,151 (42)	1,914	37.6 (1.3)
1986	3,643	3,157 (31)	86.7 (0.8)	75	75	2,576	432	1,220 (43)	1,937	38.6 (1.3)
1987	3,706	3,192 (32)	86.1 (0.9)	124	152	2,538	378	1,163 (43)	2,028	36.4 (1.3)
1988	3,676	3,184 (34)	86.6 (0.9)	72	170	2,590	351	1,155 (47)	2,028	36.3 (1.4)
1989	3,633	3,139 (34)	86.4 (0.9)	129	132	2,499	378	1,255 (48)	1,883	40.0 (1.5)
1990	3,792	3,367 (31)	88.8 (0.8)	157	196	2,604	411	1,414 (47)	1,953	42.0 (1.4)
1991	3,796	3,267 (34)	86.0 (0.9)	100	143	2,642	382	1,354 (47)	1,913	41.4 (1.4)
1992	3,832	3,339 (33)	87.1 (0.9)	135	127	2,688	390	1,408 (47)	1,931	42.2 (1.4)
1993	3,857	3,306 (34)	85.7 (0.9)	116	136	2,651	403	1,451 (48)	1,856	43.9 (1.4)
1994[1]	4,044	3,597 (32)	88.9 (0.8)	359	194	2,601	442	1,704 (50)	1,893	47.4 (1.3)
1995[1]	4,224	3,697 (34)	87.5 (0.8)	385	226	2,578	507	1,830 (51)	1,867	49.5 (1.3)
1996[1]	4,185	3,621 (36)	86.5 (0.9)	290	202	2,652	477	1,870 (53)	1,750	51.7 (1.4)
1997[1]	4,141	3,667 (34)	88.5 (0.8)	368	219	2,616	465	2,007 (53)	1,660	54.7 (1.4)
1998[1]	4,087	3,624 (33)	88.7 (0.8)	442	211	2,437	535	2,044 (53)	1,579	56.4 (1.4)
1999[1]	4,037	3,571 (34)	88.4 (0.8)	376	212	2,557	426	2,027 (52)	1,544	56.8 (1.4)
2000[1]	3,989	3,495 (34)	87.6 (0.9)	359	206	2,447	484	2,065 (52)	1,431	59.1 (1.4)
2001[1]	3,987	3,456 (35)	86.7 (0.9)	363	179	2,474	440	1,970 (52)	1,485	57.0 (1.4)

—Not available.

[1]Data collected using new procedures. May not be comparable with figures prior to 1994.

[2]Enrollment data include only those students in preprimary programs.

Note: Data are based on sample surveys of the civilian noninstitutional population. Although cells with fewer than 75,000 children are subject to wide sampling variation, they are included in the table to permit various types of aggregations. Detail may not sum to totals due to rounding. Standard errors appear in parentheses.

SOURCE: Thomas D. Snyder and Charlene M. Hoffman, "Table 43.—Enrollment of 3–, 4–, and 5–year–old children in preprimary programs, by level and control of program and by attendance status: October 1965 to October 2001," in *Digest of Education Statistics, 2002,* NCES 2003-060, U.S. Department of Education, National Center for Education Statistics, Washington, DC, June 2003

dropouts, 17.3 percent were unemployed, compared to 10.7 percent of high school graduates and 6.7 percent of college graduates. (See Table 2.15.)

Minority students who drop out are at even higher economic risk. In 2001 the proportion of black high school dropouts who were unemployed was 32.3 percent, while about 15.3 percent of Hispanic dropouts ages 16 to 24 were unemployed. In comparison, 14 percent of non-Hispanic white dropouts in the same age range were not working. (See Table 2.15.)

Persons without high school diplomas tend to earn considerably less than those with more education. In 2000 the median income (half earned more; half earned less) of males ages 25 and over who attended high school but did not graduate was $21,365, which is 70 percent of the annual median earnings of male high school completers ($30,665). Females with less than a high school education earned $12,736, just 69 percent of the earnings of females who completed high school ($18,393). (See Table 2.16.)

Many significant consequences of dropping out of school cannot be measured statistically. Some of those who drop out may likely experience lifelong poverty. Some who are poorly prepared to compete in society may turn to crime or substance abuse. Some become teenage parents without the ability to offer their children more than they had, possibly contributing to a cycle of dependence. Furthermore, it deprives the U.S. economy of the literate, technically trained, and dedicated workers it needs to compete internationally. Finally, those without a high school diploma generally do not have the opportunities available to the more highly educated.

FACTORS RELATED TO DROPPING OUT. Prepared by the NCES, the National Education Longitudinal Study of

TABLE 2.13

High school graduates compared with population 17 years of age, by sex and control of school, 1869–70 to 2001–02

[Numbers in thousands]

School year	Population 17 years old[1]	Total[2]	Sex		Control		Graduates as a percent of 17-year-old population
			Male	Female	Public[3]	Private[4]	
1	2	3	4	5	6	7	8
1869–70	815	16	7	9	—	—	2.0
1879–80	946	24	11	13	—	—	2.5
1889–90	1,259	44	19	25	22	22	3.5
1899–1900	1,489	95	38	57	62	33	6.4
1909–10	1,786	156	64	93	111	45	8.8
1919–20	1,855	311	124	188	231	80	16.8
1929–30	2,296	667	300	367	592	75	29.0
1939–40	2,403	1,221	579	643	1,143	78	50.8
1947–48	2,261	1,190	563	627	1,073	117	52.6
1949–50	2,034	1,200	571	629	1,063	136	59.0
1951–52	2,086	1,197	569	627	1,056	141	57.4
1953–54	2,135	1,276	613	664	1,129	147	59.8
1955–56	2,242	1,415	680	735	1,252	163	63.1
1956–57	2,272	1,434	690	744	1,270	164	63.1
1957–58	2,325	1,506	725	781	1,332	174	64.8
1958–59	2,458	1,627	784	843	1,435	192	66.2
1959–60	2,672	1,858	895	963	1,627	231	69.5
1960–61	2,892	1,964	955	1,009	1,725	239	67.9
1961–62	2,768	1,918	938	980	1,678	240	69.3
1962–63	2,740	1,943	956	987	1,710	233	70.9
1963–64	2,978	2,283	1,120	1,163	2,008	275	76.7
1964–65	3,684	2,658	1,311	1,347	2,360	298	72.1
1965–66	3,489	2,665	1,323	1,342	2,367	298	76.4
1966–67	3,500	2,672	1,328	1,344	2,374	298	76.3
1967–68	3,532	2,695	1,338	1,357	2,395	300	76.3
1968–69	3,659	2,822	1,399	1,423	2,522	300	77.1
1969–70	3,757	2,889	1,430	1,459	2,589	300	76.9
1970–71	3,872	2,938	1,454	1,484	2,638	300	75.9
1971–72	3,973	3,002	1,487	1,515	2,700	302	75.6
1972–73	4,049	3,035	1,500	1,535	2,729	306	75.0
1973–74	4,132	3,073	1,512	1,561	2,763	310	74.4
1974–75	4,256	3,133	1,542	1,591	2,823	310	73.6
1975–76	4,272	3,148	1,552	1,596	2,837	311	73.7
1976–77	4,272	3,152	1,548	1,604	2,837	315	73.8
1977–78	4,286	3,127	1,531	1,596	2,825	302	73.0
1978–79	4,327	3,101	1,517	1,584	2,801	300	71.7
1979–80	4,262	3,043	1,491	1,552	2,748	295	71.4
1980–81	4,212	3,020	1,483	1,537	2,725	295	71.7
1981–82	4,134	2,995	1,471	1,524	2,705	290	72.4
1982–83	3,962	2,888	1,437	1,451	2,598	290	72.9

1988 (NELS:88) focused on students from the eighth grade through their high school years and beyond. Follow-up surveys were conducted in 1990, 1992, 1994, and 2000.

The earlier studies found that school-related reasons were usually given for dropping out, such as "did not like school," "failing in school," "could not get along with teachers," or "school expulsion and suspension." Other reasons the students gave were family or job-related, such as "pregnancy or became a parent," "got married," or "found a job." The U.S. Department of Education, in *Dropout Rates in the United States: 1992,* states that "dropping out is a process, not an event" and the reasons given by students "may not be the true causes but rationalizations or simplifications of more complex circumstances."

In a 2002 report based on the NELS:88, *Coming of Age in the 1990s: The Eighth-Grade Class of 1988 12 Years Later,* the National Center for Education Statistics found that the decision to drop out of high school was related to educational experiences before high school, in addition to personal and family background characteristics. Students who exhibited high mathematics achievement, attended a private school, or participated in extracurricular activities in eighth grade were more likely to complete high school than students who lacked those academic characteristics. Students from disadvantaged backgrounds (low income, parents who did not attend college, single-parent households, having an older sibling who dropped out of high school, spending three or more hours home alone after school per day, or being a Limited-English Proficient [LEP] student) were more likely to drop out of school than students from more advantaged backgrounds. Figure 2.1 shows the event dropout rate by family income of 15- to 24-year-olds from 1972 until

TABLE 2.13

High school graduates compared with population 17 years of age, by sex and control of school, 1869–70 to 2001–02 [CONTINUED]

[Numbers in thousands]

School year	Population 17 years old[1]	High school graduates					Graduates as a percent of 17-year-old population
		Total[2]	Sex		Control		
			Male	Female	Public[3]	Private[4]	
1	2	3	4	5	6	7	8
1983–84	3,784	2,767	—	—	2,495	272	73.1
1984–85	3,699	2,677	—	—	2,414	263	72.4
1985–86	3,670	2,643	—	—	2,383	260	72.0
1986–87	3,754	2,694	—	—	2,429	265	71.8
1987–88	3,849	2,773	—	—	2,500	273	72.0
1988–89	3,842	2,744	—	—	2,459	285	71.4
1989–90	3,505	2,589	—	—	2,320	269	73.9
1990–91	3,421	2,493	—	—	2,235	258	72.9
1991–92	3,391	2,478	—	—	2,226	252	73.1
1992–93	3,447	2,480	—	—	2,233	247	72.0
1993–94	3,459	2,464	—	—	2,221	243	71.2
1994–95	3,588	2,520	—	—	2,274	246	70.2
1995–96	3,641	2,518	—	—	2,273	245	69.2
1996–97	3,773	2,612	—	—	2,358	254	69.2
1997–98	3,930	2,704	—	—	2,439	265	68.8
1998–99	3,965	2,759	—	—	2,486	273	69.6
1999–2000	4,018	2,823	—	—	2,546	277	70.3
2000–01[5]	4,004	2,847	—	—	2,568	279	71.1
2001–02[5]	3,983	2,889	—	—	2,609	280	72.5

—Not available.

[1]Derived from *Current Population Reports,* Series P-25. 17-year-old population adjusted to reflect October 17-year-old population by a weighted average of adjacent years of July data for 17-year-olds.

[2]Includes graduates of public and private schools.

[3]Data for 1929–30 and preceding years are from *Statistics of Public High Schools* and exclude graduates of high schools which failed to report to the Office of Education.

[4]For most years, private school data have been estimated based on periodic private school surveys.

[5]Public high school graduates based on state estimates.

Note: Includes graduates of regular day school programs. Excludes graduates of other programs, when separately reported, and recipients of high school equivalency certificates. Some data have been revised from previously published figures. Detail may not sum to totals due to rounding.

SOURCE: Thomas D. Snyder and Charlene M. Hoffman, "Table 103.—High school graduates compared with population 17 years of age, by sex and control of school: 1869–70 to 2001–02," in *Digest of Education Statistics, 2002,* NCES 2003-060, U.S. Department of Education, National Center for Education Statistics, Washington, DC, June 2003

2000, demonstrating that children and youth in the lowest income brackets have consistently been much more likely to drop out of school.

Detached Youth

Some young people drop out not only from school, but also from work. The Federal Interagency Forum on Child and Family Statistics applies the term "detached youth" to persons ages 16 to 19 "who are neither enrolled in school nor working." The proportion of youth fitting this description is one measure of the amount of young people who are at risk. Since 1980 this has been a persistent problem; however, the proportion declined from 1991 to 1998, and since then it has been stable. By 2002 the proportion of detached youth was 9 percent. Females tend to be more likely to be detached from school and work activities than males, although the decrease in detached youth from 1984 to 2002 occurred mostly because of a decline in the proportion of young women who fit this description. Non-Hispanic black youths and Hispanic youths were more likely than white youths to be detached. However, both black and Hispanic youth were less likely to be "detached" in 2002 than they had been in 1984. (See Figure 2.2.)

HEALTH

The behavioral choices teens make can put their health and success in life at risk. In 1997 the U.S. Bureau of the Census identified six indicators of risk to children's welfare. These included poverty, welfare dependence, absent parents, single-parent families, having an unwed mother, and having parents who have not completed high school. Children who grow up with one or more of these conditions may be statistically at greater risk of dropping out of school, being unemployed, or, for girls, becoming teenage mothers.

Both the Adolescent Health Program at the University of Minnesota (Minneapolis) and the CDC monitor teen risk behaviors. The Adolescent Health Program conducts the National Longitudinal Study on Adolescent Health (Add Health), and the CDC's Youth Risk Behavior Surveillance System (YRBSS) conducts and analyzes biennial surveys of youth.

TABLE 2.14

Percent of high school dropouts among persons 16 to 24 years old, by sex and race/ethnicity, April 1960 to October 2001

Year	Total				Men				Women			
	All races	White, non-Hispanic	Black, non-Hispanic	Hispanic origin	All races	White, non-Hispanic	Black, non-Hispanic	Hispanic origin	All races	White, non-Hispanic	Black, non-Hispanic	Hispanic origin
1	2	3	4	5	6	7	8	9	10	11	12	13
1960[1]	27.2 —	— —	— —	— —	27.8 —	— —	— —	— —	26.7 —	— —	— —	— —
1967[2]	17.0 —	15.4 —	28.6 —	— —	16.5 —	14.7 —	30.6 —	— —	17.3 —	16.1 —	26.9 —	— —
1968[2]	15.2 —	13.6 —	26.7 —	— —	14.3 —	12.6 —	26.9 —	— —	16.0 —	14.6 —	26.7 —	— —
1969[2]	15.2 —	13.6 —	26.7 —	— —	14.3 —	12.6 —	26.9 —	— —	16.0 —	14.6 —	26.7 —	— —
1970[2]	14.7 —	13.4 —	23.7 —	— —	14.2 —	12.6 —	25.5 —	— —	15.2 —	14.2 —	22.1 —	— —
1971[2]	14.7 —	13.4 —	23.7 —	— —	14.2 —	12.6 —	25.5 —	— —	15.2 —	14.2 —	22.1 —	— —
1972	14.6 (0.3)	12.3 (0.3)	21.3 (1.1)	34.3 (2.2)	14.1 (0.4)	11.6 (0.4)	22.3 (1.6)	33.7 (3.2)	15.1 (0.4)	12.8 (0.4)	20.5 (1.4)	34.8 (3.1)
1973	14.1 (0.3)	11.6 (0.3)	22.2 (1.1)	33.5 (2.2)	13.7 (0.4)	11.5 (0.4)	21.5 (1.5)	30.4 (3.2)	14.5 (0.4)	11.8 (0.4)	22.8 (1.5)	36.4 (3.2)
1974	14.3 (0.3)	11.9 (0.3)	21.2 (1.0)	33.0 (2.1)	14.0 (0.4)	12.0 (0.4)	20.1 (1.5)	33.8 (3.0)	14.3 (0.4)	11.8 (0.4)	22.1 (1.5)	32.2 (2.9)
1975	13.9 (0.3)	11.4 (0.3)	22.9 (1.1)	29.2 (2.0)	13.3 (0.4)	11.0 (0.4)	23.0 (1.6)	26.7 (2.8)	14.5 (0.4)	11.8 (0.4)	22.9 (1.4)	31.6 (2.9)
1976	14.1 (0.3)	12.0 (0.3)	20.5 (1.0)	31.4 (2.0)	14.1 (0.4)	12.1 (0.4)	21.2 (1.5)	30.3 (2.9)	14.2 (0.4)	11.8 (0.4)	19.9 (1.4)	32.3 (2.8)
1977	14.1 (0.3)	11.9 (0.3)	19.8 (1.0)	33.0 (2.0)	14.5 (0.4)	12.6 (0.4)	19.5 (1.5)	31.6 (2.9)	13.8 (0.4)	11.2 (0.4)	20.0 (1.4)	34.3 (2.8)
1978	14.2 (0.3)	11.9 (0.3)	20.2 (1.0)	33.3 (2.0)	14.6 (0.4)	12.2 (0.4)	22.5 (1.5)	33.6 (2.9)	13.9 (0.4)	11.6 (0.4)	18.3 (1.3)	33.1 (2.8)
1979	14.6 (0.3)	12.0 (0.3)	21.1 (1.0)	33.8 (2.0)	15.0 (0.4)	12.6 (0.4)	22.4 (1.5)	33.0 (2.8)	14.2 (0.4)	11.5 (0.4)	20.0 (1.3)	34.5 (2.8)
1980	14.1 (0.3)	11.4 (0.3)	19.1 (1.0)	35.2 (1.9)	15.1 (0.4)	12.3 (0.4)	20.8 (1.5)	37.2 (2.7)	13.1 (0.4)	10.5 (0.4)	17.7 (1.3)	33.2 (2.6)
1981	13.9 (0.3)	11.3 (0.3)	18.4 (0.9)	33.2 (1.8)	15.1 (0.4)	12.5 (0.4)	19.9 (1.4)	36.0 (2.6)	12.8 (0.4)	10.2 (0.4)	17.1 (1.2)	30.4 (2.5)
1982	13.9 (0.3)	11.4 (0.3)	18.4 (1.0)	31.7 (1.9)	14.5 (0.4)	12.0 (0.4)	21.2 (1.5)	30.5 (2.7)	13.3 (0.4)	10.8 (0.4)	15.9 (1.3)	32.8 (2.7)
1983	13.7 (0.3)	11.1 (0.3)	18.0 (1.0)	31.6 (1.9)	14.9 (0.4)	12.2 (0.4)	19.9 (1.5)	34.3 (2.8)	12.5 (0.4)	10.1 (0.4)	16.2 (1.3)	29.1 (2.6)
1984	13.1 (0.3)	11.0 (0.4)	15.5 (0.9)	29.8 (1.9)	14.0 (0.4)	11.9 (0.4)	16.8 (1.4)	30.6 (2.8)	12.3 (0.4)	10.1 (0.4)	14.3 (1.2)	29.0 (2.6)
1985	12.6 (0.3)	10.4 (0.3)	15.2 (0.9)	27.6 (1.9)	13.4 (0.4)	11.1 (0.4)	16.1 (1.4)	29.9 (2.8)	11.8 (0.4)	9.8 (0.4)	14.3 (1.2)	25.2 (2.7)
1986	12.2 (0.3)	9.7 (0.3)	14.2 (0.9)	30.1 (1.9)	13.1 (0.4)	10.3 (0.4)	15.0 (1.3)	32.8 (2.7)	11.4 (0.4)	9.1 (0.4)	13.5 (1.2)	27.2 (2.6)
1987	12.6 (0.3)	10.4 (0.3)	14.1 (0.9)	28.6 (1.8)	13.2 (0.4)	10.8 (0.4)	15.0 (1.3)	29.1 (2.6)	12.1 (0.4)	10.0 (0.4)	13.3 (1.2)	28.1 (2.6)
1988	12.9 (0.3)	9.6 (0.3)	14.5 (1.0)	35.8 (2.3)	13.5 (0.4)	10.3 (0.5)	15.0 (1.5)	36.0 (3.2)	12.2 (0.4)	8.9 (0.4)	14.0 (1.4)	35.4 (3.3)
1989	12.6 (0.3)	9.4 (0.3)	13.9 (1.0)	33.0 (2.2)	13.6 (0.5)	10.3 (0.5)	14.9 (1.5)	34.4 (3.1)	11.7 (0.4)	8.5 (0.4)	13.0 (1.3)	31.6 (3.1)
1990	12.1 (0.3)	9.0 (0.3)	13.2 (0.9)	32.4 (1.9)	12.3 (0.4)	9.3 (0.4)	11.9 (1.3)	34.3 (2.7)	11.8 (0.4)	8.7 (0.4)	14.4 (1.3)	30.3 (2.7)
1991	12.5 (0.3)	8.9 (0.3)	13.6 (0.9)	35.3 (1.9)	13.0 (0.4)	8.9 (0.4)	13.5 (1.4)	39.2 (2.7)	11.9 (0.4)	8.9 (0.4)	13.7 (1.3)	31.1 (2.7)
1992[3]	11.0 (0.3)	7.7 (0.3)	13.7 (0.9)	29.4 (1.9)	11.3 (0.4)	8.0 (0.4)	12.5 (1.3)	32.1 (2.7)	10.7 (0.4)	7.4 (0.4)	14.8 (1.4)	26.6 (2.6)
1993[3]	11.0 (0.3)	7.9 (0.3)	13.6 (0.9)	27.5 (1.8)	11.2 (0.4)	8.2 (0.4)	12.6 (1.3)	28.1 (2.5)	10.9 (0.4)	7.6 (0.4)	14.4 (1.3)	26.9 (2.5)
1994[3]	11.4 (0.3)	7.7 (0.3)	12.6 (0.8)	30.0 (1.2)	12.3 (0.4)	8.0 (0.4)	14.1 (1.1)	31.6 (1.6)	10.6 (0.4)	7.5 (0.4)	11.3 (1.0)	28.1 (1.7)
1995[3]	12.0 (0.3)	8.6 (0.3)	12.1 (0.7)	30.0 (1.1)	12.2 (0.4)	9.0 (0.4)	11.1 (1.0)	30.0 (1.6)	11.7 (0.4)	8.2 (0.4)	12.9 (1.1)	30.0 (1.7)
1996[3]	11.1 (0.3)	7.3 (0.3)	13.0 (0.8)	29.4 (1.2)	11.4 (0.4)	7.3 (0.4)	13.5 (1.2)	30.3 (1.7)	10.9 (0.4)	7.3 (0.4)	12.5 (1.1)	28.3 (1.7)
1997[3]	11.0 (0.3)	7.6 (0.3)	13.4 (0.8)	25.3 (1.1)	11.9 (0.4)	8.5 (0.4)	13.3 (1.2)	27.0 (1.6)	10.1 (0.4)	6.7 (0.4)	13.5 (1.1)	23.4 (1.6)
1998[3]	11.8 (0.3)	7.7 (0.3)	13.8 (0.8)	29.5 (1.1)	13.3 (0.4)	8.6 (0.4)	15.5 (1.2)	33.5 (1.6)	10.3 (0.4)	6.9 (0.4)	12.2 (1.1)	25.0 (1.6)
1999[3]	11.2 (0.3)	7.3 (0.3)	12.6 (0.8)	28.6 (1.1)	11.9 (0.4)	7.7 (0.4)	12.1 (1.1)	31.0 (1.6)	10.5 (0.4)	6.9 (0.4)	13.0 (1.1)	26.0 (1.5)
2000[3]	10.9 (0.3)	6.9 (0.3)	13.1 (0.8)	27.8 (1.1)	12.0 (0.4)	7.0 (0.4)	15.3 (1.2)	31.8 (1.6)	9.9 (0.4)	6.9 (0.4)	11.1 (1.0)	23.5 (1.5)
2001[3]	10.7 (0.3)	7.3 (0.3)	10.9 (0.7)	27.0 (1.1)	12.2 (0.4)	7.9 (0.4)	13.0 (1.1)	31.6 (1.6)	9.3 (0.3)	6.7 (0.4)	9.0 (0.9)	22.1 (1.4)

— Not available.

[1]Based on the April 1960 decennial census. Data for other years are based on October counts.

[2]White and Black include persons of Hispanic origin.

[3]Because of changes in data collection procedures, data may not be comparable with figures for earlier years.

Note: "Status" dropouts are 16- to 24-year-olds who are not enrolled in school and who have not completed a high school program regardless of when they left school. People who have received GED credentials are counted as high school completers. Standard errors appear in parentheses.

SOURCE: Thomas D. Snyder and Charlene M. Hoffman, "Table 108. Percent of high school dropouts (status dropouts) among persons 16 to 24 years old, by sex and race/ethnicity: April 1960 to October 2001," in *Digest of Education Statistics, 2002*, U.S. Department of Education, National Center for Education Statistics, Washington, DC, 2003

The Add Health study, as reported in the "Protecting Adolescents from Harm" (Michael D. Resnick et al., *Journal of the American Medical Association,* vol. 278, no. 10, September 10, 1997), found certain home conditions statistically associated with risk behaviors. For example, access to guns in the home was linked to suicidal tendencies and violence, and access to substances at home was related to teens' use of cigarettes, alcohol, and marijuana. Working 20 hours or more a week was linked to emotional distress and use of cigarettes, alcohol, and marijuana.

Adolescents who felt strongly connected to family and school were protected to some extent against health-risk behaviors. Parental disapproval of early sexual activity was associated with later onset of sexual activity, and parental expectations of school achievement were linked to lower levels of risk behavior. The presence of parents before school, after school, at dinner, and at bedtime was associated with lower levels of emotional distress, suicidal thoughts, and suicide attempts. Feeling "connected" at school also was associated with lower levels of these behaviors.

Health Studies

Funded by the National Institute on Drug Abuse (NIDA) in Washington, D.C., the Institute for Social Research at the University of Michigan conducts an

TABLE 2.15

Unemployment rate by demographic characteristics, 1999, 2000, and 2001

Sex, race/ethnicity, and educational attainment	Percent unemployed, 1999[1]				Percent unemployed, 2000[1]				Percent unemployed, 2001[1]			
	16- to 24-year-olds[2]			25 years old and over	16- to 24-year-olds[2]			25 years old and over	16- to 24-year-olds[2]			25 years old and over
	Total	16 to 19 years	20 to 24 years		Total	16 to 19 years	20 to 24 years		Total	16 to 19 years	20 to 24 years	
1	2	3	4	5	6	7	8	9	10	11	12	13
All persons												
All education levels	9.9	13.9	7.5	3.1	9.3	13.1	7.1	3.0	10.6	14.7	8.3	3.7
Less than a high school completion	16.0	16.5	14.6	6.7	15.3	15.6	14.4	6.4	16.8	17.3	15.7	7.3
High school completer, no college	9.7	12.3	8.6	3.5	9.3	11.6	8.3	3.5	10.7	13.2	9.5	4.2
Some college, no degree	5.9	7.3	5.4	3.0	5.5	6.7	5.1	2.9	6.4	8.1	5.9	3.5
Associate degree	4.7	6.7	4.6	2.5	3.2	3.2	3.2	2.3	4.6	5.9	4.6	2.9
Bachelor's degree or higher	4.7	—	4.8	1.8	4.2	—	4.2	1.7	5.7	—	5.7	2.3
Men												
All education levels	10.3	14.7	7.7	3.0	9.7	14.0	7.3	2.8	11.4	15.9	8.9	3.6
Less than a high school completion	15.6	17.0	12.2	5.8	15.2	16.5	12.2	5.5	17.3	18.7	14.7	6.5
High school completer, no college	9.7	12.3	8.6	3.3	9.2	11.7	8.2	3.4	10.7	13.0	9.8	4.3
Some college, no degree	6.2	8.2	5.7	2.8	5.7	7.2	5.4	2.7	6.9	9.1	6.4	3.4
Associate degree	5.3	9.1	5.2	2.5	3.2	7.7	3.0	2.3	5.2	7.7	5.2	3.1
Bachelor's degree or higher	5.6	—	5.7	1.8	4.2	—	4.2	1.5	6.7	—	6.8	2.2
Women												
All education levels	9.5	13.2	7.2	3.3	8.9	12.1	7.0	3.2	9.7	13.4	7.5	3.7
Less than a high school completion	16.6	15.9	19.1	8.2	15.4	14.5	18.6	7.8	16.2	15.7	17.7	8.5
High school completer, no college	9.8	12.3	8.6	3.7	9.5	11.5	8.5	3.5	10.6	13.5	9.2	4.0
Some college, no degree	5.6	6.8	5.2	3.2	5.2	6.3	4.9	3.0	5.9	7.4	5.5	3.6
Associate degree	4.2	5.3	4.2	2.5	3.2	—	3.3	2.4	3.9	4.8	3.9	2.7
Bachelor's degree or higher	4.1	—	4.1	1.8	4.2	—	4.3	1.8	4.9	—	4.9	2.3
White, non-Hispanic												
All education levels	7.8	10.9	5.9	2.5	7.4	10.4	5.5	2.4	8.6	11.8	6.7	3.0
Less than a high school completion	13.0	13.0	12.7	5.2	12.7	12.7	13.1	5.2	14.0	13.9	14.3	5.7
High school completer, no college	7.6	9.5	6.7	2.8	7.2	9.1	6.4	2.8	8.9	10.5	8.2	3.5
Some college, no degree	4.8	5.9	4.5	2.6	4.5	5.3	4.3	2.5	5.2	6.8	4.8	3.2
Associate degree	4.4	8.7	4.2	2.3	3.0	4.5	3.0	2.0	4.5	7.1	4.4	2.4
Bachelor's degree or higher	4.6	—	4.6	1.7	4.0	—	4.0	1.5	5.4	—	5.4	2.1
Black[3]												
All education levels	19.2	27.9	14.6	5.7	18.2	24.7	15.0	5.4	20.4	29.0	16.2	6.3
Less than a high school completion	31.2	32.3	28.7	11.6	29.1	28.4	30.3	10.7	32.3	33.0	31.1	11.9
High school completer, no college	18.6	24.6	16.4	6.3	18.3	23.9	16.4	6.5	19.3	26.4	16.9	7.5
Some college, no degree	10.8	15.4	10.0	4.7	9.7	11.1	9.4	4.2	12.2	16.7	11.4	5.1
Associate degree	8.0	20.0	7.4	3.8	6.3	—	6.4	3.5	7.5	—	7.6	5.0
Bachelor's degree or higher	5.7	—	5.7	2.7	5.6	—	5.7	2.5	7.1	—	7.2	2.7
Hispanic origin[4]												
All education levels	11.8	18.7	8.3	5.0	10.6	16.7	7.5	4.4	11.4	17.7	8.2	5.3
Less than a high school completion	16.1	21.3	11.1	7.1	14.4	19.9	9.6	6.3	15.3	20.2	10.9	7.5
High school completer, no college	10.2	15.4	8.3	4.7	9.1	12.6	7.9	3.9	9.9	16.2	7.4	4.4
Some college, no degree	7.2	11.4	6.1	3.4	6.4	10.4	5.1	3.2	7.3	8.8	6.8	3.8
Associate degree	4.3	—	4.4	3.1	2.4	—	2.5	2.9	1.9	—	2.0	3.6
Bachelor's degree or higher	4.1	—	4.1	2.5	4.6	—	4.7	2.2	6.3	—	6.3	3.6

—Not available.

[1] The unemployment rate is the percent of individuals in the labor force who are not working and who made specific efforts to find employment sometime during the prior 4 weeks. The labor force includes both employed and unemployed persons.
[2] Excludes persons enrolled in school.
[3] Includes persons of Hispanic origin.
[4] Persons of Hispanic origin may be of any race.

SOURCE: Thomas D. Snyder and Charlene M. Hoffman, "Table 380.—Unemployment rate of persons 16 years old and over, by age, sex, race/ethnicity, and educational attainment: 1999, 2000, and 2001," in *Digest of Education Statistics, 2002,* NCES 2003-060, U.S. Department of Education, National Center for Education Statistics, Washington, DC, June 2003

annual survey of substance use among students called Monitoring the Future (Lloyd D. Johnson, Patrick M. O'Malley, and Jerald G. Bachman, National Institute on Drug Abuse, Bethesda, MD, August 2003).

The CDC also reported on risk behaviors among young people in *Youth Risk Behavior Surveillance— United States, 1999* (Jo Anne Grunbaum, Laura Kann, Steven A. Kinchen, Barbara I. Williams, James G. Ross, Richard Lowry, and Lloyd J. Kolbe, *CDC Surveillance Summaries,* vol. 51, No. SS-4, June 28, 2002).

ATTITUDES TOWARD DRUGS. According to Monitoring the Future (MTF), in 2002 fewer students considered substance use extremely dangerous than in 1991. The proportions of those who saw great risk in the use of marijuana decreased significantly in all grades between 1991 and 2002; only 19.9 percent of 2002 tenth graders said

TABLE 2.16

Median earnings (in current dollars) for persons 25 years old and over, by selected characteristics, 2000

	Male				Female			
Highest degree attained	Total	White	Black	Hispanic	Total	White	Black	Hispanic
All education levels	$35,842	$36,668	$28,167	$23,425	$22,887	$23,078	$22,028	$16,601
9th to 12th grade, no diploma	21,365	21,837	19,072	20,459	12,736	12,753	12,677	11,973
High school completer, no college	30,665	31,295	25,466	24,973	18,393	18,627	17,822	16,757
Some college, no degree	35,463	36,051	30,915	30,591	22,308	22,242	22,960	21,860
Associate degree	38,472	40,270	30,583	35,100	25,398	25,480	25,411	22,347
Bachelor's degree or higher	55,059	55,906	42,591	42,518	35,691	35,472	37,898	32,035
Bachelor's degree	50,441	51,099	40,360	41,244	32,163	31,892	35,788	28,531
Master's degree	60,320	60,450	47,170	47,946	41,048	40,844	41,980	42,269

Note: White category includes persons who identified themselves as both White and of Hispanic origin and Black category includes persons who identified themselves as both Black and of Hispanic origin. Hispanic origin includes anyone who identified themselves as Hispanic.

SOURCE: Kathryn Hoffman, Charmaine Llagas, and Thomas D. Snyder, "Median earnings (in current dollars) for persons 25 years old and over, by sex, race/ethnicity, and educational attainment: 2000," in *Status and Trends in the Education of Blacks*, NCES 2003-034, U.S. Department of Education, National Center for Education Statistics, Institute of Education Sciences, Washington, DC, September 2003

that trying marijuana once or twice was very risky, down from 30 percent in 1991. In 2002 the proportion (64.3 percent) of tenth graders who saw great risk in smoking one or more packs of cigarettes a day had increased slightly from 1991, when it was 60.3 percent. All students in 2002 perceived daily drinking and binge drinking as less risky than they did in 1991. However, a slightly higher proportion of eighth-grade students considered using heroin dangerous in 2002 than in 1995, when heroin was first added to the survey. (See Table 2.17.)

In 2001 Hispanic high school students (34 percent) were more likely than white (28 percent) or black (22 percent) high school students to report that drugs were made available to them on school property during the previous 12 months, according to the CDC. (See Figure 2.3.)

MARIJUANA. In 2002 the proportion of eighth-grade students who reported having used marijuana at least once during their lifetimes was 19.2 percent, with 38.7 percent of tenth graders and 47.8 percent of twelfth graders reporting this same behavior. These rates represented increases from 1991, when 10.2 percent of eighth graders, 23.4 percent of tenth graders, and 36.7 percent of twelfth graders said they had used marijuana at least once in their lives. (See Table 2.18.)

Black youth (40.2 percent) were slightly less likely to report lifetime marijuana use than either white (42.8 percent) or Hispanic (44.7 percent) students. Less than one-quarter of students of all races reported using marijuana in the past 30 days—whites, 24.4 percent; blacks, 21.8 percent; and Hispanics, 24.6 percent. A lower percentage of females (20 percent) than males (27.9 percent) were current users in 2001. (See Table 2.19.)

INHALANTS. The proportion of eighth, tenth, and twelfth graders who used inhalants, such as glues, sol-

vents, and aerosols, peaked in 1995 and then began to decline. Inhalants are most often used in the earlier grade levels. For example, 15.2 percent of eighth graders reported using an inhalant during their lifetimes, compared to 13.5 percent of tenth graders and 11.7 percent of twelfth graders in 2002. (See Figure 2.4.) Because most inhalants are common household products, young people may not understand that they are potentially lethal.

ALCOHOL. From 1993 to 2001, the proportion of high school students who reported using alcohol at school declined slightly. Students were much less likely to use alcohol on school property than elsewhere. (See Figure 2.4.)

In 2002 the proportion of eighth graders who reported having tried alcohol in their lifetimes was 47 percent, with 66.9 percent of tenth graders and 78.4 percent of twelfth graders reporting this same behavior. When asked if they had been drunk in their lives, 21.3 percent of eighth graders, 44 percent of tenth graders, and 61.6 percent of twelfth graders reported that they had. (See Table 2.18.)

In 2001 black high school students (32.7 percent) reported lower levels of current alcohol use than either white (50.4 percent) or Hispanic students (49.2 percent). Black teenagers (11.1 percent) were also less likely to report binge drinking (five or more drinks in a row on at least one occasion during the month preceding the survey) than were white (34 percent) or Hispanic students (30.1 percent). Female students were slightly less likely than males to be current drinkers and considerably less likely to be binge drinkers across all ethnicities. (See Table 2.19.)

TOBACCO USE AMONG AMERICAN MIDDLE AND HIGH SCHOOL STUDENTS. Cigarette smoking among high school students declined slowly but steadily from 1975 to

FIGURE 2.1

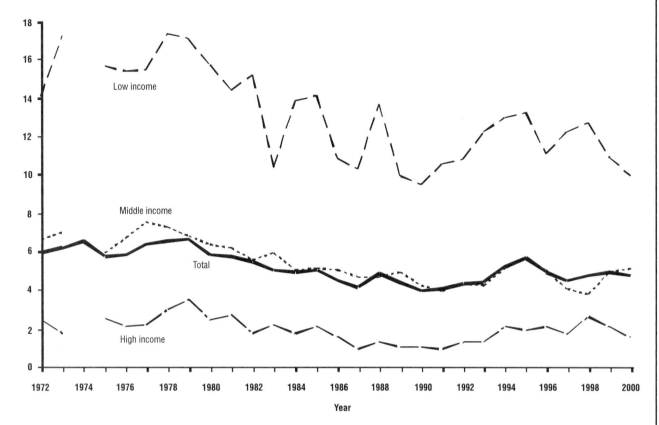

Event dropout rates of 15- through 24-year-olds who dropped out of grades 10–12, by family income*, October 1972–October 2000

Low income

Middle income

Total

High income

*Low income is defined as the bottom 20 percent of all family incomes for the year; middle income is between 20 and 80 percent of all family incomes; and high income is the top 20 percent of all family incomes.

NOTE: Data on family income are missing for 1974. Numbers for years 1987 through 2000 reflect new editing procedures instituted by the U.S. Census Bureau for cases with missing data on school enrollment items. Numbers for years 1992 through 2000 reflect new wording of the educational attainment item in the CPS beginning in 1992. Numbers for years 1994 through 2000 reflect changes in the CPS due to newly instituted computer-assisted interviewing and the change in population controls used in the 1990 Census-based estimates, with adjustment for undercounting in the 1990 Census.

SOURCE: Philip Kaufman, Martha Naomi Alt, and Christopher D. Chapman, "Figure 1.—Event dropout rates of 15- to 24-year-olds who dropped out of grades 10-12, by family income:* October 1972 to October 2000," in *Dropout Rates in the United States: 2000*, NCES 2002-114, U.S. Department of Education, National Center for Education Statistics, November 2001

the early 1990s, but the rates grew during the mid-1990s. The rates began to drop significantly again from 1997 to 2002. The proportion of students who reported using cigarettes during their lifetimes was 31.4 percent for eighth graders, 47.4 for tenth graders, and 57.2 percent for seniors in 2002. (See Table 2.18.)

In 2002 about one-half to two-thirds of students (rising with each grade level) believed that smoking one or more packs of cigarettes a day represented a great risk, a slight increase from 1991. (See Figure 2.5.) Although students in higher grades were more likely to say that there was "great risk" in smoking one or more packs a day, students in the younger grades were somewhat more likely than seniors to "disapprove" of daily cigarette smoking. (See Figure 2.6.)

In 2001 white students (31.9 percent) and Hispanic students (26.6 percent) were more likely than black teens

(14.7 percent) to have smoked cigarettes at least once in the 30 days preceding the survey. White students were also more likely to be frequent cigarette smokers (17.2 percent). (See Table 2.20.)

Seniors were most likely to be current (35.2 percent) and frequent (21 percent) smokers. Males and females were almost equally likely to be frequent smokers in ninth and tenth grades, but in eleventh and twelfth grades, males were more likely to smoke frequently. (See Table 2.20.)

SEXUAL ACTIVITY. *Great Transitions: Preparing Adolescents for a New Century* (Carnegie Council on Adolescent Development, New York, 1995) pointed out that the age of first intercourse declined during the years between 1965 and 1995. Since that time the proportion of students who reported having initiated sexual intercourse before 13 years of age has declined from 9 percent in

FIGURE 2.2

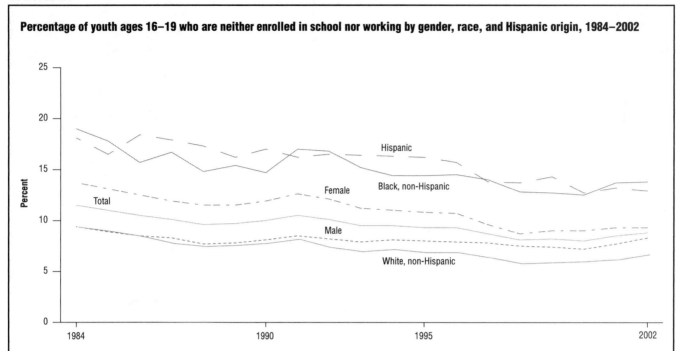

Percentage of youth ages 16–19 who are neither enrolled in school nor working by gender, race, and Hispanic origin, 1984–2002

SOURCE: Federal Interagency Forum on Child and Family Statistics, "Indicator ED6 Percentage of you ages 16 to 19 who are neither enrolled in school nor working by gender, race, and Hispanic origin, 1984–2002," in *America's Children: Key National Indicators of Well-Being, 2003,* Federal Interagency Forum on Child and Family Statistics, Washington, DC, July 2003

1995 to 6.6 percent in 2001. In its *Youth Risk Behavior Surveillance—United States, 2001,* the CDC reported that about 4 percent of females and 9.3 percent of males had first experienced sexual intercourse before age 13. About one-third (33.4 percent) of both high school females and males claimed they were currently sexually active. The proportion of females who reported that they had had four or more sexual partners was 11.4 percent, and for males, the percentage was 17.2. About 83.9 percent of females and 88.5 percent of males reported exercising responsible sexual behavior. Older students tended to be more sexually active than younger students with 47.9 percent of high school seniors stating that they were currently sexually active. Black students (60.8 percent) were more likely than white (43.2 percent) or Hispanic (48.4 percent) students to be sexually active. (See Table 2.21.)

TEEN PREGNANCY. From 1960 through 1986, the number of live births per 1,000 females ages 15 to 17 generally declined. The rate increased during the late 1980s and early 1990s before starting to decline again after 1995. The National Center for Health Statistics reported that in 2001 there were 25.3 live births per 1,000 females ages 15 to 17. (See Table 2.22.)

In 2001 mothers under age 20 accounted for a total of 455,158 live births. Non-Hispanic white teenagers had a birthrate of 30 births per 1,000 females ages 15 through 19, while Hispanic females experienced a birthrate of 92 births per 1,000 females in the same age group. The birthrate for non-Hispanic black teenage mothers was not available for 2001, but in 2000 it was 82 births per 1,000 females ages 15 through 19. (See Figure 2.7.)

Most teenage mothers are unmarried and lack the resources to give their children adequate care. The National Center for Health Statistics reported that in 2000 about 79 percent of all teen births occurred outside of marriage. In 2000 the nonmarital birthrate of females ages 15 through 19 was 40 per 1,000 females. Very few teens ages 15–19 were married, but birthrates among married teens (291 per 1,000 females) were much higher than nonmarital teenage birthrates in 2000. (See Table 2.23.)

AIDS AND OTHER SEXUALLY TRANSMITTED DISEASES. The CDC identifies certain diseases as "notifiable," meaning that state and local medical authorities must report each occurrence to the CDC. Sexually transmitted diseases (STDs) are included in the notifiable disease list. Human immunodeficiency virus (HIV, the virus that causes AIDS) is probably the best known STD, but it is not the most common. Syphilis, chlamydia, and gonorrhea are the three most common STDs reported to the CDC.

According to *HIV/AIDS Surveillance Report* (Centers for Disease Control and Prevention, vol. 13, no. 2, 2001), adolescents and young adults are at a higher risk for acquiring STDs than older adults. Chlamydia and gonorrhea are the most common STD among teenagers. The CDC reported in *Sexually Transmitted Disease Surveillance, 2002* (Centers for Disease Control and Prevention, September

TABLE 2.17

Trends in harmfulness of drugs as perceived by eighth and tenth graders, 1991–2002

Q. HOW MUCH DO YOU THINK PEOPLE RISK HARMING THEMSELVES (PHYSICALLY OR IN OTHER WAYS), IF THEY . . .

Percentage saying "great risk"[1]

8th grade

	1991	1992	1993	1994	1995	1996	1997	1998	1999	2000	2001	2002	'01–'02 change
Try marijuana once or twice	40.4	39.1	36.2	31.6	28.9	27.9	25.3	28.1	28.0	29.0	27.7	28.2	+0.5
Smoke marijuana occasionally	57.9	56.3	53.8	48.6	45.9	44.3	43.1	45.0	45.7	47.4	46.3	46.0	-0.3
Smoke marijuana regularly	83.8	82.0	79.6	74.3	73.0	70.9	72.7	73.0	73.3	74.8	72.2	71.7	-0.5
Try inhalants once or twice[2]	35.9	37.0	36.5	37.9	36.4	40.8	40.1	38.9	40.8	41.2	45.6	42.8	-2.8s
Try inhalants regularly[2]	65.6	64.4	64.6	65.5	64.8	68.2	68.7	67.2	68.8	69.9	71.6	69.9	-1.7
Try LSD once or twice[3]	—	—	42.1	38.3	36.7	36.5	37.0	34.9	34.1	34.0	31.6	29.6	-2.0
Take LSD regularly[3]	—	—	68.3	65.8	64.4	63.6	64.1	59.6	58.8	57.5	52.9	49.3	-3.6
Try MDMA (Ecstasy) once or twice[4]	—	—	—	—	—	—	—	—	—	—	35.8	38.9	+3.1
Take MDMA (Ecstasy) occasionally[4]	—	—	—	—	—	—	—	—	—	—	55.5	61.8	+6.4sss
Try crack once or twice[2]	62.8	61.2	57.2	54.4	50.8	51.0	49.9	49.3	48.7	48.5	48.6	47.4	-1.2
Take crack occasionally[2]	82.2	79.6	76.8	74.4	72.1	71.6	71.2	70.6	70.6	70.1	70.0	69.7	-0.2
Try cocaine powder once or twice[2]	55.5	54.1	50.7	48.4	44.9	45.2	45.0	44.0	43.3	43.3	43.9	43.2	-0.7
Take cocaine powder occasionally[2]	77.0	74.3	71.8	69.1	66.4	65.7	65.8	65.2	65.4	65.5	65.8	64.9	-0.9
Try heroin once or twice without using a needle[3]	—	—	—	—	60.1	61.3	63.0	62.8	63.0	62.0	61.1	62.6	+1.5
Take heroin occasionally without using a needle[3]	—	—	—	—	76.8	76.6	79.2	79.0	78.9	78.6	78.5	78.5	0.0
Try one or two drinks of an alcoholic beverage (beer, wine, liquor)	11.0	12.1	12.4	11.6	11.6	11.8	10.4	12.1	11.6	11.9	12.2	12.5	+0.3
Take one or two drinks nearly every day	31.8	32.4	32.6	29.9	30.5	28.6	29.1	30.3	29.7	30.4	30.0	29.6	-0.4
Have five or more drinks once or twice each weekend	59.1	58.0	57.7	54.7	54.1	51.8	55.6	56.0	55.3	55.9	56.1	56.4	+0.4
Smoke one or more packs of cigarettes per day[5]	51.6	50.8	52.7	50.8	49.8	50.4	52.6	54.3	54.8	58.8	57.1	57.5	+0.4
Use smokeless tobacco regularly	35.1	35.1	36.9	35.5	33.5	34.0	35.2	36.5	37.1	39.0	38.2	39.4	+1.1
Take steroids[6]	64.2	69.5	70.2	67.6	—	—	—	—	—	—	—	—	—
Approx. N (in thousands)=	17.4	18.7	18.4	17.4	17.5	17.9	18.8	18.1	16.7	16.7	16.2	15.1	

10th grade

	1991	1992	1993	1994	1995	1996	1997	1998	1999	2000	2001	2002	'01–'02 change
Try marijuana once or twice	30.0	31.9	29.7	24.4	21.5	20.0	18.8	19.6	19.2	18.5	17.9	19.9	+2.0s
Smoke marijuana occasionally	48.6	48.9	46.1	38.9	35.4	32.8	31.9	32.5	33.5	32.4	31.2	32.0	+0.8
Smoke marijuana regularly	82.1	81.1	78.5	71.3	67.9	65.9	65.9	65.8	65.9	64.7	62.8	60.8	-2.0
Try inhalants once or twice[2]	37.8	38.7	40.9	42.7	41.6	47.2	47.5	45.8	48.2	46.6	49.9	48.7	-1.2
Try inhalants regularly[2]	69.8	67.9	69.6	71.5	71.8	75.8	74.5	76.3	76.3	75.0	76.4	73.4	-3.0ss
Try LSD once or twice[3]	—	—	48.7	46.5	44.7	45.1	44.5	43.5	45.0	43.0	41.3	40.1	-1.2
Take LSD regularly[3]	—	—	78.9	75.9	75.5	75.3	73.8	72.3	73.9	72.0	68.8	64.9	-3.9ss
Try MDMA (Ecstasy) once or twice[4]	—	—	—	—	—	—	—	—	—	—	39.4	43.5	+4.1s
Take MDMA (Ecstasy) occasionally[4]	—	—	—	—	—	—	—	—	—	—	64.8	67.3	+2.6
Try crack once or twice[2]	70.4	69.6	66.6	64.7	60.9	60.9	59.2	58.0	57.8	56.1	57.1	57.4	+0.3
Take crack occasionally[2]	87.4	86.4	84.4	83.1	81.2	80.3	78.7	77.5	79.1	76.9	77.3	75.7	-1.7
Try cocaine powder once or twice[2]	59.1	59.2	57.5	56.4	53.5	53.6	52.2	50.9	51.6	48.8	50.6	51.3	+0.7
Take cocaine powder occasionally[2]	82.2	80.1	79.1	77.8	75.6	75.0	73.9	71.8	73.6	70.9	72.3	71.0	-1.4
Try heroin once or twice without using a needle[3]	—	—	—	—	70.7	72.1	73.1	71.7	73.7	71.7	72.0	72.2	+0.1
Take heroin occasionally without using a needle[3]	—	—	—	—	85.1	85.8	86.5	84.9	86.5	85.2	85.4	83.4	-2.0
Try one or two drinks of an alcoholic beverage (beer, wine, liquor)	9.0	10.1	10.9	9.4	9.3	8.9	9.0	10.1	10.5	9.6	9.8	11.5	+1.8ss
Take one or two drinks nearly every day	36.1	36.8	35.9	32.5	31.7	31.2	31.8	31.9	32.9	32.3	31.5	31.0	-0.5
Have five or more drinks once or twice each weekend	54.7	55.9	54.9	52.9	52.0	50.9	51.8	52.5	51.9	51.0	50.7	51.7	+1.0
Smoke one or more packs of cigarettes per day[5]	60.3	59.3	60.7	59.0	57.0	57.9	59.9	61.9	62.7	65.9	64.7	64.3	-0.4
Use smokeless tobacco regularly	40.3	39.6	44.2	42.2	38.2	41.0	42.2	42.8	44.2	46.7	46.2	46.9	+0.7
Take steroids[6]	67.1	72.7	73.4	72.5	—	—	—	—	—	—	—	—	—
Approx. N (in thousands)=	14.7	14.8	15.3	15.9	17.0	15.7	15.6	15.0	13.6	14.3	14.0	14.3	

Notes: Level of significance of difference between the two most recent classes: s = .05, ss = .01, sss = .001. '—' indicates data not available.

Any apparent inconsistency between the change estimate and the prevalence of use estimates for the two most recent classes is due to rounding error.

[1]Answer alternatives were: (1) No risk, (2) Slight risk, (3) Moderate risk, (4) Great risk, and (5) Can't say, drug unfamiliar.

[2]Beginning in 1997, data based on two-thirds of N indicated due to changes in questionnaire forms.

[3]Data based on one of two forms in 1993–96; N is one-half of N indicated. Beginning in 1997, data based on two-thirds of N indicated.

[4]Data based on one-third of N indicated due to changes in questionnaire forms.

[5]Beginning in 1999, data based on two-thirds of N indicated due to changes in questionnaire forms.

[6]Data based on one of two forms in 1991 and 1992. Data based on one of two forms in 1993 and 1994; N is one-half of N indicated.

SOURCE: Lloyd D. Johnston, Patrick M. O'Malley, and Jerald G. Bachman, "Table 8–1. Trends in Harmfulness of Drugs as Perceived by Eighth and Tenth Graders, 1991–2002," in Monitoring the Future: National Survey Results on Drug Use 1975–2002, Volume I: Secondary School Students, NIH Publication No. 03-5375, National Institute on Drug Abuse, Bethesda, MD, August 2003. Data from The Monitoring the Future Study, the University of Michigan

FIGURE 2.3

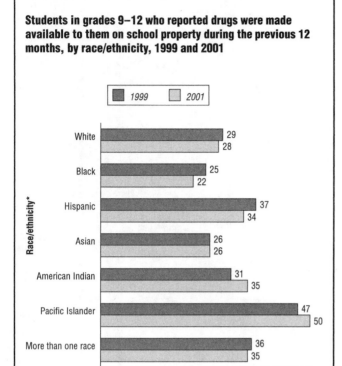

Students in grades 9–12 who reported drugs were made available to them on school property during the previous 12 months, by race/ethnicity, 1999 and 2001

*American Indian includes Alaska Native, Black includes African American, Pacific Islander includes Native Hawaiian, and Hispanic includes Latino. Race categories exclude Hispanic origin unless specified.
Note: "On school property" was not defined for survey respondents.

SOURCE: Jill F. DeVoe, Katharin Peter, Phillip Kaufman, Sally A. Ruddy, Amanda K. Miller, Mike Planty, Thomas D. Snyder, and Michael R. Rand, "Figure 19.2. Percentage of students in grades 9-12 who reported drugs were made available to them on school property during the previous 12 months, by race/ethnicity: 1999 and 2001," in *Indicators of School Crime and Safety: 2003,* NCES 2004-04/NCJ 201257, U.S. Department of Education, National Center for Education Statistics and U.S. Department of Justice, Bureau of Justice Statistics, Washington, DC, October 2003

FIGURE 2.4

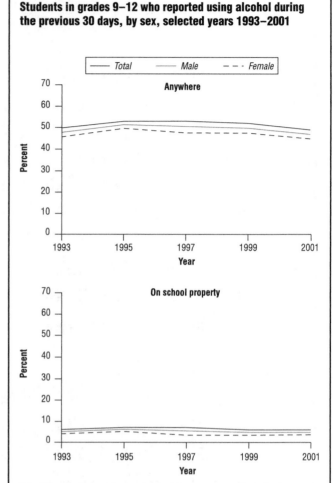

Students in grades 9–12 who reported using alcohol during the previous 30 days, by sex, selected years 1993–2001

Note: "On school property" was not defined for survey respondents. The term "anywhere" is not used in the YRBS questionnaire. Rather, students are simply asked during the past 30 days, on how many days did they have at least one drink of alcohol.

SOURCE: Jill F. DeVoe, Katharin Peter, Phillip Kaufman, Sally A. Ruddy, Amanda K. Miller, Mike Planty, Thomas D. Snyder, and Michael R. Rand, "Figure 17.1. Percentage of students in grades 9-12 who reported using alcohol during the previous 30 days, by sex, selected years 1993–2001," in *Indicators of School Crime and Safety: 2003,* NCES 2004-04/NCJ 201257, U.S. Department of Education, National Center for Education Statistics and U.S. Department of Justice, Bureau of Justice Statistics, Washington, DC, October 2003

2003) that there were 299,863 cases of chlamydia, 96,325 cases of gonorrhea, and 351 cases of syphilis among those 15 to 19 years of age in 2002. Although antibiotics can cure many STDs, they can still have serious health consequences, including an increase in a victim's risk of contracting HIV if exposed. Also, females might contract pelvic inflammatory disease, which can lead to infertility.

HIV/AIDS remains the most dangerous STD. Young people who are sexually active and/or inject drugs are at great risk of contracting the virus. Through December 2001 the CDC reported that a cumulative total of 4,428

AIDS cases had been diagnosed in youths 13 to 19 years of age. More males (2,555 cases) were diagnosed than were females (1,873 cases). (See Table 2.24.) Countless more are infected with HIV, the virus that causes AIDS. Because of the long incubation period from the time of infection and the onset of symptoms, many people who develop AIDS in their early twenties were probably infected with HIV as teenagers.

TABLE 2.18

Trends in lifetime prevalence of use of various drugs for eighth, tenth, and twelfth graders, 1991–2002

(Entries are percentages)

| | Lifetime | | | | | | | | | | | '01–'02 | |
	1991	1992	1993	1994	1995	1996	1997	1998	1999	2000	2001	2002	change
Any illicit drug [1]													
8th grade	18.7	20.6	22.5	25.7	28.5	31.2	29.4	29.0	28.3	26.8	26.8	24.5	-2.3s
10th grade	30.6	29.8	32.8	37.4	40.9	45.4	47.3	44.9	46.2	45.6	45.6	44.6	-1.1
12th grade	44.1	40.7	42.9	45.6	48.4	50.8	54.3	54.1	54.7	54.0	53.9	53.0	-0.9
Any illicit drug other than marijuana [1,2]													
8th grade	14.3	15.6	16.8	17.5	18.8	19.2	17.7	16.9	16.3	15.8	*17.0	13.7	-3.3sss
10th grade	19.1	19.2	20.9	21.7	24.3	25.5	25.0	23.6	24.0	23.1	*23.6	22.1	-1.5
12th grade	26.9	25.1	26.7	27.6	28.1	28.5	30.0	29.4	29.4	29.0	*30.7	29.5	-1.2
Any illicit drug including inhalants [1,3]													
8th grade	28.5	29.6	32.3	35.1	38.1	39.4	38.1	37.8	37.2	35.1	34.5	31.6	-2.9ss
10th grade	36.1	36.2	38.7	42.7	45.9	49.8	50.9	49.3	49.9	49.3	48.8	47.7	-1.1
12th grade	47.6	44.4	46.6	49.1	51.5	53.5	56.3	56.1	56.3	57.0	56.0	54.6	-1.4
Marijuana/hashish													
8th grade	10.2	11.2	12.6	16.7	19.9	23.1	22.6	22.2	22.0	20.3	20.4	19.2	-1.2
10th grade	23.4	21.4	24.4	30.4	34.1	39.8	42.3	39.6	40.9	40.3	40.1	38.7	-1.4
12th grade	36.7	32.6	35.3	38.2	41.7	44.9	49.6	49.1	49.7	48.8	49.0	47.8	-1.1
Inhalants [3,4]													
8th grade	17.6	17.4	19.4	19.9	21.6	21.2	21.0	20.5	19.7	17.9	17.1	15.2	-1.9s
10th grade	15.7	16.6	17.5	18.0	19.0	19.3	18.3	18.3	17.0	16.6	15.2	13.5	-1.6s
12th grade	17.6	16.6	17.4	17.7	17.4	16.6	16.1	15.2	15.4	14.2	13.0	11.7	-1.4
Nitrites [5]													
8th grade	—	—	—	—	—	—	—	—	—	—	—	—	—
10th grade	—	—	—	—	—	—	—	—	—	—	—	—	—
12th grade	1.6	1.5	1.4	1.7	1.5	1.8	2.0	2.7	1.7	0.8	1.9	1.5	-0.4
Hallucinogens [2,6]													
8th grade	3.2	3.8	3.9	4.3	5.2	5.9	5.4	4.9	4.8	4.6	* 5.2	4.1	-1.0
10th grade	6.1	6.4	6.8	8.1	9.3	10.5	10.5	9.8	9.7	8.9	* 8.9	7.8	-1.0
12th grade	9.6	9.2	10.9	11.4	12.7	14.0	15.1	14.1	13.7	13.0	*14.7	12.0	-2.7s
LSD													
8th grade	2.7	3.2	3.5	3.7	4.4	5.1	4.7	4.1	4.1	3.9	3.4	2.5	-1.0s
10th grade	5.6	5.8	6.2	7.2	8.4	9.4	9.5	8.5	8.5	7.6	6.3	5.0	-1.4s
12th grade	8.8	8.6	10.3	10.5	11.7	12.6	13.6	12.6	12.2	11.1	10.9	8.4	-2.5ss
Hallucinogens other than LSD [2]													
8th grade	1.4	1.7	1.7	2.2	2.5	3.0	2.6	2.5	2.4	2.3	* 3.9	3.3	-0.6
10th grade	2.2	2.5	2.8	3.8	3.9	4.7	4.8	5.0	4.7	4.8	* 6.6	6.3	-0.3
12th grade	3.7	3.3	3.9	4.9	5.4	6.8	7.5	7.1	6.7	6.9	*10.4	9.2	-1.2
PCP [5]													
8th grade	—	—	—	—	—	—	—	—	—	—	—	—	—
10th grade	—	—	—	—	—	—	—	—	—	—	—	—	—
12th grade	2.9	2.4	2.9	2.8	2.7	4.0	3.9	3.9	3.4	3.4	3.5	3.1	-0.5
MDMA (Ecstasy) [7]													
8th grade	—	—	—	—	—	3.4	3.2	2.7	2.7	4.3	5.2	4.3	-0.9
10th grade	—	—	—	—	—	5.6	5.7	5.1	6.0	7.3	8.0	6.6	-1.4
12th grade	—	—	—	—	—	6.1	6.9	5.8	8.0	11.0	11.7	10.5	-1.2
Cocaine													
8th grade	2.3	2.9	2.9	3.6	4.2	4.5	4.4	4.6	4.7	4.5	4.3	3.6	-0.7
10th grade	4.1	3.3	3.6	4.3	5.0	6.5	7.1	7.2	7.7	6.9	5.7	6.1	+0.5
12th grade	7.8	6.1	6.1	5.9	6.0	7.1	8.7	9.3	9.8	8.6	8.2	7.8	-0.4
Crack													
8th grade	1.3	1.6	1.7	2.4	2.7	2.9	2.7	3.2	3.1	3.1	3.0	2.5	-0.4
10th grade	1.7	1.5	1.8	2.1	2.8	3.3	3.6	3.9	4.0	3.7	3.1	3.6	+0.5
12th grade	3.1	2.6	2.6	3.0	3.0	3.3	3.9	4.4	4.6	3.9	3.7	3.8	+0.1
Other cocaine [8]													
8th grade	2.0	2.4	2.4	3.0	3.4	3.8	3.5	3.7	3.8	3.5	3.3	2.8	-0.5
10th grade	3.8	3.0	3.3	3.8	4.4	5.5	6.1	6.4	6.8	6.0	5.0	5.2	+0.2
12th grade	7.0	5.3	5.4	5.2	5.1	6.4	8.2	8.4	8.8	7.7	7.4	7.0	-0.4
Heroin [9]													
8th grade	1.2	1.4	1.4	2.0	2.3	2.4	2.1	2.3	2.3	1.9	1.7	1.6	-0.1
10th grade	1.2	1.2	1.3	1.5	1.7	2.1	2.1	2.3	2.3	2.2	1.7	1.8	+0.2
12th grade	0.9	1.2	1.1	1.2	1.6	1.8	2.1	2.0	2.0	2.4	1.8	1.7	-0.1

TABLE 2.18

Trends in lifetime prevalence of use of various drugs for eighth, tenth, and twelfth graders, 1991–2002 [CONTINUED]

(Entries are percentages)

					Lifetime							'01–'02	
	1991	1992	1993	1994	1995	1996	1997	1998	1999	2000	2001	2002	change
With a needle [10]													
8th grade	—	—	—	—	1.5	1.6	1.3	1.4	1.6	1.1	1.2	1.0	-0.1
10th grade	—	—	—	—	1.0	1.1	1.1	1.2	1.3	1.0	0.8	1.0	+0.2
12th grade	—	—	—	—	0.7	0.8	0.9	0.8	0.9	0.8	0.7	0.8	+0.1
Without a needle [10]													
8th grade	—	—	—	—	1.5	1.6	1.4	1.5	1.4	1.3	1.1	1.0	-0.1
10th grade	—	—	—	—	1.1	1.7	1.7	1.7	1.6	1.7	1.3	1.3	+0.1
12th grade	—	—	—	—	1.4	1.7	2.1	1.6	1.8	2.4	1.5	1.6	+0.1
Other narcotics [11]													
8th grade	—	—	—	—	—	—	—	—	—	—	—	—	—
10th grade	—	—	—	—	—	—	—	—	—	—	—	—	—
12th grade	6.6	6.1	6.4	6.6	7.2	8.2	9.7	9.8	10.2	10.6	9.9	10.1	+0.2[i]
Amphetamines [11]													
8th grade	10.5	10.8	11.8	12.3	13.1	13.5	12.3	11.3	10.7	9.9	10.2	8.7	-1.5s
10th grade	13.2	13.1	14.9	15.1	17.4	17.7	17.0	16.0	15.7	15.7	16.0	14.9	-1.1
12th grade	15.4	13.9	15.1	15.7	15.3	15.3	16.5	16.4	16.3	15.6	16.2	16.8	+0.5
Methamphetamine [13,14]													
8th grade	—	—	—	—	—	—	—	—	4.5	4.2	4.4	3.5	-0.9
10th grade	—	—	—	—	—	—	—	—	7.3	6.9	6.4	6.1	-0.3
12th grade	—	—	—	—	—	—	—	—	8.2	7.9	6.9	6.7	-0.2
Ice [14]													
8th grade	—	—	—	—	—	—	—	—	—	—	—	—	—
10th grade	—	—	—	—	—	—	—	—	—	—	—	—	—
12th grade	3.3	2.9	3.1	3.4	3.9	4.4	4.4	5.3	4.8	4.0	4.1	4.7	+0.6
Sedatives (Barbiturates) [11]													
8th grade	—	—	—	—	—	—	—	—	—	—	—	—	—
10th grade	—	—	—	—	—	—	—	—	—	—	—	—	—
12th grade	6.2	5.5	6.3	7.0	7.4	7.6	8.1	8.7	8.9	9.2	8.7	9.5	+0.9
Methalqualone [5,11]													
8th grade	—	—	—	—	—	—	—	—	—	—	—	—	—
10th grade	—	—	—	—	—	—	—	—	—	—	—	—	—
12th grade	1.3	1.6	0.8	1.4	1.2	2.0	1.7	1.6	1.8	0.8	1.1	1.5	+0.4
Tranquilizers [2,11]													
8th grade	3.8	4.1	4.4	4.6	4.5	5.3	4.8	4.6	4.4	4.4	‡5.0	4.3	-0.7
10th grade	5.8	5.9	5.7	5.4	6.0	7.1	7.3	7.8	7.9	8.0	‡9.2	8.8	-0.3
12th grade	7.2	6.0	6.4	6.6	7.1	7.2	7.8	8.5	9.3	8.9	‡10.3	11.4	+1.2
Rohypnol [5,15,16]													
8th grade	—	—	—	—	—	1.5	1.1	1.4	1.3	1.0	1.1	0.8	-0.3
10th grade	—	—	—	—	—	1.5	1.7	2.0	1.8	1.3	1.5	1.3	-0.2
12th grade	—	—	—	—	—	1.2	1.8	3.0	2.0	1.5	1.7	—	—
Alcohol [17]													
Any use													
8th grade	70.1	69.3	*55.7	55.8	54.5	55.3	53.8	52.5	52.1	51.7	50.5	47.0	-3.5ss
10th grade	83.8	82.3	*71.6	71.1	70.5	71.8	72.0	69.8	70.6	71.4	70.1	66.9	-3.2ss
12th grade	88.0	87.5	*80.0	80.4	80.7	79.2	81.7	81.4	80.0	80.3	79.7	78.4	-1.3
Been Drunk [14]													
8th grade	26.7	26.8	26.4	25.9	25.3	26.8	25.2	24.8	24.8	25.1	23.4	21.3	-2.1s
10th grade	50.0	47.7	47.9	47.2	46.9	48.5	49.4	46.7	48.9	49.3	48.2	44.0	-4.2sss
12th grade	65.4	63.4	62.5	62.9	63.2	61.8	64.2	62.4	62.3	62.3	63.9	61.6	-2.3
Cigarettes													
Any use													
8th grade	44.0	45.2	45.3	46.1	46.4	49.2	47.3	45.7	44.1	40.5	36.6	31.4	-5.1sss
10th grade	55.1	53.5	56.3	56.9	57.6	61.2	60.2	57.7	57.6	55.1	52.8	47.4	-5.4sss
12th grade	63.1	61.8	61.9	62.0	64.2	63.5	65.4	65.3	64.6	62.5	61.0	57.2	-3.9ss
Smokeless Tobacco [5,8]													
8th grade	22.2	20.7	18.7	19.9	20.0	20.4	16.8	15.0	14.4	12.8	11.7	11.2	-0.5
10th grade	28.2	26.6	28.1	29.2	27.6	27.4	26.3	22.7	20.4	19.1	19.5	16.9	-2.6s
12th grade	—	32.4	31.0	30.7	30.9	29.8	25.3	26.2	23.4	23.1	19.7	18.3	-1.4

TABLE 2.18

Trends in lifetime prevalence of use of various drugs for eighth, tenth, and twelfth graders, 1991–2002 [CONTINUED]

(Entries are percentages)

						Lifetime						'01–'02	
	1991	1992	1993	1994	1995	1996	1997	1998	1999	2000	2001	2002	change
Steroids[14]													
8th grade	1.9	1.7	1.6	2.0	2.0	1.8	1.8	2.3	2.7	3.0	2.8	2.5	-0.3
10th grade	1.8	1.7	1.7	1.8	2.0	1.8	2.0	2.0	2.7	3.5	3.5	3.5	0.0
12th grade	2.1	2.1	2.0	2.4	2.3	1.9	2.4	2.7	2.9	2.5	3.7	4.0	+0.3

Notes: Level of significance of difference between the two most recent classes: s = .05, ss = .01, sss = .001.

'—' indicates data not available.

'*' indicates some change in the question. See relevant footnote for that drug.

Any apparent inconsistency between the change estimate and the prevalence of use estimates for the two most recent classes is due to rounding error.

[1]For 12th graders only: Use of "any illicit drug" includes any use of marijuana, LSD, other hallucinogens, crack, other cocaine, or heroin, *or* any use of other narcotics, amphetamines, sedatives (barbiturates), or tranquilizers not under a doctor's orders. For 8th and 10th graders: The use of other narcotics and barbiturates has been excluded, because these younger respondents appear to overreport use (perhaps because they include the use of nonprescription drugs in their answers).

[2]In 2001 the question text was changed on half of the questionnaire forms for each grade. "Other psychedelics" was changed to "other hallucinogens" and "shrooms" was added to the list of examples. For the tranquilizer list of examples, Miltown was replaced with Xanax. The 2001 data presented here are based on the changed forms only; N is one-half of N indicated. In 2002 the remaining forms were changed to the new wording. The 2002 data are based on all forms. Data for "any illicit drug other than marijuana" and "hallucinogens" are also affected by these changes and have been handled in a parallel manner.

[3]For 12th graders only: Data based on five of six forms in 1991-98; N is five-sixths of N indicated. Beginning in 1999, data based on three of six forms; N is one-half of N indicated.

[4]Inhalants are unadjusted for underreporting of amyl and butyl nitrites.

[5]For 12th graders only: Data based on one of six forms; N is one-sixth of N indicated.

[6]Hallucinogens are unadjusted for underreporting of PCP.

[7]For 8th and 10th graders only: Data based on one of two forms in 1996; N is one-half of N indicated. In 1997–2001, data based on one-third of N indicated due to changes on the questionnaire forms. Data based on two of four forms in 2002; N is one-half of N indicated. For 12th graders only: Data based on one of six forms in 1996–2001; N is one-sixth of N indicated. Data based on two of six forms in 2002; N is two-sixths of N indicated.

[8]For 12th graders only: Data based on four of six forms; N is four-sixths of N indicated.

[9]In 1995, the heroin question was changed in three of six forms for 12th graders and in one of two forms for 8th and 10th graders. Separate questions were asked for use with injection and without injection. Data presented here represent the combined data from all forms. In 1996, the heroin question was changed in all remaining 8th and 10th grade forms.

[10]For 8th and 10th graders only: Data based on one of two forms in 1995; N is one-half of N indicated. Data based on all forms beginning in 1996. For 12th graders only: Data based on three of six forms; N is one-half of N indicated.

[11]Only drug use not under a doctor's orders is included here.

[12]In 2002 the question text was changed in half of the questionnaire forms. The list of examples of narcotics other than heroin was updated: Talwin, laudanum, and paregoric—all of which had negligible rates of use by 2001—were replaced with Vicodin, Oxycontin, and Percocet. The 2001 data presented here are based on all forms. The 2002 estimates are based on the 2001 prevalence of use rate plus the increase observed from 2001 to 2002 in the half-sample in which the question did not change. Thus, the change score given in the right-hand column is the difference between the data from the unchanged forms only in both 2001 and 2002.

[13]For 8th and 10th graders only: Data based on one of four forms; N is one-third of N indicated.

[14]For 12th graders only: Data based on two of six forms; N is two-sixths of N indicated.

[15]For 8th and 10th graders only: Data based on one of two forms in 1996; N is one-half of N indicated. Data based on three of four forms in 1997–98; N is two-thirds of N indicated. Data based on two of four forms in 1999–2001; N is one-third of N indicated. Data based on one of four forms in 2002; N is one-sixth of N indicated.

[16]For 12th graders only: Data for Rohypnol for 2001 and 2002 are not comparable due to changes in the questionnaire forms.

[17]In 1993, the question text was changed slightly in half of the forms to indicate that a "drink" meant "more than a few sips." The 1993 data are based on the changed forms only; N is one-half of N indicated. In 1994 the remaining forms were changed to the new wording. Beginning in 1994, the data are based on all forms.

[18]For 8th and 10th graders only: Data based on one of two forms for 1991–96 and on two of four forms beginning in 1997; N is one-half of N indicated.

[19]For 12th graders only: Data based on two of six forms in 2000; N is two-sixths of N indicated. Data based on three of six forms in 2001; N is one-half of N indicated. Data based on one of six forms in 2002; N is one-sixth of N indicated.

[20]For 12th graders only: Data based on two of six forms in 2000; N is two-sixths of N indicated. Data based on three of six forms beginning in 2001; N is one-half of N indicated.

[21]Daily use is defined as use on twenty or more occasions in the past thirty days except for cigarettes and smokeless tobacco, for which actual daily use is measured, and for 5+ drinks, for which the prevalence or having five or more drinks in a row in the last two weeks is measured.

SOURCE: Lloyd D. Johnston, Patrick M. O'Malley, and Jerald G. Bachman, "Table 5–5a. Trends in Lifetime Prevalence of Use of Various Drugs for Eighth, Tenth, and Twelfth Graders," in *Monitoring the Future: National Survey Results on Drug Use 1975–2002, Volume I: Secondary School Students*, NIH Publication No. 03-5375, National Institute on Drug Abuse, Bethesda, MD, August 2003. Data from The Monitoring the Future Study, the University of Michigan

TABLE 2.19

Percentage of high school students who drank alcohol and used marijuana, by various criteria, from Youth Risk Criteria Survey, 2001

Category	Lifetime alcohol use[1]			Current alcohol use[2]			Episodic heavy drinking[3]			Lifetime marijuana use[4]			Current marijuana use[5]		
	Female	Male	Total	Female	Male	Total	Female	Male	Total	Female	Male	Total	Female	Male	Total
Race/Ethnicity															
White[6]	79.6	80.7	**80.1**	48.3	52.6	**50.4**	30.5	37.7	**34.0**	39.2	46.4	**42.8**	20.6	28.4	**24.4**
	(±1.9)[1]	(±1.6)	**(±1.5)**	(±2.4)	(±3.1)	**(±2.2)**	(±2.1)	(±3.2)	**(±2.0)**	(±2.7)	(±2.3)	**(±2.2)**	(±2.4)	(±2.2)	**(±2.0)**
Black[6]	69.7	68.4	**69.1**	30.6	35.0	**32.7**	7.5	15.1	**11.1**	34.3	46.7	**40.2**	16.0	28.2	**21.8**
	(±5.5)	(±4.7)	**(±4.4)**	(±5.3)	(±4.9)	**(±4.6)**	(±2.0)	(±3.8)	**(±2.2)**	(±6.9)	(±5.9)	**(±5.8)**	(±3.9)	(±5.1)	**(±4.1)**
Hispanic	80.1	81.6	**80.8**	48.8	49.5	**49.2**	28.7	31.4	**30.1**	39.7	50.0	**44.7**	22.4	26.8	**24.6**
	(±3.3)	(±3.2)	**(±2.9)**	(±3.1)	(±4.1)	**(±3.0)**	(±2.8)	(±3.3)	**(±2.5)**	(±3.6)	(±3.5)	**(±2.3)**	(±3.1)	(±2.7)	**(±1.6)**
Grade															
9	72.0	74.5	**73.1**	40.0	42.2	**41.1**	23.0	26.2	**24.5**	28.6	37.3	**32.7**	16.5	22.6	**19.4**
	(±3.8)	(±3.7)	**(±2.9)**	(±4.0)	(±4.4)	**(±3.6)**	(±3.1)	(±4.2)	**(±2.8)**	(±3.5)	(±3.4)	**(±2.8)**	(±2.7)	(±2.9)	**(±2.4)**
10	76.9	75.6	**76.3**	43.5	46.9	**45.2**	26.3	30.1	**28.2**	37.5	46.1	**41.7**	21.5	28.3	**24.8**
	(±2.2)	(±2.3)	**(±1.6)**	(±3.1)	(±3.1)	**(±2.5)**	(±3.0)	(±3.5)	**(±2.6)**	(±2.6)	(±3.5)	**(±2.6)**	(±2.5)	(±3.3)	**(±2.2)**
11	79.3	81.4	**80.4**	45.1	53.6	**49.3**	26.1	38.5	**32.2**	42.6	51.7	**47.2**	21.4	30.2	**25.8**
	(±3.7)	(±3.6)	**(±3.2)**	(±3.0)	(±4.3)	**(±3.3)**	(v2.9)	(±4.6)	**(±3.4)**	(±3.4)	(±4.2)	**(±3.4)**	(±2.7)	(±3.2)	**(±2.6)**
12	85.5	84.7	**85.1**	53.9	56.6	**55.2**	31.8	42.0	**36.7**	48.9	54.2	**51.5**	21.8	32.3	**26.9**
	(±2.3)	(±2.6)	**(±1.9)**	(±4.3)	(±3.1)	**(±3.0)**	(±4.9)	(±4.2)	**(±3.7)**	(±5.4)	(±3.1)	**(±3.9)**	(±4.6)	(±3.3)	**(±3.5)**
Total	**77.9**	**78.6**	78.2	**45.0**	**49.2**	47.1	**26.4**	**33.5**	29.9	**38.4**	**46.5**	42.4	**20.0**	**27.9**	23.9
	(±1.8)	**(±1.9)**	(±1.7)	**(±2.2)**	**(±2.8)**	(±2.2)	**(±1.9)**	**(±2.9)**	(±2.0)	**(±2.1)**	**(±2.0)**	(±1.9)	**(±1.7)**	**(±1.6)**	(±1.5)

[1] Ever had ≥1 drinks of alcohol.
[2] Drank alcohol on ≥1 of the 30 days preceding the survey.
[3] Drank ≥5 drinks of alcohol on ≥1 occasions on ≥1 of the 30 days preceding the survey.
[4] Ever used marijuana.
[5] Used marijuana ≥1 times during the 30 days preceding the survey.
[6] Non-Hispanic.
[7] 95% confidence interval.

SOURCE: Jo Anne Grunbaum, Laura Kann, Steven A. Kinchen, Barbara Williams, James G. Ross, Richard Lowry, and Lloyd Kolbe, "Table 20. Percentage of high school students who drank alcohol and used marijuana, by sex, race/ethnicity, and grade—United States, Youth Risk Behavior Survey, 2001," in "Youth Risk Behavior Surveillance—United States, 2001," *Surveillance Summaries, MMWR* 2002, vol. 51, no. SS-4, June 28, 2002

FIGURE 2.5

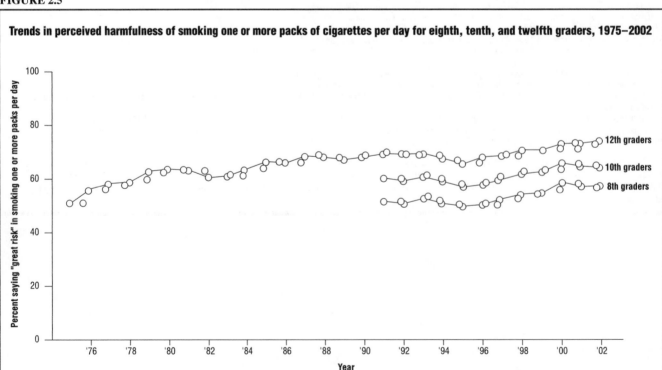

Trends in perceived harmfulness of smoking one or more packs of cigarettes per day for eighth, tenth, and twelfth graders, 1975–2002

SOURCE: Lloyd D. Johnston, Patrick M. O'Malley, and Jerald G. Bachman, "Figure 8–10a. Trends in Perceived Harmfulness of Smoking One or More Packs of Cigarettes per Day for Eighth, Tenth, and Twelfth Graders," in *Monitoring the Future: National Survey Results on Drug Use, 1975–2002, Volume I: Secondary School Students,* NIH Publication No. 03-5375, National Institute on Drug Abuse, Bethesda, MD, August 2003

FIGURE 2.6

Trends in disapproval of smoking one or more packs of cigarettes per day for eighth, tenth, and twelfth graders, 1975–2002

Eighth, Tenth, and Twelfth Graders

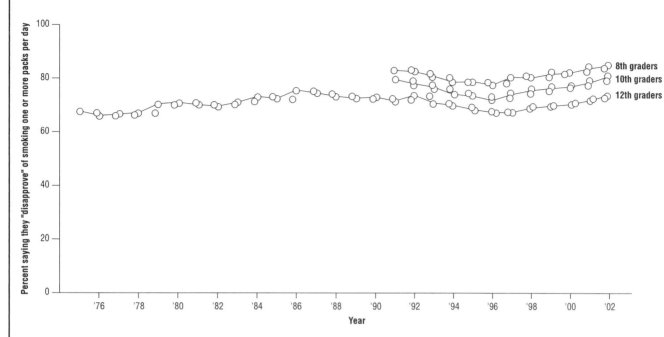

SOURCE: Lloyd D. Johnston, Patrick M. O'Malley, and Jerald G. Bachman, "Figure 8–10b. Trends in Disapproval of Smoking One or More Packs of Cigarettes per Day for Eighth, Tenth, and Twelfth Graders," in *Monitoring the Future: National Survey Results on Drug Use, 1975–2002, Volume I: Secondary School Students,* NIH Publication No. 03-5375, National Institute on Drug Abuse, Bethesda, MD, August 2003

TABLE 2.20

Percentage of high school students who used tobacco by sex, race/ethnicity, and grade, from Youth Risk Behavior Survey, 2001

Category	Lifetime cigarette use[1]			Lifetime daily cigarette use[2]			Current cigarette use[3]			Current frequent cigarette use[4]			Smoked >10 cigarettes/day[5]		
	Female	Male	Total	Female	Male	Total	Female	Male	Total	Female	Male	Total	Female	Male	Total
Race/Ethnicity															
White[6]	62.2	67.4	**64.8**	23.2	24.7	**23.9**	31.2	32.7	**31.9**	16.2	18.1	**17.2**	4.0	6.6	**5.3**
	(2.9)[1]	(2.9)	**(±2.6)**	(±2.6)	(±2.6)	**(±2.3)**	(±2.5)	(±3.0)	**(±2.3)**	(±2.3)	(±2.2)	**(±1.9)**	(±1.3)	(±1.3)	**(±1.0)**
Black[6]	56.7	59.9	**58.3**	6.5	9.0	**7.7**	13.3	16.3	**14.7**	3.1	6.2	**4.6**	0.7	1.5	**1.1**
	(±5.9)	(±4.2)	**(±4.6)**	(±1.7)	(±3.2)	**(±1.9)**	(±3.4)	(±3.2)	**(±2.8)**	(±1.3)	(±2.7)	**(±1.7)**	(±0.4)	(±1.0)	**(±0.5)**
Hispanic	67.8	70.9	**69.3**	11.5	13.4	**12.4**	26.0	27.2	**26.6**	5.9	8.8	**7.3**	1.7	1.9	**1.8**
	(±3.9)	(±5.4)	**(±4.0)**	(±2.5)	(±3.4)	**(±2.4)**	(±3.7)	(±7.0)	**(±4.3)**	(±2.0)	(±2.7)	**(±1.8)**	(±1.3)	(±0.9)	**(±0.8)**
Grade															
9	55.9	61.3	**58.4**	13.6	15.2	**14.3**	23.6	24.3	**23.9**	8.3	9.6	**8.9**	1.7	2.9	**2.2**
	(±5.3)	(±3.4)	**(±3.8)**	(±3.2)	(±3.5)	**(±2.9)**	(±3.8)	(±3.1)	**(±2.9)**	(±2.3)	(±2.7)	**(±2.1)**	(±1.0)	(±1.1)	**(±0.9)**
10	59.8	65.4	**62.6**	19.2	19.1	**19.1**	28.4	25.4	**26.9**	12.3	12.4	**12.3**	2.4	4.7	**3.6**
	(±3.9)	(±4.3)	**(±3.5)**	(±3.0)	(±2.5)	**(±1.9)**	(±3.8)	(±3.5)	**(±3.2)**	(±2.0)	(±2.4)	**(±1.8)**	(±1.5)	(±1.4)	**(±1.2)**
11	63.5	68.2	**65.9**	20.5	23.6	**22.1**	27.3	32.3	**29.8**	12.9	17.5	**15.2**	3.2	6.4	**4.8**
	(±3.3)	(±3.7)	**(±2.8)**	(±3.2)	(±4.3)	**(±3.3)**	(±3.3)	(±5.0)	**(±3.7)**	(±2.2)	(±3.6)	**(±2.6)**	(±1.3)	(±2.1)	**(±1.3)**
12	69.7	72.5	**71.1**	26.1	27.8	**26.9**	33.1	37.5	**35.2**	20.0	22.0	**21.0**	5.7	7.5	**6.6**
	(±5.0)	(±3.4)	**(±3.9)**	(±4.3)	(±4.8)	**(±4.1)**	(±5.3)	(±4.6)	**(±4.1)**	(±4.3)	(±4.2)	**(±3.6)**	(±1.8)	(±2.4)	**(±1.6)**
Total	**61.6**	**66.3**	**63.9**	**19.2**	**20.9**	**20.0**	**27.7**	**29.2**	**28.5**	**12.9**	**14.9**	**13.8**	**3.1**	**5.2**	**4.1**
	(±2.3)	**(±2.3)**	**(±2.1)**	**(±1.9)**	**(±2.2)**	**(±1.9)**	**(±2.1)**	**(±2.6)**	**(±2.0)**	**(±1.6)**	**(±1.9)**	**(±1.6)**	**(±0.9)**	**(±1.0)**	**(±0.8)**

[1]Ever tried cigarette smoking, even one or two puffs.
[2]Ever smoked >1 cigarettes every day for 30 days.
[3]Smoked cigarettes on >1 of the 30 days preceding the survey.
[4]Smoked cigarettes on >20 of the 30 days preceding the survey.
[5]Smoked >10 cigarettes per day on the days smoked during the 30 days preceding the survey.
[6]Non-Hispanic.
[7]95% confidence interval.

SOURCE: Jo Anne Grunbaum, Laura Kann, Steven A. Kinchen, Barbara Williams, James G. Ross, Richard Lowry, and Lloyd Kolbe, "Table 14. Percentage of high school students who used tobacco, by sex, race/ethnicity, and grade—United States, Youth Risk Behavior Survey, 2001," in "Youth Risk Behavior Surveillance—United States, 2001," *Surveillance Summaries, MMWR* 2002, vol. 51, no. SS-4, June 28, 2002

TABLE 2.21

Percentage of high school students who engaged in sexual behaviors, by sex, race/ethnicity, and grade, from Youth Risk Behavior Survey, 2001

Category	Ever had sexual intercourse			First sexual intercourse before age 13 years			≥4 sex partners during lifetime			Currently sexually active[1]			Responsible sexual behavior[2]		
	Female	Male	Total	Female	Male	Total	Female	Male	Total	Female	Male	Total	Female	Male	Total
Race/Ethnicity															
White[3]	41.3	45.1	**43.2**	3.3	6.2	**4.7**	11.1	12.8	**12.0**	32.3	30.0	**31.3**	84.2	89.3	**86.6**
	(±3.2)[4]	(±2.7)	**(±2.5)**	(±1.3)	(±1.2)	**(±1.1)**	(±1.8)	(±1.5)	**(±1.4)**	(±2.8)	(±2.3)	**(±2.2)**	(±1.7)	(±1.5)	**(±1.1)**
Black[3]	53.4	68.8	**60.8**	7.6	25.7	**16.3**	15.6	38.7	**26.6**	39.5	52.3	**45.6**	84.8	85.9	**85.2**
	(±5.1)	(±8.4)	**(±6.6)**	(±2.2)	(±5.0)	**(±2.6)**	(±3.6)	(±5.7)	**(±3.7)**	(±5.1)	(±7.2)	**(±5.4)**	(±2.8)	(±3.1)	**(±2.6)**
Hispanic	44.0	53.0	**48.4**	4.1	11.4	**7.6**	9.5	20.6	**14.9**	34.5	37.3	**35.9**	82.1	85.2	**83.6**
	(±5.0)	(±4.9)	**(±4.5)**	(±1.3)	(v3.6)	**(±2.0)**	(±2.0)	(±2.8)	**(±1.7)**	(±4.2)	(±3.6)	**(±3.2)**	(±3.3)	(±3.4)	**(±2.8)**
Grade															
9	29.1	40.5	**34.4**	5.4	13.7	**9.2**	5.8	13.9	**9.6**	19.9	25.9	**22.7**	93.5	92.2	**92.8**
	(±4.0)	(±4.6)	**(±3.6)**	(±1.3)	(±2.8)	**(±1.5)**	(±1.7)	(±2.3)	**(±1.6)**	(±3.4)	(±4.1)	**(±3.1)**	(±1.7)	(±1.8)	**(±1.2)**
10	39.3	42.2	**40.8**	4.7	10.6	**7.5**	10.4	15.0	**12.6**	30.7	28.6	**29.7**	85.4	91.4	**88.3**
	(±3.1)	(±4.1)	**(±3.0)**	(±1.7)	(±1.6)	**(±1.4)**	(±2.0)	(±2.4)	**(±1.8)**	(±2.9)	(±4.1)	**(±2.9)**	(±2.7)	(±1.7)	**(±1.8)**
11	49.7	54.0	**51.9**	2.9	6.4	**4.6**	12.6	17.8	**15.2**	38.1	37.8	**38.1**	82.1	87.0	**84.5**
	(±3.9)	(±3.6)	**(±2.9)**	(±1.2)	(±1.4)	**(±1.1)**	(±2.3)	(±2.4)	**(±1.5)**	(±3.6)	(±2.9)	**(±2.6)**	(±2.9)	(±2.0)	**(±1.8)**
12	60.1	61.0	**60.5**	2.2	5.0	**3.6**	19.5	23.6	**21.6**	51.0	44.6	**47.9**	70.1	81.9	**75.8**
	(±5.4)	(±4.3)	**(±4.0)**	(±0.8)	(±1.1)	**(±0.7)**	(±3.2)	(±3.6)	**(±2.4)**	(±5.4)	(±4.3)	**(±4.0)**	(±4.0)	(±2.5)	**(±2.2)**
Total	**42.9**	**48.5**	**45.6**	**4.0**	**9.3**	**6.6**	**11.4**	**17.2**	**14.2**	**33.4**	**33.4**	**33.4**	**83.9**	**88.5**	**86.1**
	(±2.8)	**(±2.7)**	**(±2.3)**	**(±0.9)**	**(±1.3)**	**(±0.9)**	**(±1.5)**	**(±1.6)**	**(±1.2)**	**(±2.5)**	**(±2.3)**	**(±2.0)**	**(±1.6)**	**(±1.3)**	**(±1.1)**

[1]Sexual intercourse during the 3 months preceding the survey.
[2]This includes students who had never had sexual intercourse, had had sexual intercourse but not during the 3 months preceding the survey, or had used a condom the last time they had sexual intercourse during the 3 months preceding the survey.
[3]Non-Hispanic.
[4]95% confidence interval.

SOURCE: Jo Anne Grunbaum, Laura Kann, Steven A. Kinchen, Barbara Williams, James G. Ross, Richard Lowry, and Lloyd Kolbe, "Table 30. Percentage of high school students who engaged in sexual behaviors, by sex, race/ethnicity, and grade— United States, Youth Risk Behavior Survey, 2001," in "Youth Risk Behavior Surveillance—United States, 2001," *Surveillance Summaries, MMWR* 2002, vol. 51, no. SS-4, June 28, 2002

TABLE 2.22

Teen birth rate (births per 1,000 females), selected years, 1940–2001

Ages	1940	1950	1960	1970	1980	1986	1990	1991	1995	1996	1997	1998	1999	2000	2001
15–19	54.1	81.6	89.1	68.3	53.0	50.2	59.9	62.1	56.8	54.4	52.3	51.1	49.6	48.5	45.9
15–17	—	—	43.9	38.8	32.5	30.5	37.5	38.7	36.0	33.8	32.1	30.4	28.7	27.4	25.3
18–19	—	—	166.7	114.7	82.1	79.6	88.6	94.4	89.1	86.0	83.6	82.0	80.3	79.2	75.8

SOURCE: Angela Romano Papillo, Kerry Franzetta, Jennifer Manlove, Kristin Anderson Moore, Elizabeth Terry-Humen, and Suzanne Ryan, "Teen Birth Rate (Births per 1,000 Females Ages 15–19, 15–17, and 18–19)," in *Facts at a Glance*, Child Trends, Inc., Washington, DC, September 2002. Reproduced with permission.

TABLE 2.23

Marital and nonmarital birth rates (births per 1,000 females), selected years 1960–2000

Rated by marital status and age	1960	1970	1980	1990	1991	1992	1993	1994	1995	1996	1997	1998	1999	2000
Marital, ages 15–19	531	444	350	420	410	398	388	351	362	344	323	322	311	291
Nonmarital, ages 15–19	15	22	28	43	45	45	45	46	44	43	42	42	40	40
Nonmarital, ages 20–24	40	38	41	65	68	69	69	72	70	71	71	72	73	75
Nonmarital, ages 15–44	22	26	29	44	45	45	45	47	45	45	44	44	44	45

SOURCE: Angela Romano Papillo, Kerry Franzetta, Jennifer Manlove, Kristin Anderson Moore, Elizabeth Terry-Humen, and Suzanne Ryan, "Marital and Nonmarital Birth Rates (Births per 1,000 Females)," in *Facts at a Glance*, Child Trends, Inc., Washington, DC, September 2002. Reproduced with permission.

FIGURE 2.7

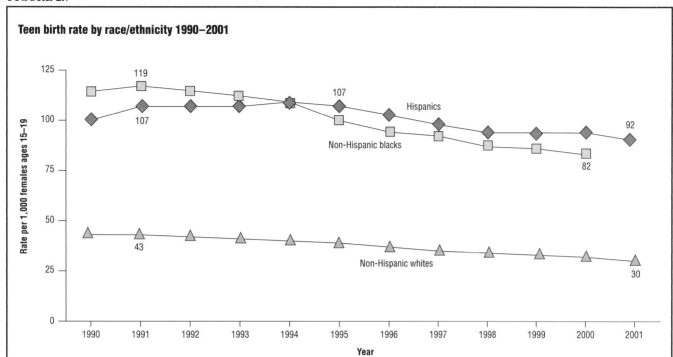

Teen birth rate by race/ethnicity 1990–2001

SOURCE: Angela Romano Papillo, Kerry Franzetta, Jennifer Manlove, Kristin Anderson Moore, Elizabeth Terry-Humen, and Suzanne Ryan, "U.S. Teen Birth Rate by Race/Ethnicity, 1990–2001," in *Facts at a Glance,* Child Trends, Inc., Washington, DC, September 2002. Reproduced with permission.

TABLE 2.24

AIDS cases, by demographic characteristics, reported through December 2001

Age at diagnosis (years)	White, not Hispanic		Black, not Hispanic		Hispanic		Asian/Pacific Islander		American Indian/ Alaska Native		Total[1]	
	No.	(%)	No.	(%)	No.	(%)	No.	(%)	No.	(%)	No.	(%)
Male												
Under 5	535	(0)	2,165	(1)	783	(1)	17	(0)	12	(1)	3,515	(1)
5–12	346	(0)	498	(0)	284	(0)	10	(0)	6	(0)	1,146	(0)
13–19	916	(0)	1,020	(0)	570	(0)	26	(0)	23	(1)	2,555	(0)
20–24	7,938	(3)	7,590	(3)	4,520	(4)	181	(3)	84	(4)	20,337	(3)
25–29	38,967	(12)	26,595	(12)	17,138	(14)	675	(13)	351	(17)	83,794	(12)
30–34	71,345	(23)	46,088	(20)	28,377	(23)	1,161	(22)	536	(26)	147,600	(22)
35–39	71,995	(23)	51,302	(22)	27,047	(22)	1,169	(22)	473	(23)	152,124	(23)
40–44	52,653	(17)	41,395	(18)	19,215	(16)	927	(17)	303	(15)	114,585	(17)
45–49	32,116	(10)	24,839	(11)	10,937	(9)	558	(10)	134	(7)	68,635	(10)
50–54	17,498	(6)	12,959	(6)	5,861	(5)	301	(6)	63	(3)	36,718	(5)
55–59	9,337	(3)	6,987	(3)	3,242	(3)	177	(3)	37	(2)	19,801	(3)
60–64	5,139	(2)	3,819	(2)	1,769	(1)	76	(1)	18	(1)	10,829	(2)
65 or older	4,249	(1)	3,242	(1)	1,455	(1)	76	(1)	17	(1)	9,048	(1)
Male subtotal	313,034	(100)	228,499	(100)	121,198	(100)	5,354	(100)	2,057	(100)	670,687	(100)
Female												
Under 5	502	(2)	2,153	(3)	770	(3)	17	(2)	13	(3)	3,460	(2)
5–12	196	(1)	521	(1)	223	(1)	10	(1)	0	(0)	953	(1)
13–19	295	(1)	1,250	(1)	316	(1)	8	(1)	4	(1)	1,873	(1)
20–24	1,774	(6)	4,844	(6)	1,625	(6)	46	(6)	36	(8)	8,328	(6)
25–29	4,831	(16)	11,876	(14)	4,364	(15)	116	(14)	69	(14)	21,266	(15)
30–34	6,818	(22)	18,055	(21)	6,418	(22)	146	(18)	105	(22)	31,564	(22)
35–39	6,244	(20)	18,351	(22)	5,878	(21)	142	(18)	95	(20)	30,733	(21)
40–44	4,199	(14)	13,221	(16)	3,950	(14)	121	(15)	61	(13)	21,560	(15)
45–49	2,307	(7)	6,922	(8)	2,249	(8)	74	(9)	48	(10)	11,607	(8)
50–54	1,309	(4)	3,447	(4)	1,245	(4)	37	(5)	22	(5)	6,062	(4)
55–59	816	(3)	1,865	(2)	750	(3)	29	(4)	18	(4)	3,479	(2)
60–64	519	(2)	1,103	(1)	411	(1)	29	(4)	5	(1)	2,069	(1)
65 or older	1,044	(3)	1,073	(1)	355	(1)	28	(3)	4	(1)	2,507	(2)
Female subtotal	30,854	(100)	84,681	(100)	28,554	(100)	803	(100)	480	(100)	145,461	(100)
Total[2]	**343,889**		**313,180**		**149,752**		**6,157**		**2,537**		**816,149**	

[1] Includes 545 males and 89 females whose race/ethnicity is unknown.
[2] Includes 1 person whose sex is unknown.

SOURCE: Centers for Disease Control and Prevention, "Table 7. AIDS cases by sex, age at diagnosis, and race/ethnicity, reported through December 2001, United States," in *HIV/AIDS Surveillance Report*, vol. 13, no. 2, 2001

CHAPTER 3
VIOLENCE, CRIME, AND VICTIMIZATION IN SOCIETY

For some young people, their teenage and young adult years are difficult and challenging times. While their peers are playing baseball, going to proms, singing in the school choir, heading to college, and making plans for the future, some juveniles and youths are, for whatever reason, committing crimes and having brushes with the law. When dealing with young offenders, each state has its own definition of the term juvenile: most states put the upper age limit at 17 years old, although some states set it as low as 14. The Federal Bureau of Investigation (FBI) considers those under the age of 18 to be juveniles when reporting its national crime statistics. The FBI often breaks its juvenile crime statistics into age-based subcategories, such as 16 or older and 15 or younger, to demonstrate how juvenile offenses vary with age. The FBI does the same with youth, who are often defined as 18 to 24. However, some organizations and studies classify youth age ranges differently, citing youths as those 18 to 21 or 18 to 25.

The U.S. Department of Justice defines crime as all behaviors and acts for which society provides formally approved punishments. Written law, both federal and state, defines which behaviors are criminal and which are not. Some behaviors—murder, robbery, and burglary—have always been considered criminal. Other actions, such as domestic violence or driving under the influence of drugs or alcohol, became classified as criminal actions more recently. Other changes in society have also influenced crime. For example, the widespread use of computers provides new opportunities for white-collar "cybercrime," including identity theft and the spread of computer viruses and worms.

Crime can range from actions as simple as taking a candy bar from a store without paying for it, to those as severe and violent as murder. Most people have broken some law, wittingly or unwittingly, at some time in their lives. Therefore, the true extent of criminality is impossible to measure. Researchers can only keep records of what is reported by victims or known to the police.

THE UCR AND NCVS

Two main government sources collect crime statistics. The FBI compiles the Uniform Crime Reports (UCR) annually. Begun in 1930, the UCR now collects data from more than 17,000 city, county, and state law enforcement agencies. In 2002 the UCR covered approximately 93.4 percent of the U.S. population as calculated by the Census Bureau.

The second set of crime statistics is the National Crime Victimization Survey (NCVS), prepared by the Bureau of Justice Statistics (BJS). Established in 1972, the survey is an annual federal statistical study that measures the levels of victimization resulting from criminal activity in the United States. The survey was previously known as the National Crime Survey, but it was renamed to emphasize the measurement of victimization experienced by citizens. The survey was created because of a concern that the FBI's Uniform Crime Reports (UCR) did not fully portray the true volume of crime. The UCR provides data on crimes reported to law enforcement authorities, but it does not estimate how many crimes went unreported.

The NCVS is designed to complement the FBI's Uniform Crime Reports. It measures the levels of criminal victimization of persons and households for the crimes of rape, robbery, assault, burglary, motor vehicle theft, and larceny. Murder is not included because the NCVS data are gathered through interviews with victims. Definitions for these crimes are the same as those established by the FBI's UCR.

Some observers believe the NCVS is a better indicator of the volume of crime in the United States than the FBI statistics. Nonetheless, like all surveys, it is subject to error. The survey depends on people's memories of incidents that happened up to six months earlier. Many times, a victim is not sure what happened, even moments after the crime occurred. In addition, the NCVS limits the data to victims age 12 and older, an admittedly arbitrary age selection. Despite these factors, however, the BJS claims a

TABLE 3.1

Index of crime, offense and population distribution by region, 2002

Region	Population	Crime Index	Modified Crime Index[1]	Violent crime[2]	Property crime[2]	Murder and non-negligent man-slaughter	Forcible rape	Robbery	Aggravated assault	Burglary	Larceny-theft	Motor vehicle theft	Arson[1]
United States total	100.0	100.0		100.0	100.0	100.0	100.0	100.0	100.0	100.0	100.0	100.0	
Northeast	18.8	13.2		15.8	12.8	13.6	13.5	19.2	14.6	11.5	13.2	13.1	
Midwest	22.6	21.3		19.4	21.6	20.4	25.3	19.5	18.7	20.7	22.3	18.8	
South	35.8	41.1		41.4	41.0	43.1	37.5	38.5	43.1	44.8	40.9	35.2	
West	22.8	24.4		23.4	24.6	23.0	23.7	22.8	23.7	22.9	23.6	32.9	

[1]Although arson data are included in the trend and clearance tables, sufficient data are not available to estimate totals for this offense.
[2]Violent crimes are offenses of murder, forcible rape, robbery, and aggravated assault. Property crimes are offenses of burglary, larceny-theft, and motor vehicle theft.
[3]Because of rounding, the percentages may not add to 100.0.

SOURCE: "Table 3. Index of crime, offense and population distribution by region, 2002," in *Crime in the United States 2002: Uniform Crime Reports,* Federal Bureau of Investigation, Washington, DC, 2003

90 to 95 percent confidence level in the data reported in the NCVS.

In 2002 the NCVS reported that "U.S. residents age 12 or older experienced about 23 million violent and property victimizations" (Callie Marie Rennison and Michael R. Rand, *Criminal Victimization, 2002,* U.S. Department of Justice, Office of Justice Programs, Washington, DC, August 2003). "These criminal victimizations included an estimated 17.5 million property crimes (burglary, motor vehicle theft, and theft), 5.3 million violent crimes (rape, sexual assault, robbery, aggravated assault, and simple assault), and 155,000 personal thefts (pocket picking and purse snatching)." The authors also note that the 2002 figures "continued a downward trend that began in 1994."

According to the NCVS, between 1999–2000 and 2001–2002 the average yearly rate of violent crimes per 1,000 persons 12 or older decreased substantially for all age categories, especially among 12- to-15 year-olds (from 67.2 per 1,000 to 49.7 per 1,000, for a decrease of 26 percent). Those 16 to 19 also experienced substantially fewer violent victimizations, moving from 70.8 per 1,000 in 1999–2000 to 57 per 1,000 in 2001–2002, for a drop of 19.5 percent. Among those 20 to 24, the rate lowered from 58.8 per 1,000 to 46.1 per 1,000 for a drop of 21.6 percent.

The UCR reported that violent crime—including murder, rape, robbery, and aggravated assault—dropped about 1 percent between 2001 and 2002. In addition, the 2002 figure was down nearly 26 percent from 1993. In a 30-year comparison (between 1973 and 2002), the NCVS observed that violent crime was at its lowest level in 2002—22.8 per 1,000 people age 12 and older. The rate in 1973 was 47.7 per 1,000, with the highest levels being reached in 1981 (52.3 per 1,000) and 1994 (51.2 per 1,000).

Property crimes remained about the same between 2001 and 2002, per the UCR, but were about 14.5 percent lower than they were in 1993. The UCR's Crime Index,

which includes select offenses (murder/nonnegligent manslaughter, forcible rape, robbery, aggravated assault, burglary, larceny-theft, and motor vehicle theft), stood at an estimated 11,877,218 offenses in 2002.

The South experienced the highest proportion of violent crime in 2002 (41.4 percent), followed by the West (23.4 percent), Midwest (19.4 percent), and Northeast (15.8 percent). (See Table 3.1.) The South also led in property crime (41 percent), followed by the West (24.6 percent), the Midwest (21.6 percent), and the Northeast (12.8 percent).

HISTORICAL TRENDS

According to the FBI, from the mid-1980s through the mid-1990s youth violence and crime grew at rapid rates. In *Juvenile Offenders and Victims: 1999 National Report* (Howard N. Snyder and Melissa Sickmund, U.S. Department of Justice, National Center for Juvenile Justice, Office of Juvenile Justice and Delinquency Prevention, Washington, DC, September 1999), the authors looked at juvenile homicide trends. They found that between 1980 and 1997, murders by juveniles were highest in 1993 and 1994. In murders involving juvenile offenders during that 18-year span, most involved a lone offender, but 39 percent featured two or more offenders. (See Figure 3.1.) The report also notes that 51 percent of the murder victims of juvenile offenders were young as well, falling into the 13–24 age group. (See Figure 3.2.) About 30 percent fell into the 18–24 age group.

That report further examines violent crime trends during the early to mid-1990s in 12 select states (Alabama, Colorado, Idaho, Illinois, Iowa, Massachusetts, Michigan, North Dakota, South Carolina, Utah, Vermont, and Virginia). They considered violent crime to include "murder, violent sexual assault, robbery, aggravated assault, and simple assault." They found that in these 12 states, violent crimes involving those under 18 and resulting in injuries occurred most often around 3 P.M., or shortly after the end

FIGURE 3.1

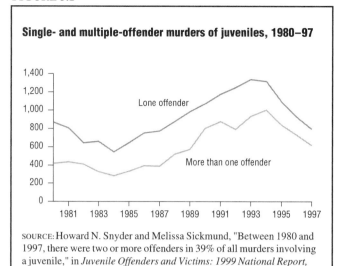

Single- and multiple-offender murders of juveniles, 1980–97

FIGURE 3.2

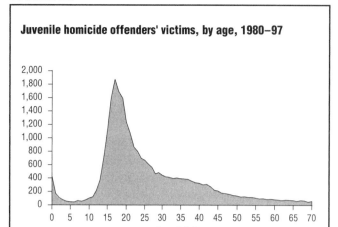

Juvenile homicide offenders' victims, by age, 1980–97

of school. (See Figure 3.3.) For adults, the peak time was around 11 P.M.

The Office of Juvenile Justice and Delinquency Prevention (OJJDP) has also reported on specific trends between 1980 to 1999. For example, it noted that juvenile offenders during that time period were responsible for 9 percent of the murders of people over 50 years of age. The proportion of juveniles and adults committing murders together also grew during that time span and then began to taper off. The peak year for such teaming for murders was in 1994 when 31 percent of murders involved both juvenile and adult killers.

The OJJDP also observed that between 1980 and 1999, some 93 percent of known juvenile killers were male and 42 percent were 17 years of age. Male and female juvenile murderers often targeted acquaintances (55 percent and 46 percent respectively), yet young female killers were more likely to murder family members (39 percent) than were their male counterparts (9 percent). Among juveniles, blacks represented the largest percentage of murderers during that time span (56 percent). However, by 1998, the percentage of white and black juvenile murderers had evened out, returning to 1985 levels. The significantly increased number of murders committed by juveniles during the mid-1980s to mid-1990s were mainly committed using guns.

The surge in youth crime and violence caused much concern in society. Various groups—public and private— undertook the mission of trying to uncover the reasons why. Lawmakers responded by toughening existing laws and finding ways to try more juveniles as adults. Courts levied stricter sentences, while parents and educators looked into various programs and methods geared to help

their children and students deal with the situation. The end result was that violent crime in general has decreased substantially since the mid-1990s. However, such actions by youthful offenders still occur in great numbers. Figure 3.4 and Figure 3.5 outline the trends in nonfatal violent victimizations and homicides by select age groups between 1976 and 2000.

CAUSES OF DEATH

Although violent crime has diminished, it still plays a significant role as a cause of death for youth. In 2001, however, the main cause of death among both males and females under the age of 24 was accidents, also reported as unintentional injuries, according to the *National Vital Statistics Reports* (vol. 52, no. 9, November 7, 2003). Of the ten leading causes of death, homicides and suicides account for many abbreviated lives as well, and these deaths increase in number among older youth. (See Table 3.2 and Table 3.3.) Of the deaths among males 1–4, 36 percent were accidental while 8.2 percent were homicides. Females in the same age group were most likely to die of injuries sustained in accidents (30.3) as well, though homicides (8 percent) were the fourth-leading cause of death of girls in this age group. No suicides were reported in this age range.

The rate of homicide decreased for both males and females in the 5–9 year range. A greater percentage of females in this age group (4.5 percent) were murdered than males (4.3 percent). Again, no suicides were observed for this age group. Suicides are recorded in the 10–14 year group. It became the third-leading cause of death for males in this age group (8.5 percent) and the

FIGURE 3.3

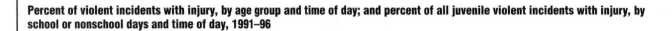

Percent of violent incidents with injury, by age group and time of day; and percent of all juvenile violent incidents with injury, by school or nonschool days and time of day, 1991–96

Percent of violent incidents with injury in age group

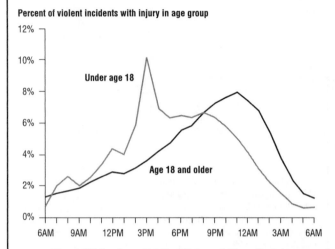

Percent of all juvenile violent incidents with injury

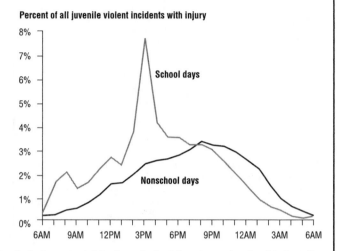

SOURCE: Howard N. Snyder and Melissa Sickmund, "Juveniles injure more victims in the hours around the close of school than at any other time," in *Juvenile Offenders and Victims: 1999 National Report,* U.S. Department of Justice, National Center for Juvenile Justice, Office of Juvenile Justice and Delinquency Prevention, Washington, DC, September 1999

sixth-leading factor for females (4.2 percent). Homicide (4.8 percent) was lower than suicide among males, but higher among females 10–14 (4.5 percent).

Homicide became the number two killer of males 15–19 (16.7 percent), followed by suicide (13.8 percent). Murder and suicide tied for third- and fourth-place in deaths among females of that age group (7 percent each). The homicide rate climbed to 10.9 percent among females 20–24, while suicide decreased slightly to 6.6 percent. Among males 20–24, homicides rose to 20.5 percent, with suicides growing to 14.5 percent.

HOMICIDE

According to the Bureau of Justice Statistics, overall death rates from homicide doubled from the mid-1960s to the late 1970s, fell until the mid-1980s, rose again until 1991, then declined sharply through 2000, reaching an overall rate of 5.5 per 100,000 population in 2000. The 2000 figure brought the rate back down to the late 1960s level.

In its report on homicide trends between 1976 and 2000, available via the BJS Web site, the bureau observed the following patterns:

Blacks are disproportionately represented as both homicide victims and offenders. In terms of rates per 100,000, blacks are six times more likely to be victimized and about eight times more likely to commit homicide than are whites.

Males represent three-quarters of homicide victims and nearly ninety percent of offenders. In terms of rates per

100,000, males are three times more likely to be killed, and almost eight times more likely to commit homicide than are females.

Approximately one-third of murder victims and almost half the offenders are under the age of 25. For both victims and offenders, the rate per 100,000 peaks in the 18–24 year-old age group.

Those aged 0–17 years old made up 9.8 percent of homicide victims, 10.7 percent of homicide offenders, and 26.8 percent of the general population over the period 1976–2000. Homicide has been and is the leading cause of death for black teenagers, both males and females, though victimization rates for black teens declined dramatically between the early 1990s and 2000.

In its *National Vital Statistics Reports* (vol. 52, no. 3, September 18, 2003) the National Center for Health Statistics (NCHS) of the Centers for Disease Control and Prevention (CDC) noted that homicide was the 13th leading cause of death overall in 2001. Homicide had moved up one notch since 2000, when it was 14th. However, the terrorist attacks of September 11, 2001, contributed significantly to that change.

The NCHS also reported homicide trends for select years between 1950 and 2001. Among those 15–19, the homicide rate increased from 3.9 per 100,000 people in the resident population in 1950 to 17.8 in 1995 before declining to 9.4 in 2001. For those 20–24, the rate in 1950 was 8.5 per 100,000 reaching 22.2 in 1990 before decreasing to 17.3 in 2001. For males 15–19, the rate in 1950 was 5.5

FIGURE 3.4

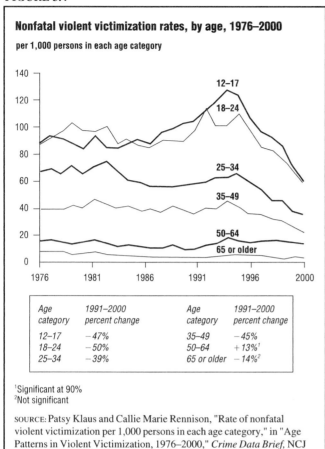

Nonfatal violent victimization rates, by age, 1976–2000

per 1,000 persons in each age category

Age category	1991–2000 percent change	Age category	1991–2000 percent change
12–17	−47%	35–49	−45%
18–24	−50%	50–64	+13%[1]
25–34	−39%	65 or older	−14%[2]

[1]Significant at 90%
[2]Not significant

SOURCE: Patsy Klaus and Callie Marie Rennison, "Rate of nonfatal violent victimization per 1,000 persons in each age category," in "Age Patterns in Violent Victimization, 1976–2000," *Crime Data Brief,* NCJ 190104, U.S. Department of Justice, Office of Justice Programs, Washington, DC, February 2002

FIGURE 3.5

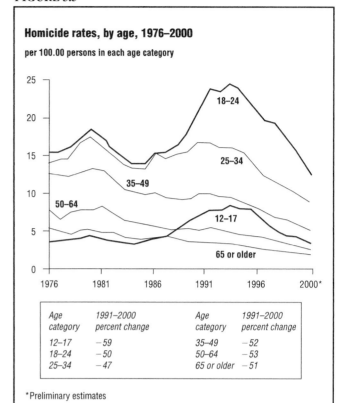

Homicide rates, by age, 1976–2000

per 100.00 persons in each age category

Age category	1991–2000 percent change	Age category	1991–2000 percent change
12–17	−59	35–49	−52
18–24	−50	50–64	−53
25–34	−47	65 or older	−51

*Preliminary estimates

SOURCE: Patsy Klaus and Callie Marie Rennison, "Rate of homicide per 100,000 persons in each age category," in "Age Patterns in Violent Victimization, 1976–2000," *Crime Data Brief,* NCJ 190104, U.S. Department of Justice, Office of Justice Programs, Washington, DC, February 2002

per 100,000 then climbed to 29.1 in 1995 before diminishing to 15.7 in 2001. The 20–24 age group among males was significantly higher, starting at 13.5 per 100,000 in 1950, surging to 36.9 in 1990, and then falling to 28.9 in 2001. Females have seen far less change during the 51-year period. For those 15–19, the rate in 1950 was 2.4 per 100,000, then grew to 5.8 in 1995 before moving back down to 2.7 in 2001. The 20–24 age group among females also saw higher numbers, beginning at 3.7 per 100,000 in 1950, reaching 8.2 in 1980, and decreasing to 5.1 in 2001.

Homicide rates between racial groups varied considerably between 1950 and 2001 as well. Starting at 3.2 per 100,000 in 1950, the rate for white males 15–24 reached 15.9 in 1995 before dropping to 11.2 in 2001. Rates for black males in the same age range were much higher: 53.8 per 100,000 in 1950, 137.1 in 1990, and 85.7 in 2001. The levels for American Indian/Alaskan Native males in that age category were also higher than for white males: 35.4 per 100,000 in 1980 and 16.1 in 2001. (Data for American Indian/Alaskan Natives is only available from 1980 onward. The same is true for Asian and Pacific Islanders.) The rate for Asian/Pacific Islander males was 9.3 in 1980, rising to 17.2 in 1995, then decreasing below its 1980 level to 9.1 in 2001. Hispanic data, compiled since 1990,

revealed a high rate of 55.4 per 100,000 for males 15–24 in 1990, falling to 30.5 in 2001.

White females 15–24 experienced homicide rates of 1.3 per 100,000 in 1950, 4.7 in 1980, and 3 in 2001. Black females in the same age group saw higher numbers: 16.5 per 100,000 in 1950, 18.9 in 1990, and 8.9 in 2001. Hispanic females in that age range decreased from 8.1 per 100,000 in 1990 to 4 in 2001. The rates for American Indian/Alaskan Native females as well as Asian/Pacific Islander females were too low to be reliable and were, therefore, not presented.

UCR on Murder

The FBI defines murder and nonnegligent manslaughter as "the willful (nonnegligent) killing of one human being by another." The figures do not include "deaths caused by negligence, suicide, or accident; justifiable homicides; and attempts to murder or assaults to murder, which are scored as aggravated assaults." In 2002, according to the UCR, approximately 16,204 murders occurred, representing a 1 percent increase from 2001, but a 33.9 percent decrease since 1993. The UCR also received supplementary homicide data on 14,054 murder victims, of which nearly 10 percent were juveniles.

TABLE 3.2

Ten leading causes of death for males, all races, aged 1–19, 2001

[Rates per 100,000 population in specified group.]

Rank[1]	Cause of death (Based on the *International Classification of Diseases, Tenth Revision*, 1992), race, sex, and age	Number[2]	Percent of total deaths	Rate[2]
	All races, male, 1–4 years			
. . .	All causes	2,899	100.0	37.0
1	Accidents (unintentional injuries) (V01–X59,Y85–Y86)	1,045	36.0	13.3
2	Congenital malformations, deformations and chromosomal abnormalities (Q00–Q99)	282	9.7	3.6
3	Assault (homicide) ([3]U01–[3]U02,X85–Y09,Y87.1)	238	8.2	3.0
4	Malignant neoplasms (C00–C97)	229	7.9	2.9
5	Diseases of heart (I00–I09,I11,I13,I20–I51)	121	4.2	1.5
6	Septicemia (A40–A41)	60	2.1	0.8
7	Influenza and pneumonia (J10–J18)	57	2.0	0.7
8	Certain conditions originating in the perinatal period (P00–P96)	44	1.5	0.6
9	In situ neoplasms, benign neoplasms and neoplasms of uncertain or unknown behavior (D00–D48)	30	1.0	0.4
10	Chronic lower respiratory diseases (J40–J47)	29	1.0	0.4
. . .	All other causes (Residual)	764	26.4	9.7
	All races, male, 5–9 years			
. . .	All causes	1,727	100.0	16.7
1	Accidents (unintentional injuries) (V01–X59,Y85–Y86)	786	45.5	7.6
2	Malignant neoplasms (C00–C97)	253	14.6	2.4
3	Congenital malformations, deformations and chromosomal abnormalities (Q00–Q99)	101	5.8	1.0
4	Assault (homicide) ([3]U01–[3]U02,X85–Y09,Y87.1)	75	4.3	0.7
5	Diseases of heart (I00–I09,I11,I13,I20–I51)	43	2.5	0.4
6	In situ neoplasms, benign neoplasms and neoplasms of uncertain or unknown behavior (D00–D48)	26	1.5	0.3
7	Chronic lower respiratory diseases (J40–J47)	24	1.4	0.2
8	Influenza and pneumonia (J10–J18)	23	1.3	0.2
9	Cerebrovascular diseases (I60–I69)	21	1.2	0.2
10	Septicemia (A40–A41)	17	1.0	*
. . .	All other causes (Residual)	358	20.7	3.5

TABLE 3.2

Ten leading causes of death for males, all races, aged 1–19, 2001 [CONTINUED]

[Rates per 100,000 population in specified group.]

Rank[1]	Cause of death (Based on the *International Classification of Diseases, Tenth Revision*, 1992), race, sex, and age	Number[2]	Percent of total deaths	Rate[2]
	All races, male, 10–14 years			
. . .	All causes	2,441	100.0	22.8
1	Accidents (unintentional injuries) (V01–X59,Y85–Y86)	1,017	41.7	9.5
2	Malignant neoplasms (C00–C97)	280	11.5	2.6
3	Intentional self-harm (suicide) ([3]U03,X60–X84,Y87.0)	207	8.5	1.9
4	Assault (homicide) ([3]U01–[3]U02,X85–Y09,Y87.1)	118	4.8	1.1
5	Congenital malformations, deformations and chromosomal abnormalities (Q00–Q99)	109	4.5	1.0
6	Diseases of heart (I00–I09,I11,I13,I20–I51)	95	3.9	0.9
7	Chronic lower respiratory diseases (J40–J47)	37	1.5	0.3
8	In situ neoplasms, benign neoplasms and neoplasms of uncertain or unknown behavior (D00–D48)	26	1.1	0.2
9	Influenza and pneumonia (J10–J18)	24	1.0	0.2
10	Septicemia (A40–A41)	22	0.9	0.2
. . .	All other causes (Residual)	506	20.7	4.7
	All races, male, 15–19 years			
. . .	All causes	9,766	100.0	93.7
1	Accidents (unintentional injuries) (V01–X59,Y85–Y86)	4,722	48.4	45.3
2	Assault (homicide) ([3]U01–[3]U02,X85–Y09,Y87.1)	1,632	16.7	15.7
3	Intentional self-harm (suicide) ([3]U03,X60–X84,Y87.0)	1,345	13.8	12.9
4	Malignant neoplasms (C00–C97)	447	4.6	4.3
5	Diseases of heart (I00–I09,I11,I13,I20–I51)	223	2.3	2.1
6	Congenital malformations, deformations and chromosomal abnormalities (Q00–Q99)	161	1.6	1.5
7	Chronic lower respiratory diseases (J40–J47)	43	0.4	0.4
8	Cerebrovascular diseases (I60–I69)	36	0.4	0.3
8	Influenza and pneumonia (J10–J18)	36	0.4	0.3
10	Septicemia (A40–A41)	31	0.3	0.3
. . .	All other causes (Residual)	1,090	11.2	10.5

[1]Rank based on number of deaths.
[2]Figures for age not stated are included in "all ages" but not distributed among age groups.
[3]Figure does not meet standards of reliability or precision.
. . . Category not applicable.

SOURCE: Adapted from Robert N. Anderson and Betty L. Smith, "Table 1. Deaths, percentage of total deaths, and death rates for the 10 leading causes of death in selected age groups, by race and sex: United States, 2001," in "Deaths: Leading Causes for 2001," *National Vital Statistics Reports,* vol. 52, no. 9, November 7, 2003

Some 15,813 people in 2002 were identified as murder offenders, including 770 males and 77 females under the age of 18, and 3,128 males and 269 females under the age of 22. (See Table 3.4.) Since the identity of all murder offenders is not known, such figures are presumably lower than they would be if all offenders had been identified. The reports also show that those under age 22 represented 21.5 percent of all murder offenders. Further breakdowns reveal that 26 murder offenders fell into the 9 to 12 age group, 18 male and 7 female; 446 into the 13 to 16 age group, 401 males and 45 females; and 1,507 into the 17 to 19 age group, 1,412 males and 92 females.

Of the age groups presented in Table 3.4, the 20- to 24-year-old age group represented the most murder offenders (2,916 or 18.4 percent of the total number). Of that group, 2,656 were male and 256 were female. The second highest age group of murder offenders was 25 to 29 (1,644), of which 1,492 were male and 150 were female. In all, people in their 20s accounted for 28.8 percent of all murder offenders.

Overall, males comprised 65 percent of all known murder offenders. While less than 5 percent of the known murder offenders were males under age 18, nearly 20 percent were males under age 22. Females represented 7 percent of known murder offenders in 2002. The identity of the remaining 28 percent was unknown. In general, among various age groups, the offender and victim were usually of the same race.

Of the supplementary data that the UCR maintained on 14,054 murder victims in 2002, 1,357 victims were under age 18, including 867 males, 489 females, and 1 unknown. (See Table 3.5.) The number of murder victims more than doubles for those under 22. Of the 3,398

TABLE 3.3

Ten leading causes of death for females, all races, aged 1–19, 2001

[Rates per 100,000 population in specified group.]

Rank[1]	Cause of death (Based on the *International Classification of Diseases, Tenth Revision*, 1992), race, sex, and age	Number[2]	Percent of total deaths	Rate[2]
	All races, female, 1–4 years			
. . .	All causes	2,208	100.0	29.5
1	Accidents (unintentional injuries) (V01–X59,Y85–Y86)	669	30.3	8.9
2	Congenital malformations, deformations and chromosomal abnormalities (Q00–Q99)	275	12.5	3.7
3	Malignant neoplasms (C00–C97)	191	8.7	2.5
4	Assault (homicide) ([3]U01–[3]U02,X85–Y09,Y87.1)	177	8.0	2.4
5	Diseases of heart (I00–I09,I11,I13,I20–I51)	104	4.7	1.4
6	Influenza and pneumonia (J10–J18)	55	2.5	0.7
7	Septicemia (A40–A41)	48	2.2	0.6
8	Cerebrovascular diseases (I60–I69)	29	1.3	0.4
9	In situ neoplasms, benign neoplasms and neoplasms of uncertain or unknown behavior (D00–D48)	28	1.3	0.4
9	Certain conditions originating in the perinatal period (P00–P96)	28	1.3	0.4
. . .	All other causes (Residual)	604	27.4	8.1
	All races, female, 5–9 years			
. . .	All causes	1,366	100.0	13.9
1	Accidents (unintentional injuries) (V01–X59,Y85–Y86)	497	36.4	5.0
2	Malignant neoplasms (C00–C97)	240	17.6	2.4
3	Congenital malformations, deformations and chromosomal abnormalities (Q00–Q99)	81	5.9	0.8
4	Assault (homicide) ([3]U01–[3]U02,X85–Y09,Y87.1)	62	4.5	0.6
5	Diseases of heart (I00–I09,I11,I13,I20–I51)	55	4.0	0.6
6	In situ neoplasms, benign neoplasms and neoplasms of uncertain or unknown behavior (D00–D48)	26	1.9	0.3
7	Influenza and pneumonia (J10–J18)	23	1.7	0.2
8	Chronic lower respiratory diseases (J40–J47)	18	1.3	*
9	Cerebrovascular diseases (I60–I69)	17	1.2	*
10	Anemias (D50–D64)	13	1.0	*
. . .	All other causes (Residual)	334	24.5	3.4

TABLE 3.3

Ten leading causes of death for females, all races, aged 1–19, 2001 [CONTINUED]

[Rates per 100,000 population in specified group.]

Rank[1]	Cause of death (Based on the *International Classification of Diseases, Tenth Revision*, 1992), race, sex, and age	Number[2]	Percent of total deaths	Rate[2]
	All races, female, 10–14 years			
. . .	All causes	1,561	100.0	15.3
1	Accidents (unintentional injuries) (V01–X59,Y85–Y86)	536	34.3	5.3
2	Malignant neoplasms (C00–C97)	235	15.1	2.3
3	Congenital malformations, deformations and chromosomal abnormalities (Q00–Q99)	85	5.4	0.8
4	Diseases of heart (I00–I09,I11,I13,I20–I51)	79	5.1	0.8
5	Assault (homicide) ([3]U01–[3]U02,X85–Y09,Y87.1)	71	4.5	0.7
6	Intentional self-harm (suicide) ([3]U03,X60–X84,Y87.0)	65	4.2	0.6
7	In situ neoplasms, benign neoplasms and neoplasms of uncertain or unknown behavior (D00–D48)	27	1.7	0.3
8	Chronic lower respiratory diseases (J40–J47)	25	1.6	0.2
9	Influenza and pneumonia (J10–J18)	22	1.4	0.2
10	Cerebrovascular diseases (I60–I69)	21	1.3	0.2
. . .	All other causes (Residual)	395	25.3	3.9
	All races, female, 15–19 years			
. . .	All causes	3,789	100.0	38.5
1	Accidents (unintentional injuries) (V01–X59,Y85–Y86)	1,924	50.8	19.5
2	Malignant neoplasms (C00–C97)	285	7.5	2.9
3	Assault (homicide) ([3]U01–[3]U02,X85–Y09,Y87.1)	267	7.0	2.7
4	Intentional self-harm (suicide) ([3]U03,X60–X84,Y87.0)	266	7.0	2.7
5	Diseases of heart (I00–I09,I11,I13,I20–I51)	124	3.3	1.3
6	Congenital malformations, deformations and chromosomal abnormalities (Q00–Q99)	94	2.5	1.0
7	Pregnancy, childbirth and the puerperium (O00–O99)	37	1.0	0.4
8	Cerebrovascular diseases (I60–I69)	32	0.8	0.3
9	Chronic lower respiratory diseases (J40–J47)	31	0.8	0.3
10	Influenza and pneumonia (J10–J18)	30	0.8	0.3
. . .	All other causes (Residual)	699	18.4	7.1

[1]Rate based on number of deaths.
[2]Figures for age not stated are included in "all ages" but not distributed among age groups.
[3]Figure does not meet standards of reliability or precision.
. . . Category not applicable.

SOURCE: Adapted from Robert N. Anderson and Betty L. Smith, "Table 1. Deaths, percentage of total deaths, and death rates for the 10 leading causes of death in selected age groups, by race and sex: United States, 2001," in "Deaths: Leading Causes for 2001," *National Vital Statistics Reports*, vol. 52, no. 9, November 7, 2003

murder victims in that age range, 2,624 were known to be male and 772 were female. While the percentage of murder victims under 18 is nearly 10 percent of the total, those under 22 comprise 24 percent. Further breakdowns reveal that those 9 to 12 accounted for 92 victims, of whom 50 were male and 42 were female. Of those 390 victims who were 13 to 16, 281 were male and 109 were female. The number of victims 17 to 19 rose to 1,184, including 1,018 males and 166 females.

The 20- to 24-year-old age group contained the most murder victims (2,756), of which 2,356 were male and 398 were female. This age group represented nearly 20 percent of total victims. The second highest number of murder victims was in the 25 to 29 age group (2,059). While the number of male murder victims drops significantly for this age group to 1,746, the number of females does not (313). Overall, people in their 20s comprised 34.3 percent of all murder victims for 2002. In all, males accounted for 76.7 percent of all murder victims.

Nearly equal numbers of whites (6,757) and blacks (6,730) were murdered in 2002. More blacks (5,579) than whites (5,356) were murder offenders that year. (See Table 3.4.) In the under 18 age category, more whites (689) than blacks (610) were murdered. The reverse is true in the under 22 age category, when more blacks (1,683) than whites (1,581) were murdered. Black and white murder victims under 18 each represented less than 5 percent of the total, while white victims under 22 encompassed 11.2 percent of the total and black victims 12 percent.

TABLE 3.4

Murder offenders by age, sex, and race, 2002

Age	Total	Sex			Race			
		Male	Female	Unknown	White	Black	Other	Unknown
Total	15,813	10,285	1,108	4,420	5,356	5,579	274	4,604
Percent distribution[1]	100.0	65.0	7.0	28.0	33.9	35.3	1.7	29.1
Under 18[2]	848	770	77	1	389	424	26	9
Under 22[2]	3,402	3,128	269	5	1,499	1,770	94	39
18 and over[2]	9,525	8,511	996	18	4,714	4,464	241	106
Infant (under 1)	0	0	0	0	0	0	0	0
1 to 4	1	0	1	0	0	1	0	0
5 to 8	1	1	0	0	0	1	0	0
9 to 12	26	18	7	1	7	18	0	1
13 to 16	446	401	45	0	227	198	15	6
17 to 19	1,507	1,412	92	3	648	802	42	15
20 to 24	2,916	2,656	256	4	1,265	1,547	73	31
25 to 29	1,644	1,492	150	2	769	819	37	19
30 to 34	1,120	986	132	2	573	506	27	14
35 to 39	865	749	116	0	460	385	13	7
40 to 44	638	522	115	1	367	242	21	8
45 to 49	493	425	68	0	298	172	20	3
50 to 54	311	262	44	5	195	103	7	6
55 to 59	168	150	18	0	117	41	6	4
60 to 64	83	72	11	0	59	22	2	0
65 to 69	49	41	8	0	38	9	2	0
70 to 74	45	38	6	1	32	12	0	1
75 and over	60	56	4	0	48	10	2	0
Unknown	5,440	1,004	35	4,401	253	691	7	4,489

[1]Because of rounding, the percentages may not add to 100.0.
[2]Does not include unknown ages.

SOURCE: "Table 2.6. Murder Offenders by Age, Sex, and Race, 2002," in *Crime in the United States, 2002: Uniform Crime Reports*, Federal Bureau of Investigation, Washington, DC, 2002

Juvenile gang killings, according to the UCR, totaled 625 in 1998 then dropped to 580 in 1999, then rose steadily to 653 in 2000, 862 in 2001, and 911 in 2002. More than 95 percent of victims in 2002 were male (869).

Victim-Offender Relationship

In *Juvenile Offenders and Victims: 1999 National Report* (Howard N. Snyder and Melissa Sickmund, U.S. Department of Justice, National Center for Juvenile Justice, Office of Juvenile Justice and Delinquency Prevention, Washington, DC, September 1999), data were made available on the victim-offender relationships of those age 0–17 who were murdered between 1980 and 1997. Overall, 36 percent were murdered by an acquaintance, 22 percent by a parent, 11 percent by a stranger, and 5 percent by another family member. (See Table 3.6.) Parents were most likely to murder children in the 0–5 age group and in the 6–11 age group. Acquaintances were the most likely individuals to murder those in the 12–17 age range. Males were most often murdered by acquaintances (38 percent), while females were murdered equally by parents and acquaintances (32 percent each). Clearly, victims 0–17 are mainly murdered by someone they know.

Weapons Used in Murders

The number of youths dying as a result of firearms increased 152 percent from 1985 to 1993 before begin-ning a decline. During those peak years, the overwhelming majority of deaths among young black males were firearm-related, and American teenage boys were more likely to die from gunshot wounds than from all natural causes combined. One out of every four deaths among 15- to 24-year-olds, and six of ten deaths among black males 15–19 years old, were inflicted through the use of firearms.

According to the NCHS, in 2001 a total of 29,573 persons died from firearm injuries in the United States, representing an increase from 28,663 persons in 2000. The NCHS's *National Vital Statistics Reports* (vol. 52, no. 3, September 18, 2003) observed that: "Firearm suicide and homicide, the two major component causes, accounted for 57 and 38.4 percent, respectively, of all firearm injury deaths in 2001. In 2001 the age-adjusted death rate for firearm injuries was 10.3 deaths per 100,000 U.S. standard population. Males had an age-adjusted rate that was 6.6 times that for females, the black population had a rate that was 2 times that of the white population, and the non-Hispanic population had a rate that was 1.3 times that of the Hispanic population."

The overall number of deaths for those 15–24 in 2001 was 32,252, of which 206 were caused by the accidental discharge of firearms. Another 4,200 (or 13 percent) were the result of firearm-related homicides. Moreover, 2,130

TABLE 3.5

Murder victims, by age, sex, and race, 2002

Age	Total	Sex				Race			
		Male	Female	Unknown		White	Black	Other	Unknown
Total	14,054	10,779	3,251	24		6,757	6,730	377	190
Percent distribution[1]	100.0	76.7	23.1	0.2		48.1	47.9	2.7	1.4
Under 18[2]	1,357	867	489	1		689	610	45	13
Under 22[2]	3,398	2,624	772	2		1,581	1,683	104	30
18 and over[2]	12,406	9,703	2,699	4		5,945	6,009	331	121
Infant (under 1)	180	96	84	0		102	71	4	3
1 to 4	328	180	147	1		176	134	14	4
5 to 8	86	35	51	0		50	33	3	0
9 to 12	92	50	42	0		53	35	4	0
13 to 16	390	281	109	0		180	196	11	3
17 to 19	1,184	1,018	166	0		519	615	39	11
20 to 24	2,756	2,356	398	2		1,115	1,560	58	23
25 to 29	2,059	1,746	313	0		809	1,173	48	29
30 to 34	1,587	1,212	375	0		667	851	54	15
35 to 39	1,337	976	359	2		676	624	23	14
40 to 44	1,137	812	325	0		621	470	40	6
45 to 49	856	624	232	0		487	337	25	7
50 to 54	566	412	154	0		333	214	16	3
55 to 59	353	246	107	0		237	98	14	4
60 to 64	245	181	64	0		170	60	10	5
65 to 69	162	103	59	0		116	44	2	0
70 to 74	156	96	60	0		115	35	4	2
75 and over	289	146	143	0		208	69	7	5
Unknown	291	209	63	19		123	111	1	56

[1] Because of rounding, the percentages may not add to 100.0.
[2] Does not include unknown ages.

SOURCE: "Table 2.5. Murder Victims by Age, Sex, and Race, 2002," in *Crime in the United States, 2002: Uniform Crime Reports,* Federal Bureau of Investigation, Washington, DC, 2002

deaths (or 6.6 percent) in that age group occurred as a result of firearm-related suicides.

The FBI reports that firearms were used in the vast majority of juvenile and young adult murders in 2002. Nearly 49 percent of murder victims under the age of 18 and more than two-thirds of those under age 22 (69.4 percent) were killed with firearms. (See Table 3.7.) Among those murdered between ages 17 to 19, more than 82 percent of the deaths involved firearms. The figure was also high (76.7 percent) among 13- to 16-year-olds. The most firearm-related murders were in the 20 to 24 age group (2,244 deaths), followed by those 25 to 29 (1,628) and 30 to 34 (1,168). However, the greatest percentage of firearm-related murders was among those 17 to 19.

Other weapons most frequently used to kill those under 18 included personal weapons (22 percent) and knives (6.6 percent). Personal weapons involve the use of hands, feet, fists, etc. In the under-22 age group, personal weapons accounted for about 10 percent of the murders, knives about 7.5 percent. More than half of murdered infants 0–4 were killed with personal weapons. For all older age groups, firearms become the weapon of choice for those murdered.

Homicide and Suicide Rates for Juveniles Worldwide

In *Juvenile Offenders and Victims: 1999 National Report,* the authors present data pertaining to the homi-

TABLE 3.6

Offender relationship to juvenile homicide victims, by age and gender of victims, 1980–97

Offender relationship to victim	Age of victim				Victim ages 0–17	
	0–17	0–5	6–11	12–17	Males	Females
Total	100%	100%	100%	100%	100%	100%
Parent	22	54	31	3	18	32
Other family member	5	6	12	4	4	7
Acquaintance	36	25	25	44	38	32
Stranger	11	3	12	16	13	8
Unknown	25	13	20	34	27	21

Note: Detail may not total 100% because of rounding.

SOURCE: Howard N. Snyder and Melissa Sickmund, "Between 1980 and 1997, most murdered children younger than age 6 were killed by a family member, while most older juveniles were killed by an acquaintance or a stranger," in *Juvenile Offenders and Victims: 1999 National Report,* U.S. Department of Justice, National Center for Juvenile Justice, Office of Juvenile Justice and Delinquency Prevention, Washington, DC, September 1999

cide and suicide rates of the United States compared to 25 other industrialized nations worldwide. Such comparisons are compiled infrequently, and the information dates from the mid-1990s, but it contributes to the overall understanding of violence patterns worldwide for juveniles.

According to the authors, their findings are based on statistics compiled by the CDC. In the study "each country

TABLE 3.7

Murder victims by age and weapon, 2002

Age	Total murder victims	Firearms	Knives or cutting instruments	Blunt objects (clubs, hammers, etc.)	Personal weapons (hands, fists, feet, etc.)[1]	Poison	Explosives	Fire	Narcotics	Strangulation	Asphyxiation	Other weapon or weapon not stated[2]
Total	14,054	9,369	1,767	666	933	23	11	104	48	143	103	887
Percent distribution[3]	100.0	66.7	12.6	4.7	6.6	0.2	0.1	0.7	0.3	1.0	0.7	6.3
Under 18[4]	1,357	661	90	52	299	5	5	21	11	16	41	156
Under 22[4]	3,398	2,358	256	94	345	6	5	29	14	23	47	221
18 and over[4]	12,406	8,568	1,646	595	607	18	6	76	36	125	58	671
Infant (under 1)	180	9	4	12	91	0	1	0	3	0	19	41
1 to 4	328	45	10	19	166	2	1	7	3	2	12	61
5 to 8	86	26	14	2	11	2	2	7	1	2	7	12
9 to 12	92	56	11	2	4	1	0	7	0	3	0	13
13 to 16	390	299	30	11	17	0	0	2	3	6	2	17
17 to 19	1,184	972	101	23	32	1	1	5	4	6	3	38
20 to 24	2,756	2,244	250	55	72	0	3	3	7	7	5	104
25 to 29	2,059	1,628	227	42	56	0	0	9	2	16	7	70
30 to 34	1,587	1,168	197	45	57	0	2	11	5	15	4	80
35 to 39	1,337	864	193	74	78	2	0	14	5	25	11	78
40 to 44	1,137	663	221	63	84	3	1	7	1	13	8	71
45 to 49	856	461	151	80	74	0	0	9	1	15	3	63
50 to 54	566	312	101	48	50	2	0	8	2	15	1	44
55 to 59	353	172	66	46	23	0	0	3	0	7	2	36
60 to 64	245	107	41	37	16	0	0	1	1	7	4	25
65 to 69	162	67	27	20	15	1	0	7	3	5	5	19
70 to 74	156	53	35	28	14	0	0	0	0	6	2	18
75 and over	289	83	57	40	46	9	0	4	6	3	4	37
Unknown	291	140	31	19	27	0	0	7	1	2	4	60

[1] Pushed is included in personal weapons.
[2] Includes drowning.
[3] Because of rounding, the percentages may not add to 100.0.
[4] Does not include unknown ages.

SOURCE: "Table 2.11. Murder Victims by Age, by Weapon, 2002," in *Crime in the United States, 2002: Uniform Crime Reports,* Federal Bureau of Investigation, Washington, DC, 2002

TABLE 3.8

Rates of homicide, suicide, and firearm-related death among children 0–14 years old: United States and 25 other industrialized countries*, 1996

(per 100,000 children for one year between 1990 and 1995)

Age group (yrs)	Total homicide	Total suicide	Firearm-related deaths				
			Homicide	Suicide	Unintentional	Intention undetermined	Total
0–4							
U.S.	4.10	0	0.43	0	0.15	0.01	0.59
Non-U.S.	0.95	0	0.05	0	0.01	0.01	0.07
Ratio U.S.:Non-U.S.	4.3:1		8.6:1		15.0:1	1.0:1	8.4:1
5–14							
U.S.	1.75	0.84	1.22	0.49	0.46	0.06	2.23
Non-U.S.	0.30	0.40	0.07	0.05	0.05	0.01	0.18
Ratio U.S.:Non-U.S.	5.8:1	2.1:1	17.4:1	9.8:1	9.2:1	6.0:1	12.4:1
0–14							
U.S.	2.57	0.55	0.94	0.32	0.36	0.04	1.66
Non-U.S.	0.51	0.27	0.06	0.03	0.04	0.01	0.14
Ratio U.S.:Non-U.S.	5.0:1	2.0:1	15.7:1	10.7:1	9.0:1	4.0:1	11.9:1

* All countries classified in the high-income group with populations ≥1 million that provided complete data (Australia, Austria, Belgium, Canada, Denmark, England and Wales, Finland, France, Germany, Hong Kong, Ireland, Israel, Italy, Japan, Kuwait, Netherlands, New Zealand, Northern Ireland, Norway, Scotland, Singapore, Sweden, Spain, Switzerland, and Taiwan). In this analysis, Hong Kong, Northern Ireland, and Taiwan are considered as countries.

SOURCE: "Rates of Homicide, Suicide, and Firearms-Related Death Among Children—26 Industrialized Countries," *Morbidity and Mortality Weekly Report,* vol. 46, no. 5, February 7, 1997

reported data for 1 year between 1990 and 1995; U.S. data were reported for 1993. The number of homicides per 100,000 children under age 15 in the U.S. was five times the number in the other countries combined (2.57 vs. 0.51). The rate of child homicides involving a firearm, however, was almost 16 times greater in the U.S. than in the other countries combined (0.94 vs. 0.06)." (See Table 3.8.)

The report also notes that the suicide rate of juveniles 0–14 in the United States was twice the rate recorded in all the other surveyed countries totaled. Figure 3.6 depicts how the United States compared with other countries during the survey. It is important to note, however, that violent crime in the United States has decreased substantially since the mid-1990s. Some attribute the lower rate of juvenile firearm-related deaths and suicides in other nations to strict gun control laws there.

SUICIDE

In 2001, according to the *National Vital Statistics Reports* (vol. 52, no. 9, November 7, 2003), suicide was not one of the 10 leading causes of death overall. However, it ranked 8th among males and 19th among females. Some 24,672 males committed suicide in 2001, representing 2.1 percent of the total male deaths that year, while 5,950 females (or 0.5 percent) took their own lives that year. As a leading cause of death, suicide ranked high among American Indians and Asian/Pacific Islanders (8th leading cause for both), slightly lower for whites (10th) and Hispanics (13th), and still lower among blacks (16th).

Suicide also played a significant role as a cause of death for younger Americans. According to the *National*

Vital Statistics Reports, "Intentional self-harm (suicide) is important for age groups from 10–14 to 25–34. Unintentional injuries, homicide, and suicide combined account for 75 percent of deaths for those 15–19 years of age, 72 percent of deaths for those 20–24 years of age, and 53 percent of deaths for those 25–34 years of age."

The likelihood that a juvenile will commit suicide increases with the presence of certain factors in his or her profile. Among the factors whose presence may indicate heightened risk are depression, substance abuse, behavioral disorders, the presence of a handgun in the home, and a tendency toward perfectionism. The suicide rate among male homosexual teens is believed to be extremely high, although this is based entirely on professional estimates. Statistical data on the subject are difficult to compile because sexual orientation is not part of public records and is often unknown to family members.

According to the May 2000 report of the Council of Economic Advisers, for teens of all ages, suicidal thoughts are higher among those who do not feel close to a parent. The report shows that younger teens who regularly ate dinner with their parents were about half as likely as other teens to think about suicide. Among teens ages 12 to 14, those who did not feel close to their parents were about three times as likely to think about suicide. Teens ages 17 to 19 who did not feel close to at least one parent were more than twice as likely to think about suicide. A *New York Times*/CBS News poll of American teenagers reported in January 2000 that nearly half (46 percent) of respondents knew of someone their age who had attempted suicide.

FIGURE 3.6

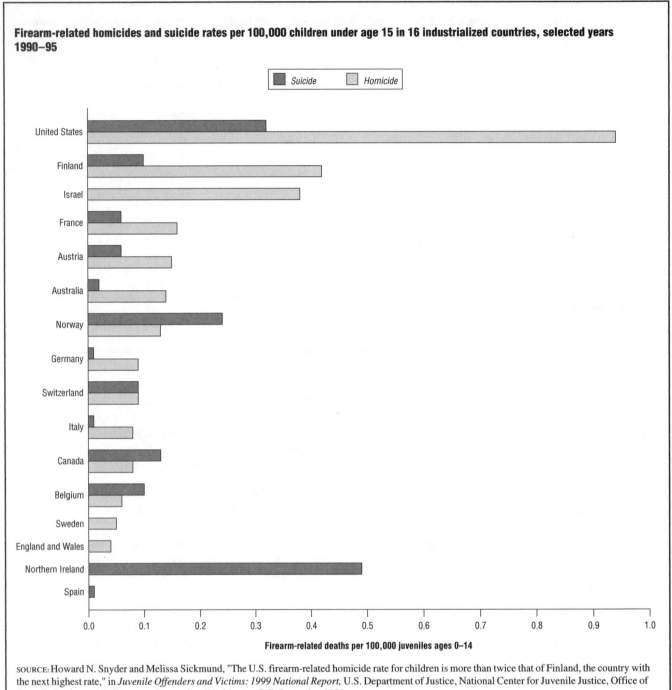

Firearm-related homicides and suicide rates per 100,000 children under age 15 in 16 industrialized countries, selected years 1990–95

Legend: Suicide / Homicide

Firearm-related deaths per 100,000 juveniles ages 0–14

SOURCE: Howard N. Snyder and Melissa Sickmund, "The U.S. firearm-related homicide rate for children is more than twice that of Finland, the country with the next highest rate," in *Juvenile Offenders and Victims: 1999 National Report*, U.S. Department of Justice, National Center for Juvenile Justice, Office of Juvenile Justice and Delinquency Prevention, Washington, DC, September 1999

RAPE

The FBI defines forcible rape as "the carnal knowledge of a female forcibly against her will. Assaults or attempts to commit rape by force or threat of force are included; however, statutory rape (without force) [sex with a consenting minor] and other sex offenses are excluded." Rape is a crime of violence in which the victim may suffer serious physical injury and long-term psychological pain. In 2002 the UCR recorded 95,136 rape offenses, an increase of 4.7 per-cent from 2001. This represents a rate of 33 per 100,000 inhabitants.

The NCVS reports that rape/sexual assault in 2002 occurred at a rate of 2.1 per 1,000 people among those 12–15, 5.5 per 1,000 people among those 16–19, and 2.9 per 1,000 people among those 20–24. NCVS data also include rapes committed against males. (See Table 3.9.) Females 16 to 19 experienced the highest rates (10.4 per 1,000). (See Table 3.10.) Among whites in that age group, the rate was 3.4 per 1,000 persons; for blacks, the

TABLE 3.9

Rates of violent crime and personal theft, by gender, age, race, and Hispanic origin, 2002

		Victimizations per 1,000 persons age 12 or older						
		Violent crimes						
			Rape/ sexual assault		Assault			Personal theft
Characteristic of victim	Population	All		Robbery	Total	Aggravated	Simple	
Gender								
Male	112,241,930	25.5	0.3	2.9	22.3	5.2	17.1	0.6
Female	119,347,330	20.8	1.8	1.6	17.4	3.4	14	0.7
Race								
White	192,956,980	22.8	0.8	1.9	20	4.1	15.9	0.7
Black	28,871,440	27.9	2.5	4.1	21.3	6.7	14.6	0.7*
Other	9,760,850	14.7	1.2*	2.4*	11	0.9*	10.1	0.4*
Hispanic origin								
Hispanic	26,991,490	23.6	0.7*	3.2	19.7	6.1	13.7	0.4*
Non-Hispanic	203,062,880	23	1.1	2.1	19.8	4.1	15.8	0.7
Age								
12–15	16,676,560	44.4	2.1	3	39.3	5	34.3	0.9*
16–19	16,171,800	58.2	5.5	4	48.6	11.9	36.7	0.6*
20–24	19,317,740	47.4	2.9	4.7	39.8	10.1	29.7	1.6*
25–34	37,329,720	26.3	0.6*	2.8	22.8	5.2	17.6	0.5*
35–49	65,263,580	18.1	0.5*	1.5	16.1	3.5	12.7	0.7
50–64	43,746,850	10.7	0.2*	1.6	8.9	1.7	7.2	0.3*
65 or older	33,083,000	3.4	0.1*	1	2.2	0.7*	1.5	0.6*

Note: The National Crime Victimization Survey includes as violent crime rape, sexual assault, robbery, and assault. Because the NCVS interviews persons about their victimizations, murder and manslaughter cannot be included.
*Based on 10 or fewer sample cases.

SOURCE: Callie Marie Rennison and Michael R. Rand, "Table 6. Rates of violent crime and personal theft, by gender, age, race, and Hispanic origin, 2002," in *Criminal Victimization, 2002*, NCJ 199994, U.S. Department of Justice, Bureau of Justice Statistics, Washington, DC, August 2003

rate was substantially higher (18.1 per 1,000). (See Table 3.11.)

Among victims 12 to 19, some 82.6 percent reported taking some form of self-protective measures. Such measures can include, according to the survey:

- Attacked offender with weapon
- Attacked offender without weapon
- Threatened offender with weapon
- Threatened offender without weapon
- Resisted or captured offender
- Scared or warned offender
- Persuaded or appeased offender
- Ran away or hid
- Got help or gave alarm
- Screamed from pain or fear
- Took other measures

The NCVS found that 55.3 percent of those 12 to 19 who acknowledged being victims of rape/sexual assault reported the incident to police. (See Table 3.12.) In its arrest reports, the UCR notes that 20,162 people were arrested for forcible rape in 2002. Of that number, 6.2 percent were under age 15, 16.7 percent were under age 18,

31.4 percent were under age 21, and 46.1 percent were under age 25.

For several reasons, the statistics on rape are incomplete. The crime often goes unreported. The BJS estimates that only about one-third of the cases of completed or attempted rape are ever reported to police. Because its data are collected through interviews, the BJS recognizes an underreporting in its statistics as well. Homosexual rape and date rape (sex forced on a woman by her escort) are not included in the BJS data. According to David Beatty, public policy director of the National Victims Center, acquaintance rape is far more common than stranger rape. Most experts conclude that in 80 to 85 percent of all rape cases, the victims knows the defendant.

AGGRAVATED ASSAULT

The FBI defines aggravated assault as "an unlawful attack by one person upon another for the purpose of inflicting severe or aggravated bodily injury. This type of assault is usually accompanied by the use of a weapon or by means likely to produce death or great bodily harm. Attempts involving the display or threat of a gun, knife, or other weapon are included because serious personal injury would likely result if the assault were completed." In 2002 the UCR recorded 894,348 aggravated assault offenses, a decrease of 1.6 percent from 2001. This represents a rate of 310.1 per 100,000 inhabitants.

TABLE 3.10

Victimization rates for persons age 12 and over, by gender and age of victims and type of crime, 2002

Gender and age	Total population	Crimes of violence	Completed violence	Attempted/ threatened violence	Rape/ sexual assault[1]	Robbery Total	With injury	Without injury	Assault Total	Aggra- vated	Simple	Purse snatching/ pocket picking
Male												
12–15	8,603,860	46.1	13.2	33.0	0.0*	4.9	1.8*	3.1*	41.2	5.4	35.8	1.8*
16–19	8,210,100	58.4	16.6	41.7	0.8*	4.9	3.0*	1.9*	52.6	16.3	36.3	1.2*
20–24	9,583,970	56.7	18.2	38.5	0.4*	7.2	2.5*	4.7*	49.1	13.2	35.9	1.9*
25–34	18,406,060	29.4	8.6	20.8	0.1*	3.2	0.8*	2.4*	26.0	6.6	19.4	0.4*
35–49	32,213,630	18.7	4.9	13.9	0.4*	2.0	1.1	0.9*	16.3	3.1	13.2	0.4*
50–64	21,052,670	11.4	3.0	8.4	0.3*	1.6	0.5*	1.1*	9.5	2.0	7.5	0.4*
65 and over	14,171,630	3.9	1.0*	2.9	0.0*	1.0*	0.6*	0.3*	2.9	1.2*	1.7*	0.0*
Female												
12–15	8,072,700	42.6	12.3	30.3	4.3	0.9*	0.3*	0.6*	37.3	4.5	32.8	0.0*
16–19	7,961,700	58.1	24.8	33.2	10.4	3.2*	1.0*	2.2*	44.5	7.4	37.1	0.0*
20–24	9,733,770	38.3	14.6	23.7	5.4	2.2*	1.3*	0.9*	30.7	7.0	23.7	1.3*
25–34	18,923,660	23.2	9.3	13.9	1.1*	2.4*	1.4*	1.0*	19.8	3.9	15.9	0.7*
35–49	33,049,950	17.6	6.2	11.4	0.6*	1.1	0.3*	0.8*	16.0	3.9	12.1	1.0*
50–64	22,694,180	10.0	3.9	6.1	0.1*	1.5	0.8*	0.7*	8.4	1.4	7.0	0.3*
65 and over	18,911,370	3.0	1.4*	1.6	0.2*	1.1*	0.1*	1.0	1.7	0.2*	1.4*	1.1*

Note: Detail may not add to total shown because of rounding.
*Estimate is based on about 10 or fewer sample cases.
[1]Includes verbal threats of rape and threats of sexual assault.

SOURCE: "Table 4. Personal crimes, 2002: Victimization rates for persons age 12 and over, by gender and age of victims and type of crime," in *Criminal Victimization in the United States, 2002 Statistical Tables*, NCJ 200561, U.S. Department of Justice, Bureau of Justice Statistics, Washington, DC, December 2003

TABLE 3.11

Victimization rates for persons age 12 and over, by race and age of victims and type of crime, 2002

Race and age	Total population	Crimes of violence	Completed violence	Attempted/ threatened violence	Rape/ sexual assault[1]	Robbery Total	With injury	Without injury	Assault Total	Aggra- vated	Simple	Purse snatching/ pocket picking
White												
12–15	12,991,380	47.5	13.6	33.9	2.0*	2.6	1.1*	1.5*	43.0	5.3	37.6	1.2*
16–19	13,032,600	56.6	19.9	36.7	3.4	4.2	2.3*	2.0*	49.0	10.9	38.1	0.8*
20–24	15,676,290	49.8	18.0	31.8	3.1	4.8	2.1	2.7*	41.9	11.2	30.7	1.9*
25–34	30,125,710	26.4	9.1	17.2	0.7*	2.5	1.0*	1.5	23.2	4.8	18.4	0.3*
35–49	54,144,220	18.3	5.5	12.8	0.3*	1.4	0.6*	0.8	16.6	3.3	13.3	0.7
50–64	37,611,120	10.3	3.1	7.2	0.1*	1.1	0.4*	0.8*	9.1	1.6	7.5	0.3*
65 and over	29,375,650	2.8	0.7*	2.1	0.2*	0.5*	0.2*	0.3*	2.2	0.6*	1.6	0.7*
Black												
12–15	2,937,540	39.6	9.7*	29.8	3.0*	4.5*	1.5*	3.0*	32.0	4.7*	27.4	0.0*
16–19	2,405,340	73.9	28.9	45.0	18.1	4.3*	1.3*	3.0*	51.5	21.1	30.4	0.0*
20–24	2,670,870	34.5	7.3*	27.2	1.5*	2.8*	0.0*	2.8*	30.3	7.1*	23.1	0.0*
25–34	5,223,930	31.9	10.6	21.3	0.7*	5.6*	2.2*	3.5*	25.5	9.2	16.3	1.9*
35–49	8,261,960	19.5	6.0	13.6	1.0*	2.1*	1.3*	0.8*	16.5	5.9	10.5	0.8*
50–64	4,513,150	14.4	6.5*	7.9	0.9*	5.1*	3.3*	1.8*	8.4	1.7*	6.6*	0.0*
65 and over	2,858,650	9.2*	6.9*	2.3*	0.0*	5.9*	1.4*	4.5*	3.3 *	1.6*	1.8*	0.8*

Note: Detail may not add to total shown because of rounding.
Excludes data on persons of "Other" races.
*Estimate is based on about 10 or fewer sample cases.
[1]Includes verbal threats of rape and threats of sexual assault.

SOURCE: "Table 9. Personal crimes, 2002: Victimization rates for persons age 12 and over, by race and age of victims and type of crime," in *Criminal Victimization in the United States, 2002 Statistical Tables*, NCJ 200561, U.S. Department of Justice, Bureau of Justice Statistics, Washington, DC, December 2003

TABLE 3.12

Percent of victimizations reported to police by type of crime and age of victims, 2002

Type of crime	Percent of victimizations reported to the police				
	12–19	20–34	35–49	50–64	65 and over
All personal crimes	**37.8%**	**53.8%**	**50.8%**	**55.9%**	**58.1%**
Crimes of violence	38.1	54.1	50.5	55.5	58.7
Completed violence	54.0	62.8	62.6	66.0	66.9*
Attempted/threatened violence	30.5	49.6	45.2	50.4	54.1
Rape/sexual assault[1]	55.3	54.6	60.4*	0.0*	50.4*
Robbery	68.3	72.3	80.3	63.2	64.3*
Completed/property taken	72.2	78.3	79.4	73.7	65.8*
With injury	74.7	81.0	91.6*	82.0*	31.7*
Without injury	69.4*	76.4	70.9	64.5*	77.0*
Attempted to take property	59.4*	53.9*	84.2*	29.9*	59.4*
With injury	100.0*	100.0*	69.2*	100.0*	100.0*
Without injury	45.0*	29.8*	100.0*	19.7*	0.0*
Assault	34.2	51.9	47.4	55.4	56.6
Aggravated	39.4	65.7	56.7	70.4	66.0*
With injury	41.4	66.0	64.6	91.1*	0.0*
Threatened with weapon	38.6	65.5	53.8	57.6*	73.1*
Simple	33.0	47.5	44.8	51.9	52.5*
With minor injury	51.3	56.1	56.3	54.1	100.0*
Without injury	26.4	44.7	40.9	51.2	41.5*
Purse snatching/pocket picking	11.8*	42.4*	59.1*	69.3*	55.1*

*Estimate is based on about 10 or fewer sample cases.
[1]Includes verbal threats of rape and threats of sexual assault.

SOURCE: "Table 96. Personal crimes, 2002: Percent of victimizations reported to the police, by type of crime and age of victims," in *Criminal Victimization in the United States, 2002 Statistical Tables*, NCJ 200561, U.S. Department of Justice, Bureau of Justice Statistics, Washington, DC, December 2003

The NCVS reports that aggravated assault in 2002 occurred at a rate of 5 per 1,000 people among those 12–15, 11.9 per 1,000 people among those 16–19, and 10.1 per 1,000 people among those 20–24. (See Table 3.9.) Among males, those aged 16 to 19 experienced the highest rates (16.3 per 1,000); among females, the same age group also endured the most aggravated assaults (7.4 per 1,000). (See Table 3.10.) For whites the rate was highest among those 20 to 24 (11.2 per 1,000); for blacks, those 16 to 19 had the highest rates (21.1 per 1,000). (See Table 3.11.)

Among victims 12 to 19, some 69.8 percent reported taking some form of self-protective measures. The NCVS found that 39.4 percent of those 12 to 19 who acknowledged being victims of aggravated assault reported the incident to police. (See Table 3.12.) In its arrest reports, the UCR notes that 339,437 people were arrested for aggravated assault in 2002. Of that number, 4.7 percent were under age 15, 13 percent were under age 18, 24.2 percent were under age 21, and 39.3 percent were under age 25.

Simple Assaults

Simple assaults, according to the FBI, are "assaults and attempted assaults where no weapon was used or which did not result in serious or aggravated injury to the victim." These include acts such as assault and battery, resisting or obstructing the police, hazing, etc. The NCVS reports that in 2002 simple assault occurred at a rate of 34.3 per 1,000 people among those 12–15, 36.7 per 1,000 people among those 16–19, and 29.7 per 1,000 people among those 20–24. (See Table 3.9.) Among males, those aged 16 to 19 experienced the highest rates (36.3 per 1,000). The same age group experienced the highest simple assaults among females (37.1 per 1,000). (See Table 3.10.) Among whites and blacks, the rate was highest among those 16 to 19 (38.1 per 1,000 and 30.4 per 1,000, respectively). (See Table 3.11.)

Among victims 12 to 19, some 68.6 percent reported taking some form of self-protective measures. The NCVS found that 33 percent of the simple assaults among those 12 to 19 were reported to police. (See Table 3.12.) In its arrest reports, the UCR lists a category called "other assaults" (to differentiate between these types of assaults and aggravated assaults). The FBI notes that 921,676 people were arrested for other assaults in 2002. Of that number, 7.8 percent were under age 15, 18.3 percent were under age 18, 28.3 percent were under age 21, and 42.3 percent were under age 25.

ROBBERY

The FBI defines robbery as "the taking or attempting to take anything of value from the care, custody, or control of a person or persons by force or threat of force or violence and/or by putting the victim in fear." In 2002 the UCR recorded 420,637 robbery offenses, a decrease of 0.7 percent from 2001. This represents a rate of 145.9 per 100,000 inhabitants.

The NCVS reports that robbery in 2002 occurred at a rate of 3 per 1,000 people among those 12–15, 4 per 1,000 people among those 16–19, and 4.7 per 1,000 people among those 20–24. (See Table 3.9.) Among males, those aged 20 to 24 experienced the highest rates (7.2 per 1,000). The highest rate for females occurred among those 16 to 19 (3.2 per 1,000). (See Table 3.10.) Among whites, robbery victimizations were highest among those 20 to 24 (4.8 per 1,000). For blacks, the 65 and older age group was robbed most often (5.9 per 1,000). Among those 12 to 15, whites were robbed about 2.6 per 1,000 and blacks 4.5 per 1,000. (See Table 3.11.)

Among victims 12 to 19, some 69.9 percent reported taking some form of self-protective measures. The NCVS found that 68.3 percent of those 12 to 19 who acknowledged being victims of robbery reported the incident to police. (See Table 3.12.) In its arrest reports, the UCR notes that 77,342 people were arrested for robbery in 2002. Of that number, 5.6 percent were under age 15, 23.1 percent were under age 18, 44.5 percent were under age 21, and 61.4 percent were under age 25.

BURGLARY

The FBI defines burglary as "the unlawful entry of a structure to commit a felony or theft. The use of force to gain entry is not required to classify an offense as a burglary." In 2002 the UCR recorded 2,151,875 burglary offenses, an increase of 1.7 percent from 2001. This represents a rate of 746.2 per 100,000 inhabitants.

The NCVS reports that household burglaries in 2002 occurred at a rate of 64.1 per 1,000 households headed by people ages 12–19 and 35.4 per 1,000 households headed by people ages 20–34. In its arrest reports, the UCR notes that 206,136 people were arrested for burglary in 2002. Of that number, 10.9 percent were under age 15, 30 percent were under age 18, 48.9 percent were under age 21, and 62.6 percent were under age 25.

LARCENY-THEFT

The FBI defines larceny-theft as "the unlawful taking, carrying, leading, or riding away of property from the possession or constructive possession of another. It includes crimes such as shoplifting, pocket-picking, purse-snatching, thefts from motor vehicles, thefts of motor vehicle parts and accessories, bicycle thefts, etc., in which no use of force, violence, or fraud occurs." It does not include embezzlement, "con" games, forgery, and passing bad checks. In 2002 the UCR recorded 7,052,922 larceny-theft offenses, a decrease of 0.6 percent from 2001. This represents a rate of 2,445.8 per 100,000 inhabitants.

The NCVS, which uses a category called "personal theft," states that in 2002 such thefts occurred at a rate of 0.9 per 1,000 people among those 12–15, 0.6 per 1,000 people among those 16–19, and 1.6 per 1,000 people among those 20–24. (See Table 3.9.) In its arrest reports, the UCR notes that 845,009 people were arrested for larceny-theft in 2002. Of that number, 11.3 percent were under age 15, 29.5 percent were under age 18, 44.8 percent were under age 21, and 56.3 percent were under age 25.

Pocket-Picking and Purse-Snatching

According to the NCVS, those 20 to 24 experienced the highest rates of pocket picking and purse snatching in 2002. In that age group, the rate for males was 1.9 per 1,000; for females, it was 1.3 per 1,000. (See Table 3.10.) Among whites, those aged 20 to 24 experienced the most occurrences of these crimes (1.9 per 1,000). (See Table 3.11.) The NCVS found that 11.8 percent of those 12 to 19 who acknowledged being victims of purse snatching/pocket picking reported the incident to police. (See Table 3.12.)

MOTOR-VEHICLE THEFT

The FBI defines motor-vehicle theft as "the theft or attempted theft of a motor vehicle. This offense includes the stealing of automobiles, trucks, buses, motorcycles, motorscooters, snowmobiles, etc. The taking of a motor vehicle for temporary use by persons having lawful access is excluded from this definition." In 2002 the UCR recorded 1,246,096 motor-vehicle theft offenses, an increase of 1.4 percent from 2001. This represents a rate of 432.1 per 100,000 inhabitants.

In its arrest reports, the UCR notes that 107,187 people were arrested for motor-vehicle theft in 2002. Of that number, 7.7 percent were under age 15, 30.4 percent were under age 18, 49.1 percent were under age 21, and 63.8 percent were under age 25.

OTHER CRIMES

Bank Robberies

The FBI's UCR also contains information on other crimes, including bank robberies and sniper shootings. Between 1996 and 2000, some 3,869 individuals were bank robbery offenders, of which 204 (or 5.3 percent) were known to be female and 2,962 (or 76.6 percent) were known to be male. (See Table 3.13.) Information about the remainder is unknown. Of the total, 140 bank robbers were between the ages of 12 and 17, including 8 females and 131 males. Another 65 female and 766 male bank robbers were between the ages of 18 and 24. In fact, the highest number of known bank robbers, for both males and females, fell into the 18 to 24 age group.

According to the UCR: "one-third of all bank robbery offenders are between 18 and 29 years of age. This is all the more astonishing because there are 703 offenders contained in the denominator that are either unknown or listed as missing data. If we drop the unknown and missing data from the denominator and recalculate the percentage, we find that 41.7 percent of bank robbery offenders reported in NIBRS [National Incident Based Reporting System] data are 18–29-year-old males."

Sniper Attacks

The UCR also presented data on sniper attacks between 1982 and 2001. This study does not include the Washington, D.C.-area sniper attacks, which occurred in October of 2002. Some 379 people were murdered by snipers during that period, including 295 males and 84 females. (See Table 3.14.) Two of five victims were 24 or younger. Of the male victims, 35 were under 18 and 82 were between 18 and 24. Among female victims, 15 under 18 and 21 were between 18 and 24. Some 27 victims were whites under 18 and another 21 were blacks under 18. Victims between the ages of 18 and 24 included 49 whites and 50 blacks.

The FBI also reported 224 sniper-attack murder offenders between 1982 and 2001. (See Table 3.15.) Of this number, 54.9 percent were 24 and under and 53.1

TABLE 3.13

Bank robberies by age and gender of offender, 1996–2000

Age	Female	Female %	Male	Male %	Unknown	Unknown %	Missing Values	Missing Values %	Total
12–17	8	0.21	131	3.39	1	0.03		0.00	140
18–24	65	1.68	766	19.80	5	0.13		0.00	836
25–29	42	1.09	554	14.32	7	0.18		0.00	603
30–34	31	0.80	406	10.49	4	0.10		0.00	441
35–39	14	0.36	261	6.75		0.00		0.00	275
40–44	8	0.21	183	4.73	1	0.03		0.00	192
45–49	6	0.16	99	2.56		0.00		0.00	105
50–54	7	0.18	51	1.32	8	0.21		0.00	66
55–59	5	0.13	25	0.65	1	0.03		0.00	31
60–64		0.00	5	0.13		0.00		0.00	5
over 64	2	0.05	14	0.36	1	0.03		0.00	17
Unknown	16	0.41	467	12.07	167	4.32	508	13.13	1,158
Total	**204**	**5.27**	**2,962**	**76.56**	**195**	**5.04**	**508**	**13.13**	**3,869**

SOURCE: "Table 5.10. Bank robberies by age and gender of offender, 1996–2000," in *Crime in the United States 2002: Uniform Crime Reports,* Federal Bureau of Investigation, Washington, DC, 2003

TABLE 3.14

Sniper-attack murder victims by age, sex, and race, 1982–2001

Age	Total	Sex			Race				
		Male	Female	Unknown	White	Black	American Indian/ Alaskan Native	Asian/ Pacific Islander	Unknown
Total	**379**	**295**	**84**	**0**	**199**	**167**	**1**	**9**	**3**
Under 10	8	4	4	0	3	5	0	0	0
10 to 12	13	8	5	0	11	2	0	0	0
13	1	1	0	0	1	0	0	0	0
14	3	3	0	0	0	2	0	0	1
15	1	0	1	0	0	1	0	0	0
16	9	6	3	0	5	3	0	1	0
17	15	13	2	0	7	8	0	0	0
18	20	15	5	0	11	8	1	0	0
19	14	12	2	0	6	8	0	0	0
20	13	13	0	0	5	7	0	1	0
21	9	4	5	0	5	4	0	0	0
22	15	12	3	0	6	9	0	0	0
23	17	13	4	0	10	7	0	0	0
24	15	13	2	0	6	7	0	1	1
25 to 29	59	48	11	0	28	30	0	1	0
30 to 34	55	46	9	0	28	26	0	1	0
35 to 39	35	26	9	0	19	15	0	1	0
40 to 44	31	24	7	0	20	10	0	0	1
45 to 49	15	11	4	0	8	6	0	1	0
50 to 54	8	7	1	0	3	3	0	2	0
55 to 59	8	5	3	0	5	3	0	0	0
60 to 64	6	5	1	0	6	0	0	0	0
65 and over	7	4	3	0	5	2	0	0	0
Unknown	2	2	0	0	1	1	0	0	0

SOURCE: "Table 5.18. Sniper-attack murder victims by age, sex, and race, 1982–2001," in *Crime in the United States 2002: Uniform Crime Reports*, Federal Bureau of Investigation, Washington, DC, 2003

percent were males 24 and under. The proportion of white and black offenders age 24 and under was close—24.6 percent and 25.9 percent respectively. Overall, female sniper-attack murderers numbered 7 (or 3.1 percent). In general, snipers were most likely to attack strangers (46.6 percent) and acquaintances (9 percent), though in 166 cases the relationship between sniper and victim was unknown. (See Table 3.16.)

Bombings

The Bureau of Alcohol, Tobacco, Firearms and Explosives (ATF) maintains data on juveniles involved in bombing incidents. (See Table 3.17.) Although the data are several years old, they illuminate the trends in juvenile bombings during some of the higher crime and violence years. During the five-year period studied, for example, 4,631 such bombings occurred or were attempted, the

TABLE 3.15

Sniper-attack murder offenders by age, sex, and race, 1982–2001

Age	Total	Sex			Race				
		Male	Female	Unknown	White	Black	American Indian/ Alaskan Native	Asian/ Pacific Islander	Unknown
Total	224	217	7	0	117	94	2	2	9
Under 10	0	0	0	0	0	0	0	0	0
10 to 12	1	1	0	0	1	0	0	0	0
13	5	4	1	0	5	0	0	0	0
14	2	2	0	0	1	1	0	0	0
15	8	7	1	0	5	1	0	0	2
16	6	6	0	0	3	3	0	0	0
17	7	7	0	0	2	5	0	0	0
18	15	15	0	0	7	5	1	0	2
19	20	19	1	0	7	12	0	0	1
20	17	17	0	0	5	10	0	2	0
21	9	9	0	0	1	7	0	0	1
22	15	14	1	0	5	9	1	0	0
23	6	6	0	0	5	1	0	0	0
24	12	12	0	0	8	4	0	0	0
25 to 29	36	35	1	0	19	17	0	0	0
30 to 34	17	16	1	0	13	4	0	0	0
35 to 39	11	11	0	0	7	4	0	0	0
40 to 44	6	6	0	0	6	0	0	0	0
45 to 49	6	6	0	0	5	1	0	0	0
50 to 54	5	5	0	0	3	2	0	0	0
55 to 59	1	1	0	0	1	0	0	0	0
60 to 64	2	2	0	0	1	1	0	0	0
65 and over	3	3	0	0	2	1	0	0	0
Unknown	14	13	1	0	5	6	0	0	3

SOURCE: "Table 5.19. Sniper-attack murder offenders by age, sex, and race, 1982–2001," in *Crime in the United States 2002: Uniform Crime Reports*, Federal Bureau of Investigation, Washington, DC, 2003

most happening in 1994 (1,126 incidents). In all, juveniles killed 18 and injured another 446 in such incidents during that time period, and were responsible for more than $2.3 million in property damage.

Law Enforcement Officers Killed

In a special report, the UCR also included statistics on the number of law enforcement officers feloniously killed between 1993 and 2002. During that 10-year period, some 785 officers were killed—the highest number (114) occurred in 1994, representing 14.5 percent of the total killed. (See Table 3.18.) In 2002 some 61 officers were feloniously killed, representing 7.8 percent of the 10-year total. Those 24 years of age and under were responsible for killing 47.5 percent of the officers between 1993 and 2002, including 49.1 percent of those officers killed in 1994. In 2002 those 24 and under were responsible for 42.6 percent of such deaths.

Computer Hacking

Illegally accessing a computer, known as hacking, is a crime committed frequently by juveniles. When it is followed by manipulation of the information of private, corporate, or government databases and networks, it can be quite costly. Another means of computer hacking involves creation of what is known as a "virus" program. The virus program is one that resides inside another program, activated by some predetermined code to create havoc in the host computer. Virus programs can be transmitted either through the sharing of disks and programs or through electronic mail.

Cases of juvenile hacking have been reported since the 1980s and have included: six teens gaining access to more than 60 computer networks such as those for the Memorial Sloan-Kettering Cancer Center and Los Alamos National Laboratory in 1983; several juvenile hackers accessing AT&T's computer network in 1987; and teens hacking into computer networks and Web sites for the National Aeronautics and Space Administration (NASA), the Korean Atomic Research Institute, America Online, the U.S. Senate, the White House, the U.S. Army, and the U.S. Department of Justice in the 1990s.

In 1998 the U.S. Secret Service filed the first criminal case against a juvenile for a computer crime. The unnamed hacker shut down the Worcester, Massachusetts, airport in 1997 for six hours. The airport was integrated into the Federal Aviation Administration (FAA) traffic system by telephone lines. The accused gained access to the communication system and disabled it by sending a series of computer commands that changed the data carried on the system. As a result, the airport could not

TABLE 3.16

Sniper-attack murder victim/offender relationship by year, 1982–2001

Year	Total confrontations	Within family* Father	Outside Family but Known to Victim											Stranger	Unknown relationship
			Neighbor	Acquaintance	Boyfriend	Girlfriend	Ex-Husband	Ex-Wife	Employee	Employer	Friend	Homosexual relationship	Other		
1982	18	0	0	3	0	0	0	0	0	0	0	0	0	13	2
1983	17	0	0	2	0	0	0	0	0	0	0	0	2	5	8
1984	40	0	0	8	0	0	0	0	0	0	0	0	0	29	3
1985	11	0	0	0	0	0	0	0	0	0	0	0	0	6	5
1986	9	0	0	0	0	0	0	0	0	0	0	0	0	4	5
1987	39	0	0	0	0	0	0	0	0	0	0	0	0	32	7
1988	67	0	0	1	0	0	0	0	0	0	5	0	3	27	31
1989	57	0	0	1	0	0	0	0	0	0	1	0	7	23	25
1990	46	0	1	1	0	0	0	0	0	0	1	0	2	19	22
1991	12	0	0	1	0	0	0	0	0	0	0	0	3	3	5
1992	37	0	0	4	0	0	0	0	0	0	0	0	0	11	22
1993	6	0	0	0	0	0	0	0	0	0	0	0	0	3	3
1994	5	0	0	3	0	0	0	0	0	0	0	0	0	2	0
1995	12	0	0	3	1	0	0	0	0	0	0	0	0	2	6
1996	15	0	0	4	0	0	0	0	0	0	0	0	0	9	2
1997	4	0	0	0	0	0	0	0	0	0	0	0	0	0	4
1998	22	0	0	7	0	0	0	0	0	0	0	0	0	9	6
1999	7	0	0	0	0	0	0	0	0	0	0	0	0	4	3
2000	8	0	1	1	0	0	0	0	0	0	0	0	0	0	6
2001	12	1	0	1	0	0	0	0	0	0	0	0	3	6	1
Total	444	1	2	40	1	0	0	0	0	0	7	0	20	207	166

*Possible relationships within the family are husband, wife, common-law husband, common-law wife, mother, father, son, daughter, brother, sister, in-law, stepfather, stepmother, stepson, stepdaughter, and other family. All entries except father were zero; therefore, they were omitted from the table.

SOURCE: "Table 5.20. Sniper-attack murder victim/offender relationship by year, 1982–2001," in *Crime in the United States 2002: Uniform Crime Reports,* Federal Bureau of Investigation, Washington, DC, 2003

function. (No accidents occurred during that time, however.) According to the Department of Justice, the juvenile pled guilty in return for two years probation, a fine, and community service.

U.S. Attorney Donald K. Stern, lead lawyer on the case against the juvenile, observed that: "Computer and telephone networks are at the heart of vital services provided by the government and private industry, and our critical infrastructure. They are not toys for the entertainment of teenagers. Hacking a computer or telephone network can create a tremendous risk to the public and we will prosecute juvenile hackers in appropriate cases."

Drug Abuse

Various studies show that many violent offenders are substance abusers. For some people, drugs and alcohol may cause such tendencies to surface. In a study prepared by the Office of National Drug Control Policy of the Executive Office of the President, 28.4 percent of teens between 12 and 17 reported having ever used any illicit drugs. (See Table 3.19.)

Marijuana/hashish use was highest (19.7 percent), followed by nonmedical use of psychotherapeutics (11.6 percent), which include pain relievers, tranquilizers, stimulants, and sedatives. Inhalants (8.6 percent), hallucinogens (5.7 percent), and cocaine (2.3 percent) rounded out

TABLE 3.17

Juvenile bombing incidents, 1992–1996

	1992	1993	1994	1995	1996	Total
Bombings	659	803	888	698	618	3,666
Attempted bombings	61	87	151	110	129	538
Incendiary bombings	44	72	55	77	46	294
Attempted incendiary	10	20	32	46	25	133
Total bombings	**774**	**982**	**1,126**	**931**	**818**	**4,631**
Killed	3	4	6	2	3	18
Injured	81	83	103	99	80	446
Property damage	$163,364	1,249,328	287,270	418,745	223,041	2,341,748

SOURCE: "Juvenile Bombing Incidents 1992–1996," Bureau of Alcohol, Tobacco, Firearms and Explosives, Washington, DC, [Online] http://www.atf.gov/pub/fire-explo_pub/eir/juvenile.htm [accessed February 7, 2004]

the top five. One in five juveniles between 12 and 17 reported any illicit drug use within the past year, while 1 in 10 reported such use during the last month.

Other drugs gaining popularity in recent years include so-called "club drugs," such as ecstasy (MDMA), Rohypnol (known as the date rape drug), GHB, and ketamine. These have been popular among teenagers at dance clubs and raves. Because each of these club drugs is scheduled under the Controlled Substances Act (Title II of the Comprehensive Drug Abuse Prevention and Control Act of 1970), they are illegal and their use constitutes a criminal offense. In 2001, some 3.2 percent of 12- to

TABLE 3.18

Law enforcement officers feloniously killed, profile of known assailants, age groups, 1993–2002

Known assailants	Total	1993	1994	1995	1996	1997	1998	1999	2000	2001	2002
Total	785	93	114	93	85	76	77	49	64	73	61
Age											
Under 18 years	83	16	18	17	7	3	11	3	4	2	2
18–24 years	290	32	38	31	37	25	27	24	20	32	24
25–30 years	150	12	24	14	23	19	17	10	11	10	10
31–40 years	117	9	15	17	6	17	10	10	8	13	12
Over 40 years	109	13	13	11	10	12	11	2	14	10	13
Age not reported	36	11	6	3	2	0	1	0	7	6	0
Average years of age	28	28	27	27	27	30	27	27	32	29	32

Note: The 72 deaths that resulted from the events of September 11, 2001, are not included in the table.

SOURCE: "Table 38. Law Enforcement Officers Feloniously Killed, Profile of Known Assailants, Age Groups, 1993–2002," in *Law Enforcement Officers Killed and Assaulted, 2002,* Federal Bureau of Investigation, Washington, DC, 2002.

17-year-olds reported they had ever used ecstasy. (See Table 3.19.)

In its arrest reports, the UCR noted that 1,103,017 people were arrested on drug abuse violations in 2002. Of that number, 2 percent were under age 15, 12.1 percent were under age 18, 31 percent were under age 21, and 49 percent were under age 25.

VICTIMIZATION

Between 1973 and 2002, the rate of violent victimizations dropped in all age categories. (See Table 3.20.) In 1973 the violent victimization rate for those aged 12 to 15 was 81.8 per 1,000. The rate peaked in 1994 at 118.6 per 1,000 then dropped steadily to 44.4 per 1,000 in 2002, its lowest point in the thirty years recorded. For those 16 to 19, the rate in 1973 was 81.7. That group also reached its zenith in 1994 at 123.9 and then decreased steadily to 55.9 in 2001, then rose to 58.3 in 2002. The highest rate in 1973 was among 20- to 24-year-olds (87.6). This age group reached its highest point in 1991 with 103.6 and then fluctuated before dropping to 47.6 in 2002.

In 1973, 16- to 19-year-olds were about twice as likely to be victimized by violent crime as persons 35 to 49 years of age; in 2002, they were about three times as likely. Victims of half of the age groups experienced their lowest rates in 2002. That includes those 12 to 15 (44.4), 25 to 34 (26.4), and 35 to 49 (18.2). The year 2001 marked the lowest rates since 1973 for those 16 to 19 (55.9), 20 to 24 (44.9), and 50 to 64 (9.5). For those 65 and older, their lowest victimization rate occurred in 1998 (2.8).

The Trauma of Victimization

The Office of Juvenile Justice and Delinquency Prevention in Washington, D.C., notes that when someone is victimized as an adolescent, long-term consequences result. When compared to adults who were not victimized as adolescents, adults who were adolescent victims are more likely to have drug problems and to perpetrate violence. (See Figure 3.7.) They are also expected to commit more acts of domestic violence and become victims of domestic violence more often than adults who were not victimized as adolescents. In addition, they are nearly twice as likely to become victims of violent crime and nearly three times as likely to commit property offenses. Their risk of developing posttraumatic stress disorder (PTSD) is also greater.

Becoming a victim of crime can have serious consequences—outcomes that the victim neither asks for nor deserves. A victim rarely expects to be victimized and seldom knows where to turn for help. Victims may end up in the hospital to be treated and released, or they may be confined to bed for days, weeks, or longer. Injuries may be temporary, or they may be permanent and forever change the way the victim lives his or her life. Victims may lose money or property, or they may even lose their lives. In some cases they lose their confidence, self-esteem, and feelings of security.

The effects of crime are not limited to the victim, however. The family is frequently devastated, and the psychological trauma may affect everyone connected to a victim. Victims and their families may experience feelings of fear, anger, shame, self-blame, helplessness, and depression—emotions that can scar life and health for years after the event. Those who were attacked in their homes or whose homes were entered illegally may no longer feel secure anywhere. They often blame themselves, feeling that they could have handled themselves better, or done something differently to prevent being victimized.

In the aftermath of crime, when victims most need support and comfort, there is often no one available who understands. Parents or spouses may be dealing with their own feelings of guilt and anger for not being able to protect their loved ones. Friends may withdraw, not knowing what to say or do. As a result, victims may lose their sense of self-esteem and no longer trust other people.

TABLE 3.19

Past illicit drug use among 12- to 17-year-olds, 2001

Drug	Ever used	Past year	Past month
Any illicit drug	28.4%	20.8%	10.8%
Marijuana/hashish	19.7	15.2	8.0
Cocaine	2.3	1.5	0.4
Crack	0.6	0.4	0.1
Heroin	0.3	0.2	0.0
Hallucinogens	5.7	4.0	1.2
LSD (lysergic acid diethylamide)	3.1	1.9	0.4
PCP (phencyclidine)	1.0	0.5	0.1
MDMA (ecstasy)	3.2	2.4	0.6
Inhalants	8.6	3.5	1.0
Methamphetamine	1.4	0.8	0.2
Nonmedical use of			
psychotherapeutics	11.6	7.9	3.2
Pain relievers	9.4	6.4	2.6
Tranquilizers	2.6	1.7	0.5
Stimulants	3.7	2.2	0.7
Sedatives	0.7	0.3	0.1

SOURCE: Michele Spiess, "Table 1. Past illicit drug use among 12- to 17-year-olds, 2001," in "Juveniles and Drugs," *ONDCP Drug Policy Information Clearinghouse Fact Sheet*, NCJ 196879, Executive Office of the President, Office of National Drug Control Policy, Rockville, MD, June 2003 [Online] http://www.whitehousedrugpolicy.gov/publications/factsht/juvenile/196879.pdf [accessed January 23, 2004]

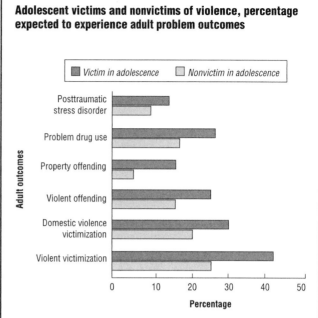

FIGURE 3.7

Adolescent victims and nonvictims of violence, percentage expected to experience adult problem outcomes

SOURCE: Scott Menard, "Adolescent Victims and Nonvictims of Violence; Percentage Expected to Experience Adult Problem Outcomes," in *Short- and Long-Term Consequences of Adolescent Victimization*, Youth Violence Research Bulletin, U.S. Department of Justice, Office of Justice Programs, Office of Juvenile Justice and Delinquency Prevention, Washington, D.C, February 2002

Fear of crime has permeated society. This factor is evidenced in the many polls reporting that neighborhood crime is a major problem today. The fear of becoming a victim of crime, however, is often much greater than the likelihood of being one.

Child Maltreatment

According to many behavioral experts, child maltreatment is believed to contribute to the chances of someone becoming violent later in life. The Administration of Children and Families (ACF) of the U.S. Department of Health and Human Services reported the victimization rates by maltreatment types for children between the years 1997 and 2001 in Figure 3.8. The ACF learned that physical abuse decreased from 3.3 per 1,000 children in 1997 to 2.3 per 1,000 in 2001. The number of neglect victims also lessened, from 7.5 per 1,000 in 1997 to 7.1 per 1,000 in 2001, although neglect still represents the highest rate of child maltreatment. Sexual abuse also diminished—from 1.7 per 1,000 in 1997 to 1.2 per 1,000 in 2001, while psychological maltreatment remained a constant 0.9 per 1,000.

WARNING SIGNS OF VIOLENT BEHAVIOR

Various government entities, schools, student and parent organizations, and research groups have devoted countless hours to the issue of youth violence. One of their goals is to find ways to recognize the potential for violent behavior in youth before it becomes a serious problem. They work individually and sometimes collectively to outline trends in youth violence as well as what factors lead to violent behavior.

The U.S. Departments of Education and Justice teamed to produce the publication *Safeguarding Our Children: An Action Guide* (K. Dwyer and D. Osher, Washington, DC, 2000). In this report, the authors note that between 10 and 15 percent of students exhibit behavioral problems that point out the need for an early intervention. They describe the early warning signs of potential violence as follows.

- Social withdrawal
- Excessive feelings of isolation or being alone
- Excessive feelings of rejection
- Being a victim of violence
- Feelings of being picked on and persecuted
- Low school interest and poor academic performance
- Expression of violence in writing and drawings
- Uncontrolled anger
- Patterns of impulsive and chronic hitting, intimidating, and bullying behaviors
- History of discipline problems
- History of violent and aggressive behavior
- Intolerance for differences and prejudicial attitudes
- Drug use and alcohol use
- Affiliation with gangs

TABLE 3.20

Violent victimization rates by age, 1973–2002

Year	Age of victim						
	12–15	16–19	20–24	25–34	35–49	50–64	65+
1973	81.8	81.7	87.6	52.4	38.8	17.2	9.1
1974	77.5	90.6	83.5	58.6	37.5	15.5	9.5
1975	80.3	85.7	80.9	59.5	36.9	17.8	8.3
1976	76.4	88.8	79.7	61.5	35.9	16.1	8.1
1977	83.0	90.2	86.2	63.5	35.8	16.8	8.0
1978	83.7	91.7	91.1	60.5	35.8	15.0	8.4
1979	78.5	93.4	98.4	66.3	38.2	13.6	6.2
1980	72.5	91.3	94.1	60.0	37.4	15.6	7.2
1981	86.0	90.7	93.7	65.8	41.6	17.3	8.3
1982	75.6	94.4	93.8	69.6	38.6	13.8	6.1
1983	75.4	86.3	82.0	62.2	36.5	11.9	5.9
1984	78.2	90.0	87.5	56.6	37.9	13.2	5.2
1985	79.6	89.4	82.0	56.5	35.6	13.0	4.8
1986	77.1	80.8	80.1	52.0	36.0	10.8	4.8
1987	87.2	92.4	85.5	51.9	34.7	11.4	5.2
1988	83.7	95.9	80.2	53.2	39.1	13.4	4.4
1989	92.5	98.2	78.8	52.8	37.3	10.5	4.2
1990	101.1	99.1	86.1	55.2	34.4	9.9	3.7
1991	94.5	122.6	103.6	54.3	37.2	12.5	4.0
1992	111.0	103.7	95.2	56.8	38.1	13.2	5.2
1993	115.5	114.2	91.6	56.9	42.5	15.2	5.9
1994	118.6	123.9	100.4	59.1	41.3	17.6	4.6
1995	113.1	106.6	85.8	58.5	35.7	12.9	6.4
1996	95.0	102.8	74.5	51.2	32.9	15.7	4.9
1997	87.9	96.3	68.0	47.0	32.3	14.6	4.4
1998	82.5	91.3	67.5	41.6	29.9	15.4	2.8
1999	74.4	77.5	68.7	36.4	25.3	14.4	3.8
2000	60.1	64.4	49.5	34.9	21.9	13.7	3.7
2001	55.1	55.9	44.9	29.4	23.0	9.5	3.2
2002	44.4	58.3	47.6	26.4	18.2	10.7	3.4

Note: Rate per 1,000 persons in age group.

SOURCE: "Violent victimization rates by age, 1973–2002," in *Key Facts at a Glance,* U.S. Department of Justice, Bureau of Justice Statistics, Washington, DC, 2004 [Online] http://www.ojp.usdoj.gov/bjs/glance/tables/vagetab.htm [accessed February 8, 2004]

• Inappropriate access to, possession of, and use of firearms

• Serious threats of violence

Those involved in the study of youth violence are quick to point out, however, that people need to be cautious when reacting to someone exhibiting such warning signs. Although it is important to provide help to youth with violent tendencies, harm could be caused by mislabeling a student as being violent or by overreacting to a set of circumstances.

Safeguarding Our Children also addresses the imminent warning signs of violence. The report lists these as:

• Serious physical fighting with peers or family members

• Severe destruction of property

• Severe rage for seemingly minor reasons

• Detailed threats of lethal violence

• Possession and/or use of firearms or threats of suicide

• Other self-injurious behaviors or threats of suicide

U.S. Surgeon General

In response to the Columbine school shootings in 1999, the U.S. Surgeon General began a comprehensive study of the status of youth and violence in the nation. Issued in 2001, *Youth Violence: A Report of the Surgeon General* addresses many aspects of crime and violence, including risk factors for violence among youth aged 15–18. (See Table 3.21.) The report contains detailed information on early onset factors (ages 6 to 11), which include exposure to violence on television and substance abuse, as well as late onset factors (ages 12 to 14), which include aggression in general, antisocial attitudes, and abusive parents.

FIGURE 3.8

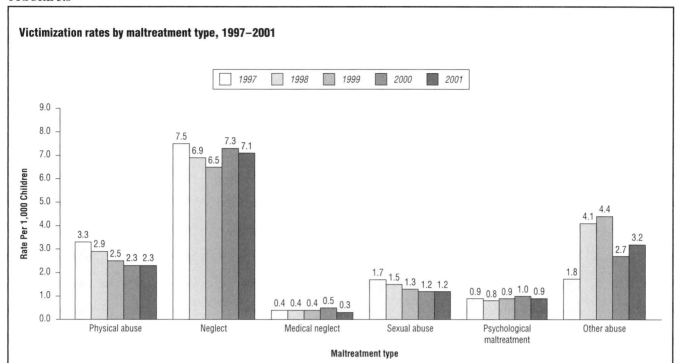

Victimization rates by maltreatment type, 1997–2001

SOURCE: "Figure 3-3. Victimization Rates by Maltreatment Type, 1997–2001," in *Child Maltreatment 2001,* U.S. Department of Health and Human Services, Administration for Children and Families, Administration on Children, Youth and Families, Children's Bureau, Washington, DC, 2003

TABLE 3.21

Risk factors for violence among youth age 15 to 18

Domain	Risk factor		Protective factor[1]
	Early onset (age 6–11)	Late onset (age 12–14)	

Individual	General offenses
	Substance use
	Being male
	Aggression[2]
	Psychological condition
	  Hyperactivity
	Problem (antisocial)
	  behavior
	Exposure to television
	  violence
	Medical, physical
	Low IQ
	Antisocial attitudes, beliefs
	  Dishonesty[2]
		General offenses
		Psychological condition
		  Restlessness
		  Difficulty concentrating[2]
		  Risk taking
		Aggression[2]
		Being male
		Physical violence
		Antisocial attitudes, beliefs
		Crimes against persons
		Problem (antisocial) behavior
		Low IQ
		Substance use
			Intolerant attitude toward
			  deviance
			High IQ
			Being female
			Positive social orientation
			Perceived sanctions for
			  transgressions

Family	Low socioleconomic
	  status poverty
	Antisocial parents
	Poor parent-child relations
	  Harsh, lax, or inconsistent
	  discipline
	Broken home
	  Separation from parents
	Other conditions
	Abusive parents
	  Neglect
		Poor parent-child relations
		  Harsh, lax discipline: poor
		  monitoring, supervision
		Low parental involvement
		Antisocial parents
		Broken home
		Low socioeconomic
		  status poverty
		Abusive parents
		Other conditions
		  Family conflict[2]
			Warm, supportive
			  relationships with
			  parents or other adults
			Parents' positive
			  evaluation of peers
			Parental monitoring

School	Poor attitude, performance	Poor attitude, performance
		  Academic failure
			Commitment to school
			Recognition for
			  involvement in
			  conventional activities

Peer group	Weak social ties Antisocial peers	Weak social ties Antisocial, delinquent peers Gang membership	Friends who engage in conventional behavior
Community		Neighborhood crime, drugs Neighborhood disorganization	

[1]Age of onset not known
[2]Males only

SOURCE: Box 4-1, in *Youth Violence: A Report of the Surgeon General,* U.S. Department of Health and Human Services, Office of the Surgeon General, Rockville, MD, 2001.

CHAPTER 4

VIOLENCE, CRIME, VICTIMIZATION, AND SAFETY IN SCHOOLS

School is supposed to be a safe haven where young people can go to learn the basics of mathematics, literature, science, and other subjects, without fearing for their safety, feeling intimidated, or being harassed. Although school administrators and teachers work toward making the environment safe and secure, crime and violence do find their way into the hallways and classrooms and onto school grounds. Despite media emphasis on topics like school shootings, fatal violence at schools is relatively low. Nonfatal crime, however, occurs in far greater numbers, sometimes even more frequently at school than away from school.

Safety is and will continue to be a concern at schools. The rash of school shootings and bomb threats that occurred in the 1990s brought increasing attention to school safety issues and what needs to be done to protect students. Various studies about school violence and crime were issued in the late 1990s and early 2000s as researchers examined past trends and tried to predict patterns for the future. Surveys range from how many children bring weapons to school to how many children were injured in fights, are afraid to go to school, or are subjected to disciplinary actions. Educators, school administrators, parents, and students themselves remain vigilant in striving to make schools safe places where youth are able to learn and prepare for the future.

So, how much crime and violence exist at schools today? Has it increased or decreased in recent years? What effect did the Columbine High School shootings have on students and public opinion in general? And, is there a danger that students, educators, and school officials will underreport school crime and violence to police? The answers to these questions and more follow.

VICTIMIZATIONS AT SCHOOL

Homicides and Suicides

In a study of school years from mid-1992 to mid-2000, "youth ages 5–19 were at least 70 times more likely

to be murdered away from school than at school," according to *Indicators of School Crime and Safety: 2003* (J.F. DeVoe, K. Peter, P. Kaufman, S.A. Ruddy, A.K. Miller, M. Planty, T.D. Snyder, and M.R. Rand, U.S. Departments of Education and Justice, Washington, DC, 2003). During that time span, 234 homicides and 43 suicides of school-aged youth (5–19) occurred at school, compared to 24,406 homicides and 16,735 suicides of school-aged youth occurring away from school.

Overall, 390 school-associated violent deaths occurred between mid-1992 and mid-2000 at elementary and secondary schools in the United States. "School-associated violent deaths include a homicide, suicide, legal intervention [involving a law enforcement officer], or unintentional firearm-related death in which the fatal injury occurred on the campus of a functioning elementary or secondary school in the United States, while the victim was on the way to or from regular sessions at such a school, or while the victim was attending or traveling to or from an official school-sponsored event," according to the report. "Victims included students, staff members, and other nonstudents."

During the 1999–2000 school year, preliminary reports show that 16 homicides and 6 suicides of youth (5–19) occurred at school, compared to 2,124 homicides and 1,922 suicides taking place away from school. (See Figure 4.1.) The most school-associated deaths (including staff, students, and nonstudents) in any year of the study was 57, which occurred during both the 1992–1993 and 1997–1998 school years. (See Table 4.1.) Those years also tied for having the most homicides of school-aged children at school in any of the surveyed years—34.

Nonfatal Crimes

Between 1992 and 2001, the rate of nonfatal crimes against students (12–18) "at school" (in the building, on school property, and en route to and from school) has

FIGURE 4.1

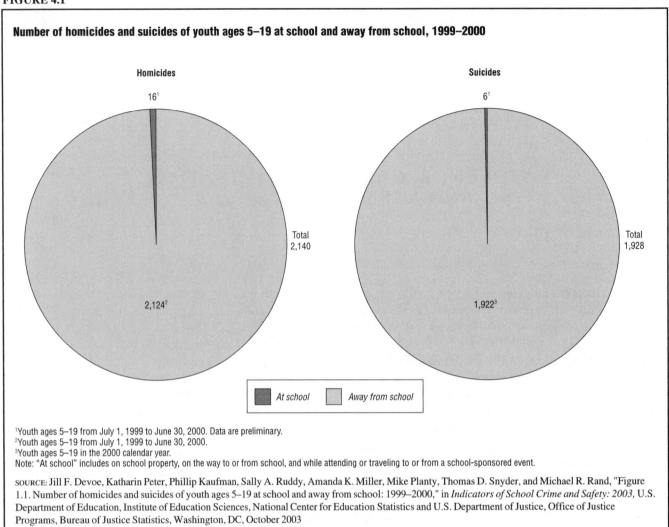

Number of homicides and suicides of youth ages 5–19 at school and away from school, 1999–2000

Homicides

16[1]

Total
2,140

2,124[2]

Suicides

6[1]

Total
1,928

1,922[3]

☐ *At school*   ☐ *Away from school*

[1]Youth ages 5–19 from July 1, 1999 to June 30, 2000. Data are preliminary.
[2]Youth ages 5–19 from July 1, 1999 to June 30, 2000.
[3]Youth ages 5–19 in the 2000 calendar year.
Note: "At school" includes on school property, on the way to or from school, and while attending or traveling to or from a school-sponsored event.

SOURCE: Jill F. Devoe, Katharin Peter, Phillip Kaufman, Sally A. Ruddy, Amanda K. Miller, Mike Planty, Thomas D. Snyder, and Michael R. Rand, "Figure 1.1. Number of homicides and suicides of youth ages 5–19 at school and away from school: 1999–2000," in *Indicators of School Crime and Safety: 2003,* U.S. Department of Education, Institute of Education Sciences, National Center for Education Statistics and U.S. Department of Justice, Office of Justice Programs, Bureau of Justice Statistics, Washington, DC, October 2003

generally declined. (See Figure 4.2.) This is based on data obtained from the National Crime Victimization Survey (NCVS), produced by the U.S. Department of Justice. Survey data show that although thefts often occur more frequently "at school" than they do away from school, the reverse is true of violent crimes, including those that are seriously violent. According to *Indicators of School Crime and Safety: 2003,* "Violent crimes include serious violent crimes and simple assault." Seriously violent crimes refer to sexual assault, rape, aggravated assault, and robbery.

The total number of nonfatal crimes against students (12–18) at school in 1992 was 3,409,200 (including 245,400 seriously violent crimes), compared to 3,286,800 (including 750,200 seriously violent crimes) away from school. (See Table 4.2.) In 2001 the number of nonfatal crimes against students at school had decreased to 2,001,300 (including 160,900 seriously violent crimes) while those occurring against students away from school stood at 1,670,500 (including 290,300 seriously violent crimes).

In the years surveyed, males consistently experienced higher rates of victimization in nonfatal crimes (theft, violent, and seriously violent crimes) at school than females. For example, in 1992 males were subjected to 60.4 percent of nonfatal crimes at school in general, including 56.5 percent of thefts and 74.7 percent of seriously violent crime. Male victimization at school dropped to 55.2 percent overall in 2001, which meant that the percentage of female victimization increased. The percentage of male victimization at school also held at 55 percent for thefts and serious violence, indicating a higher proportion of serious violence being directly against females at school in 2001 than occurred in 1992. The report also notes that older students were more likely to be victimized away from school in 2001, while younger students were more likely to be victimized at school.

Physical Fights, Injuries, and Forcible Rape

According to the Centers for Disease Control and Prevention (CDC), in 2001 some 33.2 percent of students nationwide reported being in one or more physical fights

TABLE 4.1

Number of school-associated violent deaths occurring at school and away from school, 1992–2002

Year	Total student, staff, and nonstudent school-associated violent deaths	Homicides of youth ages 5–19		Suicides of youth ages 5–19	
		Homicides[2] at school	Homicides[2] away from school	Suicides[2] at school	Suicides[3] away from school
Total 1992–2000	390	234	24,406	43	16,735
1992–93	57	34	3,583	6	2,199
1993–94	48	29	3,806	7	2,263
1994–95	48	28	3,546	7	2,220
1995–96	53	32	3,303	6	2,113
1996–97	48	28	2,950	1	2,108
1997–98	57	34	2,728	6	2,055
1998–99	47	33	2,366	4	1,855
1999–2000	32[4]	16[4]	2,124	6[4]	1,922
2000–01	27[4]	10[4]	2,045	5[4]	—
2001–02	31[4]	14[4]	—	3[4]	—

—Not available.

[1]School-associated violent deaths include a homicide, suicide, legal intervention, or unintentional firearm-related death in which the fatal injury occurred on the campus of a functioning elementary or secondary school in the United States, while the victim was on the way to or from regular sessions at such a school, or while the victim was attending or traveling to or from an official school-sponsored event. Victims included students, staff members, and other nonstudents. Total school-associated violent deaths include: in 1992–93, 47 homicides and 10 suicides; 1993–94, 38 homicides and 10 suicides; 1994–95, 39 homicides, 8 suicides, and 1 unintentional death; 1995–96, 46 homicides, 6 suicides, and 1 legal intervention; 1996–97, 45 homicides, 2 suicides, and 1 legal intervention; 1997–98, 47 homicides, 9 suicides, and 1 legal intervention; 1998–99, 38 homicides, 6 suicides, 2 legal intervention, and 1 unintentional death; 1999–2000, 24 homicides and 8 suicides; 2000–01, 20 homicides, 6 suicides, and 1 legal intervention; 2001–02, 23 homicides, 7 suicides, and 1 legal intervention.

[2]Youth ages 5–19 from July 1, 1992 to June 30, 2002.

[3]Youth ages 5–19 in the calendar year from 1993 to 2002.

[4]Data are preliminary.

Note: "At school" includes on school property, on the way to or from school, and while attending or traveling to or from a school-sponsored event.

SOURCE: Jill F. Devoe, Katharin Peter, Phillip Kaufman, Sally A. Ruddy, Amanda K. Miller, Mike Planty, Thomas D. Snyder, and Michael R. Rand, "Table 1.1. Number of school-associated violent deaths occurring at school and away from school: 1992–2002," in *Indicators of School Crime and Safety: 2003*, U.S. Department of Education, Institute of Education Sciences, National Center for Education Statistics and U.S. Department of Justice, Office of Justice Programs, Bureau of Justice Statistics, Washington, DC, October 2003

anywhere during the last 12 months (*Morbidity and Mortality Weekly Report: Youth Risk Behavior Surveillance, United States, 2001*, Centers for Disease Control and Prevention, Atlanta, GA: June 28, 2002). Male students were more likely to report this behavior (43.1 percent) than female students (23.9 percent). (See Table 4.3.) Along racial lines, more black students (36.5 percent) acknowledged such fighting than did Hispanic students (35.8 percent) or white students (32.2 percent). However, proportionally American Indians (49.2 percent) and Pacific Islanders (51.7 percent) were more likely to report being in physical fights. The proportions of students fighting, however, decreased in each higher grade level. Ninth grade students (39.5 percent) fought the most, followed by tenth graders (34.7 percent), eleventh graders (29.1 percent), and twelfth graders (26.5 percent). Reports of physical fights anywhere decreased significantly among males, females, and all grade levels between 1993 and 2001.

In 2001 some 12.5 percent of students acknowledged engaging in a physical fight on school property one or more times in the past 12 months, including 18 percent of male students and 7.2 percent of female students. (See Table 4.3.) Black students reported more fights at school (16.8 percent) while Hispanic students (14.1 percent) and white students (11.2) reported less. Proportionally, fighting at school was highest among American Indians (18.2

percent) and Pacific Islanders (29.1 percent). The proportion of fighting decreased with each grade level, beginning with 17.3 percent of ninth graders, then moving to 13.5 percent among tenth graders, 9.4 of eleventh graders, and 7.5 percent of twelfth graders.

Some 4 percent of students in 2001 noted that they had been injured in a physical fight and required treatment by a doctor or nurse one or more times in the last 12 months, including 5.2 percent of male students and 2.9 percent of female students. (See Table 4.4.) Black students reported the highest percentage of injuries (5.3 percent), with 4.4 percent of Hispanic students and 3.4 percent of white students being injured as well. Tenth graders (4.6 percent) were most likely to be injured in a physical fight, followed closely by ninth graders (4.5 percent). Twelfth graders (3.4 percent) and eleventh graders (3.1 percent) reported fewer injuries.

Overall, 9.5 percent of students claimed that they had been physically hurt by a boyfriend or girlfriend on purpose (hit, slapped, or otherwise physically hurt) one or more times in the last 12 months, including 9.8 percent of female students and 9.1 percent of male students. (See Table 4.4.) Black students (11.2 percent) were most likely to be hurt, followed by Hispanic students (9.9 percent) and white students (9.1 percent). The survey also found that the higher the grade level, the higher the percentage

FIGURE 4.2

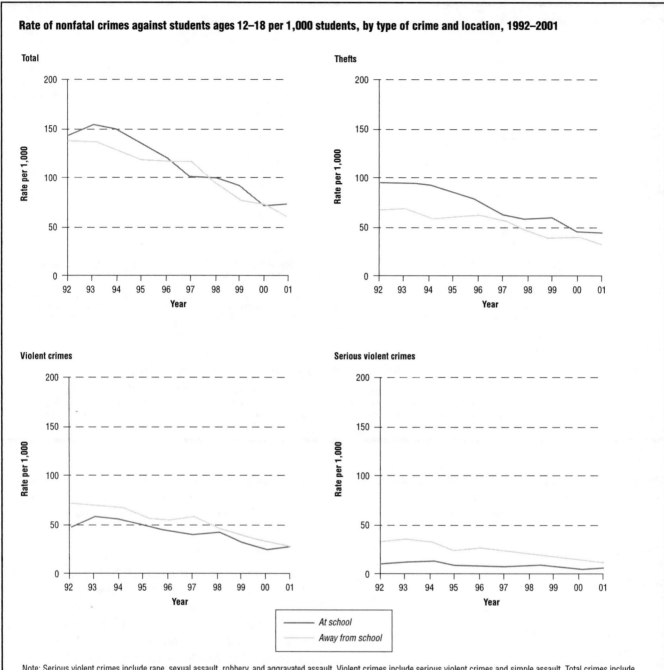

Rate of nonfatal crimes against students ages 12–18 per 1,000 students, by type of crime and location, 1992–2001

Note: Serious violent crimes include rape, sexual assault, robbery, and aggravated assault. Violent crimes include serious violent crimes and simple assault. Total crimes include violent crimes and theft. "At school" includes inside the school building, on school property, or on the way to or from school.

SOURCE: Jill F. Devoe, Katharin Peter, Phillip Kaufman, Sally A. Ruddy, Amanda K. Miller, Mike Planty, Thomas D. Snyder, and Michael R. Rand, "Figure 2.1. Rate of nonfatal crimes against students ages 12-18 per 1,000 students, by type of crime and location: 1992-2001," in *Indicators of School Crime and Safety: 2003,* U.S. Department of Education, Institute of Education Sciences, National Center for Education Statistics and U.S. Department of Justice, Office of Justice Programs, Bureau of Justice Statistics, Washington, DC, October 2003

of students getting hurt—twelfth graders (10.7 percent), eleventh graders (9.5 percent), tenth graders (9.3 percent), and ninth graders (8.5 percent).

The CDC study also asked students if they had ever been forced to have sexual intercourse. Overall, 7.7 percent of students acknowledged being forced, including 10.3 percent of female students and 5.1 percent of male students. (See Table 4.4.) Black students (9.6 percent) reported this more frequently than Hispanic students (8.9 percent) or white students (6.9 percent). Seniors experienced the most forcible rape (9 percent), followed by sophomores (7.5 percent), freshmen (7.3 percent), and juniors (7.1 percent).

Crimes against Teachers

Teachers sometimes fall victim to crimes at school. Between 1997 and 2001, some 1,290,600 crimes were

TABLE 4.2

Number of nonfatal crimes against students ages 12–18 occurring at school or on the way to or from school, by type of crime and selected student characteristics, 1992–2001

Student characteristics	1992 Total	1992 Theft	1992 Violent	1992 Serious violent[1]	1995 Total	1995 Theft	1995 Violent	1995 Serious violent[1]	2000 Total	2000 Theft	2000 Violent	2000 Serious violent[1]	2001 Total	2001 Theft	2001 Violent	2001 Serious violent[1]
Total	3,409,200	2,260,500	1,148,600	245,400	3,467,900	2,177,900	1,290,000	222,500	1,946,400	1,246,600	699,800	128,400	2,001,300	1,237,600	763,700	160,900
Sex																
Male	2,058,400	1,278,000	780,400	183,200	1,995,600	1,216,200	779,400	144,800	1,122,400	654,400	468,000	98,900	1,105,600	680,900	424,700	88,800
Female	1,350,700	982,500	368,200	62,200	1,472,300	961,700	510,500	77,600	824,000	592,200	231,800	29,600[3]	895,700	556,600	339,100	72,200
Age																
12–14	1,858,900	1,134,200	724,700	172,000	2,046,300	1,195,900	850,400	145,900	952,900	568,700	384,100	57,200	997,500	573,900	423,600	84,400
15–18	1,550,300	1,126,400	423,900	73,300	1,421,600	982,000	439,600	76,600	993,600	677,800	315,700	71,200	1,003,700	663,600	340,100	76,500
Race/ethnicity[2]																
White	2,526,700	1,694,300	832,400	148,000	2,512,200	1,594,400	917,800	123,000	1,310,500	852,700	457,800	60,000	1,399,800	888,100	511,700	88,600
Black	443,300	262,300	181,000	71,500	449,300	258,800	190,500	53,300	307,500	197,200	110,300	19,800[3]	274,100	165,300	108,800	30,500[3]
Hispanic	299,200	191,300	107,900	25,900[3]	373,500	222,200	151,300	36,900	251,500	135,200	116,400	43,100	269,100	130,700	138,400	39,300
Other	111,600	95,300	16,300[3]	#	110,800	85,800	25,100	9,300[3]	47,000	37,000	10,000[3]	2,500[3]	58,300	53,400	4,900[3]	2,500[3]
Urbanicity																
Urban	883,000	572,300	310,700	95,600	890,000	547,900	342,000	95,200	515,000	347,700	167,800	56,700	551,900	330,000	222,000	52,500
Suburban	1,809,200	1,226,700	582,500	115,000	1,907,600	1,197,800	709,800	93,400	1,059,000	665,500	393,500	54,200	1,092,000	685,600	406,400	81,100
Rural	717,000	461,500	255,500	34,700[3]	670,300	432,200	238,100	33,800	372,000	233,400	138,600	17,500[3]	357,300	222,000	135,400	27,300[3]
Household income																
Less than $7,500	249,300	132,800	116,400	27,400[3]	141,300	52,700	88,600	27,800	61,500	32,800	28,600[3]	6,200[3]	48,800	24,700	24,100[3]	8,200[3]
$7,500–14,999	335,800	196,700	139,200	38,300[3]	284,900	164,400	120,500	35,600	110,600	59,900	50,700	9,200[3]	101,600	60,900	40,700	6,500[3]
$15,000–24,999	415,200	199,700	215,600	53,100	443,500	275,400	168,000	23,800[3]	237,800	159,400	78,400	13,200	226,500	107,900	118,600	25,400[3]
$25,000–34,999	489,800	334,700	155,100	16,900[3]	538,800	328,000	210,800	42,000	218,600	125,200	93,500	18,300[3]	209,700	122,900	86,800	12,700[3]
$35,000–49,999	765,000	564,000	201,000	38,600[3]	678,800	429,900	248,900	35,000	334,800	200,100	134,700	23,200[3]	304,700	168,800	135,900	40,500
$50,000–74,999	511,100	406,500	104,600	12,000[3]	620,800	415,000	205,700	34,500	390,800	266,800	124,100	26,600[3]	363,000	269,600	93,400	24,800[3]
$75,000 or more	382,300	252,000	130,300	31,000[3]	495,600	341,300	154,300	13,600[3]	371,900	268,600	103,300	18,900[3]	477,200	318,800	158,400	20,100[3]

#No cases are reported in this cell, although the event defined by this cell could have been reported by some students with these characteristics had a different sample been drawn.

[1]Serious violent crimes are also included in violent crimes.

[2]Other includes Asians, Pacific Islanders, and American Indians (including Alaska Natives). Race categories exclude Hispanic origin unless specified.

[3]Estimate based on fewer than 10 cases.

Note: Serious violent crimes include rape, sexual assault, robbery, and aggravated assault. Violent crimes include serious violent crimes and simple assault. Total crimes include violent crimes and theft. "At school" includes inside the school building, on school property, or on the way to or from school. Population sizes are 23,740,000 students ages 12–18 in 1992; 24,558,000 in 1993; 25,327,000 in 1994; 25,715,000 in 1995; 26,151,000 in 1996; 26,548,000 in 1997; 26,806,000 in 1998; 27,013,000 in 1999; 27,169,000 in 2000, and 27,380,000 in 2001. Detail may not sum to totals because of rounding and missing cases. Numbers are rounded to the nearest 100.

SOURCE: Jill F. Devoe, Katharin Peter, Phillip Kaufman, Sally A. Ruddy, Amanda K. Miller, Mike Planty, Thomas D. Snyder, and Michael R. Rand, "Table 2.1. Number of nonfatal crimes against students ages 12–18 occurring at school or on the way to or from school, by type of crime and selected student characteristics: 1992—2001," in *Indicators of School Crime and Safety: 2003*, U.S. Department of Education, Institute of Education Sciences, National Center for Education Statistics and U.S. Department of Justice, Office of Justice Programs, Bureau of Justice Statistics, Washington, DC, October 2003

TABLE 4.3

Percentage of students in grades 9–12 who reported having been in a physical fight during the previous 12 months, by selected student characteristics, selected years 1993–2001

Student characteristics	Anywhere					On school property				
	1993	1995	1997	1999	2001	1993	1995	1997	1999	2001
Total	41.8	38.7	36.6	35.7	33.2	16.2	15.5	14.8	14.2	12.5
Sex										
Male	51.2	46.1	45.5	44.0	43.1	23.5	21.0	20.0	18.5	18.0
Female	31.7	30.6	26.0	27.3	23.9	8.6	9.5	8.6	9.8	7.2
Race/ethnicity[1]										
White	(²)	(²)	(²)	33.1	32.2	(²)	(²)	(²)	12.3	11.2
Black	(²)	(²)	(²)	41.4	36.5	(²)	(²)	(²)	18.7	16.8
Hispanic	(²)	(²)	(²)	39.9	35.8³	(²)	(²)	(²)	15.7	14.1³
Asian	(²)	(²)	(²)	22.7	22.3	(²)	(²)	(²)	10.4	10.8
American Indian	(²)	(²)	(²)	48.7	49.2	(²)	(²)	(²)	16.2	18.2
Pacific Islander	(²)	(²)	(²)	50.7	51.7	(²)	(²)	(²)	25.3	29.1³
More than one race	(²)	(²)	(²)	40.2	39.6	(²)	(²)	(²)	16.9	14.7
Grade										
9th	50.4	47.3	44.8	41.1	39.5	23.1	21.6	21.3	18.6	17.3
10th	42.2	40.4	40.2	37.7	34.7	17.2	16.5	17.0	17.2	13.5
11th	40.5	36.9	34.2	31.3	29.1	13.8	13.6	12.5	10.8	9.4
12th	34.8	31.0	28.8	30.4	26.5	11.4	10.6	9.5	8.1	7.5

[1]American Indian includes Alaska Native, Black includes African American, Pacific Islander includes Native Hawaiian, and Hispanic includes Latino. Race categories exclude Hispanic origin unless specified. While there appear to be large differences among racial/ethnic groups, some of these estimates are associated with large standard errors and should be interpreted with caution.
[2]The response categories for race/ethnicity changed in 1999 making comparisons of some categories with earlier years problematic.
[3]Revised from previously published estimates.
Note: "On school property" was not defined for survey respondents.

SOURCE: Jill F. Devoe, Katharin Peter, Phillip Kaufman, Sally A. Ruddy, Amanda K. Miller, Mike Planty, Thomas D. Snyder, and Michael R. Rand, "Table 5.1. Percentage of students in grades 9–12 who reported having been in a physical fight during the previous 12 months, by selected student characteristics: selected years 1993–2001," in *Indicators of School Crime and Safety: 2003,* U.S. Department of Education, Institute of Education Sciences, National Center for Education Statistics and U.S. Department of Justice, Office of Justice Programs, Bureau of Justice Statistics, Washington, DC, October 2003

committed against teachers, including 817,300 thefts, 473,300 violent actions, and 48,100 seriously violent actions, according to the NCVS. This amounts to an average annual rate of 58 crimes per 1,000 teachers overall, including 37 thefts per 1,000, 21 violent crimes per 1,000, and 2 seriously violent actions per 1,000. (See Table 4.5.) Although female teachers experienced 71.1 percent of crimes between 1997 and 2001, including 60.5 percent of all seriously violent crimes, male teachers annually averaged 70 crimes per 1,000 teachers while females averaged 54 per 1,000.

Proportionally, Hispanic teachers (147 per 1,000) experienced the most victimizations annually, followed by white teachers (60 per 1,000) and black teachers (47 per 1,000). Both middle/junior high schools and senior high schools reported the most victimizations on average annually (78 per 1,000). Violent crimes against teachers at middle/junior high schools (33 per 1,000) and at senior high schools (31 per 1,000) were more than double those at elementary schools (12 per 1,000) annually. However, the largest number of seriously violent victimizations of teachers between 1997 and 2001 was reported at elementary schools (30,700). Proportionally, urban schools (70 per 1,000) were far more likely annually to experience teacher victimizations than rural schools (38 per 1,000). This was true of violent crimes as well.

The U.S. Department of Education also gathers information about teacher victimizations (actual or threatened) in its Schools and Staffing Survey (SASS). During 1999–2000 the SASS observed that 10 percent of public school teachers said that students from school had threatened them with injury during the last 12 months. However, the rate was far lower at private schools—4 percent. (See Figure 4.3.) Central city public school teachers reported the most threats (13 percent) compared to urban fringe (8 percent) and rural public school teachers (9 percent). At private schools, urban fringe teachers acknowledged the most threats (5 percent), followed by rural (4 percent) and central city teachers (3 percent).

The study also showed that 4 percent of public school teachers and 2 percent of private school teachers were actually physically attacked by students from school during the last 12 months in 1999–2000. In the public sector, central city teachers were attacked more frequently (6 percent) than urban fringe (4 percent) and rural teachers (3 percent). In private schools, urban fringe teachers were attacked most often (3 percent), with central city and rural teachers (2 percent each) experiencing fewer attacks on average.

Time of Victimizations

When it comes to the time of day that most victimizations occur at school, *Are America's Schools Safe? Students*

TABLE 4.4

Percentage of high school students who engaged in violence and in behaviors resulting from violence, by sex, race/ethnicity, and grade, 2001

Category	In a physical fight[1]			Injured in a physical fight[1,2]			Physically hurt by a boyfriend or girlfriend on purpose[3]			Forced to have sexual intercourse		
	Female	Male	Total	Female	Male	Total	Female	Male	Total	Female	Male	Total
Race/ethnicity												
White[4]	21.7 (±2.4)[5]	43.1 (±2.1)	32.2 (±1.9)	2.1 (±0.6)	4.8 (±0.8)	3.4 (±0.5)	9.4 (±1.1)	8.9 (±1.1)	9.1 (±0.9)	9.8 (±1.6)	3.8 (±0.9)	6.9 (±1.1)
Black[4]	29.6 (±3.8)	43.9 (±4.3)	36.5 (±3.1)	4.8 (±1.3)	5.8 (±1.2)	5.3 (±0.8)	11.7 (±1.9)	10.7 (±2.7)	11.2 (±1.7)	10.6 (±2.7)	8.5 (±2.1)	9.6 (±1.2)
Hispanic	29.3 (±2.8)	42.4 (±2.4)	35.8 (±1.8)	3.8 (±1.2)	5.1 (±1.5)	4.4 (±1.1)	10.7 (±2.9)	9.1 (±1.8)	9.9 (±1.4)	11.6 (±1.9)	6.2 (±3.2)	8.9 (±2.0)
Grade												
9	30.3 (±3.2)	50.0 (±3.1)	39.5 (±2.5)	2.8 (±0.7)	6.5 (±1.2)	4.5 (±0.7)	9.2 (±2.0)	7.7 (±1.9)	8.5 (±1.5)	8.6 (±1.9)	5.9 (±2.7)	7.3 (±1.6)
10	24.9 (±2.6)	45.0 (±4.0)	34.7 (±2.7)	3.9 (±1.2)	5.4 (±1.4)	4.6 (±1.0)	10.6 (±2.1)	8.0 (±1.7)	9.3 (±1.3)	10.7 (±1.9)	4.1 (±1.0)	7.5 (±1.2)
11	20.3 (±1.9)	38.0 (±2.9)	29.1 (±2.2)	2.6 (±1.0)	3.7 (±1.2)	3.1 (±0.8)	9.4 (±1.7)	9.6 (±1.4)	9.5 (±1.2)	9.9 (±1.9)	4.3 (±1.1)	7.1 (±1.1)
12	16.9 (±3.2)	36.5 (±2.3)	26.5 (±2.0)	1.9 (±0.8)	5.0 (±1.2)	3.4 (±0.8)	9.8 (±2.0)	11.7 (±2.4)	10.7 (±1.3)	12.2 (±2.3)	5.8 (±1.4)	9.0 (±1.2)
Total	**23.9 (±1.9)**	**43.1 (±1.6)**	**33.2 (±1.4)**	**2.9 (±0.5)**	**5.2 (±0.7)**	**4.0 (±0.4)**	**9.8 (±0.9)**	**9.1 (±0.8)**	**9.5 (±0.6)**	**10.3 (±1.2)**	**5.1 (±1.3)**	**7.7 (±0.9)**

[1]One or more times during the 12 months preceding the survey.
[2]Students who were injured seriously enough to be treated by a doctor or nurse.
[3]During the 12 months preceding the survey.
[4]Non-Hispanic.
[5]95% confidence interval.

SOURCE: "Table 8. Percentage of high school students who engaged in violence and in behaviors resulting from violence, by sex, race/ethnicity, and grade," in *Morbidity and Mortality Weekly Report: Youth Risk Behavior Surveillance, United States, 2001*, Centers for Disease Control and Prevention, Atlanta, GA, June 28, 2002

Speak Out: 1999 School Crime Supplement (Lynn A. Addington, Sally A. Ruddy, Amanda K. Miller, and Jill F. DeVoe, U.S. Department of Education, National Center for Education Statistics, Washington, DC, 2002) reports that 39.7 percent of victimizations occurred between noon and 3 P.M. in 1999. (See Figure 4.4.) Another 30.2 percent of school victimizations transpired between the hours of 6 A.M. and noon. Another 17.2 percent are categorized as "unknown," because the exact times for various thefts and other property crimes are not always apparent. Between 3 to 6 P.M., the fewest victimizations were reported—9.9 percent.

AVOIDANCE AND FEAR

In the United States in 2001, 6.6 percent of students reported missing one or more days of school in the last 30 days because they believed it was too unsafe at school or going to and from school. The CDC also reports that more female students (7.4 percent) than male students (5.8 percent) were likely to experience this. (See Table 4.6.) Concern was about twice as high among Hispanic students (10.2 percent) and black students (9.8 percent) than it was among white students (5 percent). Fear also diminished with age, registering at 8.8 percent among ninth graders, 6.3 percent among tenth graders, 5.9 percent among eleventh graders, and 4.4 percent among twelfth graders. Fear was greatest among female students in all racial and grade classifications.

The NCVS also addresses the issue of fear of attack or harm at school or en route to and from school. As reported in *Indicators of School Crime and Safety: 2003*, 6.4 percent of students (12–18) reported such concern during the previous six months in the 2001 NCVS. (See Table 4.7.) This was down significantly from 1995 levels (11.8 percent). In 2001 males and females were equally concerned about being harmed (6.4 percent each), while Hispanic students (10.6 percent) were more likely than black (8.9 percent) or white students (4.9 percent) to be afraid. Fear levels among black and Hispanic students were generally cut in half between 1995 and 2001. Such concern also diminished within all grade levels during that time span as well. In 2001 the rate of fear decreased with each higher grade, ranging from 10.6 percent among sixth graders, to 5.5 percent among ninth graders, to 2.9 percent among twelfth graders. That year also saw urban students (9.7 percent) expressing more concern about attack or harm than either suburban (4.8 percent) or rural students (6 percent). Fear was also highest at public schools (6.6 percent).

The NCVS also maintains statistics on students who report being afraid of harm away from school. Such fear diminished between 1999, when 5.7 percent of students reported being fearful, and 2001, when 4.6 percent of students expressed fear. (See Table 4.7.) Females (5.6

TABLE 4.5

Number of nonfatal crimes against teachers and average annual rate of crimes per 1,000 teachers at school, by type of crime and selected teacher and school characteristics, 1997–2001

Teacher or school characteristics	Total crimes 1997–2001				Average annual rate of crimes per 1,000 teachers			
	Total	Theft	Violent	Serious violent[1]	Total	Theft	Violent	Serious violent[1]
Total	1,290,600	817,300	473,300	48,100	58	37	21	2
Sex								
Male	373,300	164,200	209,100	19,000	70	31	39	4[2]
Female	917,300	653,100	264,200	29,100	54	39	16	2
Race/ethnicity[3]								
White	1,102,000	697,800	404,100	41,900	60	38	22	2
Black	96,800	71,100	25,700	4,000	47	35	12[2]	2[2]
Hispanic	85,500	44,800	40,700	2,200	147	77	70	4[2]
Other	6,400	3,600	2,800	#	6	3	2[2]	#
Instructional level								
Elementary	462,300	325,700	136,600	30,700	40	28	12	3
Middle/junior high	362,600	211,500	151,000	6,200	78	46	33	1[2]
Senior high	465,700	280,100	185,700	11,100	78	47	31	2[2]
Urbanicity[4]								
Urban	744,300	442,800	301,500	25,100	70	42	28	2[2]
Suburban	368,300	257,100	111,200	18,700	53	37	16	3[2]
Rural	139,800	92,800	47,100	#	38	26	13	#

#No cases are reported in this cell, although the event defined by this cell could have been reported by some students with these characteristics had a different sample been drawn.
[1]Serious violent crimes are also included in violent crimes.
[2]The estimate was based on fewer than 10 cases.
[3]Other includes Asians, Pacific Islanders, and American Indians (including Alaska Natives). Race categories exclude Hispanic origin unless specified.
[4]Teachers teaching in more than one school across more than one type of urbanicity are not included.
Note: Serious violent crimes include rape, sexual assault, robbery, and aggravated assault. Violent crimes include serious violent crimes and simple assault. Total crimes include violent crimes and theft. "At school" includes inside the school building, on school property, at work site, or while working. For thefts, "while working" was not considered since thefts of teacher's property kept at school can occur when teachers are not present. The data were aggregated from 1997–2001 due to the small number of teachers in each year's sample. On average, there were about 4.4 million teachers per year over the 5-year period for a total population size of 22,220,000 teachers. The population reported here includes teachers from any sector part-time teachers, and other instructional and support staff. Detail may not sum to totals because of rounding and missing cases. Total crime numbers are rounded to the nearest 100.

SOURCE: Jill F. Devoe, Katharin Peter, Phillip Kaufman, Sally A. Ruddy, Amanda K. Miller, Mike Planty, Thomas D. Snyder, and Michael R. Rand, "Table 9.1. Number of nonfatal crimes against teachers and average annual rate of crimes per 1,000 teachers at school, by type of crime and selected teacher and school characteristics: 1997–2001," in *Indicators of School Crime and Safety: 2003*, U.S. Department of Education, Institute of Education Sciences, National Center for Education Statistics and U.S. Department of Justice, Office of Justice Programs, Bureau of Justice Statistics, Washington, DC, October 2003

percent) were more likely than males (3.7 percent) to be afraid away from school in 2001, while Hispanics (6.5 percent) and blacks (6.3 percent) were more concerned than whites (3.7 percent). Of the various grade levels, sixth graders (6.3 percent) were the most fearful, followed by seventh graders (5.5 percent) and eleventh graders (4.7 percent). Urban students (7.4 percent) expressed concern more frequently than suburban or rural students. Private school students (5.1 percent) were more fearful away from school than public (4.6 percent). The trends indicate that in most categories students are more afraid in school or en route to and from school than they are away from school.

NCVS statistics also cover the percentage of students (12–18) who reported avoiding one or more places at school during the previous 6 months. Such places include hallways, stairways, entrances, restrooms, sections of the cafeteria, and other areas inside the school building. Between 1995 and 2001 the percentage of students acknowledging such fear decreased substantially from 8.7 percent to 4.7 percent. (See Table 4.8.) In 2001 the proportion of males and females admitting concern was nearly equal at 4.7 percent and 4.6 percent respectively.

Blacks (6.6 percent) and Hispanics (5.5 percent) were more likely than whites (3.9 percent) to report such avoidance behaviors, as were younger students. Urban students (6 percent) and public school children (4.9 percent) were also more likely to avoid certain places at school.

DRUGS AT SCHOOL

A greater proportion of eighth-, tenth-, and twelfth-grade students used illicit drugs in 2002 than did in 1991, according to the Office of National Drug Control Policy of the Executive Office of the President. (See Table 4.9.) Among eighth graders, illicit drug use increased from 11.3 percent in 1991 to 17.7 percent in 2002; among tenth graders, use increased from 21.4 percent to 34.8 percent during the same time span; and among twelfth graders, the rate grew from 29.4 percent in 1991 to 41 percent in 2002. However, the 2002 levels for 8th, 10th, and twelfth graders are actually lower than experienced in most of the previous years. Illicit drug use for eighth graders was highest in 1996 at 23.6 percent; highest for tenth graders in 1997 at 38.5 percent; and highest for twelfth graders in 1997 at 42.4 percent.

FIGURE 4.3

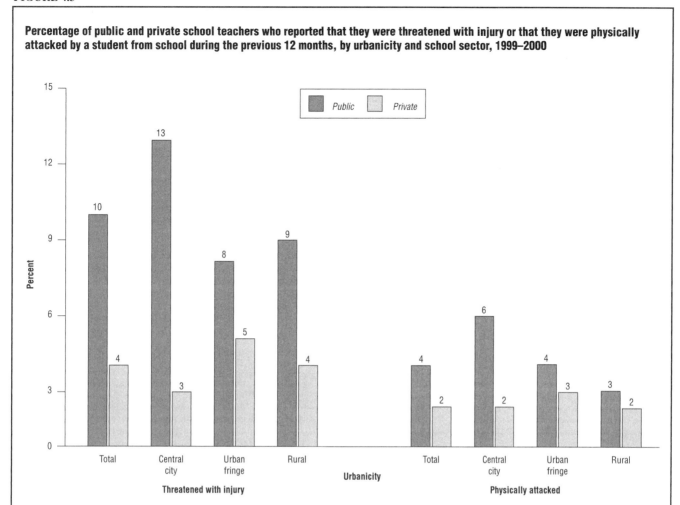

Percentage of public and private school teachers who reported that they were threatened with injury or that they were physically attacked by a student from school during the previous 12 months, by urbanicity and school sector, 1999–2000

SOURCE: Jill F. Devoe, Katharin Peter, Phillip Kaufman, Sally A. Ruddy, Amanda K. Miller, Mike Planty, Thomas D. Snyder, and Michael R. Rand, "Figure 10.2. Percentage of public and private school teachers who reported that they were threatened with injury or that they were physically attacked by a student from school during the previous 12 months, by urbanicity and school sector: 1999–2000," in *Indicators of School Crime and Safety: 2003*, U.S. Department of Education, Institute of Education Sciences, National Center for Education Statistics and U.S. Department of Justice, Office of Justice Programs, Bureau of Justice Statistics, Washington, DC, October 2003

Between 1993 and 2001, according to the CDC, males were more likely than females to admit that drugs were made available to them on school property within the last 12 months. Among students in ninth to twelfth grades, proportionally Pacific Islander students (50 percent) acknowledged the highest percentage of offers, followed by American Indians (35 percent), Hispanics (34 percent), whites (28 percent), Asians (26 percent), and blacks (22 percent).

WEAPONS IN SCHOOL

Violence at school makes students feel vulnerable and intimidated. Sometimes it makes them want to carry weapons to school for self-protection. The Gun-Free Schools Act of 1994 required states to pass laws forcing school districts to expel any student who brings a firearm to school. A 2002 report from the U.S. Department of Education revealed that 2,837 students were expelled from school in school year 1999–2000 for carrying a gun to school (*Report on State/Territory Implementation of the Gun-Free Schools Act: School Year 1999–2000*). Fifty-seven percent of the expulsions were students in high school, 31 percent were in junior high, and 12 percent were in elementary school. The number of expulsions was down 50 percent from the 1996–1997 school year, when 5,724 students were expelled.

A September 2000 report by the Hamilton Fish Institute, a federally financed research group, claimed that school principals are underreporting the number of students with guns because they are unwilling to tarnish their schools' reputations. The authors stated that there were "100 times more guns in the hands of children attending American schools than principals have been reporting to Congress" (Paul M. Kingery and Mark B. Coggeshall, "School-Based Surveillance of Violence, Injury, and Disciplinary Actions," Hamilton Fish Institute, January 2001).

FIGURE 4.4

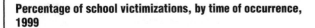

Percentage of school victimizations, by time of occurrence, 1999

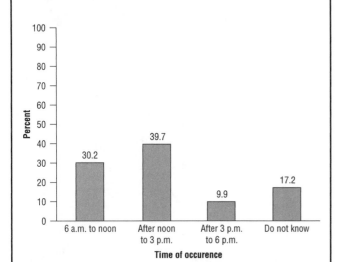

Note: Figure does not include categories with too few cases for reliable estimates.

SOURCE: Lynn A. Addington, Sally A. Ruddy, Amanda K. Miller, and Jill F. DeVoe, "Figure 9. Percentage of school victimizations, by time of occurrence: 1999," in *Are America's Schools Safe? Students Speak Out: 1999 School Crime Supplement,* U.S. Department of Education, National Center for Education Statistics, Washington, DC, 2002.

TABLE 4.6

Percentage of high school students who felt too unsafe to go to school, by sex, race/ethnicity, and grade, 2001

Category	Felt too unsafe to go to school[1]		
	Female	Male	Total
Race/ethnicity			
White[2]	5.6	4.2	5.0
	(±1.3)[3]	(±1.3)	(±1.2)
Black[2]	10.0	9.6	9.8
	(±2.3)	(±1.9)	(±1.5)
Hispanic	11.4	9.0	10.2
	(±1.6)	(±1.6)	(±1.3)
Grade			
9	9.6	8.0	8.8
	(±2.1)	(±2.0)	(±1.7)
10	7.0	5.6	6.3
	(±1.7)	(±1.6)	(±1.3)
11	6.8	5.0	5.9
	(±1.8)	(±1.6)	(±1.2)
12	5.0	3.9	4.4
	(±1.1)	(±1.2)	(±0.7)
Total	**7.4**	**5.8**	**6.6**
	(±1.3)	**(±1.1)**	**(±1.0)**

[1]On ≥ 1 of the 30 days preceding the survey
[2]Non-Hispanic.
[3]95% confidence interval.

SOURCE: Adapted from "Table 10. Percentage of high school students who engaged in violence and in behaviors resulting from violence on school property, by sex, race/ethnicity, and grade," in *Morbidity and Mortality Weekly Report: Youth Risk Behavior Surveillance, United States, 2001,* Centers for Disease Control and Prevention, Atlanta, GA: June 28, 2002

So, just how many students bring weapons to school? According to *Indicators of School Crime and Safety: 2003,* about 6.4 percent of students in grades 9–12 reported carrying a weapon on school property at least 1 day during the previous 30 days in 2001. This was a significant drop from 1993 when 11.8 percent of students reported carrying a weapon to school. (See Table 4.10.) Based on data from the CDC, the report compares data from select years between 1993 and 2001. The report also noted that the percentage of students who reported carrying a weapon anywhere decreased from 22.1 percent in 1993 to 17.4 percent in 2001.

Males were most likely to carry weapons on school property in all years reported, moving from a high of 17.9 percent in 1993 to a low of 10.2 percent in 2001. They were also most likely to carry weapons anywhere, though this dropped from 34.3 percent in 1993 to 29.3 percent in 2001. Females were far less likely to carry weapons on school property (5.1 percent in 1993 compared to 2.9 percent in 2001) or anywhere else (9.2 percent in 1993 and 6.2 percent in 2001).

In general, ninth graders carried weapons on school property most often (12.6 percent in 1993 and 6.7 percent in 2001). Tenth graders tied with ninth graders in 2001, reaching 6.7 percent as well. Ninth graders were also more likely to carry weapons anywhere in all but one of the years surveyed (1999). In that year, tenth graders reported a slightly higher percentage rate.

Various reasons could explain why students carried fewer guns to school in 2001. These include enhanced security measures at school, such as metal detectors and locker searches, added in the wake of the highly publicized school shootings in the 1990s. Another reason could be the stricter punishment given to those found with guns in school. Many schools have adopted "zero tolerance" rules, resulting in the immediate expulsion of someone who is found breaking those guidelines.

High school students report a number of reasons why they carry weapons according to *High School Youths, Weapons, and Violence: A National Survey* (National Institute of Justice, Washington, DC, 1998). The most frequent reason they cited was that they needed a weapon for protection (43 percent of gun carriers). (See Table 4.11.) Other reasons included that they were holding the weapon for someone else (35 percent), that they wanted to scare someone (18 percent), or that the weapon made them feel important (10 percent).

For some students, obtaining guns is fairly easy. The Office of Juvenile Justice and Delinquency Prevention (OJJDP) notes that young people attempt various methods to secure guns, including stealing them from cars, houses, apartments, stores and pawnshops, and family members. They also buy guns from family members, drug dealers or addicts, stores, gang members, family friends, and others.

TABLE 4.7

Percentage of students ages 12–18 who reported being afraid at school or on the way to and from school and away from school during the previous 6 months, by selected student characteristics, 1995, 1999, and 2001

Student characteristics	At school or on the way to and from school			Away from school	
	1995	1999	2001	1999	2001
Total	**11.8**	**7.3**	**6.4**	**5.7**	**4.6**
Sex					
Male	10.8	6.5	6.4	4.1	3.7
Female	12.8	8.2	6.4	7.4	5.6
Race/ethnicity[1]					
White	8.1	5.0	4.9	4.3	3.7
Black	20.3	13.5	8.9	8.7	6.3
Hispanic	20.9	11.7	10.6	8.9	6.5
Other	13.5	6.7	6.4	5.4	6.6
Grade					
6th	14.3	10.9	10.6	7.8	6.3
7th	15.3	9.5	9.2	6.1	5.5
8th	13.0	8.1	7.6	5.5	4.4
9th	11.6	7.1	5.5	4.6	4.5
10th	11.0	7.1	5.0	4.8	4.2
11th	8.9	4.8	4.8	5.9	4.7
12th	7.8	4.8	2.9	6.1	3.3
Urbanicity					
Urban	18.4	11.6	9.7	9.1	7.4
Suburban	9.8	6.2	4.8	5.0	3.8
Rural	8.6	4.8	6.0	3.0	3.0
Sector					
Public	12.2	7.7	6.6	5.8	4.6
Private	7.3	3.6	4.6	5.0	5.1

[1]Other includes Asians, Pacific Islanders, and American Indians (including Alaska Natives). Race categories exclude Hispanic origin unless specified.
Note: In 1995 and 1999, students reported fear of "attack or harm" at school or on the way to and from school during the previous 6 months. In 2001, students reported fear of "attack or threat of attack" at school or on the way to and from school during the previous 6 months. Includes students who reported that they sometimes or most of the time feared being victimized in this way. Fear of attack away from school was not collected in 1995. Population sizes for students ages 12–18 are 23,601,000 in 1995, 24,614,000 in 1999, and 24,315,000 in 2001.

SOURCE: Jill F. Devoe, Katharin Peter, Phillip Kaufman, Sally A. Ruddy, Amanda K. Miller, Mike Planty, Thomas D. Snyder, and Michael R. Rand, "Table 12.1. Percentage of students ages 12–18 who reported being afraid at school or on the way to and from school and away from school during the previous 6 months, by selected student characteristics, 1995, 1999, and 2001," in *Indicators of School Crime and Safety: 2003,* U.S. Department of Education, Institute of Education Sciences, National Center for Education Statistics and U.S. Department of Justice, Office of Justice Programs, Bureau of Justice Statistics, Washington, DC, October 2003

TABLE 4.8

Percentage of students ages 12–18 who reported that they avoided one or more places in school during the previous 6 months, by selected student characteristics, 1995, 1999, and 2001

Student characteristics	1995	1999	2001
Total	**8.7**	**4.6**	**4.7**
Sex			
Male	8.8	4.6	4.7
Female	8.5	4.6	4.6
Race/ethnicity[1]			
White	7.1	3.8	3.9
Black	12.1	6.7	6.6
Hispanic	12.9	6.2	5.5
Other	11.1	5.4	6.2
Grade			
6th	11.6	5.9	6.8
7th	11.8	6.1	6.2
8th	8.8	5.5	5.2
9th	9.5	5.3	5.0
10th	7.8	4.7	4.2
11th	6.9	2.5	2.8
12th	4.1	2.4	3.0
Urbanicity			
Urban	11.7	5.8	6.0
Suburban	7.9	4.7	4.3
Rural	7.0	3.0	3.9
Sector			
Public	9.3	5.0	4.9
Private	2.2	1.6	2.0

[1]Other includes Asians, Pacific Islanders, and American Indians (including Alaska Natives). Race categories exclude Hispanic origin unless specified.
Note: Places include the entrance, any hallways or stairs, parts of the cafeteria, restrooms, and other places inside the school building. Population sizes for students ages 12–18 are 23,601,000 in 1995, 24,614,000 in 1999, and 24,315,000 in 2001.

SOURCE: Jill F. Devoe, Katharin Peter, Phillip Kaufman, Sally A. Ruddy, Amanda K. Miller, Mike Planty, Thomas D. Snyder, and Michael R. Rand, "Table 13.1. Percentage of students ages 12–18 who reported that they avoided one or more places in school during the previous 6 months, by selected student characteristics: 1995, 1999, and 2001," in *Indicators of School Crime and Safety: 2003,* U.S. Department of Education, Institute of Education Sciences, National Center for Education Statistics and U.S. Department of Justice, Office of Justice Programs, Bureau of Justice Statistics, Washington, DC, October 2003

Weapon Use on School Property

Nearly 9 percent of students in grades 9–12 reported being threatened or injured with a weapon on school property within the past 12 months in 2001, according to CDC data. (See Table 4.12.) This figure represents an increase from 1993, when 7.3 percent acknowledged being threatened or injured. Between 1993 and 2001 the percentage has remained in the 7 to 9 percent range, indicating no clear pattern that the situation is improving or getting worse. For purposes of the survey data, a weapon can be a gun, knife, club, or other device.

Male students received considerably more threats and injuries in all years surveyed between 1993 and 2001. In addition, the rate in 2001 (11.5 percent) is 2.3 percentage points higher than it was in 1993 (9.2 percent). Female students also reported more threats and injuries in 2001, increasing from 5.4 percent in 1993 to 6.5 percent. Proportionally, the victimization rate was highest among Pacific Islanders in 2001 (24.8 percent) and lowest among whites (8.5 percent). Racial data was only available for the years 1999 and 2001.

Ninth graders (12.7 percent) were also more likely to report threats and injuries than other students in 2001. In fact the rate of victimization decreased with each higher grade level that year. Similar patterns were observed in the other years of the survey as well. While ninth and tenth graders experienced increased threat and injury levels between 1993 and 2001, eleventh and twelfth graders experienced slight decreases.

TABLE 4.9

Past-year illicit drug use among 8th, 10th, and 12th graders, 1991–2002

Year	8th Grade	10th Grade	12th Grade
1991	11.3%	21.4%	29.4%
1992	12.9	20.4	27.1
1993	15.1	24.7	31.0
1994	18.5	30.0	35.8
1995	21.4	33.3	39.0
1996	23.6	37.5	40.2
1997	22.1	38.5	42.4
1998	21.0	35.0	41.4
1999	20.5	35.9	42.1
2000	19.5	36.4	40.9
2001	19.5	37.2	41.4
2002	17.7	34.8	41.0

SOURCE: Michele Spiess, "Table 3. Past year illicit drug use, 1991–2002," in "Juveniles and Drugs," *ONDCP Drug Policy Information Clearinghouse Fact Sheet*, NCJ 196879, Executive Office of the President, Office of National Drug Control Policy, Rockville, MD, June 2003 [Online] http://www.whitehousedrugpolicy.gov/publications/factsht/juvenile/196879.pdf [accessed January 23, 2004]

Criminal Victimization and Students Observed with Guns

Students (12–18) who report seeing another student at school with a gun are more than twice as likely to acknowledge being the victim of a criminal act at school than those who do not, according to *Are America's Schools Safe? Students Speak Out: 1999 School Crime Supplement.* (See Figure 4.5.) "The prevalence of students reporting violent victimizations was 10.7 percent for those who saw another student with a gun compared to 3.8 percent for those who did not, while the prevalence of students reporting property victimizations was 13.3 percent compared to 7.6 percent," note the authors. Rates were similar for those who reported knowing a student who brought a gun to school as well.

National Longitudinal Study of Adolescent Health

The National Longitudinal Study of Adolescent Health was the largest survey of teens ever taken in the United States. Published in the *Journal of the American Medical Association* (vol. 278, no. 10, September 1997), the survey questioned 90,000 students in grades 7–12 at 145 schools around the country. This federally funded study was conducted by researchers at the University of North Carolina, Chapel Hill, and the University of Minnesota. They found that almost one-fourth of students surveyed had easy access to guns at home. Adolescents living in homes where guns were kept were more likely to behave violently and more likely to contemplate or attempt suicide.

Teens who said they had strong family ties were less likely to be involved in interpersonal violence than those who said they did not have close family ties. Older teens (ninth through twelfth grades) who had a parent present at breakfast, after school, at dinner, and at bedtime were also less likely to behave violently.

More than 10 percent of males and more than 5 percent of females interviewed said they had committed a violent act in the previous year. These acts included participating in fights, injuring someone, threatening someone with a weapon, using a weapon in a fight, or shooting or stabbing someone.

Younger teens (seventh and eighth graders) more often reported having been involved in violent activities than older teens. Urban teens, teens whose families received welfare, and American Indian teens seemed more likely than others to have been involved in violence. About 1 in 8 students said that they brought a weapon to school in the month prior to being surveyed. Some 26 percent of students said they had either carried a weapon or been present at an incident where someone was hurt by a weapon. The researchers commented on the importance of finding that race, income, and family structure were not the most important factors influencing risky behaviors. Far more important predictors of risky behavior were failure in school, too much unstructured time, and poor family relationships.

SCHOOL SHOOTINGS

Between July 1, 1992, and June 30, 1999, some 358 school-associated violent deaths occurred in the United States, including 255 deaths of school-aged children, or about 51 such violent deaths each year. For the single year July 1, 1998, through June 30, 1999, there were 47 school-associated violent deaths in the United States. Thirty-eight were homicides, six were suicides, two involved suspects killed by a law enforcement officer in the line of duty, and one was unintentional. According to the U.S. Secret Service's National Threat Assessment Center (NTAC), between 1974 and 2000 some 37 school shootings have occurred. Despite the understandable fear generated by the media coverage of events, various reports on school shootings acknowledge that the possibility of being shot at school is very minimal.

However, Americans were shocked by the rash of school shootings in the 1990s and some were afraid to send their children to school. (For a select list of school shootings from 1996 through January of 2004, see Table 4.13.) The Bi-Partisan Working Group on Youth Violence of the 106th Congress explored the issue and in February 2000 released its final report. It stated: "While it is important to carefully review the circumstances surrounding these horrifying incidents so that we may learn from them, we must also be cautious about inappropriately creating a cloud of fear over every student in every classroom across the country. In the case of youth violence, it is important to note that, statistically speaking, schools are among the safest places for children to be."

TABLE 4.10

Percentage of students in grades 9–12 who reported carrying a weapon at least 1 day during the previous 30 days, by selected student characteristics, selected years 1993–2001

Student characteristics	Anywhere					On school property				
	1993	1995	1997	1999	2001	1993	1995	1997	1999	2001
Total	22.1	20.0	18.3	17.3	17.4	11.8	9.8	8.5	6.9	6.4
Sex										
Male	34.3	31.1	27.7	28.6	29.3	17.9	14.3	12.5	11.0	10.2
Female	9.2	8.3	7.0	6.0	6.2	5.1	4.9	3.7	2.8	2.9
Race/ethnicity[1]										
White	(2)	(2)	(2)	16.4	17.9	(2)	(2)	(2)	6.4	6.1
Black	(2)	(2)	(2)	17.2	15.2	(2)	(2)	(2)	5.0	6.3
Hispanic	(2)	(2)	(2)	18.7	16.5[3]	(2)	(2)	(2)	7.9	6.4[3]
Asian	(2)	(2)	(2)	13.0	10.6[3]	(2)	(2)	(2)	6.5	7.2
American Indian	(2)	(2)	(2)	21.8	31.2	(2)	(2)	(2)	11.6	16.4
Pacific Islander	(2)	(2)	(2)	25.3	17.4	(2)	(2)	(2)	9.3	10.0
More than one race	(2)	(2)	(2)	22.2	25.2	(2)	(2)	(2)	11.4	13.2
Grade										
9th	25.5	22.6	22.6	17.6	19.8	12.6	10.7	10.2	7.2	6.7
10th	21.4	21.1	17.4	18.7	16.7	11.5	10.4	7.7	6.6	6.7
11th	21.5	20.3	18.2	16.1	16.8	11.9	10.2	9.4	7.0	6.1
12th	19.9	16.1	15.4	15.9	15.1	10.8	7.6	7.0	6.2	6.1[3]

[1]American Indian includes Alaska Native, Black includes African American, Pacific Islander includes Native Hawaiian, and Hispanic includes Latino. Race categories exclude Hispanic origin unless specified. While there appear to be large differences among racial/ethnic groups, some of these estimates are associated with large standard errors and should be interpreted with caution.
[2]The response categories for race/ethnicity changed in 1999 making comparisons of some categories with earlier years problematic.
[3]Revised from previously published estimates.
Note: "On school property" was not defined for survey respondents. Rather, students are simply asked during the past 30 days, on how many days they carried a weapon.

SOURCE: Jill F. Devoe, Katharin Peter, Phillip Kaufman, Sally A. Ruddy, Amanda K. Miller, Mike Planty, Thomas D. Snyder, and Michael R. Rand, "Table 11.1. Percentage of students in grades 9–12 who reported carrying a weapon at least 1 day during the previous 30 days, by selected student characteristics: selected years 1993–2001," in *Indicators of School Crime and Safety: 2003,* U.S. Department of Education, Institute of Education Sciences, National Center for Education Statistics and U.S. Department of Justice, Office of Justice Programs, Bureau of Justice Statistics, Washington, DC, October 2003

Columbine

The Columbine High School shooting, however, still weighs heavy on many students' minds some five years after the incident. The tragedy began around 11:10 A.M. on April 20, 1999, as senior Eric David Harris, 18, arrived at the student parking lot at Columbine High School in Littleton, a suburb of Denver, in Colorado. A short time later, Harris' friend and classmate Dylan Bennet Klebold, 17, pulled up in his 1982 black BMW. Carrying two large duffel bags, they walked together to the school cafeteria. Each of the bags contained a 20-pound propane bomb, which was set to detonate at exactly 11:17 A.M. Harris and Klebold looked for an inconspicuous place to leave their bomb-concealing bags among the hundreds of other backpacks and bags there. After choosing a spot, Harris and Klebold returned to the parking lot to wait for the bombs to detonate.

Part of their plan was aimed at diverting the Littleton Fire Department, Jefferson County Sheriff's Office, and other emergency personnel away from Columbine as the pair stormed the school. To achieve this, they had planted pipe bombs three miles southwest of the high school set to explode and start grass fires. As the explosions began, Harris and Klebold prepared to reenter Columbine High School, this time via the west exterior steps. That location is the highest point on campus that allows a view of the student parking lots and the cafeteria's entrances and exits. Both Harris and Klebold, dressed in black trench coats, concealed 9mm semiautomatic weapons from view. As they approached, the pair pulled out shotguns from a duffel bag and opened fire toward the west doors of the school, killing 17-year-old Rachel Scott.

After entering the school, they roamed the halls, library, and cafeteria, among other areas, killing 12 other victims, including a teacher, before finally killing themselves. In the process they also injured 23 other students physically and many others emotionally. The details of the event are outlined in *The Columbine High School Shootings: Jefferson County Sheriff Department's Investigation Report,* released May 15, 2000, by the Jefferson County Sheriff's Department. Since that time, more documents and videotapes have been made available to the victims' families, the media, and others as well.

HARRIS AND KLEBOLD. Since Harris and Klebold ended their school spree by taking their own lives, they could not explain the motives behind their rampage. As a result, various law enforcement officers, reporters, and others looked into the background of these youth to see what prompted them to commit such violence and whether they were part of a larger conspiracy of students. A background check revealed that the pair had brushes with the law in the recent past. For example, Harris and Klebold were arrested for breaking into a vehicle more

TABLE 4.11

High school students' reasons for carrying a weapon, 1995

Reasons	Percentage of gun carriers (N = 40)
I needed protection	43
I was holding it for someone	35
I used the weapon in a crime	10
To scare someone	18
To get back at someone	18
Most of my friends carry them	10
It made me feel important	10
Other	15

Note: Multiple responses permitted

SOURCE: *High School Youths, Weapons, and Violence: A National Survey,* National Institute of Justice, Washington, DC, 1998

TABLE 4.12

Percentage of students in grades 9–12 who reported being threatened or injured with a weapon on school property during the previous 12 months, by selected student characteristics, selected years 1993–2001

Student characteristics	1993	1995	1997	1999	2001
Total	**7.3**	**8.4**	**7.4**	**7.7**	**8.9**
Sex					
Male	9.2	10.9	10.2	9.5	11.5
Female	5.4	5.8	4.0	5.8	6.5
Race/ethnicity[1]					
White	(2)	(2)	(2)	6.6	8.5
Black	(2)	(2)	(2)	7.6	9.3
Hispanic	(2)	(2)	(2)	9.8	8.9
Asian	(2)	(2)	(2)	7.7	11.3
American Indian	(2)	(2)	(2)	13.2	15.2
Pacific Islander	(2)	(2)	(2)	15.6	24.8
More than one race	(2)	(2)	(2)	9.3	10.3
Grade					
9th	9.4	9.6	10.1	10.5	12.7
10th	7.3	9.6	7.9	8.2	9.1
11th	7.3	7.7	5.9	6.1	6.9
12th	5.5	6.7	5.8	5.1	5.3

[1]American Indian includes Alaska Native, Black includes African American, Pacific Islander includes Native Hawaiian, and Hispanic includes Latino. Race categories exclude Hispanic origin unless specified. While there appear to be large differences among racial/ethnic groups, some of these estimates are associated with large standard errors and should be interpreted with caution.
[2]The response categories for race/ethnicity changed in 1999 making comparisons of some categories with earlier years problematic.
Note: "On school property" was not defined for survey respondents.

SOURCE: Jill F. Devoe, Katharin Peter, Phillip Kaufman, Sally A. Ruddy, Amanda K. Miller, Mike Planty, Thomas D. Snyder, and Michael R. Rand, "Table 4.1. Percentage of students in grades 9–12 who reported being threatened or injured with a weapon on school property during the previous 12 months, by selected student characteristics: selected years 1993–2001," in *Indicators of School Crime and Safety: 2003,* U.S. Department of Education, Institute of Education Sciences, National Center for Education Statistics and U.S. Department of Justice, Office of Justice Programs, Bureau of Justice Statistics, Washington, DC, October 2003

than a year before the Columbine incident. One year before the shooting, in April of 1998, the duo were fined and enrolled in a juvenile diversion program. Their punishment also included community service as well as participation in anger management classes. After successfully completing the diversion program, the two were released from the program on February 9, 1999. This meant that their juvenile records were cleared.

It was also revealed that the local sheriff's office had investigated Eric Harris following a suspicious incident report filed by resident Randy Brown in March 1998. Brown alleged that his son, Brooks, was being targeted by Harris with death threats on the Internet. On Harris' Web page, Brown alleged, the student was writing about how to make and detonate pipe bombs and use them against people. However, the sheriff's investigators were unable to substantiate the claims as they were unable to access Harris' Web site.

The Columbine investigation also led to the discovery of a diary kept by Eric Harris, which he began in the spring of 1998. In the diary, Harris wrote that he wanted to kill. He also described the preparations that he and Klebold were making in what would later become the Columbine incident. Those descriptions, part of the only entry Harris made in his diary in 1999, also included a detailed discussion of the weapons and bombs the pair was intending to use.

Also recovered were three videotapes produced by Harris and Klebold that documented their plan and ideologies. One of the tapes contained eight sessions recorded from early April 1999 to the morning of April 20, the morning of the shootings. In the tape, the pair show off some of their weapons and bombs and rehearse how the plan will unfold.

Among the people most surprised by the shootings were Klebold's family. Tom Klebold, father of Dylan, told

investigators that his son had never showed any interest in guns. The Klebolds told authorities that Dylan had been accepted at the University of Arizona and planned on studying computer science. Klebold's friends and teachers described him as a nice, normal teenager. However, authorities also learned that Klebold and Harris were often subjected to harassment and bullying from other students. Much discussion of this fact was reported by the media, which prompted various research organizations to look into the effects of bullying on juveniles. Some wondered if the ridicule from other students had prompted Harris and Klebold to seek revenge.

THE COLUMBINE LAWSUITS. Various litigation resulted from the Columbine school shootings, including five wrongful death lawsuits against the Jefferson County Sheriff's Department. Those suits alleged that the department did not respond appropriately when the shootings occurred, mishandled the rescue of students caught in the crossfire, failed to fully investigate the Web site of Eric Harris, and ignored the warning signs that a violent attack

FIGURE 4.5

Percentage of students ages 12 through 18 who reported experiencing criminal victimization at school, by student reports of knowing or seeing another student with a gun at school, 1999

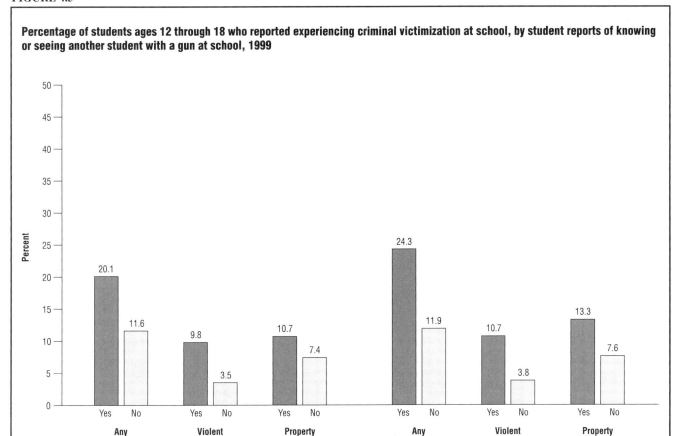

[1]Any victimization is a combination of violent and property victimization. If the student reported an incident of either, he or she is counted having experienced any victimization. If the respondent reported having experienced both, he or she is counted once under the "any victimization" category.
[2]Violent victimization includes physical attack or taking property from the student directly by force, weapons, or threats or rape, sexual assault, robbery, aggravated assault, or simple assault.
[3]Property victimization includes theft of a student's property at school.

SOURCE: Lynn A. Addington, Sally A. Ruddy, Amanda K. Miller, and Jill F. DeVoe, "Figure 6. Percentage of students ages 12 through 18 who reported experiencing criminal victimization at school, by student reports of knowing or seeing another student with a gun at school: 1999," in *Are America's Schools Safe? Students Speak Out: 1999 School Crime Supplement,* U.S. Department of Education, National Center for Education Statistics, Washington, DC, 2002.

was coming. Other legal actions were filed in federal court in Denver. Some of the litigation was filed against the parents of Harris and Klebold as well as the people who helped the shooters obtain the guns. Another lawsuit was aimed at 25 companies in the entertainment industry. In litigation filed by the family of Dave Sanders, the one teacher killed at Columbine, the suit alleged that the creators and distributors of certain violent movies and video games were responsible for creating products that could have inspired Harris and Klebold to carry out their plans. The killers were said to enjoy the violent video game "Doom" among others. In fact, the plaintiffs alleged that the shooters made a film crediting the role the militaristic "Doom" played in their planned shooting spree.

The Columbine-related lawsuits were consolidated in federal court by U.S. District Court Judge Lewis Babcock on June 1, 2000. The judge noted that video and moviemakers could not be held responsible for the actions

of Harris and Klebold and dismissed that case. In April 2001, the parents of Harris and Klebold as well as those who provided guns used in the shooting agreed to a $2.5-million settlement with 36 families of Columbine victims.

Still another suit was filed in 2002 by student Mark Taylor, who was wounded in the Columbine shooting spree. Taylor filed suit against the maker of the antidepressant that Harris was prescribed and using during the time of the Columbine incident. Taylor alleged that the pharmaceutical caused Harris to do what he did.

FBI Investigates School Shooters

Prior school shooting incidents had prompted the Federal Bureau of Investigation (FBI) to spend two years researching the phenomenon. In its 1999 report *The School Shooter: A Threat Assessment Perspective,* compiled by Mary Ellen O'Toole, the FBI asserted that the "profile" of a school shooter could not be determined, nor

TABLE 4.13

School shooting timeline: selected events February 1996 through January 2004

Date	Location	Description of event	Number killed/injured
February 2, 1996	Frontier Middle School Moses Lake, WA	14-year-old Barry Loukaitis enters a junior high algebra class armed with three guns and begins shooting. A teacher and two students are killed; a third student is injured. Loukaitis is sentenced to life in prison.	3 killed; 1 injured
February 19, 1997	Bethel High School Bethel, AK	16-year-old Evan Ramsey uses a .12-gauge shotgun at school to kill the principal and a popular student athlete. Two other students are wounded. Ramsey is sentenced to two 99-year terms.	2 killed; 2 injured
October 1, 1997	Pearl High School Pearl, MS	16-year-old Luke Woodham murders his mother before heading to class; at school, he shoots and kills two students, including his ex-girlfriend. Seven others are injured. Woodham is sentenced to life in prison.	2 killed; 7 injured assailant also killed his mother
December 1, 1997	Heath High School West Paducah, KY	14-year-old Michael Carneal shoots and kills three students and injures five others while the victims are holding a prayer circle in a hallway at school. Carneal enters a guilty plea but claims mental illness. Carneal is sentenced to life in prison.	3 killed; 5 injured
March 24, 1998	Westside Middle School Jonesboro, AR	Andrew Golden, 11, and Mitchell Johnson, 13, begin a shooting spree from the woods killing four girls and a teacher; 10 others are wounded. The shootings take place during a false fire alarm evacuation at school. Golden and Johnson receive sentences in juvenile court and can be held to age 21.	5 killed; 10 wounded
April 24, 1998	Parker Middle School Edinboro, PA	14-year-old Andrew Wurst opens fire at a graduation dance at a local restaurant. The school's 48-year-old science teacher is shot to death and three others (including another teacher) are wounded. Wurst pleads guilty and is sentenced to 30 to 60 years in prison.	1 killed; 3 wounded
May 19, 1998	Lincoln County High School Fayetteville, TN	18-year-old honor student Jacob Lee Davis fires his father's rifle in the school's parking lot and kills a fellow student. The victim, who was dating Davis's ex-girlfriend, is shot just three days before graduation. Davis is sentenced to life in prison.	1 killed
May 21, 1998	Jersey Village, TX (Near Houston)	17-year-old boy is charged with "unlawfully carrying a weapon on school property" after a gun he is carrying in his backpack "for protection" against bullies goes off in biology class, wounding a 15-year-old girl in the leg.	1 wounded
May 21, 1998	Thurston High School Springfield, OR	15-year-old Kip Kinkel fires 50 rounds in 90 seconds in the school cafeteria, killing two students and injuring 25 others. His parents are later found shot to death in their home. Kinkel, who was expelled the previous day for bringing a gun to school, is later sentenced to 111 years in prison for his crimes.	2 killed; 25 wounded; assailant also killed his mother and father
April 20, 1999	Columbine High School Littleton, CO	Eric Harris, 18, and Dylan Klebold, 17, go on a shooting rampage and detonate bombs in a suburban high school killing 12 students and 1 teacher before turning the guns on themselves; 23 others are wounded.	15 killed (including the assailants); 23 wounded
May 20, 1999	Heritage High School Conyers, GA	15-year-old T.J. Solomon enters school and fires into a crowd of his classmates; six are injured. Solomon pleads guilty but claims mental illness; he is sentenced to 40 years.	6 injured
November 19, 1999	Deming Middle School Deming, NM	12-year-old Victor Cordova Jr., dressed in camouflage clothing, uses a .22-caliber handgun to fire a single shot, killing a 13-year-old female classmate on the school's playground. Cordova is held in a juvenile-treatment facility for 3 1/2 years before being released in late 2003.	1 killed
December 6, 1999	Fort Gibson Middle School Ft. Gibson, OK	13-year-old Seth Trickey shoots some 15 bullets from his father's 9mm semiautomatic handgun, injuring four classmates. Trickey is convicted of assault.	4 injured
February 29, 2000	Buell Elementary School Mt. Morris Township, MI	6-year-old boy steals a .32-caliber handgun from his uncle's house and kills 6-year-old Kayla Rolland in class. A teacher and 22 students witness the shooting. The Buell School incident involves the youngest school shooter as of February 2004. The boy is not charged due to his age.	1 killed
May 26, 2000	Lake Worth Middle School Lake Worth, FL	13-year-old honor student Nathaniel Brazill is sent home on the last day of class for throwing water balloons. He returns to school and shoots his English teacher in the face, killing him. Brazill is sentenced to 28 years in prison.	1 killed
March 5, 2001	Santana High School Santee, CA	15-year-old Charles "Andy" Williams goes on a 6-minute shooting spree killing 2 students and wounding 13 others. He claims he brought a gun to school because he was being bullied. Williams is sentenced to serve 50 years to life.	2 killed; 13 wounded
March 7, 2001	Bishop Neumann High School Williamsport, PA	14-year-old Elizabeth Catherine Bush fires several shots from a .22-caliber revolver in the cafeteria of a Roman Catholic high school. A 13-year-old female student is wounded. The first female school shooter in recent years, Bush is sentenced in juvenile court to a psychiatric treatment facility.	1 wounded
January 16, 2002	Appalachian School of Law Grundy, VA	43-year-old student Peter Odighizuma, who had just failed law school a second time, opens fire with a semiautomatic handgun killing the dean, a professor, and a student. Three others are injured. Odighizuma is later declared mentally unfit to stand trial and is hospitalized.	3 killed; 3 injured
October 28, 2002	University of Arizona Tuscon, AZ	41-year-old Robert Flores Jr., a Gulf War veteran and a failing student in the university's nursing school, shoots and kills 3 of his professors before killing himself.	4 killed (including the assailant)
September 24, 2003	Rocori High School Cold Spring, MN	15-year-old Jason McLaughlin pulls a gun from his gym bag and shoots two students; both are fatally injured. One dies later that day, the other dies two weeks later. McLaughlin, the son of a police officer, is charged with second-degree murder.	2 killed

SOURCE: Prepared by the staff of Information Plus, January 2004.

was it possible to create a checklist of the warning signs indicating the next juvenile who would bring lethal violence to school. The intent of the report, however, is to assist people in assessing threats and to keep such incidents from being implemented.

The report uses a four-pronged approach in assessing "the totality of the circumstances" known about a student in four major areas: the student's personality, family dynamics, school dynamics, and social dynamics. "If an act of violence occurs at a school," the report notes, "the school becomes the scene of the crime. As in any violent crime, it is necessary to understand what it is about the school which might have influenced the student's decision to offend there rather than someplace else."

The FBI established the following factors in making that determination:

- The student's attachment to school: The student appears to be "detached" from school, including other students, teachers, and school activities.
- Tolerance for disrespectful behavior: The school does little to prevent or punish disrespectful behavior between individual students or groups of students.
- Inequitable discipline: Discipline is inequitably applied (or has the perception of being inequitably applied) by students and/or staff.
- Inflexible culture: The school's culture is static, unyielding, and insensitive to changes in society and the changing needs of newer students and staff.
- Pecking order among students: Certain groups of students are officially or unofficially given more prestige and respect than others.
- Code of silence: Few students feel they can safely tell teachers or administrators if they are concerned about another student's behavior or attitudes. Little trust exists between students and staff.
- Unsupervised computer access.

In addition, the report asserts that media coverage creates a number of myths concerning school shooters. Among them are:

- All school shooters are alike.
- The school shooter is always a loner.
- School shootings are exclusively revenge motivated.
- Easy access to weapons is the most significant risk factor.

Attitudes about School Violence

The Columbine school shootings appalled, yet fascinated, people who sought to know how such violence could be perpetrated in one of the nation's schools, particularly a suburban school in a fairly affluent middle-class neighborhood. The incident became, for a time, one of the most popular essay topics among applicants to colleges, according to the *Denver Post* (November 5, 2000). Prior to the Littleton tragedy, as observed by college deans, students tended to write about favorite teachers, influential relatives, or sports achievements. The report also noted that since the incident, college-bound students were concerned about school safety, gun control, and fear and vulnerability, often specifically mentioning Columbine in relation to these concerns.

Various opinion polls revealed that the Columbine shootings caused public attitudes about gun control to shift, but not in the direction that one might expect. Fewer respondents in general favored stricter gun control after the Columbine incident than before it. In a Harris poll, 69 percent of respondents in April 1998 favored stricter gun control, while only 63 percent were of that opinion in June 1999. An Associated Press (AP) poll found opinion remained stable. When the AP inquired about stricter gun control laws one week prior to Columbine, 56 percent were in favor; the same percentage were in favor four months after Columbine as well. The same AP poll asked whether better enforcement of existing gun laws or tougher gun laws would bring about a decrease in gun violence. The post-Littleton poll indicated a slight rise in the belief that those two actions would result in less gun violence.

According to researchers, the Columbine shootings did lead more Americans to rank guns/gun control and violence as major concerns. In a Harris poll, the percentage of people who ranked guns and gun control as important problems jumped from 1 percent pre-Columbine to 10 percent post-Columbine. The rankings of crime and violence as important problems soared from 7 percent to 19 percent after the incident. A Gallup Poll showed a similar rise in the crime/violence category, as did a CBS poll.

Eight months after Columbine, Public Agenda conducted a poll about who was to blame for the tragedy. Pollsters learned that the public attitude was divided. While teens were more likely to blame those involved in the shootings, adults pointed to guns and the influence of the media.

STUDENT ATTITUDES BEFORE AND AFTER COLUMBINE. As reported in *Are America's School's Safe? Students Speak Out: 1999 School Crime Supplement* (Lynn A. Addington, Sally A. Ruddy, Amanda K. Miller, and Jill F. DeVoe, U.S. Department of Education, National Center for Education Statistics, Washington, DC, 2002), a higher number of students (12–18) "feared attack or harm at school" in the few months following the April 20, 1999 Columbine school shooting. Some 4.8 percent of the student sample interviewed prior to the Columbine shootings indicated that they "feared attack or harm at school." Soon after the incident, the number rose to 6.3 percent. (See Table 4.14.)

TABLE 4.14

Percentage of students ages 12–18 who reported fearing being attacked or harmed at school, on the way to and from school, or outside school, before April 20, 1999 (the day of the Columbine school shootings) and after

Date of interview	Number of students[1] (thousands)	Feared attack or harm at school[2]			Feared attack or harm on the way to and from school[3]			Feared attack or harm outside school		
		Yes (percent)	No (percent)	Not ascertained (percent)	Yes (percent)	No (percent)	Not ascertained (percent)	Yes (percent)	No (percent)	Not ascertained (percent)
Before or on April 20, 1999	16,246	4.8	94.5	0.7	3.6	95.7	0.7	5.4	93.8	0.8
After April 20, 1999	8,361	6.3	93.1	0.6	4.4	95.0	0.6	6.2	92.9	0.8

[1]The number of students is not the same as the total number of students on previous tables. Seven cases were excluded because they did not include a date for the interview.
[2]If students responded that they sometimes or most of the time feared being attacked or harmed at school, they are included in the "Feared attack or harm at school" category.
[3]If students responded that they sometimes or most of the time feared being attacked or harmed while traveling to or from school, they are included in the "Feared attack or harm on the way to and from school" category.
Note: Detail may not sum to totals because of rounding and too few sample cases.

SOURCE: Lynn A. Addington, Sally A. Ruddy, Amanda K. Miller, and Jill F. DeVoe, "Table 19. Percentage of students ages 12 through 18 who reported fearing being attacked or harmed at school, on the way to and from school, or outside of school, by interview date: 1999," in *Are America's Schools Safe? Students Speak Out: 1999 School Crime Supplement*, U.S. Department of Education, National Center for Education Statistics, Washington, DC, 2002

TABLE 4.15

Percentage of students ages 12–18 who reported that they avoided attending school, class, or participating in extracurricular activities, before April 20, 1999 (the day of the Columbine School shootings) and after

Date of interview	Number of students* (thousands)	Avoided class			Avoided school			Avoided extracurricular activities		
		Yes (percent)	No (percent)	Not ascertained (percent)	Yes (percent)	No (percent)	Not ascertained (percent)	Yes (percent)	No (percent)	Not ascertained (percent)
Before or on April 20, 1999	16,246	0.4	98.9	0.7	2.3	97.0	0.7	0.7	98.7	0.6
After April 20, 1999	8,361	0.9	98.6	0.6	2.3	97.1	0.6	1.1	98.3	0.5

*The number of students is not the same as the total number of students on previous tables. Seven cases were excluded because they did not include a date for the interview.
Note: Detail may not sum to totals because of rounding.

SOURCE: Lynn A. Addington, Sally A. Ruddy, Amanda K. Miller, and Jill F. DeVoe, "Table 20. Percentage of students ages 12 through 18 who reported that they avoided attending school, class, or participating in extracurricular activities, by interview date: 1999," in *Are America's Schools Safe? Students Speak Out: 1999 School Crime Supplement*, U.S. Department of Education, National Center for Education Statistics, Washington, DC, 2002

Students were also asked if they feared being attacked or harmed while en route to or from school. Before the Columbine incident, 3.6 percent responded affirmatively; 4.4 percent did so after Columbine. Similar growth patterns were seen when students were asked if they feared being attacked or harmed while away from school. Some 5.4 percent acknowledged having that fear before Columbine, while 6.2 percent admitted it after the Columbine tragedy. It is important to note that pre-Columbine respondents were most likely to report being fearful of attack or harm outside school. After the Columbine incident, however, a slightly higher percentage of students feared attack or harm at school.

Researchers also studied the effects of Columbine on student participation in extracurricular activities and in class attendance. In general, the number of students reporting avoiding class, school, and extracurricular activities was low initially and continued to remain low after

Columbine. The percentage of students reporting that they avoided class nearly doubled (from 0.4 to 0.9 percent), but nonetheless represented few students. (See Table 4.15.) Students avoiding school remained the same, at 2.3 percent. However, slight growth was seen in the percentage of students avoiding extracurricular activities. Prior to Columbine, 0.7 percent of students acknowledged avoiding such events; following Columbine, the percentage climbed to 1.1 percent.

Far-Reaching Effects of School Shootings

In 1998 the Justice Policy Institute (JPI) issued a report concluding that school shootings are extremely rare and not on the rise (*School House Hype: School Shootings and the Real Risks Kids Face in America,* 1998). In a 2000 follow-up report, the JPI noted that public opinion polls continue to show that many Americans fear that their schools are likely to erupt in lethal violence whether violence is rising or falling. The perception of violence leads to legislation, and students often find themselves suspended or expelled from school for relatively trivial offenses. Students were far less likely than adults to fear that a school shooting could take place in their community, according to a 2001 IRC/ABC poll. Thirty-five percent of students reported that a school shooting was "very unlikely" compared with only 13 percent of adults ("Crime: A Nation Divided," Public Agenda Online, accessed February 11, 2003).

In a study conducted by Alfred University (Edward Gaughan, Jay D. Cerio, and Robert A. Myers, *Lethal Violence in Schools: A National Study,* Alfred University, Alfred, NY, August 2001), researchers found that concern about violence is prevalent in school. Some 37 percent of those surveyed believed that there are "kids at my school who I think might shoot someone." According to the report, "20 percent of respondents have heard rumors that another student plans to shoot someone, and 20 percent have also overheard another student actually talking about shooting someone at school." Another 8 percent acknowledged wanting to shoot someone at school themselves. Finally, only about half of the survey participants said they would inform an adult if they overheard someone's plans to shoot another person.

SCHOOL SAFETY

The Columbine incident marked the worst school shooting in U.S. history. In the wake of the shootings, schools stepped up efforts to prevent another such tragedy. Most schools opted for a long-term approach, focusing on prevention and intervention. Peer counseling and mediation programs seemed to be the overwhelming choice. Many schools implemented visitor sign-in programs while others had closed lunches, established controlled grounds, conducted drug sweeps, and installed metal detectors. Considering the most common threats to schools after Columbine were bomb threats and using school computers for counterfeiting and hacking, most schools scurried to find ways to deal with the threats.

Many schools have implemented a number of safety measures to deal with violence and crime at school. That number varies depending on the level of such problems at each school. However, critics of stepped-up surveillance in schools contend that bullying, stalking, and harassment are the real security problems in schools.

Students work with administrators and teachers on crime and violence reduction programs as well. Some form organizations aimed at reducing bullying or violence on campus, others sponsor talks and outings. Various students perform peer-on-peer mediation to help others work out their issues. When a tragic event does impact a school, many students participate in candlelight vigils to honor the victim as well as to comfort each other.

In some areas, police officers work directly in schools, such as in the School Resource Officer (SRO) program. SROs educate, counsel, and work to prevent crime at schools across the country. Various police officers make frequent visits to schools to give talks about the long-lasting effects that crime and violence have on both the perpetrator and his/her victim.

Disciplinary Problems and Actions

Schools contend with a wide range of disciplinary problems that can impact the safety and positive educational experience of students and staff alike. These include bullying, gang activities, verbal abuse of teachers, disrespectful acts against teachers, widespread disorder in the classroom, cult or extremist group activities, and racial tension. The National Center for Education Statistics of the U.S. Department of Education reviews such disciplinary problems in its School Survey on Crime and Safety (SSOCS). Its 1999–2000 survey found that 29 percent of public schools experienced problems with student bullying. (See Figure 4.6.) The highest percentage of public schools reporting bullying occurred at the middle school level (43 percent). Undesirable gang activities and student disrespect for teachers each tied with 19 percent of public schools acknowledging problems in these areas. Gang activities were most prevalent at secondary schools (37 percent), while disrespect for teachers occurred more often at middle schools (30 percent).

Student verbal abuse of teachers was reported at 13 percent of public schools, including 22 percent of middle schools and 17 percent of secondary schools. Seven percent of public schools reported disciplinary problems with undesirable cult or extremist group activities. This was most likely to occur at secondary schools (19 percent) and middle schools (13 percent) and far less likely at the elementary school level (2 percent). Widespread disorder in classrooms and student racial tensions each tied with 3 percent of public schools reporting problems in these areas.

One of the ways that schools attempt to deal with safety issues is to take serious disciplinary action against students committing crimes and violent acts. Based on data from the SSOCS, the authors of *Indicators of School Crime and Safety: 2003* noted that "about 54 percent of public schools took at least one serious disciplinary action, including suspensions lasting 5 days or more, removals with no services (i.e., expulsions), and transfers to specialized schools, for any of the offenses that occurred in the 1999–2000 school year.... Altogether, about 1,163,000 actions were taken." Suspensions occurred in 83 percent of the offenses, with 11 percent being removed with no services, and 7 percent being transferred to specialized schools.

According to the SSOCS data, 35 percent of public schools took serious disciplinary action regarding

FIGURE 4.6

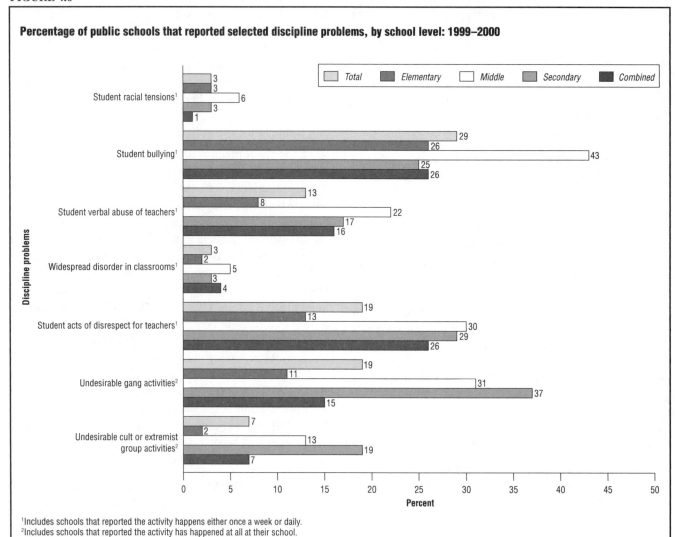

Percentage of public schools that reported selected discipline problems, by school level: 1999–2000

[1]Includes schools that reported the activity happens either once a week or daily.
[2]Includes schools that reported the activity has happened at all at their school.

SOURCE: Jill F. Devoe, Katharin Peter, Phillip Kaufman, Sally A. Ruddy, Amanda K. Miller, Mike Planty, Thomas D. Snyder, and Michael R. Rand, "Figure 16.1. Percentage of public schools that reported selected discipline problems, by school level: 1999–2000," in *Indicators of School Crime and Safety: 2003*, U.S. Department of Education, Institute of Education Sciences, National Center for Education Statistics and U.S. Department of Justice, Office of Justice Programs, Bureau of Justice Statistics, Washington, DC, October 2003

physical attacks or fights in 1999–2000. (See Figure 4.7.) Threats or intimidation (22 percent), possession or use of alcohol or illegal drugs (20 percent), possession of a weapon other than a firearm (19 percent), and insubordination (18 percent) also received significant attention. Two percent of public schools took serious disciplinary action regarding the use of a firearm or explosive device, as did 5 percent of schools regarding the use of a weapon other than a firearm.

NO CHILD LEFT BEHIND ACT: "PERSISTENTLY DANGEROUS" SCHOOLS

The No Child Left Behind Act (NCLB) was passed by Congress in 2001 and signed into law by President George W. Bush in January 2002. A reauthorization of the Elementary and Secondary Education Act (ESEA) of 1965, it mandates sweeping changes to the law defining and regulating the federal government's role in kindergarten through grade 12 education. The law is based on four basic education reform principles. The four principles, as described on the government's NCLB Web site (http://www.NoChildLeft Behind.gov/next/overview/index.html), are:

- Stronger accountability for results
- Increased flexibility and local control
- Expanded options for parents
- An emphasis on teaching methods that have proven effective.

Under the NCLB, schools are required to demonstrate "adequate yearly progress" toward statewide proficiency goals. Those that do not will face corrective action and restructuring measures. Reporting of progress will be public, so parents can stay informed about their school

FIGURE 4.7

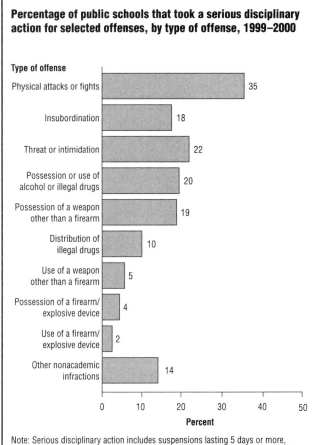

Percentage of public schools that took a serious disciplinary action for selected offenses, by type of offense, 1999–2000

Note: Serious disciplinary action includes suspensions lasting 5 days or more, removals with no services (i.e., expulsions), and transfers to specialized schools.

SOURCE: Jill F. Devoe, Katharin Peter, Phillip Kaufman, Sally A. Ruddy, Amanda K. Miller, Mike Planty, Thomas D. Snyder, and Michael R. Rand, "Figure 8.2. Percentage of public schools that took a serious disciplinary action for selected offenses, by type of offense, 1999–2000," in *Indicators of School Crime and Safety: 2003*, U.S. Department of Education, Institute of Education Sciences, National Center for Education Statistics and U.S. Department of Justice, Office of Justice Programs, Bureau of Justice Statistics, Washington, DC, October 2003

and school district. Schools that make or exceed adequate yearly progress will be eligible for awards. The ultimate goal is that all children will have a quality education by the 2013–2014 school year.

Unsafe School Choice Option (USCO)

Among the various changes that the NCLB requires is a provision mandating that states work on making schools safer. According to the NCLB Web site: "Under Title IV of ESEA as reauthorized by the No Child Left Behind Act, states are required to establish a uniform management and reporting system to collect information on school safety and drug use among young people. The states must include incident reports by school officials and anonymous student and teacher surveys in the data they collect. This information is to be publicly reported so that parents, school officials and others who are interested have information about any violence and/or drug use at

their schools. They can then assess the problems at their schools and work toward finding solutions. Continual monitoring and reports will track progress over time."

To hold schools accountable for ensuring student safety, the NCLB requires states to create a definition of "persistently dangerous" schools. States must permit students to have public school choice if their school consistently falls into this category. In addition, student victims of violent crime are also allowed public school choice even if the school isn't considered "persistently dangerous."

"PERSISTENTLY DANGEROUS" SCHOOLS: GEORGIA'S EXAMPLE. To illustrate what some states have done to fulfill the NCLB requirements pertaining to "persistently dangerous" schools, this section will focus on the Georgia Department of Education's (GDOE) efforts in that regard. According to the GDOE Web site, the state has defined persistently dangerous schools as:

Any school in which for three consecutive years:

At least 1 student is found by official tribunal action to have violated a school rule related to a violent criminal offense (including aggravated battery, aggravated child molestation, aggravated sexual battery, aggravated sodomy, armed robbery, arson, kidnapping, murder, rape, & voluntary manslaughter) either on campus or at a school-sanctioned event;

At least 2 percent of the student body or 10 students, whichever is greater, have been found to have violated school rules related to other identified criminal offenses, including non-felony drugs, felony drugs, felony weapons, terroristic threats;

Any combination of [the above]

The GDOE further outlines what happens as a consequence of a school being labeled persistently dangerous.

When a school meets the criteria for three consecutive years, local education agencies (local school systems, or LEAs) must within ten school days notify parents of each student attending the school that the state has identified the school as persistently dangerous.

Within 20 school days from the time that the LEA learns that the school has been identified as persistently dangerous, the LEA must give students the opportunity to transfer to a safe public school, including a safe public charter school, within the LEA.

The victim of a violent crime at school can transfer immediately.

Transportation will be provided only up to the limit of funds provided by the federal government for transportation.

If deemed persistently dangerous, a school will need to show significant improvements to regain its place on the safe school list. The state of Georgia has specific requirements that such schools must follow, which include taking corrective measures. After a year of showing that it is no longer dangerous, a school can reapply to the GDOE. When it filed its report in 2003, the GDOE reported that no Georgia schools were deemed persistently dangerous.

Reporting Violence and Crime at School

The unsafe school requirement of the NCLB has caused concern among some educators, parents, and police. Some believe that schools will be even more hesitant to report crimes so that they wo not be labeled as persistently dangerous. They suggest that by falling into this designation, such schools will undoubtedly lose enrollment and school funds. As such, schools may begin to underreport such crimes so that they maintain a clean rating.

In its annual survey in 2003, the National Association of School Resource Officers (NASRO) asked its members what impact the NCLB will have on school administrators reporting school-based crimes. Some 61 percent of participants believed it would result in decreased reporting of crimes at schools (Kenneth S. Trump, *School Safety Threats Persist, Funding Decreasing: NASRO 2003 National School-Based Law Enforcement Study,* National Association of School Resource Officers, Osprey, FL, August 19, 2003). Nearly 9 out of 10 (87.2 percent) believed that campus crimes were underreported in general.

Earlier studies, however, reveal that many crimes, including acts of violence, were not reported to the police even before the NCLB was passed into law. In *Indicators of School Crime and Safety: 2003,* information is presented about the percentage of schools experiencing certain types of crimes and what percentage of those crimes is actually reported to the police. For the study, school administrators were asked to comment on "crimes that took place in school buildings, on school grounds, and on school buses during normal school hours and at school-sponsored events or activities" during the 1999–2000 school year. The survey revealed that 1,466,400 violent

acts took place at public elementary and secondary schools, including 60,700 seriously violent incidents. Some 217,900 thefts at school also occurred that year.

During the school year, according to the principals of schools participating in the SSOCS, 71 percent of public schools experienced one or more violent crimes but just 36 percent reported one or more violent crimes to the police. (See Figure 4.8.) The survey also showed that 87 percent of middle schools and 92 percent of secondary schools experienced one or more violent incidents but only 56 percent of middle schools and 71 percent of secondary schools reported such events to the police. Violent incidents included physical attacks, fights with or without weapons, threats of physical violence with or without weapons, rape, sexual battery (other than rape), and robbery with or without weapons. Low-reporting trends also occurred with thefts. Whereas 46 percent of public schools experienced one or more thefts, just 28 percent reported them to the police. Secondary schools experienced and reported the most thefts, however middle schools had the highest discrepancy of thefts occurring and thefts being reported (65 percent to 40 percent).

Proportionally, schools were more likely to report seriously violent incidents to the police, presumably due to the gravity of such offenses. For example, 20 percent of public schools experienced one or more seriously violent acts and 15 percent reported the events to the police. Elementary schools were the least likely to report such acts: 14 percent experienced one or more serious acts of violence and 8 percent reported the incidents to the police.

Data were also presented based on the location of schools: city, urban fringe, town, and rural. Overall, 77 percent of city public schools experienced one or more violent events and reported 44 percent to the police. (See Figure 4.9.) Rural public schools had the biggest discrepancy between violent acts committed (70 percent) and acts reported to the police (29 percent).

FIGURE 4.8

Percentage of public schools with various types of crime and percentage of public schools that reported various types of crime to the police, by school level, 1999–2000

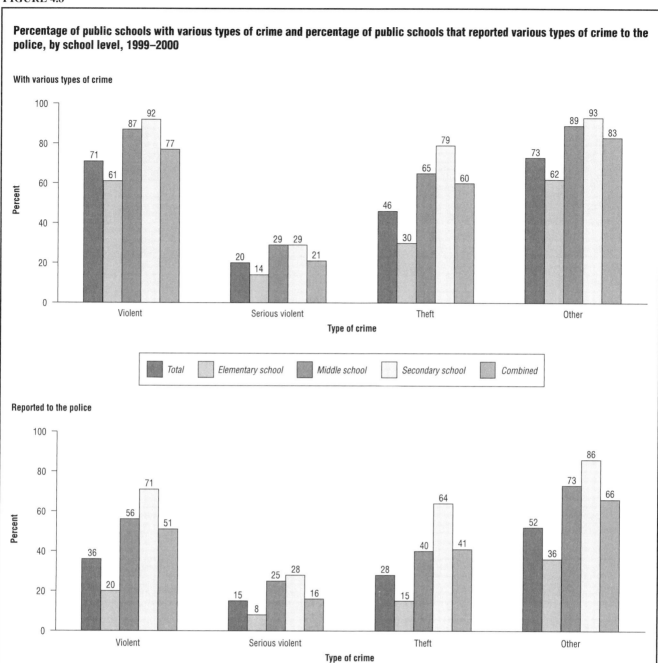

Note: Violent incidents include rape, sexual battery other than rape, physical attack or fight with or without a weapon, threat of physical attack with or without a weapon, and robbery with or without a weapon. Serious violent incidents include rape, sexual battery other than rape, physical attack or fight with a weapon, threat of physical attack with a weapon, and robbery with or without a weapon. Other incidents include possession of a firearm or explosive device, possession of a knife or sharp object, distribution of illegal drugs, possession or use of alcohol or illegal drugs, sexual harassment, or vandalism. Principals were asked to report crimes that took place in school buildings, on school grounds, and on school buses during normal school hours and at school-sponsored events or activities.

SOURCE: Jill F. Devoe, Katharin Peter, Phillip Kaufman, Sally A. Ruddy, Amanda K. Miller, Mike Planty, Thomas D. Snyder, and Michael R. Rand, "Figure 7.1. Percentage of public schools with various types of crime and percentage of public schools that reported various types of crime to the police, by school level: 1999–2000," in *Indicators of School Crime and Safety: 2003,* U.S. Department of Education, Institute of Education Sciences, National Center for Education Statistics and U.S. Department of Justice, Office of Justice Programs, Bureau of Justice Statistics, Washington, DC, October 2003.

FIGURE 4.9

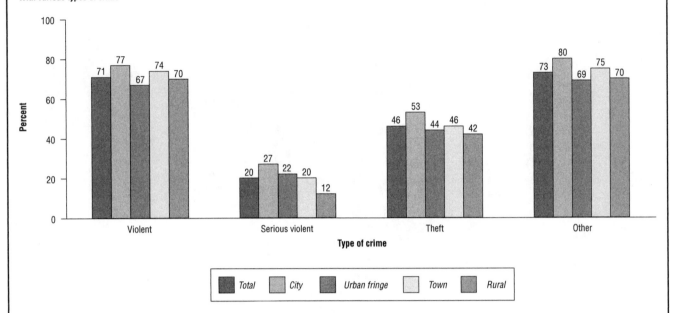

Percentage of public schools with various types of crime and percentage of public schools that reported various types of crime to the police, by urbanicity, 1999–2000

With various types of crime

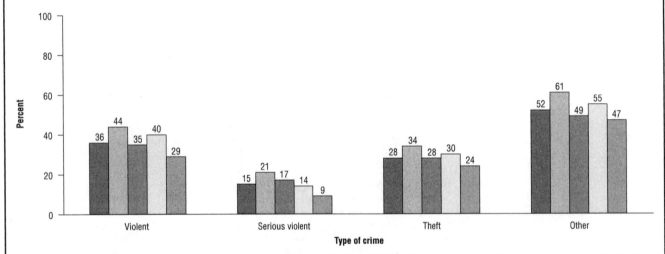

Note: Violent incidents include rape, sexual battery other than rape, physical attack or fight with or without a weapon, threat of physical attack with or without a weapon, and robbery with or without a weapon. Serious violent incidents include rape, sexual battery other than rape, physical attack or fight with a weapon, threat of physical attack with a weapon, and robbery with or without a weapon. Other incidents include possession of a firearm or explosive device, possession of a knife or sharp object, distribution of illegal drugs, possession or use of alcohol or illegal drugs, sexual harassment, or vandalism. Principals were asked to report crimes that took place in school buildings, on school grounds, and on school buses during normal school hours and at school-sponsored events or activities.

SOURCE: Jill F. Devoe, Katharin Peter, Phillip Kaufman, Sally A. Ruddy, Amanda K. Miller, Mike Planty, Thomas D. Snyder, and Michael R. Rand, "Figure 7.3. Percentage of public schools with various types of crime and percentage of public schools that reported various types of crime to the police, by urbanicity: 1999–2000," in *Indicators of School Crime and Safety: 2003*, U.S. Department of Education, Institute of Education Sciences, National Center for Education Statistics and U.S. Department of Justice, Office of Justice Programs, Bureau of Justice Statistics, Washington, DC, October 2003

CHAPTER 5
YOUTH GANGS

THE EVOLUTION OF YOUTH GANGS

Crips, Bloods, the 18th Avenue Boys, Gangsta Disciples, and Lords of Vice were all names of gangs active in the United States in 2004. Gangs and their unique names have a long history in the United States, dating back to the 1800s. As the United States became the "great melting pot," allowing people of diverse races, ethnicities, and religions to enter the country, some immigrants joined gangs to help them gain identity, defend themselves against other groups, and establish a unified presence. Although people feared street gangs of the nineteenth century, the gangs of today pose a greater threat to public safety than in years past.

The street gangs of the early twentieth century were mainly divided into small groups. The extent of their criminal activities involved delinquent acts or petty crimes, such as brawls with rival gangs. Yet, as the years rolled on, gangs began getting involved with more serious crimes. Toward the end of the twentieth century, many gang members were regarded as serious criminals who used intimidation tactics, engaged in the illegal trafficking of drugs or weapons, and used violence to pursue their goals. More and more gang members began to support themselves through dealing drugs, such as crack cocaine and heroin. Many were said to have easy access to high-powered weapons and were not afraid to use them. In addition, the proliferation of gangs in the late twentieth century meant that groups moved beyond city boundaries into suburban and rural areas as well. This movement into new territories occurred about the same time that youth violence surged in the 1980s and early 1990s.

Researchers note various reasons for the growth of gangs during the end of the twentieth century. According to "Preventing Adolescent Gang Involvement" (Finn-Aage Esbensen, *Juvenile Justice Bulletin,* U.S. Department of Justice, Office of Justice Programs, Office of Juvenile Justice and Delinquency Prevention, September

2000), "American society witnessed a reemergence of youth gang activity and media interest in this phenomenon in the 1980's and 1990's. *Colors, Boyz n the Hood,* other Hollywood productions, and MTV brought Los Angeles gang life to suburban and rural America."

During the 1970s, about 1 percent of U.S. cities and about 40 percent of the states reported having problems with youth gangs, according to the Office of Juvenile Justice and Delinquency Prevention (OJJDP). By the late 1990s, the percentage of U.S. cities with gang problems grew to 7 percent, and youth gangs were reported in all 50 states and the District of Columbia. Gang growth in cities soared in the 1980s and 1990s, increasing in number by 281 percent. During the period 1995–98, gang activity was recorded in some 1,550 cities and 450 counties where it had not been reported previously. In 1998 the West had the highest percentage of law enforcement agencies reporting active youth gangs, especially in the Pacific region. (See Figure 5.1.) The lowest percentage of agencies reporting active youth gangs was in the Northeast. Between 1996 and 1998, however, the percentage of jurisdictions reporting active gangs had decreased by 5 percent overall. The rate declined the most in the Midwest and Northwest (6 percent each).

Historically, gangs were big-city problems, but that is changing to some degree. It is still true that the larger the population, the greater the likelihood of the existence of gangs in that area. However, gangs are spreading to small towns, villages, and rural areas, some of which do not even have their own police departments.

Table 5.1 shows the correlation between jurisdiction population size and the number of gangs and gang members between 1996 and 1998. The data were drawn from the National Youth Gang Survey (NYGS) of 1998, the last year for which extensive NYGS results have been issued. The NYGS, conducted by the OJJDP, also issues annual

FIGURE 5.1

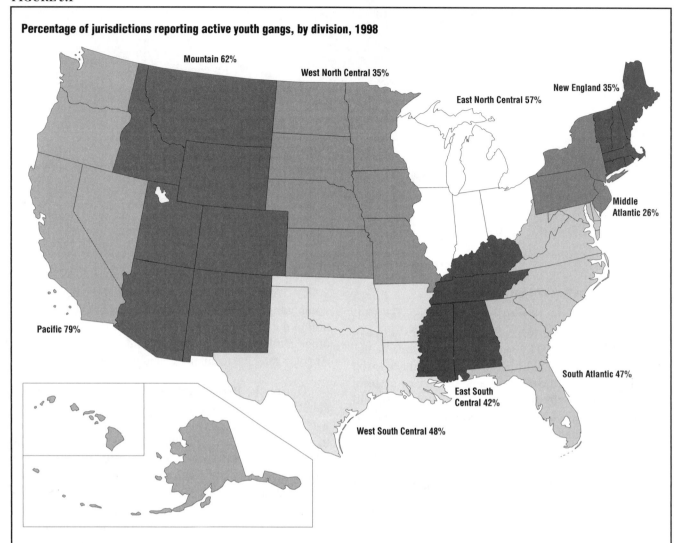

Percentage of jurisdictions reporting active youth gangs, by division, 1998

Mountain 62%

West North Central 35%

East North Central 57%

New England 35%

Middle Atlantic 26%

Pacific 79%

South Atlantic 47%

East South Central 42%

West South Central 48%

SOURCE: Adapted from "Table 3: Percentage of Jurisdictions Reporting Active Youth Gangs, by Division, 1996, 1997, and 1998," in *1998 National Youth Gang Survey*, U.S. Department of Justice, Office of Justice Programs, Office of Juvenile Justice and Delinquency Prevention, Washington, DC, November 2000

highlights as well as multi-year comparisons, such as "National Youth Gang Survey Trends from 1996 to 2000" (*OJJDP Fact Sheet,* U.S. Department of Justice, Office of Justice Programs, Office of Juvenile Justice and Delinquency Prevention, Washington, DC, February 2002).

NATIONAL YOUTH GANG SURVEY (NYGS)

In an effort to track the growth and activities of gangs, the National Youth Gang Center of OJJDP began conducting the NYGS in 1996. For purposes of the survey, researchers annually query all police and sheriff departments serving cities and counties with populations of 25,000 or more. Since gang membership is moving beyond cities, the NYGS also queries a random sample of law enforcement agencies in rural areas with populations between 2,500 and 25,000. Not all jurisdictions that receive the survey respond, but a solid majority do. Survey participants are instructed to provide information on

youth gangs within their jurisdictions. Motorcycle gangs, prison gangs, adult gangs, and hate or ideology-based groups are not to be included in the sample.

In 2000 the NYGS reported an estimated 24,500 active gangs in the United States. Although this represents an overall decline of 5 percent from 1999 levels, cities with populations of more than 25,000 reported an increase of 1 percent in the number of gangs to 12,850, the largest number reported since the survey began. Although the preliminary NYGS report for 2001 did not list actual gang numbers, it noted that "all cities with a population of 250,000 or more reported gang activity in 2001, as did 85 percent of cities with a population between 100,000 and 249,999" (Arlen Egley Jr. and Aline K. Major, "Highlights of the 2001 National Youth Gang Survey," U.S. Department of Justice, Office of Justice Programs, Office of Juvenile Justice and Delinquency Prevention, Washington, DC, April 2003). The

TABLE 5.1

Average number of youth gangs and gang members per jurisdiction, by population size, 1996–98

	1996		1997		1998	
Population size	Gangs	Gang members	Gangs	Gang members	Gangs	Gang members
250,000 or more	80 (*n*=90)	5,894 (*n*=68)	85 (*n*=88)	5,120 (*n*=77)	83 (*n*=78)	4,465 (*n*=73)
100,000–249,999	32 (*n*=167)	1,016 (*n*=141)	22 (*n*=179)	764 (*n*=159)	21 (*n*=154)	712 (*n*=148)
50,000–99,999	10 (*n*=304)	352 (*n*=221)	9 (*n*=333)	289 (*n*=286)	10 (*n*=273)	307 (*n*=235)
25,000–49,999	6 (*n*=414)	134 (*n*=302)	6 (*n*=406)	128 (*n*=332)	7 (*n*=377)	151 (*n*=320)
10,000–24,999	4 (*n*=143)	84 (*n*=91)	5 (*n*=144)	85 (*n*=99)	5 (*n*=177)	88 (*n*=131)
Less than 10,000	3 (*n*=132)	37 (*n*=85)	4 (*n*=149)	55 (*n*=113)	3 (*n*=124)	41 (*n*=109)
Overall average	15 (*n*=1,250)	741 (*n*=908)	14 (*n*=1,299)	615 (*n*=1,066)	14 (*n*=1,183)	559 (*n*=1,106)

Notes: *n* = number of observations in a particular category. The overall average takes into account all jurisdictions, regardless of population size. The particular averages take into account the population size of the jurisdiction and the number of jurisdictions for a particular population size. The overall average is not an average of particular averages.

SOURCE: "Table 11: Average Number of Youth Gangs and Gang Members per Jurisdiction, by Population Size, 1996, 1997, and 1998," in *1998 National Youth Gang Survey,* U.S. Department of Justice, Office of Justice Programs, Office of Juvenile Justice and Delinquency Prevention, Washington, DC, November 2000

percentages are smaller in cities averaging 50,000 to 99,999 residents (65 percent), cities with 25,000 to 49,999 people (44 percent), and cities with residents numbering 2,500 to 24,999 (20 percent). Respondents in suburban counties (35 percent) and rural counties (11 percent) also noted the presence of gangs.

Comparing statistics between the 1996 and 2000 surveys, NYGS researchers found that "the proportion of respondents that reported youth gangs in their jurisdiction decreased over the survey years, from 53 percent in 1996 to 40 percent in 2000" (Arlen Egley Jr., "National Youth Gang Survey Trends from 1996 to 2000," U.S. Department of Justice, Office of Justice Programs, Office of Juvenile Justice and Delinquency Prevention, Washington, DC, February 2002). Much of the decrease in the number of gangs and gang members occurred in jurisdictions with populations between 100,000 and 249,999. The report noted that all participating jurisdictions with 250,000 or more residents acknowledged having persistent gang activity during each survey year. These larger jurisdictions also experienced a drop in the average number of gang members but not in the average number of gangs.

In 2000 some 772,500 gang members were active in the United States, according to the NYGS. This represented an overall decrease of 8 percent from 1999. However, the number of gang members increased by 2 percent to an estimated total of 509,500 in cities with populations of 25,000 or more. More than 40 percent of gang cities in that year were concentrated in just four counties: Los Angeles, Riverside, and Orange counties in California, and Cook County, Illinois (which includes Chicago). The California Department of Justice estimated that 300,000 gang members lived in California in 2001, and the Chicago Crime Commission estimated that the city had about 132 gangs in 1995 with 30,000 to 50,000 "hardcore" members.

CHARACTERISTICS OF GANGS

The modern street gang, or youth gang as they are often called, takes many forms. Individual members, gang cliques, or entire gang organizations engage in trafficking in drugs; operating car theft rings; committing shootings, assaults, robbery, extortion, and other felonies; and terrorizing neighborhoods. Some of the most ambitious gangs spread out from their home jurisdictions to other cities and states. Yet, some of the movement occurs simply because the gang members' families move to other areas, especially during times of economic growth. However, many gang members come from impoverished and transitional neighborhoods, where children are born into or must contend with second- and third-generation street gangs.

The authors of "Hybrid and Other Modern Gangs" (David Starbuck et al., *Juvenile Justice Bulletin,* U.S. Department of Justice, Office of Justice Programs, Office of Juvenile Justice and Delinquency Prevention, Washington, DC, December 2001) examined survey data and current research to offer a portrait of the modern youth gang. Various stereotypes exist about gangs. For example, the stereotypical view holds that youth gangs are tightly organized groups comprised of black or Hispanic, inner-city males operating under strict codes of conduct with explicit punishments for infractions of the rules. However, the new "hybrid" gang could have members from both genders and from different racial groups as well as those having radically opposing viewpoints.

The authors noted that a modern gang might be made up of African Americans, white supremacists, and girls. The gangs are found in schools and the military and in territories as small as shopping malls. Rules or codes of conduct may be unclear. Hybrid gangs sometimes borrow the symbols, graffiti, and even the names of established Los Angeles– or Chicago-based organizations (Bloods, Crips, Latin Kings) but are actually locally based and have no connection to those organizations. Rival gangs may cooperate in criminal activities, and mergers of small gangs are common.

The 1998 National Youth Gang Survey reported that an estimated 36 percent of youth gangs had members from two or more racial/ethnic groups, and that small cities, particularly in the Midwest, had the largest proportion of gangs with mixed race/ethnicity. Other studies show that in many cases, the modern adolescent may refuse to join a gang or leave it without fear of reprisal, even though gangs try to maintain the illusion that leaving is impossible. This was borne out by OJJDP-supported longitudinal studies in Denver, Colorado (1988–1999) and Rochester, New York (1986–1997), as well as the Seattle Social Development Project in Washington (1985–2001), showing that well more than half (54–69 percent) of youths who joined gangs in those cities remained for 1 year or less, while only 9–21 percent stayed for 3 or more years.

In "Hybrid and Other Modern Gangs," the authors note that in places where gangs are a fairly recent phenomenon, drug sales and distribution are less likely to be major problems. Gang member involvement in drug sales is most prevalent in areas where gangs emerged between 1981 and 1985, at the height of the crack cocaine epidemic. Highly organized, entrepreneurial, gang control of drug distribution across wide areas and the violent crime that goes with it are mainly associated with the gangs that emerged in the 1960s and 1970s in Los Angeles and Chicago.

Definition of a Gang

Politicians, citizen groups, law enforcement officials, and researchers have yet to determine a universal definition for gangs. As such, attempts to collect data about gangs at the national level are complicated because definitions differ regarding what constitutes a gang.

Some define a gang as a group of people using a unique name and identifiable marks or symbols who claim a territory or turf as their own. These individuals associate on a regular basis and frequently engage in criminal or antisocial behavior. The Federal Bureau of Investigation (FBI) refers to gangs, whose main activities include violence and drugs, as "violent street gang/drug enterprise." Further, the bureau defines a criminal street gang as "[a] group of people who form an allegiance based on various social needs and engage in acts injurious to public health and morals. Members of street gangs engage in (or have engaged in) gang-focused criminal activity either individually or collectively; they create an atmosphere of fear and intimidation within the community."

The Bureau of Justice Statistics (BJS) of the U.S. Department of Justice says that gangs are groups of people engaged in illegal activities. In order to be classified as a gang, such groups typically exhibit five or six of the following characteristics.

- Have a recognized group leader, or certain members of the group whom the others follow
- Have a formal membership, which includes a set of rules and initiation requirements
- Wear unique clothing that signifies membership in the gang, including symbols, tattoos, group colors, haircuts, jewelry
- Have a recognized name
- Have a membership that is derived from a specific neighborhood, school, or street
- Have an established territory (or turf), which the group calls its own, that is the location of many of the group's activities

Other researchers report additional gang identifiers, including the use of:

- Hand signs, such as unique handshakes or gestures
- Unique or uncommon language (terms, phrases, or slang)
- Graffiti, including symbols and signs, on walls, lockers, homework, and notebooks

Other organizations have varying definitions. In the 1996–1998 National Youth Gang Surveys, a gang was defined as "a group of youths or young adults in [the respondent's] jurisdiction that [the respondent] or other responsible persons in [the respondent's] agency or community are willing to identify or classify as a 'gang.'" As noted earlier, survey respondents were instructed to exclude certain types of gangs.

An alternative definition was composed by gang researcher Malcolm Klein for the 1998 National Youth Gang Survey. His definition follows: "A group of youths or young adults in your jurisdiction whose involvement in illegal activities over months or years marks them in their own view and in the view of the community and police as different from most other youthful groups. Do not include motorcycle gangs, hate or ideology groups, prison gangs, or other exclusively adult gangs." The difference between the two NYGS definitions is the use of the term "illegal" in the alternative definition.

In the 1998 survey, law enforcement agencies were asked what percentage of the youth gangs they reported would fit the alternative definition. About 10 percent of agencies reported that none of their gangs met the alternative definition, demonstrating that law enforcement agencies define "gang" in different ways. Table 5.2 shows the number of gangs identified under both definitions by region. The West had the strongest correspondence (84 percent) between gangs reported under the original and the alternative definitions. The reason may be that many

TABLE 5.2

Number of youth gangs reported under two definitions of "youth gangs," by region, 1998

Region	Gangs by original definition	Gangs by alternative definition		
		Number	Percentage of original	n*
Midwest	2,611	1,892	72%	292
Northeast	795	646	81	100
South	4,680	3,491	75	346
West	6,343	5,334	84	264
Total	14,429	11,363	79	1,002

*n = number of observations reported by police departments to the OJJDP.

SOURCE: Adapted from "Table 49: Responses to the Alternative Definition of Youth Gangs, by Region, 1998," in *1998 National Youth Gang Survey*, U.S. Department of Justice, Office of Justice Programs, Office of Juvenile Justice and Delinquency Prevention, Washington, DC, November 2000

Western states use California's definition of gangs, which notes that the commission of criminal acts is one of a gang's main activities.

Specific Gang Characteristics

Researchers, law enforcement, and community groups devote time to learning about gangs and the types of characteristics they share. Much study has gone into gang slang, graffiti, hand signs, colors, and initiations, among other characteristics. The goal is to learn more about how gangs communicate and interact, both internally and externally, as well as test themselves and each other. Much can be learned about gangs from these aspects of gang culture if one knows what the characteristics represent.

GANG SLANG. Various gang members have created their own slang language. Although some terms are used in gangs throughout the country, others are only used regionally and within certain gangs. Various terms originated with the infamous Crips and Bloods gangs of Los Angeles, who have been adversaries for many years. The following is a small sampling of gang slang and what the terms represent.

- 5-O: Police
- A.K.: AK-47 semi-automatic assault rifle
- Banging: Involved in gang activities
- B.G. or Baby G. (Baby Gangster): Gang member who has not shot someone; also young gang member, usually between ages 7 and 12
- B.K. (Blood killer): Term used by "Crip" members to threaten their rivals, usually "Blood" members
- Blood: Umbrella organization of street gangs in California, signified by the color red
- Breakdown: Shotgun

- Bucket: Old, beat-up car
- Bud: Marijuana
- Bullet: One-year prison term
- Buster: Fake gang member; one who wants to be in a gang
- C.K. (Crip killer): Term used by "Blood" members to threaten their rivals, usually "Crip" members
- Clicking In/Jumping In: Gang initiation
- Clique: Gang
- Colors: Clothing of a particular color, such as jackets, shoes, or bandanas, worn by gang members to identify themselves as part of the gang
- Crib: Home, room, or prison cell
- Crip: Umbrella organization of street gangs in California, signified by the color blue
- Double Deuce: .22 caliber handgun
- Durag (Dew Rag): Bandanna
- Dusted: Killed or addicted to phencyclidine (PCP or angel dust)
- Gang Banger: Member of a gang
- Gat: Gun
- Jack: Rob or assault someone or steal something
- Mad Dog: Intimidating stare
- O.G. (Original Gangster): Gang member who has killed someone; also founding member or leader of a gang
- Peace Out: Good-bye
- Popped a Cap: To shoot at someone or something
- Posse: Gang
- Ride: Car
- R.I.P.: Rest in Peace
- Shank: Knife
- Tag: Name or moniker, usually associated with a graffiti artist
- Tagging: Marking a territory with graffiti
- Tats: Tattoos
- Trey Eight: .38 caliber handgun
- Turf: Territory

GRAFFITI. Graffiti has been a form of communication since ancient times. Meaning "little scratches" in Italian, graffiti has appeared in cave dwellings, Egyptian temples, and on other natural and human-made objects. Today, there are several categories of graffiti; each type is used to get the artists' message out to anyone who can read it. Among the various types are personal musings, political messages, "tagging," "piecing" or "bombing," and gang graffiti.

The most common type of graffiti is that of personal musings—thoughts written down quickly in public places, such as restrooms and phone booths. Sometimes humorous, this type of graffiti might be of a sexual nature, or might include memorable quotes. Often times, it concerns race relations.

Political graffiti usually appears in places accessible to the general public—on the sides of buildings, freeway overpasses, etc. The political message is generally against the establishment or authorities and may contain statements regarding labor conditions, civil rights, and religious thought.

"Tagging" is another type of graffiti. A tag is a signature, or moniker, which may incorporate the artist's physical features or symbolize his/her personality. Tags are found usually on exterior building walls in urban areas. They may also appear on mass transit systems (buses and trains), freeway overpasses, and other areas for all to see and wonder how it got there. Tagging first appeared on the East Coast in the late 1960s, making its way to the West Coast by the 1980s. Taggers feel a sense of power and fame as more and more surfaces contain their tags.

Mural-type graffiti is known as "piecing" or "bombing." The piece usually contains elaborate depictions or a montage of images. Often times, slogans appear within the piece. Whereas tags can be done quickly, piecing may take up to several hours and require numerous cans of spray paint in many colors.

Gang graffiti employs all of the aforementioned types. Gangs use graffiti for many purposes. In some instances, it may be a way of communicating messages to other gang members, like a newsletter. Tags or monikers may be used to show a gang's hierarchy. Pieces may memorialize a fallen comrade or pay tribute to the crimes committed by gang members. Some pieces may enumerate rules in the gang's society—it is often a means to advertise a gang's presence in the neighborhood. Gang graffiti may also serve as a threatening message to rival gangs—stay away from our turf.

In today's society, all types of graffiti are generally perceived as vandalism and a public nuisance, punishable by law in the United States.

HAND SIGNS. Hand signs are a way of communicating concepts or ideas without using words. However, only those individuals who are familiar with the gesture's meaning are able to understand the message being conveyed. The rise of gang hand signs began in the Los Angeles area during the 1950s. Since that time, many gangs have developed hand signs for use between members of the group. Gang members "throw" or "flash" hand signs as a way of communicating amongst themselves, sending secret messages to other members within the group. For example, placing a clenched fist over the heart means, "I'll die for you."

Each gang usually has a hand sign that symbolizes affiliation with the gang. For example, the Los Angeles Bloods use the sign "B" (creating a circle with the thumb and index finger, with the other fingers raised) to signify membership in the gang. Crips use a sign that represents the letter "C." Although this is a good way for gang members to recognize other members or affiliates, it can be used against them as well. A gang might use gestures created by a rival gang in an act called "false flagging." When this occurs, a gang member will flash a rival gang's hand sign as a way to infiltrate the opposing gang or to lure an unsuspecting adversary into a bad situation.

Most gangs recognize many universal hand signals. One such ubiquitous sign dates back to World War II (1939–45)—the sign for "victory," made by raising the index and middle fingers in the shape of a "V." Gangs use many universal gestures to intimidate or "dis" (disrespect) rival gangs. A raised fist means "power." Raising the index finger shows that the gang is "number one" and can beat all rivals. Gang hand signs may also appear prominently in gang graffiti.

FLYING THE COLORS. Throughout history, opposing armies at war have used different colors to symbolize their cause or protect their territory. Flags, uniforms, and the like were made in the color chosen to represent the nation or army at war. By donning the color of the army, soldiers were easily identified as being on one side or the other—the enemy could be spotted easily. During the American Revolution, most of the British forces wore red uniforms; thus, they were called the "Redcoats." To distinguish themselves from the British, the American colonists chose uniforms of blue.

This is also true of gangs. For many years, they have used color to distinguish themselves from rival gangs, while protecting their turf. Gang members often show support for the gang by wearing "uniforms." Sporting clothes in the gang's colors, such as bandannas, shoes, jackets, jewelry, and other articles of clothing, shows a person's membership in one gang over another. For example, the two largest gangs in the Los Angeles area are the Bloods and the Crips. The Bloods use red; the Crips use blue. The colors are a way to symbolize the gang's unity, power, and pride.

In 2004, however, "flying the colors" could be a disadvantage to gangs. Although colors make it easier for other gangs to identify rival members, they also help law enforcement and school officials recognize gang members. Police have been able to crack down on gang-related criminal activities, rounding up juveniles and youths wearing gang colors. Many schools have banned students from wearing certain colors to lessen gang intimidation and pressure in the classroom.

In response to this new threat, many gangs have opted to forego their traditional colors and are developing new methods of identification. Like the modern-day army, gang members are beginning to camouflage themselves from their rivals, making their "uniforms" less conspicuous. Wearing a hat tilted to the left may show membership in a gang whose rivals are those who wear their pants legs rolled up. Gang members also use hand signs to identify their affiliation to certain groups.

RECRUITMENT AND INITIATION. Since the dawn of time, people have organized themselves into groups of like-minded individuals to meet and participate in group-related activities. Whether the group is formed to hunt game for the village, collect stamps, or discuss the latest book club selection, the group offers fellowship—a way to bond with others who share similar interests or goals. For today's youth, this is no different. Scouting, athletics, or debate clubs offer ways for kids to meet new friends and participate in various group activities, such as camping, learning crafts, etc. The group organizers recruit members by offering experiences that a boy or girl might not have unless they are members of the group.

Although their activities are often criminal and their recruitment tactics highly aggressive, gangs operate in a similar fashion. Gang recruiters offer prospective members a chance to be a part of something—to gain a sense of belonging that might be lacking in their lives. Through the use of graffiti, the wearing of colors or tattoos, or intimidation tactics, the gang recruits new members to increase its power. In turn, some juveniles see this power in the schools or on the sides of buildings and may feel pressured into joining a gang. In some instances, gang members threaten the child or members of his/her family into joining, offering protection from bullies or rival gangs. Others might be eager to join a gang thinking it is cool and exciting to be part of a clique that engages in criminal activity.

As is common in some social clubs, many prospective gang inductees must undergo an initiation to show the members that they are worthy enough to be accepted into the group. "Jumping in" or "clicking in" to a gang usually involves some type of criminal activity for the inductee to perform. This may include stealing or damaging property, assaulting someone, or carrying and selling drugs. More radical forms of gang initiations may involve drive-by shootings or rape. In some instances, the inductee is "beat-down" by gang members using baseball bats or brass knuckles. In rare instances, a new member may be "blessed in"—not having to prove his/her worth—because a brother or sister is already a member of the gang. Some have difficulty trying to leave a gang. In these cases, the youth might be pressured to remain in the clique, or might be hesitant to leave because his/her friends and family (including parents) are in the gang.

INDICATORS OF GANG INVOLVEMENT. Many groups have compiled lists to aid parents, siblings, educators, and others in looking for signs that a youth has joined a gang. However, those groups are quick to point out that someone exhibiting only one or a few of these signs may not be a gang member or even a "wannabe" or "gonnabe" (at-risk youth). But the more signs that someone exhibits increases the likelihood that he or she is headed for gang involvement. Warning signs for youth includes one who:

- Experiences a sudden drop in school grades
- Lacks interest in school and other activities that were once important
- Becomes truant (skips school)
- Comes home late
- Acts more outwardly aggressive or outright defiant
- Develops a new circle of friends who seem more rough and tough
- Behaves more secretively and is less forthcoming
- Changes clothing style; begins wearing some colors exclusively or wears clothes in a unique way consistently (like rolling up pants legs)
- Exhibits more antisocial tendencies; becomes withdrawn or uninterested in family activities
- Suddenly acquires costly material possessions (CDs, DVDs, electronics equipment, etc.) or large amounts of cash, and the source of the funds cannot be explained
- Starts using a new nickname (or street name)
- Becomes fascinated with weapons, particularly guns
- Has new cuts and bruises indicating evidence of being in a fight; unable to provide reasonable explanation
- Sports new unusual tattoos
- Writes gang graffiti on notebooks, schoolbooks, posters
- Develops increased interest in "gangsta" rap music
- Hides stash of spray paint, permanent markers, and other graffiti supplies
- Has encounters with law enforcement
- Shows dependency on drugs or alcohol

Gang Types and Activities

In the National Assessment on Gang Prosecution, a survey sponsored by the National Institute of Justice in the early-to-mid 1990s, prosecutors were asked to note the types of gangs that operate within their jurisdictions. They were also asked to comment on whether gang members were involved in drugs or violent crime. If the gang was identified with drug trafficking, the study further asked what types of drugs were involved.

Among respondents reporting gang problems, 83 percent in large jurisdictions and 60 percent in small jurisdictions reported the presence of local black gangs. Such gangs originated in that jurisdiction, rather than migrating from California gangs, such as the Crips or Bloods. Hispanic gangs were the second most-prevalent gang type in large jurisdictions (reported by 64 percent of prosecutors), followed closely by motorcycle gangs (62 percent). Forty-nine percent of small jurisdiction prosecutors acknowledged that motorcycle gangs were present in their areas, followed by 43 percent reporting Hispanic gangs.

Some 88 percent of large- and 81 percent of small-jurisdiction prosecutors stated that Hispanic gangs in their communities trafficked in drugs. Ninety percent of motorcycle gangs in large jurisdictions and 86 percent in small jurisdictions were said to be involved in the sale of drugs.

Fifty percent of prosecutors in large jurisdictions reported the presence of Crips and Bloods gangs. Ninety percent were linked to violent crimes and 92 percent were involved in drug trafficking. The survey data did not indicate whether Crips and Bloods located in various jurisdictions had any continuing connection with the original Los Angeles gangs bearing those names. However, studies indicate that the names and colors often persist long after such gangs drop any real Los Angeles connection. Caribbean-based gangs were almost always reported to be involved in drug trafficking. Cocaine (more than 96 percent) was the drug most often dealt by such gangs.

Prosecutors indicated that Asian gangs were more likely to be involved in violent crime than drug trafficking. They cited the presence of Asian gangs in 52 percent of large jurisdictions but far fewer small jurisdictions (14 percent).

NATIONAL VICTIM ASSISTANCE ACADEMY. The *National Victim Assistance Academy Textbook* (U.S. Department of Justice, Office for Victims of Crime, Washington, DC, June 2002) discusses gang research that was conducted by Dr. Carl S. Taylor. A sociologist, Taylor categorized gangs into three types:

- Scavenger: These gangs act spontaneously and lack organization. They have frequent changes in leadership. Many members of scavenger gangs tend to be low achievers. These factors contribute to the fact that scavenger gangs are the least successful and are regarded unfavorably by other types of gangs.

- Territorial: These are highly organized gangs, prone to fighting. They live according to traditional practices, such as turfs or territories, formal initiations, etc. Formed mainly for social reasons, such gangs sometimes sell drugs to survive on the streets. Members are often poor students.

- Corporate: The most highly structured gangs, they engage in drug trafficking. They live by a strict set of rules, with harsh punishments for those who break them, and can be considered actual gangsters. Members are smart but may lack formal schooling.

CHARACTERISTICS OF INDIVIDUAL GANG MEMBERS

Gender

According to NYGS participants in 2000, 94 percent of gang members were male and 6 percent were female.

This represented a 2 percent increase in male membership in gangs since 1998 and a 2 percent decrease in female membership. In 2000 some 39 percent of such gangs had females among their ranks. Respondents also noted that about 2 percent of the gangs in their jurisdiction were composed primarily of females.

In its comprehensive 1998 report, the NYGS presented findings for gang members based on gender and area type. In terms of percentages, female gang membership was highest in small cities (12 percent versus 88 percent for males) and lowest in large cities (7 percent versus 93 percent for males). In actual numbers, female gang members were most often reported in large cities, followed by suburban counties. When location was considered, the ratio of females to males was highest in the Northeast (13 percent female to 87 percent male) and lowest in the Midwest (5 percent female to 95 percent male).

Proportionally, female-dominated gangs were most prevalent in the Northeast (4 percent) and least prevalent in the West and Midwest (1 percent apiece). The South had the largest number of female-dominated gangs (123), followed by the West (65), Midwest (33), and Northeast (26). The number of female-dominated gangs was highest in cities with 250,000 or more people (120) and lowest in areas with less than 10,000 people (3).

Age

Gangs sometimes serve as families for children whose own families may be dysfunctional. Gang members have said there is often little need to intimidate youngsters to recruit them because they know what youth need and are willing to provide it in return for the child's commitment. Gangs provide emotional support, shelter, and clothing—in essence, just what the child's family may not be providing. However, some children are intimidated into joining gangs either out of fear or for protection from other gangs.

The age of gang members is often hard to determine. Researchers, such as those involved in the NYGS, try to estimate the approximate age ranges of gang members. Age surveys are not conducted annually, just in select years. The NYGS reports that gang membership was about 50 percent juvenile and 50 percent adult in 1996, then decreased to about 37 percent juvenile in 1999. Much of the change can be attributed to an increase of youths (18–24) either staying in the gangs past their juvenile years or joining up as adults.

The NYGS also commented on the age ranges of members of youth gangs by area type where gangs operated in 1998. (See Figure 5.2.) Large cities and suburban counties reported the highest proportions of adult gang members; small cities and rural counties reported the highest proportions of juveniles, including juveniles under age 15. Between 1996 and 1998, the percentage of juveniles under age 15 decreased the most in rural counties (6 percent) and large cities (5 percent). While rural counties (1 percent) and suburban counties (4 percent) saw an increase of members aged 15–17, large cities (6 percent) and small cities (2 percent) experienced a decrease among that age group. The largest percentage growth for those aged 18–24 occurred in large cities (10 percent).

Race/Ethnicity

The NYGS also surveys its participants to determine the race of gang members in select years. Totals for 2001 show that Hispanics comprised 49 percent of gang members, followed by African Americans (34 percent), whites (10 percent), and Asians (6 percent). This represents a 2 percent increase in Hispanic gang members and a 3 percent increase in African American gang members since 1999. Whites and Asians dropped 3 percent and 1 percent respectively. However, according to the National Youth Gang Center Web site in 2004, "The newest gang-problem areas ... report, on average, a larger proportion of Caucasian/white gang members than any other racial/ethnic group." As such, this is an indication that gang membership represents the characteristics found within the gang's community or neighborhood.

In the comprehensive report of the 1998 NYGS, researchers noted that proportionally, Hispanics comprised the largest percentage of gang members in three of four area types—large city, small city, and suburban county. African Americans were highest in rural counties. In terms of location, African American gang members were more often found in the Midwest and Northeast than other groups, and Hispanics had the highest percentages in the South and West.

NATIVE AMERICAN GANGS. In an effort to learn more about Native American gangs, the National Youth Gang Center conducted a survey and presented its finding in the *2000 Survey of Youth Gangs in Indian Country* (Aline K. Major and Arlen Egley, Jr., U.S. Department of Justice, Office of Justice Programs, Office of Juvenile Justice and Delinquency Prevention, Washington, DC, June 2002). The survey included "persons of American Indian, Alaska Native, or Aleut heritage who reside within the limits of Indian reservations, pueblos, rancherias, villages, dependent Indian communities, or Indian allotments, and who together comprise a federally recognized tribe or community." The survey found that youth gangs were active in 23 percent of Indian communities. Fifty-nine percent of communities reporting active gangs estimated the number of gangs between 1 and 5; 19 percent estimated the number to be between 6 and 10; and 6 percent estimated more than 10. Sixteen percent of the communities with gangs believed the gangs consisted of more than 50 people, 12 percent estimated 26 to 50 people, and 32 percent reported 25 or fewer. Of the crimes most often reported of native peoples, graffiti, vandalism, and drug sales topped the list.

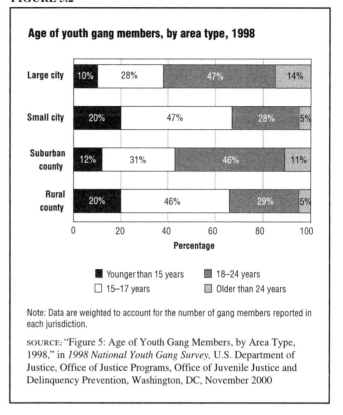

FIGURE 5.2

Age of youth gang members, by area type, 1998

Note: Data are weighted to account for the number of gang members reported in each jurisdiction.

SOURCE: "Figure 5: Age of Youth Gang Members, by Area Type, 1998," in *1998 National Youth Gang Survey*, U.S. Department of Justice, Office of Justice Programs, Office of Juvenile Justice and Delinquency Prevention, Washington, DC, November 2000

According to the survey, about 75 percent of gang members were juveniles. Females comprised 20 percent of Indian country gangs. A mix of both males and females existed in some 82 percent of the gangs. Female-dominated gangs amounted to about 10 percent of the Indian gangs. Nearly four out of five gang members in Indian country were of American Indian, Alaskan Native, or Aleut descent. The other 22 percent came from other races/ethnicities, most notably Hispanics and whites.

Stereotypes

Various stereotypes about gangs are perpetuated in the news media and the movies. For example, many gang members are depicted as constantly violent, quick to kill, emotionless, drug-crazed, highly self-destructive, and living on the edge. In "Preventing Adolescent Gang Involvement," the authors attempt to set the record straight regarding the average gang member. "For the majority of the time, gang youth engage in the same activities as other youth—sleeping, attending school, hanging out, working odd jobs. Only a fraction of their time is dedicated to gang activity." While gang youth are involved in more crimes than non-gang youth, some describe gang life as somewhat boring.

Another stereotype about gangs is that they are predominately male and that females only play an auxiliary role. In the past researchers have depicted girl gang members as tomboys or as sexually promiscuous teens. However, more research has shown that females participate in gangs at all levels. Some participate in mixed-gender gangs while others are part of female-dominated or exclusively female gangs. In some instances, female gang members have used excessive violence to show they are as tough as their male counterparts.

As more research is conducted on females in gangs, some have suggested that female membership has been underreported for a variety of reasons. First, some law enforcement officers perceived that male gang members were the biggest threat and discounted female involvement. Also, females in general engage in lower rates of crime and violence, so they have fewer encounters with the police who would report their existence in surveys. As of 2004, law enforcement, citizens groups, and researchers were beginning to take a closer look at females and their role in gang culture.

Other myths about gangs indicate that members are exclusively poor, come from large urban areas, and are from dysfunctional homes. According to the OJJDP, those notions are too restrictive. The reality is that gang members come from a variety of household situations—from single-parent families to two-parent families to recombined families (stepfamilies). Although many may come from lower-income families in urban areas, some come from families with higher-income levels in suburban and rural areas.

Many assert that young people turn to illegal activities because they do not want to work minimum-wage or low-wage jobs. Various intervention programs have proved otherwise. Throughout the country thousands of former gang members have taken such jobs. Some go back to school and use these jobs as a starting point for future career development.

REASONS FOR JOINING A GANG

Why juveniles, youths, and even adults participate in gangs is the subject of much ongoing study in the United States. Although the reasons vary greatly among gang members, some of the most common reasons follow. However, it is important to note that while these factors may cause some people to join gangs, the majority of people never do so.

- Feeling marginalized by society and seeking a commonality with others in similar situations
- Wanting power and respect
- Having friends involved in gangs and wanting to be a part of that too
- Desiring a sense of belonging when that is not available through a traditional family setting
- Seeking safety and/or protection from bullies, rival gangs, family members, or others
- Having power in numbers
- Ending poverty and joblessness by turning to criminal activities, such as stealing and drug trafficking

- Needing to feel a sense of purpose
- Having trouble or a disinterest in school
- Living in neighborhoods or communities where other troubled youth roam the streets
- Adding organization and structure to one's life
- Having feelings of low self-esteem that are diminished through encouragement from other gang members

GANGS IN SCHOOLS

The presence of street gangs is a growing concern in America's schools. Various educators and students—urban, suburban, and rural—acknowledge the presence of gangs in their schools. Such gangs are often involved in illegal activities, such as violence, drugs, and weapons trafficking. Gang presence in schools often leads to fear among non-gang-affiliated students, and may encourage non-gang members to join up in order to gain protection. In schools with significant gang presence, the level of violence is frequently higher than in schools with less gang presence.

In *Indicators of School Crime and Safety: 2003* (J.F. DeVoe, K. Peter, P. Kaufman, S.A. Ruddy, A.K. Miller, M. Planty, T.D. Snyder, and M.R. Rand, U.S. Departments of Education and Justice, Washington, DC, 2003), the authors address the issue of student reports of street gangs on campus. In 2001 urban students (29 percent) were most likely to acknowledge the presence of street gangs at school during the previous six months. (See Figure 5.3.) Suburban students (18 percent) and rural students (13 percent) followed. The percentages of students reporting gangs in public schools far eclipsed the number in private schools. Nearly one-third (32 percent) of students in urban public schools reported gangs at school compared to 5 percent of private urban school students. Proportionally, public suburban school students were five times more likely to report gang presence than private suburban school students. Among public and private rural school students, the rates were 14 percent and 7 percent respectively. However, among private schools, rural students were the most likely group to report gang presence.

In terms of race and ethnicity, Hispanics in urban schools (40.3 percent) were the most likely group to acknowledge gangs at school, while white rural students (12.1 percent) were the least likely. Among sixth to twelfth graders, ninth-grade urban school students (35.3 percent) were the most likely to report gang presence, with seventh-grade rural school students being the least likely (8.9 percent).

Are America's Schools Safe? Students Speak Out: 1999 School Crime Supplement (Lynn A. Addington, Sally A. Ruddy, Amanda K. Miller, and Jill F. DeVoe, U.S. Department of Education, National Center for Education Statistics, Washington, DC, 2002) presented comparisons of student reports on street gangs at school in 1995 and 1999. The percentage of students (12–18)

FIGURE 5.3

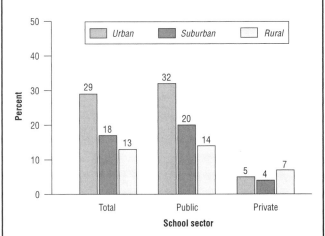

Percentage of students ages 12–18 who reported that street gangs were present at school during the previous 6 months, by urbanicity and school sector, 2001

Note: "At school" means in the school building, on school property, on a school bus, or going to and from school.

SOURCE: Jill F. Devoe, Katharin Peter, Phillip Kaufman, Sally A. Ruddy, Amanda K. Miller, Mike Planty, Thomas D. Snyder, and Michael R. Rand, "Figure 15.1. Percentage of students ages 12–18 who reported that street gangs were present at school during the previous 6 months, by urbanicity and school sector: 2001," in *Indicators of School Crime and Safety: 2003*, U.S. Department of Education, Institute of Education Sciences, National Center for Education Statistics and U.S. Department of Justice, Office of Justice Programs, Bureau of Justice Statistics, Washington, DC, October 2003

reporting gangs decreased 11.1 percent, from 28.4 in 1995 to 17.3 in 1999. (See Table 5.3.) While close percentages of males and females reported the presence of gangs in 1995 and again in 1999, the percentages decreased more than 10 percent during that time span.

Proportionally, Hispanics most often reported the presence of street gangs at school, 49.7 percent in 1995 and 28.3 percent in 1999, a decrease of more than 20 percent. In 1995 tenth graders (33.6 percent) indicated the highest incidence of gangs at school; in 1999 ninth graders (22.7 percent) were most likely to do so. In 1995 those from families with the lowest incomes (less than $7,500) acknowledged gangs at school most frequently (38.9 percent), while students of lower-middle-income ($15,000–24,999) families were most likely to report school gangs in 1999 (23.4 percent). Students who were victimized at school were also more likely to note the presence of gangs (41.3 percent) in 1995 and again in 1999 (26.1 percent). The same is true of students who know a classmate who brought a gun to school—55.2 percent in 1995 and 45.1 percent in 1999.

Indicators of Gang Presence at School

In its report "Youth Gangs in Schools" (James C. Howell and James P. Lynch, *Juvenile Justice Bulletin*, Office of Juvenile Justice and Delinquency Prevention,

August 2000), the OJJDP notes that even in elementary and secondary schools, youth gangs can present serious crime problems. The authors describe various studies that asked surveyed students to explain why they thought gangs were present. The students' responses indicating the presence of gangs included:

- The gang has a recognized name (80 percent)
- The surveyed student has spent time with gang members (80 percent)
- The gang members wear clothing or other items identifying their group (71 percent)
- The gang marks or tags its territory/turf with graffiti (56 percent)
- The gang has committed acts of violence (50 percent)
- The gang has a recognized territory/turf (47 percent)
- The gang members have tattoos (37 percent)
- The gang members have a recognized leader (33 percent)

Gangs and Drugs at School

"Youth Gangs in Schools" comments on the connection between drug availability and gang presence at school. The authors note: "Where none of the drugs was easy to get, only 25 percent of surveyed students said gangs were present. This percentage increased from 42 percent when only one drug was readily available to 69 percent when seven drugs were readily available." When eight and nine drugs were available at school, the percentages of students reporting gangs were 63 percent and 62 percent respectively.

Gang Criminality at School

The "Youth Gangs in Schools" bulletin also contains information regarding survey respondents' impressions about the presence of gangs in school and crime. According to the publication: "The students reported that most of the gangs they see at school are actively involved in criminal activities. About two-thirds of the students reported that gangs are involved in none or only one of three types of criminal acts: violence, drug sales, or carrying guns. Nevertheless, students said that a small proportion of gangs in schools (8 percent) are involved in all three types of crimes, and these gangs are probably responsible for the most disruption and violent victimizations in and around schools." The report's authors also noted that other studies include a variety of other criminal activities known to be perpetrated by gang members.

The report states that gangs contribute substantially to victimizations at school. It is believed that some students join gangs to avoid persecution by gang members. For them, gang membership serves as a form of protection from other students who may have threatened them or wished them harm.

TABLE 5.3

Percentage of students ages 12–18 who reported the presence of street gangs at school, by selected characteristics and perceptions of conditions at school, 1995 and 1999

Student characteristics and perceptions of conditions at school	1995 Number of students (thousands)	1995 Street gangs at school Yes (percent)	No (percent)	Do not know (percent)	Not ascertained (percent)	1999 Number of students (thousands)	1999 Street gangs at school Yes (percent)	No (percent)	Do not know (percent)	Not ascertained (percent)
Total	23,601	28.4	57.2	13.4	1.0	24,614	17.3	62.9	15.9	3.9
Characteristics										
Student sex										
Male	12,142	28.9	57.6	12.5	1.0	12,631	17.5	64.0	14.2	4.2
Female	11,459	27.8	56.8	14.5	0.9	11,983	17.1	61.8	17.6	3.5
Student race/ethnicity										
White, non-Hispanic	16,196	23.0	63.1	13.1	0.8	16,211	13.1	68.8	14.6	3.4
Black, non-Hispanic	3,652	34.8	49.4	14.0	1.8	3,826	24.7	51.6	18.3	5.4
Hispanic	2,829	49.7	36.4	12.9	0.9	3,450	28.3	48.9	18.5	4.3
Other, non-Hispanic	924	31.5	48.3	19.0	1.3	1,127	17.9	59.9	18.0	4.2
Student grade										
6th	2,312	15.7	67.8	14.7	1.7	2,109	9.2	70.5	16.3	4.0
7th	3,736	26.5	57.2	15.4	0.9	4,040	12.0	67.7	16.1	4.3
8th	3,784	28.8	58.8	11.9	0.4	4,032	12.9	68.6	14.2	4.3
9th	3,678	32.4	51.4	15.1	1.1	3,838	22.7	56.4	17.2	3.7
10th	3,654	33.6	52.7	12.7	1.0	3,677	22.1	57.4	16.8	3.7
11th	3,422	30.3	57.4	11.5	0.7	3,586	19.6	61.4	15.9	3.1
12th	2,737	27.3	58.1	13.5	1.1	3,332	20.0	60.9	14.9	4.2
Other	277	15.9	73.1	8.4	†	–	–	–	–	–
Student household income										
Less than $7,500	1,432	38.9	44.3	15.8	1.0	985	21.3	62.1	13.5	3.1
$7,500–9,999	761	30.5	45.8	20.2	3.4	468	17.3	58.0	17.1	7.6
$10,000–14,999	1,635	30.9	53.5	15.3	0.3	1,413	23.2	53.4	17.3	6.1
$15,000–24,999	3,087	30.0	54.8	13.7	1.5	2,848	23.4	55.2	17.8	3.6
$25,000–29,999	1,689	30.2	58.0	11.0	0.9	1,358	18.0	62.1	14.2	5.7
$30,000–49,999	6,206	27.6	58.5	13.2	0.6	5,511	17.2	62.8	16.0	3.9
$50,000 or more	6,529	24.6	61.7	13.0	0.7	8,534	13.2	69.1	14.8	2.8
Not ascertained	2,263	28.5	58.3	11.7	1.5	3,496	18.4	59.4	17.3	4.9
Student place of residence										
Urban	6,208	40.5	43.5	15.0	1.1	6,541	25.1	50.6	19.1	5.2
Suburban	11,209	26.3	59.8	13.2	0.7	12,936	15.8	65.3	15.9	3.0
Rural	6,185	19.9	66.4	12.4	1.3	5,138	11.1	72.6	11.7	4.6
Student school type										
Public	21,400	30.6	54.4	14.2	0.8	22,232	18.6	60.7	16.9	3.8
Private	2,150	6.8	86.6	6.3	†	2,372	4.4	84.3	6.3	5.0
Not ascertained	51	†	17.5	†	73.6	11	†	†	†	†
Perceptions of conditions at school										
Student reports of any victimization at school[1]										
Yes	3,456	41.3	46.6	11.6	0.5	21,488	26.1	55.7	15.2	3.0
No	20,013	26.3	59.4	13.8	0.4	3,008	16.1	64.2	16.0	3.6
Not ascertained	133	†	†	†	89.5	119	†	23.1	†	70.2
Student reports of violent victimization at school[2]										
Yes	1,002	50.5	36.9	11.6	1.1	23,445	36.3	43.8	18.3	1.6
No	22,460	27.5	58.5	13.6	0.4	988	16.4	63.8	15.8	4.0
Not ascertained	140	†	7.8	†	84.9	182	21.3	58.4	15.9	4.4
Student reports of property victimization at school[3]										
Yes	2,757	39.7	48.6	11.4	0.3	22,611	25.4	57.8	14.3	2.5
No	20,685	27.0	58.8	13.8	0.4	1,895	16.6	63.4	16.0	4.0
Not ascertained	159	4.9	9.6	6.5	79.0	109	22.3	57.2	14.9	†
Student reports of knowing a student who brought a gun to school										
Yes	2,989	55.2	35.0	9.5	0.4	1,847	45.1	38.5	13.7	2.7
No	20,332	24.6	60.9	14.1	0.4	22,566	15.0	65.2	16.1	3.6
Not ascertained	280	13.5	29.2	10.8	46.4	202	14.0	28.7	13.4	43.9

TABLE 5.3

Percentage of students ages 12–18 who reported the presence of street gangs at school, by selected characteristics and perceptions of conditions at school, 1995 and 1999 [CONTINUED]

Student characteristics and perceptions of conditions at school	1995					1999				
	Number of students (thousands)	Street gangs at school				Number of students (thousands)	Street gangs at school			
		Yes (percent)	No (percent)	Do not know (percent)	Not ascertained (percent)		Yes (percent)	No (percent)	Do not know (percent)	Not ascertained (percent)
Student reports of seeing a student with a gun at school										
Yes	1,247	63.6	30.0	6.4	†	690	58.0	29.4	9.9	2.6
No	22,053	26.5	59.2	13.8	0.4	23,743	16.1	64.2	16.1	3.6
Do not know	41	25.1	35.7	33.6	†	27	†	26.1	47.0	†
Not ascertained	261	16.4	24.8	9.8	49.0	155	13.7	27.4	†	55.6

– Data were not collected.
† Too few sample cases.
[1] Any victimization is a combination of violent and property victimization. If the student reported an incident of either, he or she is counted as having experienced any victimization. If the respondent reported having experienced both, he or she is counted once under the "any victimization" category. Any victimization includes those cases that can be allocated to either the violent or property categories as well as those that can not.
[2] Violent victimization includes physical attack or taking property from the student directly by force, weapons, or threats, rape, sexual assault, robbery, aggravated assault, and simple assault.
[3] Property victimization includes theft of a student's property at school.
Note: Detail may not sum to totals and percentages may not sum to 100 percent due to rounding and too few cases for reliable estimates.

SOURCE: Lynn A. Addington, Sally A. Ruddy, Amanda K. Miller, and Jill F. DeVoe, "Table 8. Percentage of students ages 12–18 who reported the presence of street gangs at school, by selected characteristics and perceptions of conditions at school: 1995 and 1999," in *Are America's Schools Safe? Students Speak Out: 1999 School Crime Supplement*, U.S. Department of Education, National Center for Education Statistics, Washington, DC, 2002

GANG CRIME AND VIOLENCE

Homicides

According to the NYGS, from 1999 to 2000 at least one gang-related homicide was reported in 91 percent of cities with populations of 250,000 or more; 64 percent of cities with populations between 100,000 and 200,000; 55 percent of cities with populations between 50,000 and 100,000; and 32 percent of cities with between 25,000 and 50,000 residents. Among all cities surveyed, 47 percent reported an increase in gang homicides from 1999 to 2000. Cities with the highest rate of gang homicides included Chicago and Los Angeles.

In the 2001 NYGS, researchers noted that many cities with gang problems continued to experience gang-related murders in 2001. In cities with a population of 100,000 or more, 69 percent reported such deaths. Some 37 percent of cities averaging 50,000 to 99,999 people experienced gang-related deaths. In Los Angeles and Chicago, 698 deaths were attributed to gangs. This figure, according to the NYGS, "was greater than the total number of gang-related homicides (637) reported by 130 other gang-problem cities with a population of 100,000 or more." Gang-related deaths comprised more than half of all murders reported in Los Angeles and Chicago.

HOMICIDE TRENDS. "The number of youth gang homicides declined in the 1990s, but the trends varied by city and also varied between the early and later parts of the decade," according to the OJJDP report "Youth Gang Homicides in the 1990's" (March 2001). From 1990 to

1996 the total number of homicides decreased by 256 (almost 15 percent) in the 408 cities surveyed, from 1,748 to 1,492 incidents. A decrease was reported by 32 percent of the cities, an increase was recorded by 29 percent, and 39 percent reported no change. The authors concluded that gang homicides were a serious problem in the early part of the decade for three reasons: nearly 30 percent of the 256-homicide decrease occurred in Los Angeles, the number of cities with decreases was counterbalanced by the number of cities with increases, and many cities reported no change.

Between 1996 and 1998, 237 cities of 1,216 surveyed (19 percent) reported gang homicides in all three years (1,293 in 1996, 1,260 in 1997, and 1,061 in 1998—an 18 percent decrease over the period). Los Angeles and Chicago were conspicuous for their high numbers of gang homicides (totaling 173 and 180, respectively), but Los Angeles reported a 41 percent decrease and Chicago reported a 19 percent decrease over the period. Almost half (49 percent) of the 237 cities reported a decrease in gang homicides, 36 percent reported an increase, and 15 percent reported no change. The fact that more cities reported a decrease is attributed to gang violence prevention efforts by law enforcement and social services agencies.

As noted in *Homicide Trends in the United States* (James Alan Fox and Marianne W. Zawitz, U.S. Department of Justice, Bureau of Justice Statistics, Washington, DC, 2001), between 1976 and 1999, gang-related homicides were most often committed by white offenders (56.6 percent) followed by black offenders (39.3 percent).

Homicide victims of gang-related violence were most often white (58.1 percent), while blacks (38.4 percent) represented more than a third of the victims.

Concerning gangs and violence, the *2002 National Victim Assistance Academy Textbook* notes that "youthful gang members have 'no fear of death' and often how they die is what is important in gang dynamics. This factor contributes to retaliatory gang violence and criminal acts that are increasingly violent in nature."

Crime

Twenty-seven percent of all jurisdictions participating in the 1998 NYGS said that most or all of their gangs were involved in drug sales. This represented 30 percent of suburban county, 28 percent of large city, 26 percent of rural county, and 20 percent of small city jurisdictions. Overall, 17 percent of jurisdictions reported most of their gangs as being involved in larceny/theft, while 13 percent listed high gang involvement in burglary/breaking and entering. Rural jurisdictions reported the highest percentages in these areas: 21 percent for burglary/breaking and entering and 19 percent for larceny-theft. As noted in the NYGS for 1998: "Clearly, serious youth gang crimes are no longer concentrated only in the Nation's large cities."

Survey participants were also asked how often gangs in their areas were involved in certain types of criminal activity: aggravated assault, robbery, burglary/breaking and entering, motor vehicle theft, larceny/theft, and drug sales. Jurisdictions in the West reported the highest percentage of gangs involved in aggravated assault (18 percent) and motor vehicle theft (16 percent), while the Southern gangs topped the charts in larceny/theft (22 percent) and burglary/breaking and entering (19 percent). Northeast gangs scored highest in the drug sales category at 33 percent, followed closely by the Midwest (32 percent) and the South (31 percent).

When it comes to crime and punishment, gang members have learned to "work the system." According to the *2002 National Victim Assistance Academy Textbook*:

> Experience shows that incapacitation of individual gang members is not sufficient to control gang crime because removing individuals does not diminish the influence of the gang on the street. In addition, gangs have learned the procedural differences between juvenile and adult court and have used these to their advantage. Since gangs consist of both juvenile and adult members, many gangs have come to use juveniles extensively in the commission of crimes. This ensures lenient penalties for adjudicated juvenile offenders.

VICTIMIZATION IN INDIAN COUNTRY. The *2002 National Victim Assistance Academy Textbook* had this to say about Native Americans and crime: "Incidence of gang-related victimization in Indian Country is small but growing. It is difficult to stop due to isolation, drug influ-ence, and lack of alternative activities. In addition, when juveniles go to adult prison or youth detention facilities, they may learn gang activity there and bring it back to tribal lands."

DRUGS. According to the 1998 NYGS, 34 percent of its participating jurisdictions noted the presence of youth drug gangs. The term "drug gangs" was used to refer to those gangs "organized specifically for the purpose of traf-ficking in drugs." Although 300 jurisdictions reported no drug gangs, 99 asserted that 100 percent of their gangs were involved in drugs. Contrary to popular belief, the largest percentage of jurisdictions reporting drug gangs was not large cities (35 percent). Instead, rural counties claimed the highest percentage (38 percent), with subur-ban counties (31 percent) scoring higher than small cities (25 percent). However, the number of drug gangs in cities (3,082) far outweighed the number in rural counties (135).

The percentage of jurisdictions reporting drug gangs was highest in the Northeast (60 percent) and Midwest (46 percent) and lowest in the South (41 percent) and West (18 percent). In actual numbers, the South led in the number of youth gangs (1,753), compared to the Midwest (1,253), West (999), and Northeast (463).

CASE STUDIES

Big City Gangs

Details about gangs are often hard to obtain for vari-ous reasons. At times, it may be difficult for law enforce-ment to ascertain if a crime was gang related or not. When investigating the motivations behind a crime, police may suspect gang involvement but not be able to prove it. Also, gang members themselves are difficult to survey. Some may not want to participate at all while others may over- or underreport their activities and involvement. These are among the challenges that researchers need to overcome when conducting their studies.

Two studies conducted in 1995 revealed important details about gang involvement. Some of the findings, presented here for historical purposes, illuminate the dif-ferences between gang members themselves and those at risk to become gang members. One of the studies was funded by the OJJDP, the other by the National Institute of Justice (NIJ). In the studies, 50 gang members were interviewed in four communities: Aurora, Colorado; Den-ver, Colorado; Broward County, Florida; and Cleveland, Ohio. As a control, researchers also interviewed 50 youths from each area who represented the at-risk population, but who were not gang members. The results of the one-time, confidential interviews indicated that gang members were significantly more involved in crime than nonmembers.

The principal investigator of the NIJ study, Dr. C. Ronald Huff of Ohio State University, noted that 58 per-cent of Colorado and Florida gang members and 45 percent of Cleveland gang members acknowledged that they had personally stolen cars. The control group youths self-reported a much lower car theft rate. In Colorado and Florida, that rate was 12.5 percent, and in Cleveland it was 4 percent. The studies also asked about drive-by shootings. Researchers learned that 40 percent of Cleveland gang members claimed to have participated in a drive-by, compared to 2 percent of those in the control group. Among Colorado and Florida gang members, 64 percent acknowledged that members of their gangs had committed homicide. That number was far less among control-group members, 6.5 percent of whom reported that their friends had killed someone.

On the subject of guns, gang members were much more likely than nonmembers to own guns. In the study communities, more than 90 percent of gang members stated that their peers had carried concealed weapons and another 80 percent admitted that members had taken guns to school. About half of the control-group members had friends who had carried a concealed weapon, while one-third acknowledged that friends had taken guns to school.

Drug trafficking was much higher among gang members than at-risk youth. More than 70 percent of gang members reported selling drugs, while 6 to 9 percent of control-group youth said they had sold drugs.

Juveniles in Gangs

A study conducted in Seattle, Washington, tracked juveniles over the course of several years to learn more about their involvement in gang-related activities. Those findings are detailed in "Early Precursors of Gang Membership: A Study of Seattle Youth" (Karl G. Hill, Christina Lui, and J. David Hawkins, *Juvenile Justice Bulletin,* Office of Juvenile Justice and Delinquency Prevention, Washington, DC, December 2001). During the multi-year study, researchers tracked a group of 808 fifth-graders through age 18. They learned that more than 15 percent (124 students) joined a gang between the ages of 13 and 18. Of those joining gangs, about 69 percent stayed in a gang for less than one year; less than 1 percent of study participants who joined a gang at age 13 were still in a gang at age 18.

Those who stayed in a gang for several years, according to researchers, "were the most behaviorally and socially maladjusted children," often exhibiting "early signs of violent externalizing such as aggression and hyperactivity." Those associating with antisocial peers were more than twice as likely to remain in a gang for more than one year. The National Victim Assistance Academy reported in 2001 that gangs were starting to recruit younger members, sometimes as young as seven years old.

In the study, researchers also identified various risk factors potentially leading to gang involvement. These include having a learning disability, access to marijuana, low academic achievement, other youth in trouble living in the neighborhood, and a living arrangement that includes one parent along with other unrelated adults.

GANG LOITERING

Court Rulings on Gang Loitering

To combat the rise in violent and drug-related crime, which was attributed to a rise in criminal street gang activity, the city of Chicago enacted a Gang Congregation Ordinance in 1992. The ordinance prohibited "criminal street gang members from loitering with one another or with other persons in any public place," regardless of whether the others were fellow gang members. Police officers were required to order any group of people standing around "with no apparent purpose" to move along if the officers believed at least one of them belonged to a street gang. The ordinance had considerable support in the high-crime neighborhoods in which it was implemented. During the three years the law was in effect, more than 42,000 people were arrested for refusing to obey police orders to move along. In 2001 the ordinance was struck down when the U.S. Supreme Court agreed with a lower court that the ordinance was unconstitutionally vague and encompassed a great deal of harmless behavior (*Chicago v. Morales* [No. 97-1121]).

CONSEQUENCES OF BEING IN A GANG

Being in a gang can be dangerous. Former gangbangers can tell many stories about the difficulties one encounters in gang life. In addition to living a life with the potential for more violence and crime than the average youth would experience, many other consequences exist. Although such consequences might vary considerably among individuals, some of the most commonly encountered consequences follow:

- Becoming a school dropout
- Having little opportunity to secure a good, legal job
- Being unable to hold a steady job
- Becoming antisocial; having difficulty socializing outside the gang
- Having an increased likelihood of being a victim of violent crime
- Entering motherhood or fatherhood at an early age
- Ending up in prison or jail for gang crimes
- Developing a dependency on drugs and/or alcohol
- Experiencing a higher risk of premature death

CHAPTER 6
CRIME AND PUNISHMENT

Whether juveniles should be confined in prisons or jails for committing certain crimes has long been debated in the United States. The practice of trying juveniles as adults and holding convicted children in prison for life without parole are topics that evoke emotion from politicians, social reformers, and the public alike. Various people believe that juveniles who commit adult crimes should do adult time in prison or jail while others assert that confining juveniles with hardened adult convicts ensures that the youthful offender will become a hardened adult criminal too.

JUVENILE JUSTICE IN THE UNITED STATES

How old does someone have to be to understand right from wrong? Throughout the history of the United States, that question has proven difficult to answer. In the late 1700s, the public view was that children age seven or less were incapable of criminal intent. As such, they could not be punished as adults. Accordingly, in some cases, violent children were left to inflict their crimes on others in society until they reached the age when they could be punished legally. Even today many Americans continue to believe that young children are not capable of criminal intent. The idea is that young children are still developing their minds and learning the difference between right and wrong.

In the nineteenth century, as Americans continued to study the problems of youth violence and crime, a movement began based on European educational reform ideas from the sixteenth century. Many people began to view older juveniles as individuals who had not fully developed their cognitive capabilities, rather than as individuals who were "miniature adults." This movement had an impact on the U.S. prison and jail systems and juveniles were separated from adult offenders in many major U.S. city facilities.

Advent of Juvenile Courts

As the methods used for confining juvenile criminals continued to evolve, the state of Illinois passed the Juve-nile Court Act of 1899. This legislation created the first juvenile court, which was located in Cook County in northeast Illinois. The idea of such a court was based on "parens patriae," meaning "state as parent," a British doctrine. The act allowed the state to treat juvenile criminals differently from its adult offenders—it permitted the state to intervene in the lives of juveniles. In that era, the new juvenile justice system was intended to focus on the welfare of the delinquent child. It was to provide the child with the "benevolent intervention" that such a system could offer when parents failed to give their youngsters proper care and supervision. The system aimed to provide treatment and rehabilitation so that the juvenile could one day become a productive member of society.

The idea caught on in other states. Similar juvenile justice systems were operating in most states by 1925 and held exclusive jurisdiction over youthful offenders. The juvenile courts considered various factors far beyond those addressed with adult offenders. Juvenile courts examined legal factors as well as nonlegal circumstances, such as schooling and home environment conditions. Emphasizing an atmosphere of rehabilitation rather than punishment, juvenile courts were less formal in their approach than adult courts. A youth could only be tried in an adult court if the juvenile court waived its jurisdiction in the case.

Yet the success of the juvenile justice system came under attack again and again as the problems of youth violence and crime continued. In the 1950s and 1960s, for example, people questioned whether the system could really reform and rehabilitate young criminals. The rehabilitation techniques used on juvenile offenders had failed to show a uniformly effective result. Concerned citizens and politicians pointed to the population of juveniles being institutionalized indefinitely while supposedly being "reformed." That group, they said, was continuing to grow in number. More and more juveniles were being detained until adulthood because such rehabilitative treatments did not appear to be changing the offenders' deviant behaviors.

Changes to the Juvenile Court System

Following a number of U.S. Supreme Court cases, the juvenile court changed. It adopted a more formal approach in protecting juveniles' rights in waiver situations or if juveniles were to be confined. The court continued to evolve after the passage of the Juvenile Delinquency Prevention and Control Act of 1968. Through the act, Congress recommended changes be made to how "status offenders" were handled in the system. Such status offenders were youths who had not committed criminal crimes but were guilty of lesser acts, such as running away from home, being truant from school, or being "incorrigibles." The act called for status offenders to be handled outside of the juvenile court system in the future.

In response to continued concerns about juvenile crime, Congress passed the Juvenile Justice and Delinquency Prevention Act in 1974. It deemed that juvenile detainees should be separated from adults. To discourage institutionalization, community-based programs were further developed and expanded. When the act was amended in 1980, it mandated that juveniles be removed from adult jails.

RESPONSE TO CLAIMS THE SYSTEM IS TOO LENIENT. In the 1980s many citizens came to believe that the system had gotten too lenient. Serious juvenile crime appeared to be growing and the system, they thought, was not doing enough to combat the problem. According to Howard N. Snyder and Melissa Sickmund in *Juvenile Offenders and Victims: 1999 National Report* (U.S. Department of Justice, Washington, DC), this view centered on a "substantial misperception regarding increases in juvenile crime." In an effort to appease voters, state legislatures took various approaches:

> Some laws removed certain classes of offenders from the juvenile justice system and handled them as adult criminals in criminal court. Others required the juvenile justice system to be more like the criminal justice system and to treat certain classes of juvenile offenders as criminals but in juvenile court.
>
> As a result, offenders charged with certain offenses are *excluded* from juvenile court jurisdiction or face *mandatory* or *automatic waiver* to criminal court. In some States, concurrent jurisdiction provisions give prosecutors the discretion to file certain juvenile cases directly in criminal court.... In some States, some adjudicated juvenile offenders face *mandatory sentences.*

Efforts to exclude certain serious offenses from juvenile court jurisdiction continued into the 1990s. This meant that if juveniles committed certain serious crimes, they could be tried legally as adults. Whether a juvenile could be tried as an adult in certain states was determined solely by that state's prosecutor.

Laws were changed in the District of Columbia and in 47 states between 1992 and 1997. The result was the creation of an era when juvenile offenders were incarcerated at historically high rates. Only three states—Nebraska, New York, and Vermont—made no changes.

In "Juvenile Justice: A Century of Change" (*1999 National Report Series,* Office of Juvenile Justice and Delinquency Prevention, Washington, DC), the authors discuss the stricter laws that were enacted for dealing with juvenile offenders in the 1990s. They cite the areas most affected by the new, harsher laws as:

- Confidentiality—modifying or removing traditional juvenile court rules relating to confidentiality by making records and proceedings more open; adopted in 46 states

- Sentencing authority—giving criminal and juvenile courts expanded sentencing options; adopted in 31 states

- Transfer provisions—making it easier to transfer juvenile offenders to the jurisdiction of the adult criminal justice system; adopted by 45 states

- Correctional programming—allowing for the development of new detention programs for certain adult offenders and for juveniles transferred to the adult justice system

- Victims' rights—increasing the role of victims of juvenile crime in the juvenile justice system

Also, the juvenile codes in many states were amended so that juveniles are held more accountable for their crimes and are given punishments that are more in keeping with the nature or seriousness of their offenses.

According to Nancy E. Gist, director of the Bureau of Justice Assistance, most states since 1992 "have passed or amended legislation making it easier to prosecute juveniles as adults. The result is that the number of youth under 18 confined in adult prisons has more than doubled in the past decade. This phenomenon is challenging the belief, enshrined in our justice system a century ago, that children and young adolescents should be adjudicated and confined in a separate system focused on their rehabilitation." Gist's statement, made in 2003, reveals that the debate surrounding juvenile justice continues today.

WHO IS CONSIDERED A JUVENILE?

Juvenile court generally has original jurisdiction in cases involving youth who were under age 18 when the crime was committed, the youth was arrested, or the offender was referred to the court. In 1999 the majority of states (37) and the District of Columbia considered the oldest age for juveniles to be 17, according to Howard N. Snyder and Melissa Sickmund in *Juvenile Offenders and Victims: 1999 National Report* (U.S. Department of

Justice, Washington, DC). Ten other states—Georgia, Illinois, Louisiana, Massachusetts, Michigan, Missouri, New Hampshire, South Carolina, Texas, and Wisconsin—use 16. In Connecticut, New York, and North Carolina, the age is set at 15.

When youth crime surged in the 1980s, many citizens called for legislation to lower the maximum age at which children are considered juveniles. This meant that some older juvenile offenders would not fall under the jurisdiction of juvenile courts; instead, more and more would be tried as adults. Even though the youth crime rate has gone down since that time, states are reluctant to increase the maximum age.

According to the Office of Juvenile Justice and Delinquency Prevention's (OJJDP) Web site in 2003, most states have retained juvenile court jurisdiction over offenders 17 and younger. Older teens are considered to be adults. An agency within the U.S. Department of Justice, the OJJDP is an important source for data on trends and events in the juvenile justice system.

If the court deems that it is in the interests of the juvenile and the public, juvenile courts in some states may retain jurisdiction over juvenile offenders past the ages discussed earlier. Thus, such courts can handle juvenile offenders until they turn 20 in Alabama, Florida, Idaho, Michigan, New Mexico, Washington, and some 27 other jurisdictions, including the District of Columbia. According to *Juvenile Offenders and Victims,* Kansas uses age 22, while California, Montana, Oregon, and Wisconsin use 24 as the cutoff. In Colorado, Hawaii, and New Jersey, someone can remain under juvenile court jurisdiction until the term of the disposition order has ended.

Extended jurisdiction, however, may be limited by legislation to specific crimes or certain juveniles. Hence, the question of who is considered a juvenile does not have one consistent, standard answer. In various states, exceptions can be made to the age criteria. This is done so that juveniles can be tried as adults or to provide for procedures under which a prosecutor can decide whether to handle the offender as a juvenile or an adult.

Some states also acknowledge minimum ages for juvenile courts. Eleven states use age 10, while Arizona sets 8 as the cutoff. Maryland, Massachusetts, and New York observe age 7, while North Carolina uses age 6.

JUVENILE ARREST TRENDS

Since the 1980s, during the years that tougher legislation was enacted against youthful offenders, juveniles ages 0 to 17 declined from 28 percent of the total U.S. population to 25 percent of the population as of 2001, per the U.S. Bureau of the Census. That proportion is expected to decline even further by 2010 to 24 percent.

More specifically, the 10- to 17-year-old age group declined as a proportion of the total U.S. population during that time period. In 1980 the group numbered 13,482 per 100,000 people and dropped to 10,928 per 100,000 by 1990. In 2000 it had increased to 11,540 in 100,000 people, but had ultimately experienced a decrease of 1,942 per 100,000 during that 20-year span.

Because the number of juvenile crimes increased during that time, then tapered off to a degree, juvenile arrests and incarceration trends cannot be said to merely reflect the decreasing population of teenagers. Instead, a combination of factors is responsible for the crime increases, including a change in behavior by some juveniles and the resultant reaction of legislators and law enforcement officials to combat those behaviors.

According to statistics maintained by the Federal Bureau of Investigation (FBI) during that same time period, 1980–2000, the property and violent crime arrest rate for juveniles ages 10 to 17 began to rise during the 1980s. As recorded in the FBI's Property Crime Index and its Violent Crime Index, arrests per 100,000 juveniles in that age bracket decreased for both property and violent crime from around 1980 to 1983. At that point, property crime arrests began a gradual increase while violent crime started to surge in the late 1980s. Around 1995 arrest rates for both property crime and violent acts began to decrease, with violent crimes seeing the greatest reductions.

In fact, from 1994 to 2000, property crime index offenses among juveniles dropped 37 percent, per Howard N. Snyder in "Juvenile Arrests 2000" (*Juvenile Justice Bulletin,* U.S. Department of Justice, Office of Justice Programs, Office of Juvenile Justice and Delinquency Prevention, Washington, DC, November 2002). The violent crime index arrest rate for juveniles peaked in 1994, then decreased 41 percent by 2000.

As reported in *Crime in the United States 2002: Uniform Crime Reports* (Federal Bureau of Investigation, U.S. Department of Justice, Washington, DC, 2003), some 13.7 million arrests were made in 2002. That was an increase of 0.5 percent from 2001. Overall, in 2002 adults represented 83.5 percent of all arrests. That means that 16.5 percent of all arrests were among juveniles under age 18. Compared to 2001, total adult arrests increased 1.2 percent in 2002, while juvenile arrests decreased 3 percent. Nationwide, the total arrest rate was 4,783.4 arrests per 100,000 people.

Ten-year arrest trends are recorded in Table 6.1, compiled by the FBI. The number of juveniles under 18 years of age arrested between 1993 and 2002 decreased from 1.56 million to 1.39 million, or 10.9 percent. The change in arrest rates for those 18 years of age and older amounted to less than one-tenth of 1 percent. With the

TABLE 6.1

Ten-year arrest trends, 1993–2002

[7,596 agencies; 2002 estimated population 175,384,794; 1993 estimated population 157,011,564]

	Number of persons arrested								
	Total all ages			Under 18 years of age			18 years of age and over		
Offense charged	1993	2002	Percent change	1993	2002	Percent change	1993	2002	Percent change
Total[1]	8,581,290	8,413,983	-1.9	1,564,326	1,393,752	-10.9	7,016,964	7,020,231	*
Murder and nonnegligent manslaughter	15,125	8,933	-40.9	2,485	886	-64.3	12,640	8,047	-36.3
Forcible rape	23,509	17,394	-26.0	3,928	2,887	-26.5	19,581	14,507	-25.9
Robbery	96,877	69,405	-28.4	26,505	16,338	-38.4	70,372	53,067	-24.6
Aggravated assault	320,814	299,286	-6.7	49,427	38,082	-23.0	271,387	261,204	-3.8
Burglary	253,751	178,477	-29.7	89,511	54,393	-39.2	164,240	124,084	-24.4
Larceny-theft	959,452	729,825	-23.9	307,926	216,434	-29.7	651,526	513,391	-21.2
Motor vehicle theft	128,552	94,608	-26.4	57,740	28,664	-50.4	70,812	65,944	-6.9
Arson	12,646	10,055	-20.5	6,451	4,957	-23.2	6,195	5,098	-17.7
Violent crime[2]	456,325	395,018	-13.4	82,345	58,193	-29.3	373,980	336,825	-9.9
Property crime[3]	1,354,401	1,012,965	-25.2	461,628	304,448	-34.0	892,773	708,517	-20.6
Crime Index[4]	1,810,726	1,407,983	-22.2	543,973	362,641	-33.3	1,266,753	1,045,342	-17.5
Other assaults	733,037	782,294	+6.7	126,489	143,933	+13.8	606,548	638,361	+5.2
Forgery and counterfeiting	66,364	71,842	+8.3	5,341	3,070	-42.5	61,023	68,772	+12.7
Fraud	218,695	195,925	-10.4	6,449	5,258	-18.5	212,246	190,667	-10.2
Embezzlement	7,910	11,815	+49.4	510	883	+73.1	7,400	10,932	+47.7
Stolen property; buying, receiving, possession	101,613	76,137	-25.1	28,808	15,766	-45.3	72,805	60,371	-17.1
Vandalism	209,095	169,842	-18.8	97,968	65,360	-33.3	111,127	104,482	-6.0
Weapons; carrying, possessing, etc.	175,998	104,418	-40.7	42,530	22,615	-46.8	133,468	81,803	-38.7
Prostitution and commercialized vice	61,811	51,275	-17.0	755	958	+26.9	61,056	50,317	-17.6
Sex offenses (except forcible rape and prostitution)	69,072	59,193	-14.3	13,387	12,198	-8.9	55,685	46,995	-15.6
Drug abuse violations	710,922	974,082	+37.0	73,413	116,781	+59.1	637,509	857,301	+34.5
Gambling	10,348	6,500	-37.2	1,715	1,053	-38.6	8,633	5,447	-36.9
Offenses against the family and children	67,930	79,059	+16.4	3,520	5,208	+48.0	64,410	73,851	+14.7
Driving under the influence	984,141	879,210	-10.7	8,878	12,921	+45.5	975,263	866,289	-11.2
Liquor laws	316,919	385,611	+21.7	75,836	88,574	+16.8	241,083	297,037	+23.2
Drunkenness	509,543	362,979	-28.8	11,705	11,452	-2.2	497,838	351,527	-29.4
Disorderly conduct	483,676	398,728	-17.6	103,747	112,844	+8.8	379,929	285,884	-24.8
Vagrancy	13,581	15,702	+15.6	2,254	1,346	-40.3	11,327	14,356	+26.7
All other offenses (except traffic)	1,834,511	2,209,668	+20.4	221,650	239,171	+7.9	1,612,861	1,970,497	+22.2
Suspicion	6,231	2,252	-63.9	1,239	708	-42.9	4,992	1,544	-69.1
Curfew and loitering law violations	68,042	91,984	+35.2	68,042	91,984	+35.2	–	–	–
Runaways	127,356	79,736	-37.4	127,356	79,736	-37.4	–	–	–

[1]Does not include suspicion.
[2]Violent crimes are offenses of murder, forcible rape, robbery, and aggravated assault.
[3]Property crimes are offenses of burglary, larceny-theft, motor vehicle theft, and arson.
[4]Includes arson.
*Less than one-tenth of 1 percent.

SOURCE: "Table 32. Ten-year arrest trends: 1993–2002," in *Crime in the United States 2002: Uniform Crime Reports*, Federal Bureau of Investigation, Washington, DC, 2003

reduction in juvenile arrests, total arrest rates were down 1.9 percent between 1993 and 2002.

The crimes experiencing the greatest percentage reductions among juveniles between 1993 and 2002 included murder and nonnegligent manslaughter (64.3 percent); motor vehicle theft (50.4 percent); weapons carrying/possession (46.8 percent); buying, receiving, or possessing stolen property (45.3 percent); forgery and counterfeiting (42.5 percent); and vagrancy (40.3 percent). (See Table 6.1.) The number of runaways also saw a reduction—37.4 percent. The largest percentage gains were for embezzlement (73.1 percent), drug abuse violations (59.1 percent), offenses against family and children (48.0 percent), driving under the influence (45.5 percent),

curfew and loitering law violations (35.2 percent), and prostitution and commercialized vice (26.9 percent).

In terms of actual number of offenses, the greatest reductions of juvenile arrests were in larceny-theft (91,492), runaways (47,620), and burglary (35,118). (See Table 6.1.) The greatest gains were in drug abuse violations (43,368), curfew and loitering law violations (23,942), and other assaults (17,444).

Arrests Among Specific Age Groups

Crime in the United States 2002: Uniform Crime Reports also records arrest rate statistics for specific age groups—under 15, under 18, under 21, and under 25—in Table 6.2. Such statistics point out crimes that people

TABLE 6.2

Arrests of persons under 15, 18, 21, and 25 years of age, 2002

[10,372 agencies; 2002 estimated population 205,122,185]

Offense charged	Total all ages	Number of persons arrested				Percent of total all ages			
		Under 15	Under 18	Under 21	Under 25	Under 15	Under 18	Under 21	Under 25
Total	9,819,501	510,226	1,624,192	3,077,565	4,556,104	5.2	16.5	31.3	46.4
Murder and nonnegligent manslaughter	10,107	101	973	2,915	5,161	1.0	9.6	28.8	51.1
Forcible rape	20,162	1,243	3,361	6,324	9,302	6.2	16.7	31.4	46.1
Robbery	77,342	4,323	17,893	34,409	47,460	5.6	23.1	44.5	61.4
Aggravated assault	339,437	15,846	44,281	82,137	133,400	4.7	13.0	24.2	39.3
Burglary	206,136	22,389	61,843	100,886	129,124	10.9	30.0	48.9	62.6
Larceny-theft	845,009	95,090	248,861	378,668	475,903	11.3	29.5	44.8	56.3
Motor vehicle theft	107,187	8,227	32,544	52,623	68,394	7.7	30.4	49.1	63.8
Arson	11,833	3,728	5,851	7,108	8,022	31.5	49.4	60.1	67.8
Violent crime[1]	447,048	21,513	66,508	125,785	195,323	4.8	14.9	28.1	43.7
Property crime[2]	1,170,165	129,434	349,099	539,285	681,443	11.1	29.8	46.1	58.2
Crime Index[3]	1,617,213	150,947	415,607	665,070	876,766	9.3	25.7	41.1	54.2
Other assaults	921,676	71,697	168,996	261,254	390,153	7.8	18.3	28.3	42.3
Forgery and counterfeiting	83,111	457	3,652	15,737	30,841	0.5	4.4	18.9	37.1
Fraud	233,087	1,178	6,434	29,905	66,714	0.5	2.8	12.8	28.6
Embezzlement	13,416	90	1,005	3,581	5,887	0.7	7.5	26.7	43.9
Stolen property; buying, receiving, possessing	91,280	5,044	18,819	36,064	50,878	5.5	20.6	39.5	55.7
Vandalism	198,550	32,888	75,955	108,498	134,926	16.6	38.3	54.6	68.0
Weapons; carrying, possessing, etc.	118,312	8,647	25,288	46,491	67,458	7.3	21.4	39.3	57.0
Prostitution and commercialized vice	58,758	165	1,095	6,259	13,818	0.3	1.9	10.7	23.5
Sex offenses (except forcible rape and prostitution)	67,833	7,226	13,877	21,313	29,049	10.7	20.5	31.4	42.8
Drug abuse violations	1,103,017	21,836	133,754	342,204	540,142	2.0	12.1	31.0	49.0
Gambling	7,525	171	1,114	2,496	3,845	2.3	14.8	33.2	51.1
Offenses against the family and children	97,716	2,442	6,572	13,227	25,566	2.5	6.7	13.5	26.2
Driving under the influence	1,020,377	370	15,214	110,849	294,898	*	1.5	10.9	28.9
Liquor laws	463,849	10,132	106,014	331,409	366,125	2.2	22.9	71.4	78.9
Drunkenness	413,808	1,679	13,529	53,504	116,051	0.4	3.3	12.9	28.0
Disorderly conduct	482,827	56,314	139,048	203,997	277,201	11.7	28.8	42.3	57.4
Vagrancy	19,678	402	1,519	3,325	5,294	2.0	7.7	16.9	26.9
All other offenses (except traffic)	2,606,294	76,025	282,025	626,786	1,063,824	2.9	10.8	24.0	40.8
Suspicion	7,670	294	1,171	2,092	3,164	3.8	15.3	27.3	41.3
Curfew and loitering law violations	103,155	29,070	103,155	103,155	103,155	28.2	100.0	100.0	100.0
Runaways	90,349	33,152	90,349	90,349	90,349	36.7	100.0	100.0	100.0

[1]Violent crimes are offenses of murder, forcible rape, robbery, and aggravated assault.
[2]Property crimes are offenses of burglary, larceny-theft, motor vehicle theft, and arson.
[3]Includes arson.
*Less than one-tenth of 1 percent.

SOURCE: "Table 41. Arrests of persons under 15, 18, 21, and 25 years of age, 2002," in *Crime in the United States 2002: Uniform Crime Reports*, Federal Bureau of Investigation, Washington, DC, 2003

under age 25 commit consistently, yet also reveal crimes more associated with juveniles than with older youths. The chart compares the number of arrests for those four age groups against the total number of arrests for all ages in 2002. For each offense, it presents the number of actual arrests for each age group as well as what percentage of total arrests falls within each age group.

A high percentage in Table 6.2 does not necessarily indicate a high number of arrests in a category. Instead, it means that age group was responsible for a high percentage of arrests within that category. For example, 133,754 individuals under 18 were arrested on drug abuse violations, which is 12.1 percent of the total arrests in that category. Compare that to the 18,819 persons under 18 arrested for buying, receiving, and possessing stolen prop-

erty. Although the number of stolen property offenses is far less than that of drug abuse violations for those under 18, it represents 20.6 percent of the total arrests for stolen property. Such percentages help law enforcement personnel identify trends and patterns in juvenile crime.

Two categories that consistently had high arrest percentages among each of the four age groups presented in Table 6.2 were arson and vandalism. Of the 11,833 total arrests for arson in 2002, more than two-thirds (67.8 percent) involved people under 25. The percentage of arson arrests dropped to 60.1 percent for those under 21, then to 49.4 percent for those under 18. The rate further decreased for those under 15 to 31.5 percent. Vandalism arrest percentages for individuals under age 25 also amounted to more than two-thirds of the total number of vandalism arrests in 2002. Of the 198,550 people arrested for vandalism in 2002, 68 percent were under age 25, 54.6 percent were under age 21, and 38.3 percent were under age 18. The number significantly decreased for those under age 15 (16.6 percent).

Other categories with the highest arrest percentages for those under 15 include: larceny-theft (11.3 percent), disorderly conduct (11.7 percent), burglary (10.9 percent), and sex offenses (except forcible rape and prostitution) (10.7 percent). (See Table 6.2.) The under-15 group also scored high in two other categories that are not applicable to those over age 18—curfew and loitering law violations and runaway arrests. For that age group, runaway arrests totaled 36.7 percent whereas curfew and loitering law violations reached 28.2 percent.

Arrest rate data also reveal the categories having the smallest percentage of arrests. Driving under the influence for those under age 15 amounted to less than one-tenth of one percent. (See Table 6.2.) Other crimes with low arrest rates for this group include prostitution and commercialized vice (0.3 percent), forgery and counterfeiting (0.5 percent), fraud (0.5 percent), and drunkenness (0.4 percent).

For those under age 18, other categories with the highest arrest percentages were motor vehicle theft (30.4 percent), burglary (30.0 percent), and larceny-theft (29.5 percent). (See Table 6.2.) The crimes with the lowest percentages of arrests of individuals under 18 include driving under the influence (1.5 percent), prostitution and commercialized vice (1.9 percent), fraud (2.8 percent), drunkenness (3.3 percent), and forgery and counterfeiting (4.4 percent).

Among those under age 21, the arrest percentages were highest for liquor law violations (71.4 percent) and also high for motor vehicle theft (49.1 percent), burglary (48.9 percent), larceny-theft (44.8 percent), and robbery (44.5 percent). (See Table 6.2.) The arrest percentages were lowest in prostitution and commercialized vice (10.7 percent), driving under the influence (10.9 percent), fraud (12.8 percent), drunkenness (12.9 percent), and offenses against the family and children (13.5 percent).

Many of the high arrest categories were the same for those under 25. (See Table 6.2.) The highest arrest percentages occurred in liquor law violations (78.9 percent), motor vehicle theft (63.8 percent), burglary (62.6 percent), and robbery (61.4 percent). The lowest arrest percentage categories for this age group were prostitution and commercialized vice (23.5 percent), driving under the influence (28.9 percent), fraud (28.6 percent), drunkenness (28.0 percent), vagrancy (26.9 percent), and offenses against the family and children (26.2 percent).

When studying the "under 25" category, note that this age group is responsible for nearly two-thirds of all arrests for robbery, burglary, motor vehicle theft, arson,

and vandalism. (See Table 6.2.) The group also claims four-fifths of all liquor law violations. More than half of all arrests for murder/nonnegligent manslaughter, larceny-theft, stolen property, weapons violations, gambling, and disorderly conduct are attributed to this group as well.

From the 1970s to the turn of the century, adult and juvenile arrest trends were similar. As noted in the Official Crime Index, published in the *Uniform Crime Reports* (Federal Bureau of Investigation, Washington, DC), between 1980 and 2000 the violent crime rate hit its highest point in 1992 and has decreased since that time. During the same time period, property crime peaked in 1991 and has also since declined. The violent crime rate for both juveniles and adults dropped more rapidly than did the property crime rate during that time.

Arrests by Gender

In "Juvenile Arrests 2000," Howard N. Snyder shows that young males were arrested in far greater numbers than young females from 1980 to 2000 in general and specifically in three violent crime categories (aggravated assault, other [simple] assault, and weapons) as well as for drug abuse. However, juvenile female arrest rates grew proportionately more than did arrests among young males, particularly in violent crime. Snyder's findings were for juveniles between the ages of 10 and 17. In 2000 females represented 28 percent of the juveniles arrested. By 2002 the female juvenile arrest rate experienced slight growth, reaching nearly 29 percent.

The FBI reported that males (all ages) in the United States were involved in 77 percent of all arrests in 2002. Although the number of overall male arrests was nearly the same between 2001 and 2002, males represented 82.6 percent of violent crime arrests and 69.3 percent of property crime arrests. The female (all ages) arrest rate increased 2.1 percent between 2001 and 2002.

Between 1993 and 2002, the overall arrest rate for males under 18 years of age decreased by 16.4 percent. (See Table 6.3.) However, the rate for juvenile females increased 6.4 percent during that same time period. The arrest rate for all males decreased by 5.9 percent while increasing 14.1 percent for all females.

According to the FBI's 10-year arrest trends, juvenile males and females engage in many of the same types of crimes. For example, the crime most undertaken by both males and females is larceny-theft. Although numbers of arrests were down for both males and females in this category in 2002, males were arrested 130,798 times while females were arrested 85,636 times for larceny-theft. (See Table 6.3.) As such, juvenile males were responsible for 17.9 percent of these arrests, juvenile females for 11.7 percent. Together, juvenile offenders represented almost 30 percent of all larceny-theft arrests. (See Table 6.2.)

Other areas with high arrest rates of both juvenile males and females include the categories of "other assault,"

TABLE 6.3

Ten-year arrest trends by sex, 1993–2002

[7,596 agencies; 2002 estimated population 175,384,794; 1993 estimated population 157,011,564]

| | Male | | | | | | Female | | | | | |
| | Total | | | Under 18 | | | Total | | | Under 18 | | |
Offense charged	1993	2002	Percent change	1993	2002	Percent change	1993	2002	Percent change	1993	2002	Percent change
Total[1]	6,891,398	6,486,470	-5.9	1,186,822	992,153	-16.4	1,689,892	1,927,513	+14.1	377,504	401,599	+6.4
Murder and non-negligent manslaughter	13,656	7,986	-41.5	2,326	795	-65.8	1,469	947	-35.5	159	91	-42.8
Forcible rape	23,201	17,141	-26.1	3,856	2,782	-27.9	308	253	-17.9	72	105	+45.8
Robbery	88,326	62,330	-29.4	24,263	14,908	-38.6	8,551	7,075	-17.3	2,242	1,430	-36.2
Aggravated assault	272,381	238,780	-12.3	41,055	29,127	-29.1	48,433	60,506	+24.9	8,372	8,955	+7.0
Burglary	227,422	154,642	-32.0	80,681	48,136	-40.3	26,329	23,835	-9.5	8,830	6,257	-29.1
Larceny-theft	645,065	459,358	-28.8	212,145	130,798	-38.3	314,387	270,467	-14.0	95,781	85,636	-10.6
Motor vehicle theft	112,582	78,955	-29.9	49,534	23,777	-52.0	15,970	15,653	-2.0	8,206	4,887	-40.4
Arson	10,847	8,507	-21.6	5,685	4,393	-22.7	1,799	1,548	-14.0	766	564	-26.4
Violent crime[2]	397,564	326,237	-17.9	71,500	47,612	-33.4	58,761	68,781	+17.1	10,845	10,581	-2.4
Property crime[3]	995,916	701,462	-29.6	348,045	207,104	-40.5	358,485	311,503	-13.1	113,583	97,344	-14.3
Crime Index[4]	1,393,480	1,027,699	-26.2	419,545	254,716	-39.3	417,246	380,284	-8.9	124,428	107,925	-13.3
Other assaults	600,914	596,196	-0.8	93,725	97,759	+4.3	132,123	186,098	+40.9	32,764	46,174	+40.9
Forgery and counterfeiting	42,342	43,190	+2.0	3,482	1,949	-44.0	24,022	28,652	+19.3	1,859	1,121	-39.7
Fraud	120,506	105,140	-12.8	4,270	3,472	-18.7	98,189	90,785	-7.5	2,179	1,786	-18.0
Embezzlement	4,631	5,898	+27.4	296	506	+70.9	3,279	5,917	+80.5	214	377	+76.2
Stolen property; buying, receiving, possessing	88,634	63,261	-28.6	25,671	13,551	-47.2	12,979	12,876	-0.8	3,137	2,215	-29.4
Vandalism	183,817	141,782	-22.9	88,566	56,527	-36.2	25,278	28,060	+11.0	9,402	8,833	-6.1
Weapons; carrying, possessing, etc.	162,611	96,141	-40.9	39,160	20,123	-48.6	13,387	8,277	-38.2	3,370	2,492	-26.1
Prostitution and commercialized vice	22,728	18,078	-20.5	320	331	+3.4	39,083	33,197	-15.1	435	627	+44.1
Sex offenses (except forcible rape and prostitution)	63,068	54,249	-14.0	12,148	11,084	-8.8	6,004	4,944	-17.7	1,239	1,114	-10.1
Drug abuse violations	594,006	798,695	+34.5	65,051	98,383	+51.2	116,916	175,387	+50.0	8,362	18,398	+120.0
Gambling	9,314	5,954	-36.1	1,670	1,022	-38.8	1,034	546	-47.2	45	31	-31.1
Offenses against the family and children	55,344	59,802	+8.1	2,242	3,229	+44.0	12,586	19,257	+53.0	1,278	1,979	+54.9
Driving under the influence	846,497	727,089	-14.1	7,584	10,416	+37.3	137,644	152,121	+10.5	1,294	2,505	+93.6
Liquor laws	252,565	289,770	+14.7	54,032	58,648	+8.5	64,354	95,841	+48.9	21,804	29,926	+37.3
Drunkenness	452,805	313,451	-30.8	9,842	9,047	-8.1	56,738	49,528	-12.7	1,863	2,405	+29.1
Disorderly conduct	384,867	301,613	-21.6	80,673	79,064	-2.0	98,809	97,115	-1.7	23,074	33,780	+46.4
Vagrancy	11,470	12,696	+10.7	1,893	1,023	-46.0	2,111	3,006	+42.4	361	323	-10.5
All other offenses (except traffic)	1,498,770	1,730,296	+15.4	173,623	175,833	+1.3	335,741	479,372	+42.8	48,027	63,338	+31.9
Suspicion	5,200	1,748	-66.4	1,024	512	-50.0	1,031	504	-51.1	215	196	-8.8
Curfew and loitering law violations	49,007	63,454	+29.5	49,007	63,454	+29.5	19,035	28,530	+49.9	19,035	28,530	+49.9
Runaways	54,022	32,016	-40.7	54,022	32,016	-40.7	73,334	47,720	-34.9	73,334	47,720	-34.9

[1]Does not include suspicion.
[2]Violent crimes are offenses of murder, forcible rape, robbery, and aggravated assault.
[3]Property crimes are offenses of burglary, larceny-theft, motor vehicle theft, and arson.
[4]Includes arson.

SOURCE: "Table 33. Ten-year arrest trends by sex, 1993–2002," in *Crime in the United States 2002: Uniform Crime Reports*, Federal Bureau of Investigation, Washington, DC, 2003

disorderly conduct, and drug abuse violations. (See Table 6.3.) Young males were arrested 97,759 times on "other assault" charges while young females were arrested 46,174 times for that offense in 2002. Disorderly conduct resulted in 79,064 males and 33,780 females under age 18 being arrested, while drug abuse violations accounted for 98,383 young males and 18,398 young females getting arrested.

Other crimes most frequently committed by young males and females include: liquor law violations (58,648 arrests for males, 29,926 arrests for females) and curfew and loitering law violations (63,454 arrests for males, 28,530 arrests for females). (See Table 6.3.) Males also saw high numbers of arrests for vandalism (56,527 arrests), while young females were arrested 47,720 times as runaways.

Despite the high number of juvenile crimes, arrest rates for youth under age 18 were down in many categories from 1993 to 2002. Young males experienced the greatest decline in number of arrests for murder and nonnegligent manslaughter (65.8 percent); motor vehicle theft (52 percent); possessing and carrying weapons (48.6 percent); vagrancy (46.0 percent); buying, receiving, and possessing stolen property (47.2 percent); and forgery and counterfeiting (44.0 percent). (See Table 6.3.)

During that same time period, young female arrest rates dropped most in the following areas: murder and nonnegligent manslaughter (42.8 percent); motor vehicle theft (40.4 percent); forgery and counterfeiting (39.7 percent); robbery (36.2 percent); runaways (34.9 percent); gambling (31.1 percent); and buying, receiving, and possessing stolen property (29.4 percent). (See Table 6.3.)

However, various arrest categories continued to see growth, some rapid, for juveniles between 1993 and 2002. For young males, the categories seeing the biggest jump in arrests included: embezzlement (70.9 percent), drug abuse violations (51.2 percent), offenses against family and children (44.0 percent), driving under the influence (37.3 percent), and curfew and loitering law violations (29.5 percent). (See Table 6.3.)

For young females, those categories were: drug abuse violations (120.0 percent), driving under the influence (93.6 percent), embezzlement (76.2 percent), offenses against the family and children (54.9 percent), and curfew and loitering law violations (49.9 percent). (See Table 6.3.) Two other areas seeing significant growth in the young female arrest rate were prostitution/commercialized vice (44.1 percent) and forcible rape (45.8 percent). The prostitution/commercialized vice arrest rate for young males grew by 3.4 percent during the same time period, while the number of forcible rapes by juvenile males declined by 27.9 percent.

Arrests by Race/Ethnicity

The Census Bureau reported the overall U.S. population in March 2002 as 81.6 percent white, 12.8 percent black, 4.4 percent Asian/Pacific Islander, and 1.2 percent American Indian/Alaskan Native. Hispanics, who can be of any race, represented 13.3 percent of the total. *Crime in the United States 2002* noted that more than two-thirds of all arrested individuals (70.7 percent) in 2002 were white, followed by blacks at more than one-quarter or 26.9 percent. The remaining 2.4 percent of arrests were split among other races. Whites were most often arrested for driving under the influence, and blacks most often on drug charges.

The juvenile population (those under age 18), as reported by the Census Bureau in March 2002, stood at 25.7 percent. Of the juvenile population, white juveniles represented 77.8 percent; blacks, 16.1 percent; Asian/Pacific Islanders; 4.5 percent; and American Indian/Alaskan Natives, 1.6 percent. Hispanic juveniles totaled 17.7 percent. In the FBI report of juvenile arrests by race, whites (71.5 percent) had the most arrests, followed by blacks (25.7 percent), Asian/Pacific Islanders (1.6 percent), and American Indians/Alaskan Natives (1.3 percent). (See Table 6.4.)

In terms of percent distribution of the population, black juveniles had higher arrest rates for murder/nonnegligent homicide (50.1 percent) than white juveniles (45.9 percent). (See Table 6.4.) The highest percentages of arrests for white youth were for driving under the influence (93.3 percent), liquor law violations (92.2 percent), drunkenness (90.0 percent), vandalism (81.0 percent), and arson (80.7 percent). In addition to murder/nonnegligent homicide, the following categories had the highest percentage of arrests among black youths: gambling (85.7 percent); robbery (58.9 percent); prostitution and commercialized vice (54.6 percent); buying, receiving, and possessing stolen property (41.4 percent); and motor vehicle theft (38.3 percent). American Indian/Alaskan Native juveniles represented larger percentages of liquor law violations (2.5 percent) and murder and nonnegligent manslaughter (2.4 percent) than other offenses. Runaway violations (4.5 percent) and gambling (2.9 percent) were the crimes for which Asian/Pacific Islanders showed the largest percent distribution of the juvenile population.

In terms of the number of arrests, three types of crimes were consistently among the highest for all juvenile racial groups: larceny-theft, other assaults, and drug abuse violations. (See Table 6.4.) Other top arrest categories for white youths were liquor law violations (97,372) and disorderly conduct (88,761). For black juveniles, those categories included disorderly conduct (47,261) and curfew and loitering violations (29,717). Among the highest arrest categories for American Indian/Alaskan Natives under 18 were liquor law violations (2,656) and disorderly conduct (1,708), and for Asian/Pacific Islander youths, those categories included curfew and loitering law violations (1,516) and runaway arrests (4,039).

The FBI data on arrests by race did not identify arrest rates by Hispanic origin. The largest racial group among Hispanics as reported by the Census Bureau in 2002 was white.

Arrests in Geographic Locations

The FBI also compiles data on arrest rates in four geographic areas: the Midwest, the Northeast, the South, and the West. Among people of all ages, the South held the highest arrest rate in 2002 at 5,217.7 arrests per 100,000 people. The Midwest was second with 5,041.1 per 100,000 people, followed by the West at 4,628.0 per 100,000 and the Northeast at 3,942.3 per 100,000. However, the West led in violent crime, at 275.6 arrests per 100,000. The South followed with 196.8 per 100,000, then the Midwest with 193.5 per 100,000. The Northeast experienced the lowest rate at 188.9 per 100,000 people.

The Midwest and the South tied for the highest murder arrest rate at 5.7 per 100,000 people. The West (4.2

TABLE 6.4

Arrests by race, 2002

[10,370 agencies; 2002 estimated population 205,108,615]

Offense charged	Total arrests					Percent distribution[1]				
	Total	White	Black	American Indian or Alaskan Native	Asian or Pacific Islander	Total	White	Black	American Indian or Alaskan Native	Asian or Pacific Islander
Total	9,797,385	6,923,390	2,633,632	130,636	109,727	100.0	70.7	26.9	1.3	1.1
Murder and nonnegligent manslaughter	10,099	4,814	5,047	115	123	100.0	47.7	50.0	1.1	1.2
Forcible rape	20,127	12,766	6,852	240	269	100.0	63.4	34.0	1.2	1.3
Robbery	77,280	34,109	41,837	471	863	100.0	44.1	54.1	0.6	1.1
Aggravated assault	338,850	214,992	115,789	4,069	4,000	100.0	63.4	34.2	1.2	1.2
Burglary	205,873	144,958	56,647	1,992	2,276	100.0	70.4	27.5	1.0	1.1
Larceny-theft	843,066	572,515	246,946	10,345	13,260	100.0	67.9	29.3	1.2	1.6
Motor vehicle theft	107,031	64,625	39,114	1,156	2,136	100.0	60.4	36.5	1.1	2.0
Arson	11,808	9,067	2,537	100	104	100.0	76.8	21.5	0.8	0.9
Violent crime[2]	446,356	266,681	169,525	4,895	5,255	100.0	59.7	38.0	1.1	1.2
Property crime[3]	1,167,778	791,165	345,244	13,593	17,776	100.0	67.7	29.6	1.2	1.5
Crime Index[4]	1,614,134	1,057,846	514,769	18,488	23,031	100.0	65.5	31.9	1.1	1.4
Other assaults	919,691	610,946	286,787	12,201	9,757	100.0	66.4	31.2	1.3	1.1
Forgery and counterfeiting	82,882	57,125	24,148	458	1,151	100.0	68.9	29.1	0.6	1.4
Fraud	232,336	157,763	71,538	1,431	1,604	100.0	67.9	30.8	0.6	0.7
Embezzlement	13,379	9,153	3,959	64	203	100.0	68.4	29.6	0.5	1.5
Stolen property; buying, receiving, possessing	91,150	53,535	35,986	611	1,018	100.0	58.7	39.5	0.7	1.1
Vandalism	198,139	150,437	42,757	2,804	2,141	100.0	75.9	21.6	1.4	1.1
Weapons; carrying, possessing, etc.	118,148	73,140	42,810	879	1,319	100.0	61.9	36.2	0.7	1.1
Prostitution and commercialized vice	58,659	33,650	23,455	364	1,190	100.0	57.4	40.0	0.6	2.0
Sex offenses (except forcible rape and prostitution)	67,761	50,378	15,745	680	958	100.0	74.3	23.2	1.0	1.4
Drug abuse violations	1,101,547	728,797	357,725	6,848	8,177	100.0	66.2	32.5	0.6	0.7
Gambling	7,525	2,033	5,136	38	318	100.0	27.0	68.3	0.5	4.2
Offenses against the family and children	97,393	66,440	28,180	1,266	1,507	100.0	68.2	28.9	1.3	1.5
Driving under the influence	1,017,504	893,395	99,548	15,460	9,101	100.0	87.8	9.8	1.5	0.9
Liquor laws	462,215	405,275	41,204	11,397	4,339	100.0	87.7	8.9	2.5	0.9
Drunkenness	412,735	345,448	55,598	9,563	2,126	100.0	83.7	13.5	2.3	0.5
Disorderly conduct	481,932	321,117	149,393	7,883	3,539	100.0	66.6	31.0	1.6	0.7
Vagrancy	19,669	12,223	6,888	419	139	100.0	62.1	35.0	2.1	0.7
All other offenses (except traffic)	2,599,658	1,751,450	778,558	37,377	32,273	100.0	67.4	29.9	1.4	1.2
Suspicion	7,647	4,130	3,128	108	281	100.0	54.0	40.9	1.4	3.7
Curfew and loitering law violations	103,054	70,738	29,717	1,083	1,516	100.0	68.6	28.8	1.1	1.5
Runaways	90,227	68,371	16,603	1,214	4,039	100.0	75.8	18.4	1.3	4.5

per 100,000) and the Northeast (3.2 per 100,000) had lower rates. The Midwest led in forcible rape (11.2 per 100,000), followed by the South (10.1 per 100,000), Northeast (10.0 per 100,000), and the West (8.4 per 100,000). Property crime was highest in the West (596.3 per 100,000) and South (593.2 per 100,000), with the Midwest (583.6 per 100,000) and the Northeast (469.6 per 100,000) experiencing fewer arrests in that category.

The states recording the most arrests of individuals under 18 were California (227,266 arrests), Texas (180,017 arrests), Florida (123,260 arrests), Wisconsin (114,131 arrests), and Pennsylvania (100,243 arrests). However, when population size is taken into account, Wisconsin, Illinois, Wyoming, Idaho, and Utah were the states with the highest percentages of juvenile arrests.

Arrests in Cities, Suburbs, and Rural Areas

The FBI also tracked arrest data for juveniles living in cities (1,116,543 youth), suburban counties (185,198 youth), rural counties (77,308 youth), and suburban areas (482,099 youth). ("Suburban areas" cover law enforcement agencies in cities with less than 50,000 inhabitants and county law enforcement agencies within a metropolitan statistical area.) In 2002 juveniles living in cities were most often arrested for larceny-theft (188,883 arrests), other assaults (114,887 arrests), disorderly conduct (95,954 arrests), drug abuse violations (87,897 arrests), and curfew and loitering law violations (77,138 arrests).

Among city juveniles, the areas experiencing the greatest percentage drops between 2001 and 2002 were embezzlement (28.3 percent), forgery and counterfeiting (18.8 percent), vagrancy (16.4 percent), and offenses against the

TABLE 6.4

Arrests by race, 2002 [CONTINUED]

[10,370 agencies; 2002 estimated population 205,108,615]

	Arrests under 18					Percent distribution[1]				
Offense charged	Total	White	Black	American Indian or Alaskan Native	Asian or Pacific Islander	Total	White	Black	American Indian or Alaskan Native	Asian or Pacific Islander
Total	1,620,594	1,158,776	415,854	20,383	25,581	100.0	71.5	25.7	1.3	1.6
Murder and nonnegligent manslaughter	972	446	487	23	16	100.0	45.9	50.1	2.4	1.6
Forcible rape	3,355	2,079	1,207	37	32	100.0	62.0	36.0	1.1	1.0
Robbery	17,878	6,895	10,537	91	355	100.0	38.6	58.9	0.5	2.0
Aggravated assault	44,185	26,877	16,217	535	556	100.0	60.8	36.7	1.2	1.3
Burglary	61,754	44,680	15,558	689	827	100.0	72.4	25.2	1.1	1.3
Larceny-theft	248,202	173,910	65,667	3,443	5,182	100.0	70.1	26.5	1.4	2.1
Motor vehicle theft	32,487	18,949	12,428	445	665	100.0	58.3	38.3	1.4	2.0
Arson	5,837	4,711	1,026	48	52	100.0	80.7	17.6	0.8	0.9
Violent crime[2]	66,390	36,297	28,448	686	959	100.0	54.7	42.8	1.0	1.4
Property crime[3]	348,280	242,250	94,679	4,625	6,726	100.0	69.6	27.2	1.3	1.9
Crime Index[4]	414,670	278,547	123,127	5,311	7,685	100.0	67.2	29.7	1.3	1.9
Other assaults	168,641	106,119	58,518	1,942	2,062	100.0	62.9	34.7	1.2	1.2
Forgery and counterfeiting	3,644	2,845	711	33	55	100.0	78.1	19.5	0.9	1.5
Fraud	6,418	4,242	2,051	47	78	100.0	66.1	32.0	0.7	1.2
Embezzlement	1,004	696	287	1	20	100.0	69.3	28.6	0.1	2.0
Stolen property; buying, receiving, possessing	18,769	10,612	7,761	134	262	100.0	56.5	41.4	0.7	1.4
Vandalism	75,781	61,373	12,594	919	895	100.0	81.0	16.6	1.2	1.2
Weapons; carrying, possessing, etc.	25,239	16,945	7,751	207	336	100.0	67.1	30.7	0.8	1.3
Prostitution and commercialized vice	1,094	479	597	6	12	100.0	43.8	54.6	0.5	1.1
Sex offenses (except forcible rape and prostitution)	13,857	9,986	3,603	107	161	100.0	72.1	26.0	0.8	1.2
Drug abuse violations	133,494	97,766	33,208	1,152	1,368	100.0	73.2	24.9	0.9	1.0
Gambling	1,114	127	955	0	32	100.0	11.4	85.7	*	2.9
Offenses against the family and children	6,554	4,837	1,541	56	120	100.0	73.8	23.5	0.9	1.8
Driving under the influence	15,155	14,138	628	267	122	100.0	93.3	4.1	1.8	0.8
Liquor laws	105,652	97,372	4,629	2,656	995	100.0	92.2	4.4	2.5	0.9
Drunkenness	13,508	12,155	995	258	100	100.0	90.0	7.4	1.9	0.7
Disorderly conduct	138,847	88,761	47,261	1,708	1,117	100.0	63.9	34.0	1.2	0.8
Vagrancy	1,518	1,147	346	14	11	100.0	75.6	22.8	0.9	0.7
All other offenses (except traffic)	281,184	210,704	62,641	3,261	4,578	100.0	74.9	22.3	1.2	1.6
Suspicion	1,170	816	330	7	17	100.0	69.7	28.2	0.6	1.5
Curfew and loitering law violations	103,054	70,738	29,717	1,083	1,516	100.0	68.6	28.8	1.1	1.5
Runaways	90,227	68,371	16,603	1,214	4,039	100.0	75.8	18.4	1.3	4.5

[1]Because of rounding, the percentages may not add to 100.
[2]Violent crimes are offenses of murder, forcible rape, robbery and aggravated assault.
[3]Property crimes are offenses of burglary, larceny-theft, motor vehicle theft and arson.
[4]Includes arson.
*Less than one-tenth of 1 percent.

SOURCE: "Table 43. Arrests by race, 2002," in *Crime in the United States 2002: Uniform Crime Reports*, Federal Bureau of Investigation, Washington, DC, 2003

family and children (12.4 percent). The areas with the highest percentage growth during that same period were suspicion (90 percent) and gambling (26.9 percent).

Arrests among those under 18 in suburban counties were highest in the following categories: other assaults (24,965), larceny-theft (22,055), drug abuse violations (16,396), runaways (16,136), and liquor law violations (12,087). The highest percentage decreases for this group between 2001 and 2002 occurred in arrests for suspicion (54.1 percent), vagrancy (37.4 percent), gambling (25 percent), and curfew and loitering law violations (16.7 percent). The highest percentage increases were for offenses

against the family and children (25 percent) and murder and nonnegligent manslaughter (9.9 percent).

Rural counties saw the largest number of juvenile arrests in the areas of liquor law violations (9,885), other assaults (8,581), larceny-theft (6,484), drug abuse violations (6,366), and burglary (4,778). The crimes with the largest percentage decreases for this group between 2001 and 2002 were gambling (62.1 percent); suspicion (56.1 percent); buying, receiving, or possessing stolen property (21.8 percent); arson (17.7 percent); and carrying or possessing weapons (13 percent). The largest percentage gains were in prostitution and commercialized vice (300 percent), embezzlement (76.5 percent), and murder and nonnegligent manslaughter (22.2 percent). Keep in mind that percentages indicate trends but may actually represent a low number of crimes in some categories. For example, the number of actual prostitution arrests in rural counties went from 3 in 2001 to 12 in 2002, while the number of murder/nonnegligent manslaughter arrests rose by 10. The percentage changes, however, reveal patterns for police to monitor closely in the future.

In suburban areas, the highest number of juvenile arrests occurred in many of the same categories: larceny-theft (67,477), other assaults (54,667), disorderly conduct (44,087), drug abuse violations (42,024), and liquor law violations (35,855). Between 2001 and 2002 the percentage of suburban juvenile arrests decreased the most in embezzlement (14.8 percent), suspicion (13.1 percent), and forgery and counterfeiting (12.3 percent). The highest percentage gains occurred in gambling (15.4 percent) and prostitution/commercialized vice (13.1 percent).

PROSECUTING MINORS AS ADULTS

Many people believe that some crimes are so horrific that the courts should focus on the type of offense and not the age of the accused in determining the type of trial court. From 1987 to 1993, a dramatic 65 percent increase occurred in the rate of juvenile arrests for murder. Rates of other violent crimes, such as rape, robbery, and aggravated assault, also grew during this time period. The increase in violent crime among juveniles saw U.S. juvenile courts handling 84 percent more criminal homicide cases in 1995 than in 1986. Most experts believe the increases were related to a surge in violent gangs selling crack cocaine coupled with easy access to handguns.

Voters were outraged over the crime wave and lawmakers responded with tough new policies, including trying more juveniles in adult criminal courts. Historically, the states relied mainly on a judge's decision to waive delinquents to adult criminal court. However, by 2000 all 50 states and the District of Columbia had one or more laws permitting the transfer of youth to criminal courts to be tried as adults. Many states have also expanded these laws to make it easier to prosecute juveniles as adults. More than half the states have laws that specify the crimes and minimum ages for which juveniles can be prosecuted as adults.

For example, a 1995 Missouri law removed the minimum age limit, which had been 14 years of age, for trying children as adults in cases involving drug dealing, murder, rape, robbery, and first-degree assault. A Texas law allows children as young as 10 years of age to be sentenced for up to 40 years' incarceration. In Wisconsin, juveniles 10 years old can be tried in adult court for murder.

The number of cases transferred from juvenile to adult court increased 47 percent between 1987 and 1996, or roughly from 6,800 to 10,000. Despite growing numbers, however, the proportion of transferred cases overall remained fairly constant in the 1990s. In 1992 some 1.4 percent of all formally processed delinquency cases were transferred to criminal (adult) court. In 1996 and 1998, 1 percent of all formally processed delinquency cases were waived to adult court.

Does It Work?

From 1994 to 1999, the murder rate for juvenile offenders consistently declined, dropping about 68 percent. In 1993 about 3,800 juvenile-perpetrated homicides occurred compared to 1,400 in 1999. As such, some public officials believed that efforts to reduce crime through adult sentencing were working. However, many experts attribute the murder rate decline to expanded after-school crime prevention programs, the decline of crack cocaine and violent gangs, and big-city police efforts to crack down on illegal guns.

A Florida study discussed in "The Transfer of Juveniles to Criminal Court: Does It Make a Difference?" (*Crime and Delinquency,* April 1996), suggested that juveniles tried in adult courts were likely to be rearrested more quickly and more often than juveniles who went to juvenile court. The report compared the rearrest rates of juveniles transferred to criminal court to a matched sample (similar crimes, past court experience, age, gender, and race) of those retained in the juvenile system. Of the transferred youth, 30 percent were rearrested, compared to 19 percent of the nontransferred ones. Transferred youth who were rearrested had committed a new offense within 135 days of release, compared to 227 days for youth processed in juvenile courts.

In *Youth on Trial: A Developmental Perspective of Juvenile Justice* (Thomas Grisso and Robert G. Schwartz, eds., University of Chicago Press, 2000), some of the inherent problems in transferring juveniles to adult court are discussed. The authors note that juveniles have a harder time than adults making "knowing and intelligent" decisions at many junctures in the criminal justice process. In particular, problems occur when waiving Miranda rights, which allow the juvenile to remain silent and talk to a lawyer before responding to questions posed by police. When a juvenile waives such rights, this can lead to much more serious consequences in adult court than in juvenile proceedings. The authors assert that "questions must be raised regarding the juvenile's judgment, decision-making capacity, and impulse control as they relate to criminal culpability" in adult proceedings. Before deciding if a youth can be held accountable as an adult for a particular offense, according to researchers and experts in child development, it is important to understand an adolescent's intellectual, social, and emotional development.

Juvenile Records

Traditionally, juvenile hearings were closed to the public and juvenile records sealed based on the belief that delinquent behavior by a young child should not be held against him or her for the rest of the child's life. However, many states have started to allow more openness of juvenile records. According to the National Center for Juvenile Justice, in 1999, 13 states had laws or court rules that permitted or required juvenile delinquency hearings to be open to the public; 21 states opened delinquency hearings to the public but placed age and/or offense requirements on the openness of the hearing; and 9 states allowed the public release of juvenile court records without qualifying restrictions. Most states required that police departments notify school officials when a student was charged with a crime. Like lowering the age of "adult" responsibility for crimes, recent laws in this regard are intended to make juveniles more accountable for their acts.

Adult Time for Adult Crime?

A poll conducted by the Gallup Organization in 2000 sampled people's opinions about the treatment of violent juvenile offenders. Survey participants were asked if violent juveniles should be treated the same as adults or if they should be given more leniency. Two of three respondents said that juveniles should be treated the same as adults. Men (69 percent) were more likely than women (61 percent) to give that response, as were whites (67 percent) compared to blacks (52 percent). Those aged 18 to 29 (65 percent) were also more likely than those 65 and older (61 percent) to select "same as adults." College postgraduates (55 percent) were less likely to give that answer than those with some college (68 percent). Other groups least likely to advocate adult punishment fell into the following categories: highest income level (60 percent), Democrats (60 percent), Easterners (60 percent), and urban dwellers (59 percent). Other groups most likely to want violent juveniles treated like adults were individuals making $50,000–$74,999 (69 percent), living in the suburbs (69 percent), voting Independent (68 percent) or Republican (67 percent), and living in the Midwest (71 percent).

Disposition of Juveniles Arrested

In the 1970s a change occurred in the disposition of juveniles arrested. Statistics for 1972 show that 50.8 percent of arrested minors were referred to juvenile court, 45.0 percent were handled within the police department and then released, and 1.3 percent were referred to criminal or adult court. (See Figure 6.1.) From 1972 to 2000, however, those referred to juvenile court increased 20 percent, while those handled internally and then released dropped nearly 25 percent. The percentage of juvenile cases referred to criminal or adult court nearly quintupled, rising to 7 percent.

Table 6.5 shows police disposition trends of juvenile offenders taken into custody in 2002. Overall, the number of juvenile cases referred to juvenile court increased slightly from 2000 to 72.8 percent, while the total cases handled within the department and then released dropped

FIGURE 6.1

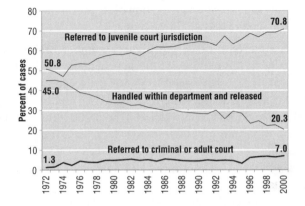

Percent distribution of juveniles taken into police custody, 1972–2000

Note: Excludes two categories: "Referred to other police agency," and "Referred to welfare agency." These categories were 1.6 and 1.3 percent respectively in 1972 and 1.1 and 0.8 percent in 2000.

SOURCE: Adapted from Ann L. Pastore and Kathleen Maguire, eds., "Table 4.26: Percent distribution of juveniles taken into police custody," in *Sourcebook of Criminal Justice Statistics 2001*, U.S. Bureau of Justice Statistics, Washington, DC, 2002 [Online] http://www.albany.edu/sourcebook/1995/wk1/t426.wk1 [accessed April 21, 2003]

to 18.1 percent. The number of cases referred to criminal or adult court remained the same at 7.0 percent. Also included on this table are statistics for the percentage of juveniles referred to a welfare agency (0.7 percent) and those referred to another police agency (1.4 percent). Statistics for city-residing juveniles are consistent with the overall totals. However, in rural counties, far more juveniles were referred to criminal or adult court (11.5 percent) and fewer were handled in the department and then released (13.5 percent).

PRISON AND JAIL

Some 10,303 juveniles were in prison or jail in 2002, according to the Bureau of Justice Statistics (Paige M. Harrison and Jennifer C. Karberg, *Prison and Jail Inmates at Midyear, 2002*, U.S. Bureau of Justice Statistics, Washington, DC, 2003). Of the 7,248 juveniles in jail, 6,112 were being held as adults. The remaining 3,055 juveniles were being held in state prisons. The number of juveniles in jail/prison increased at an average annual rate of about 4.3 percent between 1985 and 2002, while the number of juveniles ages 14 to 17 in jail/prison increased at an average annual rate of about 0.3 percent during that same period of time. Starting in 1984, the number of jailed juveniles began increasing, then surged in 1991. Although the number began to fall sharply after 1999, the figure in 2002 remains at more than 7,000 compared to under 2,000 in the early 1980s. (See Figure 6.2.)

TABLE 6.5

Police disposition of juvenile offenders taken into custody, 2002

Population group	Total[1]	Handled within department and released	Referred to juvenile court jurisdiction	Referred to welfare agency	Referred to other police agency	Referred to criminal or adult court
Total agencies: 6,073 agencies; population 130,229,927						
Number	732,282	132,825	532,940	4,779	10,183	51,555
Percent[2]	100.0	18.1	72.8	0.7	1.4	7.0
Total cities: 4,577 cities; population 92,489,061						
Number	611,897	115,191	444,336	3,956	7,901	40,513
Percent[2]	100.0	18.8	72.6	0.6	1.3	6.6

[1]Includes all offenses except traffic and neglect cases.
[2]Because of rounding, the percentages may not add to 100.0.

SOURCE: "Table 68. Police Disposition of Juvenile Offenders Taken into Custody, 2002," in *Crime in the United States 2002: Uniform Crime Reports,* Federal Bureau of Investigation, Washington, DC, 2003.

Of the 3,055 juveniles in state prisons as of mid-year 2002, 2,943 (or 96.3 percent) were male. (See Table 6.6.) That figure represented a drop of 1,084 from 1999. Although females were a small percentage of the juveniles incarcerated in state prison each year during that time, their numbers have decreased as well, from 167 in 1999 to 112 in 2002. Overall, the number of juveniles in state prison dropped by 1,139 from 1999 to 2002.

Eleven states claimed more than 100 juvenile inmates in mid-year 2002, with Connecticut (366), Florida (306), and Texas (230) having the most. (See Table 6.7.) Other states with more than 100 included: New York (210), North Carolina (200), Arizona (147), South Carolina (140), California (112), Illinois (111), Mississippi (107), and Michigan (106). Between 2001 and 2002, most of these states saw an increase in their juvenile inmate populations. The biggest increase was in Michigan (100 percent), followed by Mississippi (18.9 percent) and California (17.9 percent). Florida had the largest decrease (22.5 percent) with New York (17.3 percent) and North Carolina (5.7 percent) also seeing declining numbers. In twelve states, the juvenile inmate population numbered 10 or less; three states reported no juvenile inmates.

Detailed statistics about juveniles in adult confinement are also found in the Bureau of Justice Assistance's most recent report on the subject, *Juveniles in Adult Prisons and Jails: A National Assessment* (Office of Justice Programs, U.S. Justice Department, Washington, DC, October 2000). In this survey, conducted in 1998, juveniles were defined as those aged 17 and under. The survey recorded information for both the juvenile and adult incarcerated populations. It contains data from state prisons and participating local jail systems; the federal prison system did not participate. The study shows that among juvenile offenders in adult facilities, 3.3 percent were female. Compare that to the number held in juvenile residential facilities, which was 13 percent.

In Table 6.8, which describes the characteristics of youths and adults in state prison for 1998, data are pre-

sented for the offenses/crimes that youth and adults committed, the racial/ethnic breakdowns for those incarcerated in state prisons, and what type of housing was being used to detain them. In the offenses/crimes category, the biggest difference between the juvenile and adult prison populations occurred in the drug category. Compared to 1 in 5 adults, 1 in 10 juveniles were incarcerated on drug charges. Both youth and adults were incarcerated most often for crimes against persons (57 percent for youths and 44 percent for adults). The second largest category for youth was property crimes (21 percent). For the second largest category among adults, there was a tie: 20 percent for drugs and 20 percent for property crimes.

In the state prison survey, more than half of the youths incarcerated were blacks (55 percent), followed by whites (26 percent) and Hispanics (14 percent). (See Table 6.8.) The breakdown for adult prisoners was similar. Blacks (48 percent) accounted for nearly one-half of adult prisoners, whites represented more than one-third (35 percent), and Hispanics comprised 15 percent. The percentage of Native American juveniles incarcerated in state prisons was much higher than for adults: 4 percent versus 1 percent. The rate of incarcerated Asians was the same in both categories at 1 percent.

In terms of housing, proportionally more adults (35 percent) shared double cells than juveniles (19 percent). (See Table 6.8.) However, nearly 1 in 3 youths (30 percent) had single cells while 1 in 5 adults (22 percent) had no cell mates. More than half of the incarcerated juveniles (51 percent) slept in dormitories compared to 43 percent of adults.

SENTENCED YOUTH UNDER STATE OR FEDERAL JURISDICTION

According to *Prisoners in 2002* (Paige M. Harrison and Allen J. Beck, U.S. Department of Justice, Bureau of Justice Statistics, Washington, DC, July 2003), 37,700 youths (ages 18 and 19) were being held under state or federal jurisdiction with sentences of more than one year in

FIGURE 6.2

Juveniles under confinement in jails and prisons, 1983–2002

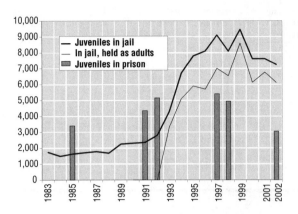

Note: Data on juveniles in prison are not available for every year. Data on juveniles held in jail as adults became available in 1990 but remained at zero until 1993. Thereafter, most juveniles held in jail were held as adults.

SOURCE: Created by Information Plus from U.S. Department of Justice, Office of Justice Programs data

---

TABLE 6.7

States with the highest number of prisoners under age 18, midyear 2002

	Number of prisoners under age 18		Percent change
	6/30/02	**6/30/01**	
Connecticut	366	330	10.9%
Florida	306	395	−22.5
Texas	230	208	10.6
New York	210	254	−17.3
North Carolina	200	212	−5.7
Arizona	147	142	3.5%
South Carolina	140	133	5.3
California	112	95	17.9
Illinois	111	110	0.9
Mississippi	107	90	18.9
Michigan	106	53	100.0

SOURCE: Paige M. Harrison and Jennifer C. Karberg, *Prison and Jail Inmates at Midyear 2002*, NCJ 198877, U.S. Department of Justice, Bureau of Justice Statistics, Washington, DC, April 2003

2002. (See Table 6.9.) Such youths represented 2.7 percent of the total number of prisoners being held in that year. Young males numbered 36,400 or 96.6 percent of total youths being held; young females, 1,300 or 3.4 percent.

Black youth (17,800) represented 47.2 percent, outnumbering white (9,500 at 25.2 percent) and Hispanic (8,600 at 22.8 percent) youth. (See Table 6.9.) Other races comprise the remaining 4.8 percent. Among males, nearly 1 in 2 sentenced youth were black (47.5 percent). White (24.2 percent) and Hispanic (23.1 percent) male youths each represented about 1 in 4 of all sentenced male youths. More than half (53.8 percent) of female youths

---

TABLE 6.6

Number of inmates under age 18 held in state and federal prisons, by gender, 1990, 1995, and 1999–2002

	Inmates under age 18		
Year	**Total**	**Male**	**Female**
2002	3,055	2,943	112
2001	3,147	3,010	137
2000	3,896	3,721	175
1999	4,194	4,027	167
1995	5,309	—	—
1990	3,600	—	—

Note: Federal prisons held 39 inmates under age 18 in 1990, but none in 1995 and 1999 to 2002.
—Not available.

SOURCE: Paige M. Harrison and Jennifer C. Karberg, "Table 5. Number of inmates under age 18 held in State and Federal prisons, by gender, June 30, 1990, 1995, and 1999–2002," in *Prison and Jail Inmates at Midyear 2002*, NCJ 198877, U.S. Department of Justice, Bureau of Justice Statistics, Washington, DC, April 2003

TABLE 6.8

Characteristics of youths and adults in state prison, 1998

	Youths		Adults		Total
	Number	**Percentage**	**Number**	**Percentage**	
Offense/Crime					
Persons	2,722	57%	473,821	44%	476,544
Property	974	21%	216,756	20%	217,730
Alcohol Related	135	3%	20,457	2%	20,592
Drug Related	467	10%	210,975	20%	211,442
Public Order	185	4%	40,468	4%	40,653
Parole/Probation	79	2%	90,260	8%	90,339
Unknown	92	2%	5,676	1%	5,768
Other	85	2%	13,327	1%	13,412
Total	4,739	100%	1,071,740	100%	1,076,479
Race/Ethnicity					
Asian	65	1%	11,056	1%	11,121
Black	2,706	55%	497,343	48%	500,050
White	1,309	26%	355,960	35%	357,269
Hispanic	689	14%	156,782	15%	157,471
Native American	176	4%	9,421	1%	9,597
Total	4,945	100%	1,030,562	100%	1,035,507
Housing Type[1]					
Single Cell	1,019	30%	120,221	22%	121,240
Double Cell	670	19%	193,754	35%	194,424
Dormitory	1,757	51%	237,801	43%	239,559
Total	3,446	100%	551,776	100%	555,222

Note: Discrepancies in totals are due to rounding.
[1] Housing type statistics are reported for 21 states that house juveniles in adult correctional facilities.

SOURCE: James Austin, Kelly Dedel Johnson, and Maria Gregoriou, "Table 7. Characteristics of State Prison Inmates, 1998," in *Juveniles in Adult Prisons and Jails: A National Assessment*, U.S. Department of Justice, Office of Justice Programs, Washington, DC, October 2000

---

under sentence were white, while black females represented nearly two-fifths (38.5 percent) and Hispanic females comprised nearly one-sixth (15.4 percent).

Overall, black males under sentence outnumber white males in all age categories shown in Table 6.9 until the age group from 45 to 54. The number of white females

---

TABLE 6.9

Number of sentenced prisoners under state or federal jurisdiction by gender, race, Hispanic origin, and age, 2002

| | Number of sentenced prisoners | | | | | | | |
| | Males | | | | Females | | | |
	Total[1]	White[2]	Black[2]	Hispanic	Total[1]	White[2]	Black[2]	Hispanic
Total	1,291,326	436,800	586,700	235,000	89,044	35,400	36,000	15,000
18-19	36,400	8,800	17,300	8,400	1,300	700	500	200
20-24	218,300	59,400	105,400	47,400	8,900	3,700	3,100	2,100
25-29	248,400	70,700	123,000	49,300	15,900	5,500	6,500	3,000
30-34	245,700	83,900	111,400	46,200	22,100	8,500	9,200	3,600
35-39	220,600	79,400	102,500	34,200	19,400	7,800	8,300	2,900
40-44	150,200	56,300	64,600	25,300	10,700	4,100	4,700	1,400
45-54	127,300	55,800	48,500	18,800	8,400	3,700	3,000	1,400
55 or older	38,900	21,500	10,800	4,800	1,900	1,200	500	200

[1]Includes American Indians, Alaska Natives, Asians, Native Hawaiians, and other Pacific Islanders.
[2]Excludes Hispanics.
Note: Estimates were rounded to the nearest hundred.

SOURCE: Paige M. Harrison and Allen J. Beck, "Table 13. Number of sentenced prisoners under State or Federal jurisdiction, by gender, race, Hispanic origin, and age, 2002," in *Prisoners in 2002*, NCJ 200248, U.S. Department of Justice, Bureau of Justice Statistics, Washington, DC, July 2003

TABLE 6.10

Number of sentenced prisoners under state or federal jurisdiction per 100,000 residents, by gender, race, Hispanic origin, and age, 2002

| | Number of sentenced prisoners per 100,000 residents of each group | | | | | | | |
| | Males | | | | Females | | | |
Age	Total[1]	White[2]	Black[2]	Hispanic	Total[1]	White[2]	Black[2]	Hispanic
Total	912	450	3,437	1,176	61	35	191	80
18-19	869	331	2,865	1,224	34	26	87	35
20-24	2,109	934	7,490	2,382	90	59	217	130
25-29	2,577	1,229	10,376	2,394	170	97	498	179
30-34	2,326	1,251	8,885	2,409	213	129	662	216
35-39	2,014	1,080	7,893	2,060	177	106	566	193
40-44	1,316	691	4,939	1,850	92	51	315	111
45-54	647	376	2,344	1,030	41	25	123	76
55 or older	141	96	479	272	5	4	17	8

[1]Includes American Indians, Alaska Natives, Asians, Native Hawaiians, and other Pacific Islanders.
[2]Excludes Hispanics.

SOURCE: Paige M. Harrison and Allen J. Beck, "Table 14. Number of sentenced prisoners under State or Federal jurisdiction per 100,000 residents, by gender, race, Hispanic origin, and age, 2002," in *Prisoners in 2002*, NCJ 200248, U.S. Department of Justice, Bureau of Justice Statistics, Washington, DC, July 2003.

under sentence is higher than that of black females in the 18–19, 20–24, 45–54, and 55 or older age categories. Black females outnumber white females under sentence in age categories from 25 to 44.

In 2002 the number of sentenced prisoners under state or federal jurisdiction per 100,000 residents was 912 for males and 61 for females. (See Table 6.10.) Among youth 18 to 19 years old, there were 869 prisoners per 100,000 males and 34 prisoners per 100,000 females. For male youths, blacks had the highest ratio at 2,865 per 100,000, followed by Hispanics (1,224 per 100,000), then whites (331 per 100,000). Proportionally, among female youth, more blacks (87 per 100,000 residents) were under sentence than Hispanics (35 in 100,000) and whites (26 in 100,000).

JUVENILES IN JAIL

Between 1983 and 2000 the number of juveniles confined in adult jails rose 339 percent, according to the Bureau

of Justice Statistics. In 1983 the number of incarcerated juveniles in adult jails stood at 1,736; by 2000 it had climbed to 7,615. (See Table 6.11.) The most growth in the juvenile category appears between 1990 and 2000 (231 percent) and the lowest between 1983 and 1990 (33 percent).

The adult jail population also experienced rapid growth, rising 177 percent between 1983 and 2000. (See Table 6.11.) The percentage of incarcerated adults, however, experienced the slowest growth between 1990 and 2000 (52 percent). The biggest jump was seen in the adult female population, which grew 350 percent between 1983 and 2000. The adult male population grew by 163 percent during that same time frame.

The Bureau of Justice Statistics Correctional Surveys chart a one-day count of the number of jail inmates for various years. The largest increase of juveniles in jail during 1990 to 2000 occurred between 1993 and 1994, when the

TABLE 6.11

Juveniles in adult jails, 1983–2000

Year	Total adult inmates	All males	All females	Juveniles
1983	221,815	206,163	15,652	1,736
1984	233,018	216,275	16,743	1,482
1985	254,986	235,909	19,077	1,629
1986	272,736	251,235	21,501	1,708
1987	294,092	270,172	23,920	1,781
1988	341,893	311,594	30,299	1,676
1989	393,248	356,050	37,198	2,250
1990	403,019	365,821	37,198	2,301
1991	424,129	384,628	39,501	2,350
1992	441,780	401,106	40,674	2,804
1993	455,600	411,500	44,100	4,300
1994	479,800	431,300	48,500	6,700
1995	499,300	448,000	51,300	7,800
1996	510,400	454,700	55,700	8,100
1997	557,974	498,678	59,296	9,105
1998	584,372	520,581	63,791	8,090
1999	596,485	528,998	67,487	9,458
2000	613,534	543,120	70,414	7,615
% Change:				
1983–1990	82	77	138	33
1990–2000	52	48	89	231
1983–2000	177	163	350	339

SOURCE: Adapted from James Austin, Kelly Dedel Johnson, Maria Gregoriou, "Table 2: Juveniles in Adult Jails, 1983–1998," in *Juveniles in Adult Prisons and Jails: A National Assessment*, U.S. Department of Justice, U.S. Bureau of Justice Assistance, Washington, DC, 2000 and "Jail populations by age and gender, 1990-2000," *Demographic Trends in Jail Populations*, U.S. Bureau of Justice Statistics [Online] http://www.ojp.usdoj.gov/bjs/glance/tables/jailagtab.htm [accessed March 5, 2003]

TABLE 6.12

Average daily population and the number of men, women, and juveniles in local jails, midyear 1995 and 2000–02

	1995	2000	2001	2002
Average daily population[1]	509,828	618,319	625,966	652,082
Number of inmates, June 30	507,044	621,149	631,240	665,475
Adults	499,300	613,534	623,628	658,228
Male	448,000	543,120	551,007	581,411
Female	51,300	70,414	72,621	76,817
Juveniles[2]	7,800	7,615	7,613	7,248
Held as adults[3]	5,900	6,126	6,757	6,112
Held as juveniles	1,800	1,489	856	1,136

Note: Data are for June 30 in 1995 and 2000; for June 29 in 2001; and June 28, for 2002. Detailed data for 1995 were estimated and rounded to the nearest 100.
[1]The average daily population is the sum of the number of inmates in a jail each day for a year, divided by the total number of days in the year
[2]Juveniles are persons defined by state statute as being under a certain age, usually 18, and subject initially to juvenile court authority even if tried as adults in criminal court. In 1994 the definition was changed to include all persons under age 18.
[3]Includes juveniles who were tried or awaiting trial as adults.

SOURCE: Paige M. Harrison and Jennifer C. Karberg, "Table 9. Average daily population and the number of men, women, and juveniles in local jails, midyear 1995 and 2000–2002," in *Prison and Jail Inmates at Midyear 2002*, NCJ 198877, U.S. Department of Justice, Bureau of Justice Statistics, Washington, DC, April 2003

number rose by 2,400. (See Table 6.11.) The biggest decrease was seen between 1999 and 2000, when the number declined from 9,458 to 7,615 (a total of 1,843 juveniles).

According to *Prison and Jail Inmates at Midyear 2002* (Paige M. Harrison and Jennifer C. Karberg, U.S. Department of Justice, Bureau of Justice Statistics, Washington, DC, April 2003), the average daily population in local prisons and jails increased more than 140,000 between 1995 and 2002. In 1995 the number of juveniles in jail stood at 7,800 compared to 7,248 in 2002, a decrease of 552. (See Table 6.12.) In fact, the number of juveniles in jail declined between 1995 and 2000 and again between 2000 and 2002.

Table 6.12 also captures information regarding the number of juvenile inmates being held as adults and those being held as juveniles. Between 1995 and 2002 the number of juveniles being held as adults rose from 5,900 to 6,112. The number was highest in 2001 at 6,757. More than 84 percent of juvenile jail inmates in 2002 were being held as adults. This means that they were either being held for trial in adult criminal court or they had been convicted as adults.

IMPRISONING JUVENILES AND ADULTS TOGETHER

A number of human rights organizations and juvenile justice groups point out the risks associated with incarcerat-

ing juveniles together with adults. Among the chief concerns is that being held with hardened adult prisoners will likely cause youths to become more violent, more tough, and repeat offenders. Instead of rehabilitation and education, such juveniles will be subjected to more physical and sexual abuse and violence, increasing their likelihood of showing violent tendencies when returning to society one day.

According to Amnesty International, "Youth in prison are notoriously a common target of sexual and physical assault by adult inmates" (*Betraying the Young: Human Rights Violations Against Children in the US Justice System*, Amnesty International Web site, accessed February 2004). Keeping youth in adult prisons and jails "plac[es] them at risk of attack by adults, and exposed to the corrupting influence of people with extensive criminal records." The Center on Juvenile and Criminal Justice echoes that sentiment. "Young people slated to be placed in adult prisons and jails are more likely to be raped, assaulted, and commit suicide."

Organizations also point out that juveniles are exposed to attack not only by adult inmates but also from prison guards. Reasons for this can include the juveniles' small stature, lack of confidence, and inexperience at living confined with hardened criminals. Juveniles sometimes resort to suicide because they may give in to despair more quickly.

JUVENILES IN DETENTION IN GENERAL

In "Detention in Delinquency Cases, 1989–1998" (*OJJDP Fact Sheet*, U.S. Department of Justice, Office of

TABLE 6.13

Delinquency cases involving detention, 1989–98

Case type	Percent of all cases involving detention			Percent change in number of cases, 1989–98		Change in number of cases involving detention, 1989–98
	1989	1994	1998	All cases	Detained cases	
Total	**21%**	**18%**	**19%**	**44%**	**25%**	**66,100**
Person	25	23	22	88	63	34,200
Property	17	15	15	11	−6	−7,400
Drugs	36	24	23	148	55	15,600
Public order	26	21	22	73	44	23,800
Male	23%	20%	20%	35%	20%	44,200
Person	27	25	24	71	49	22,800
Property	18	16	16	3	−8	−8,700
Drugs	38	25	23	142	51	12,800
Public order	26	22	22	65	40	17,400
Female	17%	14%	14%	83%	56%	21,900
Person	19	17	18	157	138	11,500
Property	12	10	9	44	8	1,300
Drugs	28	18	19	182	93	2,800
Public order	25	18	19	105	59	6,400
White	18%	16%	17%	43%	33%	49,200
Person	22	20	21	107	95	25,100
Property	15	14	13	8	−8	−5,900
Drugs	23	17	18	192	128	13,100
Public order	24	20	21	68	48	16,900
Black	29%	22%	23%	44%	15%	14,900
Person	30	26	24	63	30	7,800
Property	23	18	19	16	−1	−300
Drugs	56	36	35	80	11	2,000
Public order	30	22	21	86	32	5,400

SOURCE: Paul Harms, "Delinquency cases involving detention, 1989–1998," in *Detention in Delinquency Cases, 1989–1998,* Fact Sheet, U.S. Department of Justice, Office of Juvenile Justice and Delinquency Prevention, January 2002

Justice Programs, Washington, DC, January 2002), the OJJDP reported that the number of delinquency cases involving detention increased 25 percent during the time frame of its study. While detention cases among male juveniles increased 20 percent overall, female detention cases grew by 56 percent proportionally. (See Table 6.13.) Both males and females saw large increases for detention cases in the "person" offense category; however, female cases in that category grew 138 percent between 1989 and 1998 compared to 49 percent for male cases. The number of detention cases involving drugs increased greatly among whites (128 percent) and far less among blacks (11 percent). The percentage increase during these years in the overall number of cases detained was greater for whites (33 percent) than blacks (15 percent).

RESIDENTIAL PLACEMENT

Although 10,303 juveniles resided in prison and jail in 2002, many more were held in confinement. They represented those youths transferred to the jurisdiction of adult courts, usually by waiver or under statutorily mandated rules. According to the Census of Juveniles in Residential Placement (CJRP), last conducted in 1999 by the OJJDP, 108,931 juvenile offenders were confined in pub-

lic and private juvenile correctional, detention, and shelter facilities. Excluded from this category are juveniles in prisons and jails. So to calculate the total number of confined youth in 1999, one must add 13,900 juveniles in prison and jail that year. This brings the total population of confined youth to 122,831 in 1999. Of this number, 11 percent resided in adult facilities while the rest were held in juvenile residential facilities. In 1999 the number of residential facilities numbered 2,939, of which 1,794 were private, 1,136 were public, and 9 were tribal, according to Melissa Sickmund in "Juvenile Offenders in Residential Placement: 1997–1999" (*OJJDP Fact Sheet,* no. 07, March 2002).

The OJJDP divides crimes into delinquency offenses and status offenses. Delinquency offenses are acts that are illegal regardless of the age of the perpetrator. Status offenses are acts that are illegal only for minors, such as truancy and running away. About 96 percent of juveniles in residential placement in 1999 were delinquents. This represented an increase of 5 percent from 1997. (See Table 6.14.) The other 4 percent were status offenders (truants from school, noncriminal ordinances and rules violators, out-of-control youths, curfew violators, and runaways). Most juveniles in residential placement were held for burglary (11 percent), aggravated assault (9 percent), and robbery (8 percent) offenses. Robbery, like aggravated assault, is considered a violent crime because the threat of force is either used or implied by the perpetrator.

Among the categories with the greatest percentage increases during this time period were offenses against other persons, which rose 50 percent. (See Table 6.14.) Such offenses include violent sex acts (other than rape), kidnapping, and false imprisonment, among others. Large percentage gains were also seen for sexual assault (34 percent), arson (23 percent), and public order offenses other than those involving weapons (17 percent). The biggest declines were found in status offenses (32 percent), criminal homicide (21 percent), and robbery (13 percent). Those categories with the smallest change included drug trafficking (up 2 percent) and burglary (down 3 percent).

Details about the residential facilities housing youth appeared in "Juvenile Residential Facility Census, 2000: Selected Findings" (Melissa Sickmund, *OJJDP Bulletin*, December 2002). In that study, Sickmund reported that the number of juvenile inmates in residential facilities had increased another 1,353 since 1999, for a total of 110,284 in 2000. The number of facilities increased as well: public added 67 for 1,203 total; private grew by 54 for 1,848 total; and tribal gained 1 for 10 total. Public facilities continued to house the most juveniles (77,662 or 70.4 percent). (See Table 6.15.)

In 2000 states with the largest number of youth under 21 in residential facilities included: California (19,286), Texas (8,354), Florida (7,278), Pennsylvania (5,085), New York (5,081), and Ohio (4,890). (See Table 6.15.) These states housed more than 45 percent of all juveniles in residential detention. States with the smallest number included Hawaii (122), Vermont (158), and New Hampshire (193). However, such data need to be considered in relation to the size of the population of these states. For example, the number of juveniles in California is far greater than the number in Hawaii, but the number of California residents is much greater than that of Hawaii as well. Detailed information on juveniles being held in tribal facilities is not included in Table 6.15. Those facilities are located in Arizona, Colorado, Montana, Oklahoma, and South Dakota.

Overcrowding

The residential facility census also reported information on bed availability in 2000. Overcrowding is an issue in many centers housing juveniles. About 94 percent of the facilities supplied information. Of the 2,875 facilities participating, 1,704 were private and 1,164 were public; the rest were tribal. Overall, 39 percent of these facilities had more residents than available standard beds. Private facilities reported 40 percent and public, 37 percent. According to the census, "A single bed is counted as one standard bed and a bunk bed is counted as two standard

TABLE 6.14

Juvenile offenders in residential placement by offense, 1999

Most serious offense	Juvenile offenders in residential placement		Percent change 1997–99
	Number	Percent	
Total juvenile offenders	**108,931**	**100**	**3**
Delinquency	104,237	96	5
Person	38,005	35	7
Criminal homicide	1,514	1	-21
Sexual assault	7,511	7	34
Robbery	8,212	8	-13
Aggravated assault	9,984	9	5
Simple assault	7,448	7	12
Other person[a]	3,336	3	50
Property	31,817	29	-1
Burglary	12,222	11	-3
Theft	6,944	6	-5
Auto theft	6,225	6	-5
Arson	1,126	1	23
Other property	5,300	5	13
Drug	9,882	9	6
Drug trafficking	3,106	3	2
Other drug	6,776	6	9
Public order	10,487	10	8
Weapons	4,023	4	-4
Other public order	6,464	6	17
Technical violation[b]	14,046	13	12
Violent Crime Index[b]	27,221	25	3
Property Crime Index[b]	26,517	24	-3
Status offense	4,694	4	-32

[a] Offenses against other persons include kidnapping, violent sex acts other than forcible rape (e.g., incest, sodomy), custody interference, unlawful restraint, false imprisonment, reckless endangerment, harassment, and attempts to commit any such acts.
[b] Technical violations include violations of probation, parole, and valid court orders. Violent Crime Index offenses include criminal homicide, sexual assault, robbery, and aggravated assault. Property Crime Index offenses include burglary, theft, auto theft, and arson.

SOURCE: Melissa Sickmund, "More than one-third of juvenile offenders in residential placement were held for person offenses," in "Juvenile Offenders in Residential Placement: 1997–1999," *Juvenile Offenders and Victims National Report Series Fact Sheet #07*, U.S. Department of Justice, Office of Justice Programs, Office of Juvenile Justice and Delinquency Prevention, Washington, DC, March 2002

beds. Makeshift beds (e.g., cots, rollout beds, mattresses, and sofas) are not counted as standard beds."

Most states reported some overcrowding in their facilities overall in 2000. Rhode Island had the highest percentage of overcrowding: 80 percent overall, 100 percent in public facilities, and 78 percent in private centers. Other states reporting more than half of their facilities as being overcrowded include: Massachusetts (77 percent); Delaware (57 percent); California (56 percent); New York and Oklahoma (53 percent each); and Florida, Idaho, Tennessee, and West Virginia (all 52 percent). Delaware reported overcrowding at 100 percent of its public centers, while Mississippi recorded the same percentage in its private facilities. North Dakota (0 percent), Wisconsin (14 percent), and Wyoming (17 percent) experienced the least overcrowding overall.

Placement Status

The OJJDP classifies juveniles in residential placement into three categories: committed, detained, and

TABLE 6.15

Juvenile residential facilities by state, 2000

State	Juvenile facilities All facilities	Public	Private	Offenders younger than 21 All facilities	Public	Private	State	Juvenile facilities All facilities	Public	Private	Offenders younger than 21 All facilities	Public	Private
U.S. Total*	3,061	1,203	1,848	110,284	77,662	32,464	Missouri	65	57	8	1,540	1,290	250
Alabama	46	12	34	1,583	926	657	Montana	18	8	10	260	173	65
Alaska	19	5	14	339	261	78	Nebraska	23	6	17	789	577	212
Arizona	51	16	35	2,248	1,752	398	Nevada	15	10	5	1,176	750	426
Arkansas	45	11	34	639	295	344	New Hampshire	8	2	6	193	123	70
California	285	116	169	19,286	17,551	1,735	New Jersey	57	45	12	2,274	2,171	103
Colorado	73	12	61	2,054	1,112	940	New Mexico	27	19	8	885	838	47
Connecticut	26	5	21	1,360	900	460	New York	210	59	151	5,081	2,883	2,198
Delaware	7	3	4	295	246	49	North Carolina	67	27	40	1,555	1,237	318
Dist. of Columbia	17	3	14	272	159	113	North Dakota	13	4	9	203	105	98
Florida	166	53	113	7,278	3,269	4,009	Ohio	106	71	35	4,890	4,342	548
Georgia	50	29	21	3,270	2,593	677	Oklahoma	52	14	38	1,034	535	479
Hawaii	7	3	4	122	107	15	Oregon	48	27	21	1,637	1,415	222
Idaho	22	14	8	580	470	110	Pennsylvania	163	29	134	5,085	1,241	3,844
Illinois	46	26	20	3,402	3,074	328	Rhode Island	11	1	10	360	211	149
Indiana	97	41	56	3,334	2,239	1,095	South Carolina	42	16	26	1,592	1,072	520
Iowa	76	18	60	1,166	395	771	South Dakota	22	9	13	646	365	265
Kansas	51	17	34	1,185	831	354	Tennessee	63	28	35	1,824	1,041	783
Kentucky	58	31	27	950	757	193	Texas	138	77	61	8,354	6,475	1,879
Louisiana	64	20	44	2,663	2,105	558	Utah	51	17	34	1,135	453	682
Maine	17	3	14	300	248	52	Vermont	5	1	4	158	26	132
Maryland	43	11	32	1,492	690	802	Virginia	74	62	12	2,868	2,616	252
Massachusetts	71	18	53	1,481	567	914	Washington	42	31	11	2,064	1,938	126
Michigan	108	42	66	3,896	1,782	2,114	West Virginia	27	6	21	381	241	140
Minnesota	121	22	99	1,922	986	936	Wisconsin	94	27	67	2,017	1,271	746
Mississippi	20	19	1	787	785	2	Wyoming	24	2	22	379	173	206

Note: State is the state where the facility is located. Offenders sent to out-of-state facilities are counted in the state where the facility is located, not the state where their offense occurred.
*U.S. total includes 158 offenders in 10 tribal facilities. These offenders were located in Arizona, Colorado, Montana, Oklahoma, and South Dakota.

SOURCE: Melissa Sickmund, "In October 2000, 4 in 10 juvenile facilities were publicly operated and held 70% of juvenile offenders in custody," in "Juvenile Residential Facility Census, 2000: Selected Findings," *Juvenile Offenders and Victims National Report Series Bulletin*, U.S. Department of Justice, Office of Justice Programs, Office of Juvenile Justice and Delinquency Prevention, Washington, DC, December 2002

under a diversion agreement. According to the OJJDP in its CJRP, "Committed juveniles include those placed in the facility as part of a court ordered disposition. Detained juveniles include those held awaiting a court hearing, adjudication, disposition or placement elsewhere. Voluntarily admitted juveniles include those in the facility in lieu of adjudication as part of a diversion agreement."

In 1999, of the 108,931 juveniles in residential placement overall, 73.9 percent were committed, 25.2 percent were detained, and less than 1 percent were under diversion agreements. The largest group, "committed," were sent to residential placement by juvenile courts. Those being "detained" were part of a transitory population—those awaiting hearings, the disposition of their cases, or transfer to a different type of facility. It is likely that some of the "detained" individuals were sent to prison or jail later. Persons in confinement under diversion agreements have entered detention voluntarily. In other words, the juvenile may have "volunteered" to go to a detention center to avoid going to juvenile court.

In its research on the most serious offenses committed by those in residential placement, the OJJDP learned that delinquency offenses ranked highest among all three groups:

detained (96.5 percent), committed (95.6 percent), and diversionary (71.1 percent). The latter group, however, had a much greater proportion of status offenses (28.9 percent) than the detained (3.5 percent) and committed (4.4 percent) groups.

The largest proportion of delinquency crimes for all three groups fell under the person and property categories. The top three crimes for committed youth in these categories were burglary (9,696), aggravated assault (7,815), and robbery (6,795). For detained youth, the top crimes were burglary (2,475), aggravated assault (2,112), and simple assault (2,016). Among the diversionary group, simple assault (84), sexual assault (51), and theft (27) were highest. Status offenses for all three groups were highest in the categories of incorrigibility, running away, and truancy. Incorrigibility was the status offense that had the highest numbers for both committed and detained juveniles. Of the three status offenses, diversionary juveniles were most often detained for running away.

Demographics of Those in Residential Placement

GENDER. In 1999 juvenile detention facilities were home to a disproportionately larger number of males (86.6 percent) than females (13.4 percent), according to the CJRP.

Of the males in confinement, more than one-third (35.7 percent) had committed offenses against people and slightly less than one-third (30 percent) had committed property offenses. Females were less likely to commit person offenses (29.9 percent) and property offenses (24 percent) than males. Proportionally, among person offenses, females were more likely to commit simple assault than males (11.8 percent to 6.1 percent respectively), but far less likely to commit sexual assault (0.6 percent to 7.9 percent). Property offenses seeing the largest discrepancies between males and females included burglary (males—12.2 percent, females—4.7 percent) and theft (males—6 percent, females—8.7 percent). Males were more likely to be involved in drug and public order offenses, while females, proportionally, were more frequently detained for technical and status offenses.

RACE/ETHNICITY. In 1999 blacks represented the highest proportion of juveniles in residential placement at 39 percent, followed by whites (38 percent), Hispanics (18 percent), and American Indians and Asians/Pacific Islanders (2 percent each). (Hispanics may be of any race.) Another 1 percent fell into the "other" category, which includes those of multiple races. The CJRP also provides data on the number of detained juveniles per 100,000 juveniles in the general population for each of the racial/ethnic categories, except "other." The ratio for black youths was highest (1,004 per 100,000), followed by Native Americans (632 per 100,000), Hispanics (485 per 100,000), whites (212 per 100,000), and Asians/Pacific Islanders (182 per 100,000).

ALTERNATIVE CORRECTIONAL FACILITIES: BOOT CAMPS

Modeled after military boot camps, such facilities for juveniles began to surface in the mid-1980s. Among the first was a camp in Orleans Parish, Louisiana. Generally established for "midrange" offenders, such as those who have failed to meet the requirement of their probation, juvenile camps are intended to provide youths with structure, organization, and discipline. Certain types of youths are typically excluded, including those with a record of serious violence, armed robbery, and sex offenses.

The camps, which generally last from 90–120 days, use many activities that are common in military camps. For example, uniformed drill instructors and a platoon sergeant keep participants in line, handing out punishments when someone breaks the rules. Work details are another aspect of such camps, as are programs devoted to academic education. One of the goals of many camps is to provide youth with vocational education, job preparation, or work-skills training.

Although initially popular, boot camps have become controversial for several reasons. The recidivism (or relapse into crime) rate for youths attending boot camps has ranged between 64 and 75 percent, according to the Koch Crime Institute (KCI). "Overall, KCI researchers have found that boot camps have not been shown to reduce recidivism or deter crime. However, the recidivism rate of boot camps is only slightly higher than that of traditional juvenile facilities," according to the study *Juvenile Boot Camps: Cost and Effectiveness vs. Residential Facilities* (Brent Zaehringer, Koch Crime Institute, 1998). Various reports have also surfaced charging some camps with neglect and physical abuse of juveniles.

CHAPTER 7

A CULTURE OF VIOLENCE?:
CURRENT TOPICS OF SPECIAL INTEREST

High homicide rates, gang violence, bullies, school shootings, crimes based on hate, tales of violent hazings at school, and young people's easy access to guns are just some of the issues frequently cited by the media, lawmakers, and the public as indications that a culture of violence pervades the United States. Whether one reads a newspaper in print or online or watches television, cable, or satellite news, stories featuring crime and violence permeate those publications and broadcasts. "Breaking news" events often spur a flurry of special reports on topics related to the news event. For example, after Eric Harris and Dylan Klebold went on a shooting rampage at Columbine High School in Littleton, Colorado, in 1999, many reports focused on the easy availability of guns and youths' fascination with weapons. Or, when someone is killed in a drive-by shooting, reports often center on gang violence and what law enforcement is doing to prevent it. When the world learned the identities of the Washington, D.C.-area snipers and discovered one was a juvenile, it sparked discussion of whether juveniles should be tried as adults. During the subsequent trial of the young sniper, Lee Boyd Malvo, much debate focused on whether juveniles should be eligible for the death penalty.

Such topics might receive a lot of attention, then fade from view when another incident of a serious, but different, nature occurs. In time, many of those earlier topics are back in the news, the focus of new studies and the subject of much discussion. This chapter presents detailed information on several of the topics frequently discussed in the early twenty-first century.

HATE CRIMES

In October 1998 the lives of three 21-year-old men forever changed after reportedly meeting in a bar in Laramie, Wyoming. One was Matthew Shepard, an openly gay student at the University of Wyoming. The other two men, who were friends, were locals Aaron McKinney and Russell Henderson. After meeting, Shepard left the bar with McKinney and Henderson. The pair ultimately robbed and beat Shepard so severely that he died five days later after falling into a coma. They struck Shepard repeatedly with a gun and then tied him to a fence in the countryside, leaving him to die. Shepard was found some 18 hours later by a bicyclist, who at first glance thought Shepard was a scarecrow. The wounds were so severe that doctors could not operate. When Shepard died, the world turned its eyes on Laramie, wondering how a crime so brutal could occur in such a seemingly small, friendly town.

Many perceived the acts against Shepard to be a hate crime, committed against him because he was gay. The prosecution did not approach the case as a hate crime, however. Some people claimed the motive was robbery because McKinney and Henderson took twenty dollars off Shepard as well as his coat, shoes, and credit card. Regardless, during the subsequent trials of the perpetrators, gay and lesbian advocates as well as antigay groups flooded the town and held demonstrations. Members of the Westboro Baptist Church of Topeka, Kansas, led by the Reverend Fred Phelps, held signs saying "God Hates Fags" and "Matt in Hell." Friends of Shepard's, dressed as angels, countered the demonstrators, trying to block the protestors from sight by spreading their bed-sheet wings. Members of Phelps' congregation even protested at Shepard's funeral in Casper, Wyoming.

Both McKinney and Henderson were sent to prison. Henderson pled guilty to felony murder, thus avoiding a death sentence. McKinney made a deal with prosecutors to avoid the death penalty after being found guilty of felony murder. Shepard's parents supported the deal with McKinney. Shepard's father, Dennis, addressed the court on November 4, 1999. In his statement to the court, as recorded on an official Web site devoted to Shepard (http://www.matthewsplace.com), Dennis noted that:

"Matt became a symbol—some say a martyr, putting a boy-next-door face on hate crimes." He added, "Matt's beating, hospitalization, and funeral focused worldwide attention on hate. Good is coming out of evil. People have said 'Enough is enough.'"

Phelps and his followers, however, sought to erect a monument to Shepard in the slain student's hometown of Casper, Wyoming. The proposed Shepard monument reputedly cites scripture and says "Matthew Shepard entered Hell October 12, 1998 at age 21 in defiance of God's solemn warning...." Because a city park displayed a monument to the 10 Commandments of the Old Testament, Phelps asserted that the city had to let his group put up their memorial. The group claimed that since the city had allowed one religious monument to be placed in a public park, the door was opened for others. The group has tried to erect the antigay memorial in other cities as well, including Boise, Idaho. Viewed by many as a message of hate, such proposed memorials have cities thinking about removing the 10 Commandments monuments from their parks.

Shepard's death—and the victimization of other individuals due to bias motivation—has caused lawmakers to look at hate crimes legislation and what can be done to deter such incidents from occurring. It has also caused many antidiscrimination groups to remain ever-vigilant in the fight to stop hate.

Definition of a Hate Crime

According to the Bureau of Justice Statistics, hate crimes "also referred to as bias crimes, are criminal offenses motivated by an offender's bias against a race, religion, disability, sexual orientation, or ethnicity" (Kevin J. Strom, *Hate Crimes Reported in NIBRS, 1997–1999,* Bureau of Justice Statistics, Washington, DC, September 2001). The Anti-Defamation League's (ADL) Web site (http://www.adl.org) further notes that "hate crimes are defined under specific penal code sections as an act or an attempted act by any person against the person or property of another individual or group which in any way constitutes an expression of hostility toward the victim because of his or her race, religion, sexual orientation, national origin, disability, gender or ethnicity." The ADL further contends: "This includes, but is not limited to, threatening phone calls, hate mail, physical assaults, vandalism, cross burning, destruction of religious symbols and fire bombings."

The Federal Bureau of Investigation (FBI), charged with recording hate crimes statistics, notes that such incidents have occurred throughout history. In the foreword to *Hate Crime Statistics, 2002* (Federal Bureau of Investigation, Washington, DC), the FBI explains: "It is only recently, however, that our society has given it a name and decided to monitor it, study it, and legislate against it."

With the passage of the Hate Crime Statistics Act of 1990, Congress took steps to gain information about such crimes. The FBI published its first set of findings in *Hate Crime Statistics, 1990: A Resource Book.* That publication, however, only contained information from 11 states. In the Violent Crime and Law Enforcement Act of 1994, Congress added disabled persons to the list of bias-crime motivations. As of January 1, 1997, the FBI began recording these data as well. In its most recent study, *Hate Crime Statistics, 2002,* the FBI reports information from 12,073 agencies from 49 states and the District of Columbia.

Hate Crimes Statistics

REPORTING ISSUES. Not all hate crimes get counted, according to various antidiscrimination groups and government entities. Such organizations note that some law enforcement agencies report false zeroes and others are assigned a false zero when they fail to report. According to the Southern Law Poverty Center (SLPC) in its report *Discounting Hate,* which appears on its Web site, "In addition to the false zeroes phenomenon, there are several other factors that contribute to the systematic underreporting of hate crimes—from a lack of training in recognizing hate crimes, the false belief that relatively minor crimes need not be reported to the FBI, and an over-eagerness to write off the bias aspect of criminal incidents, to outright opposition to the very notion of hate crimes." The SLPC further asserts that although some recent reports cite about 8,000 hate crimes annually, the actual figure could be closer to 50,000. Another reason for this discrepancy is that victims are often reluctant to report such incidents. Asserting that accurate reporting is essential, the SLPC quotes hate crimes expert Jack Levin: "When we regard hate crime incidents like vandalism and desecration of cemeteries as mere childish pranks, we inadvertently cause the perpetrators to raise the ante."

Other reasons for underreporting exist as well. Many incidents cannot be verified as hate crimes. Plus, some victims are hesitant to report bias crimes because they believe the criminal justice system has its own bias against the group to which he or she belongs. In these instances, such victims believe that law enforcement officials will not help them. Researchers report that many hate crimes against gays and lesbians go unreported as well. Some do not want to make public their sexual preferences, while others are concerned about how they will be treated by police. The process of proving bias can be long and tedious, requiring extra investigation. While some individuals do not want to relive the experience through more investigation, some law enforcement agencies simply do not have the staff available to investigate allegations of hate that are not immediately apparent. If an investigator cannot find enough evidence of bias motivation, the crime is not counted as a hate crime.

ESTIMATED NUMBERS. In *Hate Crimes Statistics, 2002* the FBI presents data that were submitted by 12,073

TABLE 7.1

Agency hate crime reporting by state, 2002

Participating state	Number of participating agencies	Population covered	Agencies submitting incident reports	Total number of incidents reported
Total	**12,073**	**247,246,683**	**1,868**	**7,462**
Alabama	31	259,938	2	2
Alaska	1	267,280	1	7
Arizona	88	5,023,657	29	238
Arkansas	7	387,957	0	0
California	726	35,056,859	243	1,648
Colorado	190	4,251,762	30	96
Connecticut	84	2,838,717	50	129
Delaware	50	806,717	8	13
District of Columbia	2	570,898	2	14
Florida	489	16,660,424	93	257
Georgia	76	1,558,760	10	31
Idaho	117	1,330,416	14	43
Illinois	59	4,639,084	46	155
Indiana	163	4,476,334	25	77
Iowa	221	2,863,046	18	46
Kansas	339	2,366,821	13	55
Kentucky	341	3,663,360	38	76
Louisiana	159	3,418,556	13	15
Maine	180	1,291,128	14	36
Maryland	148	5,458,137	26	211
Massachusetts	305	5,822,308	90	430
Michigan	619	9,814,593	164	416
Minnesota	279	4,843,609	71	203
Mississippi	66	942,735	3	3
Missouri	144	2,955,399	19	64
Montana	93	881,473	6	13
Nebraska	203	1,362,661	17	74
Nevada	35	2,173,491	7	62
New Hampshire	107	654,470	19	27
New Jersey	557	8,590,300	220	570
New Mexico	49	1,180,982	3	15
New York	505	19,154,571	63	693
North Carolina	446	8,242,488	29	62
North Dakota	74	562,980	7	18
Ohio	400	8,244,818	63	263
Oklahoma	301	3,493,714	19	44
Oregon	172	3,509,432	24	61
Pennsylvania	849	11,086,040	26	92
Rhode Island	48	1,069,725	7	38
South Carolina	310	4,103,856	35	70
South Dakota	130	734,731	4	4
Tennessee	443	5,796,102	54	129
Texas	969	21,698,160	82	347
Utah	59	1,790,393	17	54
Vermont	57	565,746	10	18
Virginia	399	7,258,150	54	291
Washington	246	6,036,923	47	174
West Virginia	336	1,758,307	16	41
Wisconsin	370	5,438,068	13	32
Wyoming	31	290,607	4	5

SOURCE: "Table 2.36. Agency hate crime reporting by state, 2002," in *Crime in the United States 2002: Uniform Crime Reports,* Federal Bureau of Investigation, Washington, DC, 2003

agencies. Although the data may be incomplete, the report does illuminate trends among hate crime victims and offenders. Table 7.1 provides a breakdown of the agencies within each state reporting bias incidents and the number of incidents reported. A low number does not necessarily mean that only few hate crimes occurred in that state. It could mean that hate crimes are underreported in that state. Overall, 7,462 hate crime incidents were reported to the FBI in 2002. All but three of the crimes were single-bias incidents, meaning that the incident derived from one type of bias. The single-bias incidents resulted in 8,825 offenses being committed; seven offenses occurred during

multiple-bias incidents. Those offenses fell into three categories according to the FBI: "crimes against persons, crimes against property, and crimes against society." More than two of three crimes were committed against people, while nearly a third were against property. Crimes against society comprised less than 1 percent. (See Table 7.2.)

Crimes against people represented 5,960 of the 8,832 total offenses. Most involved intimidation (3,105), followed by simple assault (1,791), aggravated assault (1,035), murder and nonnegligent manslaughter (11), and forcible rape (8). Ten fell into the "other" category.

TABLE 7.2

TABLE 7.3

Incidents, offenses, victims, and known offenders by offense type, 2002

Offense type	Incidents[1]	Offenses	Victims[2]	Known offenders[3]
Total	**7,462**	**8,832**	**9,222**	**7,314**
Crimes against persons:	4,784	5,960	5,960	6,090
Murder and nonnegligent manslaughter	11	11	11	15
Forcible rape	8	8	8	16
Aggravated assault	800	1,035	1,035	1,498
Simple assault	1,473	1,791	1,791	2,436
Intimidation	2,484	3,105	3,105	2,117
Other[4]	8	10	10	8
Crimes against property:	2,823	2,823	3,213	1,423
Robbery	131	131	179	269
Burglary	131	131	163	86
Larceny-theft	151	151	157	95
Motor vehicle theft	9	9	9	3
Arson	38	38	47	27
Destruction/damage/vandalism	2,347	2,347	2,642	927
Other[4]	16	16	16	16
Crimes against society[4]	49	49	49	61

[1]The actual number of incidents is 7,462. However, the column figures will not add to the total because incidents may include more than one offense type, and these are counted in each appropriate offense type category.
[2]The term victim may refer to a person, business, institution, or society as a whole.
[3]The term known offender does not imply that the identity of the suspect is known, but only that an attribute of the suspect is identified, which distinguishes him/her from an unknown offender. The actual number of known offenders is 7,314. However, the column figures will not add to the total because some offenders are responsible for more than one offense type, and they are, therefore, counted more than once in this table.
[4]Includes additional offenses.

SOURCE: "Table 2.34. Incidents, offenses, victims, and known offenders by offense type, 2002," in *Crime in the United States 2002: Uniform Crime Reports*, Federal Bureau of Investigation, Washington, DC, 2003

Incidents, offenses, victims, and known offenders by bias motivation, 2002

Bias motivation	Incidents	Offenses	Victims[1]	Known offenders[2]
Total	**7,462**	**8,832**	**9,222**	**7,314**
Single-bias incidents	7,459	8,825	9,211	7,311
Race:	3,642	4,393	4,580	4,011
Anti-white	719	888	910	1,064
Anti-black	2,486	2,967	3,076	2,510
Anti-American Indian/ Alaskan Native	62	68	72	52
Anti-Asian/Pacific Islander	217	268	280	242
Anti-multiple races, group	158	202	242	143
Religion:	1,426	1,576	1,659	568
Anti-Jewish	931	1,039	1,084	317
Anti-Catholic	53	58	71	21
Anti-Protestant	55	57	58	34
Anti-Islamic	155	170	174	103
Anti-other religion	198	217	237	73
Anti-multiple religions, group	31	32	32	18
Anti-atheism/agnosticism/etc.	3	3	3	2
Sexual orientation:	1,244	1,464	1,513	1,438
Anti-male homosexual	825	957	984	1,022
Anti-female homosexual	172	207	221	172
Anti-homosexual	222	259	267	225
Anti-heterosexual	10	26	26	6
Anti-bisexual	15	15	15	13
Ethnicity/national origin:	1,102	1,345	1,409	1,247
Anti-Hispanic	480	601	639	656
Anti-other ethnicity/national origin	622	744	770	591
Disability:	45	47	50	47
Anti-physical	20	20	20	21
Anti-mental	25	27	30	26
Multiple-bias incidents[3]	3	7	11	3

[1]The term victim may refer to a person, business, institution, or society as a whole.
[2]The term known offender does not imply that the identity of the suspect is known, but only that an attribute of the suspect is identified, which distinguishes him/her from an unknown offender.
[3]A multiple-bias incident only occurs when two or more offense types are committed in a single incident. In a situation when there is more than one offense type, the agency can indicate a different bias type for each offense. In the case of a single offense type, only one bias type can be indicated.

SOURCE: "Table 2.33. Incidents, offenses, victims, and known offenders by bias motivation, 2002," in *Crime in the United States 2002: Uniform Crime Reports*, Federal Bureau of Investigation, Washington, DC, 2003

Crimes against property involved 2,823 offenses. Most involved destruction/damage/vandalism (2,347), followed by larceny-theft (151), robbery and burglary (131 each), arson (38), motor vehicle theft (9), and other (16). Forty-nine incidents were classified as crimes against society.

The majority of hate crimes were committed based on race (48.8 percent). (See Table 7.3.) Religion followed at 19.1 percent, with sexual orientation at 16.7 percent. Ethnicity/national origin was fourth with 14.8, then disability at less than 1 percent. Of the 8,832 offenses reported, 4,393 were based on race. More than two-thirds of those incidents (67.5 percent) were against blacks (2,967), while 20.2 percent (888) were against whites. Of the 1,576 offenses based on religion, two-thirds were against Jews (1,039). Less than 11 percent were against those of the Islamic religion (170). Nearly two-thirds of the 1,464 offenses involving homosexuals were committed against gay males (957), while more than 2 of 5 offenses involving ethnicity/national origin were aimed at Hispanics (601). The majority of disability incidents were leveled at those with mental impairments (27).

Of the data collected about known offenders, 61.8 percent were white, 21.8 percent were black, and 1.2 percent were Asian/Pacific Islander. (See Table 7.4.) More than 9.8 percent were of unknown race, 4.9 percent were of multiple races, and less than 1 percent were American Indian/Alaskan Native.

The FBI report also records the location of bias incidents. Residence/home topped the list with 2,198 incidents or 29.5 percent of the total, followed by highway/road/alley/street with 1,490 or 20 percent. Among those locations specified in the report, school/college came in third with 789 incidents or 10.6 percent. (See Table 7.5.) Of the nearly 800 incidents reported at schools and colleges, all were single-bias incidents. More than half were racially motivated, while 21.2 were based on sexual orientation, 18.9 on religion, 8.4 on ethnicity/national origin, and less than 1 percent on disability.

Hate at School

In *Indicators of School Crime and Safety: 2003* (J.F. DeVoe, K. Peter, P. Kaufman, S.A. Ruddy, A.K. Miller,

TABLE 7.4

Race of known offenders, 2002[1]

Known offender's race

Total	**7,314**
White	4,517
Black	1,592
American Indian/Alaskan Native	43
Asian/Pacific Islander	87
Multiple races, group[2]	355
Unknown race	720

[1]The term known offender does not imply that the identity of the suspect is known, but only that an attribute of the suspect is identified, which distinguishes him/her from an unknown offender.

[2]The term multiple races, group is used to describe a group of offenders comprised of individuals of varying races.

SOURCE: "Table 2.35. Race of known offenders, 2002," in *Crime in the United States 2002: Uniform Crime Reports,* Federal Bureau of Investigation, Washington, DC, 2003

M. Planty, T.D. Snyder, and M.R. Rand, U.S. Departments of Education and Justice, Washington, DC, 2003), students' experiences with hate crimes are recorded. Of the students (ages 12–18) surveyed in 2001, 12.3 percent acknowledged being targeted by hate-related words at school over the past 6 months. (See Table 7.6.) The definition of "school" not only includes the building itself, but school property, going to and from school, and riding on school buses.

Males reported a slightly higher incidence (12.8 percent) than females (11.7 percent), while blacks (13.9 percent) were most often affected, followed by whites (12.1 percent), then Hispanics (11 percent). Although seventh graders (14.1 percent) cited the most occurrences, tenth graders (13.1 percent) and eighth graders (13 percent) were close behind. Incidents greatly diminished among twelfth graders (7.9 percent). Rural and suburban students experienced hate-related words at the same levels (12.4 percent) while urban students (11.9 percent) were affected less often. Such events were far more common in public schools (12.7 percent) than private schools (8.2 percent).

Students were also asked to select what characteristics the hate-related words described. As such, they could choose multiple answers. The most common characteristic was race (4.2 percent), followed by gender (2.8 percent), ethnicity (2.7 percent), religion (1.8 percent), sexual orientation (1.2 percent), and disability (1.1 percent). Males most often cited race (4.6 percent), while females most frequently noted gender (4.4 percent). Blacks (7.8 percent) reported race hate-related words most often, and whites listed gender most frequently (3.3 percent). Race also topped the list for sixth through eleventh grade, with twelfth graders citing ethnicity and gender (2.3 percent each). Gender was also highest among suburban, rural, and private school students, with race highest among urban and public school students.

Indicators of School Crime and Safety: 2003 also compared the percentage of students who were targets of hate-related words with the percentage who saw hate-related graffiti at school. (See Figure 7.1.) In general, students were about three times more likely to see hate-related graffiti than to be targets of hate-related words. Some 36 percent of students 12–18 acknowledged seeing such graffiti, while about 12 percent were targets of hate-related words. The percentage of students seeing hate-related graffiti was close among genders, racial groups, and school type (urban, suburban, or rural). However, nearly 20 percent fewer students proportionally reported seeing graffiti in private schools than did students in public schools.

Age Estimates

Age data for hate crimes is included in *Hate Crimes Reported in NIBRS, 1997–1999* (Kevin J. Strom, Bureau of Justice Statistics, U.S. Department of Justice, Washington, DC, September 2001). In the report, Strom notes that most hate crime offenders are between the ages of 13 and 24 (58 percent). Four percent fall into the 0–12 age group, while 29 percent are between 13 and 17, and another 29 percent are 18 to 24. Seventeen percent were between 25 and 34, 13 percent between 35 and 44, and 9 percent were 45 or older. Some 27 percent of violent offenses and 40 percent of property offenses were committed by 13- to 17-year-olds, with 18- to 24-year-olds being responsible for 29 percent of violent offenses and 25 percent of property offenses.

Among the hate crimes committed between 1997 and 1999, 1 in 5 victims (21 percent each) were ages 18 to 24 or 25 to 34. Six percent were 0 to 12, 19 percent were 35 to 44, 17 percent were 13 to 17, and 16 percent were 45 or older. Nearly a quarter of violent hate-crime victims were ages 18 to 24, one fifth were 13 to 17, and another fifth were 25 to 34. Property crime victims were most frequently 45 or older (32 percent), 35 to 44 (24 percent), or 25 to 34 (19 percent). Those 18 to 24 reported fewer incidents of property crime (17 percent), followed by those 13 to 17 (7 percent) and 0 to 12 (1 percent).

According to Strom, "Younger victims were more likely to be victimized by persons known to them.... Of violent victims age 12 or younger, 67 percent were victimized by an acquaintance, 19 percent by a stranger, and 3 percent by a relative or friend.... Among victims age 13 to 17, 46 percent were victimized by an acquaintance, 18 percent by a stranger, and 4 percent by a relative or friend." In addition, young victims of violent hate crimes were most often targeted during the day. Among victims 17 and under, two-thirds were attacked between 7 A.M. and 6 P.M. However, most incidents occurred between 2 and 4 P.M. The time span for 18- to 24-year-olds was much later, with 1 in 4 attacks occurring between 10 P.M. and 1 A.M.

Although many hate crimes do not result in arrest, according to the National Incident-Based Reporting

TABLE 7.5

Hate crime incidents by location, 2002

| Location | Total incidents | Bias motivation | | | | | | Multiple-bias incidents* |
		Race	Religion	Sexual orientation	Ethnicity/ national origin	Disability	
Total	7,462	3,642	1,426	1,244	1,102	45	3
Air/bus/train terminal	63	38	8	10	5	2	0
Bank/savings and loan	19	9	4	4	2	0	0
Bar/night club	128	63	5	42	18	0	0
Church/synagogue/temple	284	28	241	4	10	1	0
Commercial office building	200	83	48	18	48	3	0
Construction site	19	11	2	2	4	0	0
Convenience store	114	38	9	17	49	1	0
Department/discount store	58	37	11	6	4	0	0
Drug store/Dr.'s office/hospital	51	24	10	8	9	0	0
Field/woods	69	43	6	10	10	0	0
Government/public building	82	38	20	9	14	1	0
Grocery/supermarket	51	22	10	7	12	0	0
Highway/road/alley/street	1,490	855	117	309	200	9	0
Hotel/motel/etc.	55	26	10	10	9	0	0
Jail/prison	42	26	2	4	10	0	0
Lake/waterway	12	5	1	3	3	0	0
Liquor store	14	4	1	1	8	0	0
Parking lot/garage	461	277	62	68	52	2	0
Rental storage facility	9	4	2	0	1	2	0
Residence/home	2,198	1,092	373	383	338	9	3
Restaurant	166	74	14	29	48	1	0
School/college	789	402	149	167	66	5	0
Service/gas station	78	39	13	7	18	1	0
Specialty store (TV, fur, etc.)	93	38	24	6	25	0	0
Other/unknown	915	365	284	120	138	8	0
Multiple locations	2	1	0	0	1	0	0

*A *multiple-bias incident* occurs only when two or more offense types are committed in a single incident. In a situation where there is more than one offense type, the agency can indicate a different bias for each offense. In the case of a single offense type, only one bias can be indicated.

SOURCE: "Table 10. Incidents: Bias Motivation by Location, 2002," in *Hate Crime Statistics, 2002,* Federal Bureau of Investigation, Washington, DC, 2003.

System (NIBRS), juveniles accounted for more than one in three arrests. The most common arrest of juveniles was for property crime (56 percent). They also represented 66 percent of the arrests for damage, destruction, or vandalism, 33 percent of arrests for intimidation, and 29 percent of the arrests for simple assault.

Hate's Perpetrators

Hate crimes are committed by individuals, groups of individuals, or organizations with a prejudice against people of a certain race, religion, gender, ethnicity/nationality, sexual orientation, or disability. According to the ADL, hate crime offenders fall into three categories: reactive, thrill-seeking, and mission-oriented perpetrators.

Reactive offenders believe that they are retaliating against some perceived imminent harm, threat, or danger from the victim. He or she sees the victim's race, ethnicity, religion, or lifestyle as being responsible for the perpetrator's problems in life. Such offenders often act out in opportunistic ways, such as spur-of-the-moment impulses. Often, the offender has recently used alcohol or drugs. This is the most common type of perpetrator.

The second category, young thrill seekers, are also responsible for a large number of hate crimes, according to the 1997 Leadership Conference Education Fund (LCEF). The third category, mission-oriented individuals, may or may not be members of extremist organizations. However, they act from ideologies perpetuating bigotry against some group or groups of people. Those ideologies are based on ridding the world of whatever that individual or group considers evil. This is the least common perpetrator.

Types of Hate Crimes

The Southern Poverty Law Center (SPLC) records incidents of hate crimes on its Web site in its "Hatewatch for the Record." Between April and June 2003, the site listed numerous incidents of hate crimes throughout the United States, many involving juvenile perpetrators or victims. Among the examples cited are occurrences of hate-related words being spray-painted on playgrounds, churches, schools, and homes; youth assaulting each other and using hate speech; threatening phone calls; cross burnings; threats made with weapons present; murders; robberies; hate-filled pamphlets and emails; and other incidents of harassment.

TABLE 7.6

Percentage of students ages 12–18 who reported being targets of hate-related words at school during the previous 6 months, by selected student characteristics, 2001

Student characteristics	Total[1]	Hate-related words related to student's characteristics					
		Race	Ethnicity	Religion	Disability	Gender	Sexual orientation
Total	**12.3**	**4.2**	**2.7**	**1.8**	**1.1**	**2.8**	**1.2**
Sex							
Male	12.8	4.6	3.2	2.0	1.2	1.2	1.3
Female	11.7	3.7	2.2	1.6	0.9	4.4	1.2
Race/ethnicity[2]							
White	12.1	2.8	1.6	2.0	1.2	3.3	1.6
Black	13.9	7.8	3.3	1.3	1.1	2.7	0.8
Hispanic	11.0	4.9	6.0	1.2	0.6	1.0	0.5
Other	13.6	9.7	5.9	2.7	0.4	0.8	0.0
Grade							
6th	12.1	2.7	1.9	1.1	2.1	2.1	0.4
7th	14.1	5.0	3.4	1.8	1.6	3.2	1.1
8th	13.0	5.3	3.1	2.2	1.0	2.2	1.0
9th	12.1	3.6	2.1	1.3	1.0	3.4	1.2
10th	13.1	4.6	2.6	2.1	0.8	3.1	1.9
11th	12.7	4.7	3.1	2.3	1.1	2.7	1.7
12th	7.9	2.2	2.3	1.7	0.2	2.3	1.1
Urbanicity							
Urban	11.9	5.0	3.3	1.6	0.9	2.5	0.9
Suburban	12.4	4.2	2.8	1.9	1.1	2.9	1.5
Rural	12.4	2.9	1.7	2.1	1.1	2.7	1.0
Sector							
Public	12.7	4.4	2.8	1.9	1.2	2.8	1.2
Private	8.2	1.5	1.6	1.5	0.3	2.0	1.3

[1]In the questionnaire, students were asked if they were the targets of hate-related words at school. If the students responded that they were called a hate-related word, they were asked to choose the specific characteristics that the hate-related word targeted. Students were allowed to choose more than one characteristic. If a student chose more than one characteristic, he or she is counted once under the "total" category. Therefore, the percent of students who reported being called a hate-related word is less than the sum of all the individual characteristics.

[2]Other includes Asians, Pacific Islanders, and American Indians (including Alaska Natives). Race categories exclude Hispanic origin unless specified.

Note: "At school" means in the school building, on school property, on a school bus, or going to and from school. Population size is 24,315,000 students ages 12–18 in 2001.

SOURCE: Jill F. Devoe, Katharin Peter, Phillip Kaufman, Sally A. Ruddy, Amanda K. Miller, Mike Planty, Thomas D. Snyder, and Michael R. Rand, "Table 14.1. Percentage of students ages 12–18 who reported being targets of hate-related words at school during the previous 6 months, by selected student characteristics: 2001," in *Indicators of School Crime and Safety: 2003*, U.S. Department of Education, Institute of Education Sciences, National Center for Education Statistics and U.S. Department of Justice, Office of Justice Programs, Bureau of Justice Statistics, Washington, DC, October 2003

ARSON. Arsons are often classified as hate crimes. The FBI notes that arson is "any willful or malicious burning or attempt to burn, with or without intent to defraud, a dwelling house, public building, motor vehicle or aircraft, personal property of another, etc." Arson statistics have been collected since 1979.

In 2002, according to the FBI's Uniform Crime Reports, 16.5 percent of all arsons were cleared by law enforcement personnel. Clearance can be achieved in two ways: arresting the person/persons responsible, charging those responsible, and turning them over for prosecution, or by exceptional means. Exceptional means clearance is used when sufficient evidence exists to prosecute a person as the perpetrator but the person dies, cannot be extradited, or there are other extenuating circumstances. Of the total of the arson cases cleared in 2002, 43 percent involved juvenile perpetrators. Among those arrested for arson in 2002, 49.4 percent were juveniles. That number climbs above two-thirds (67.8 percent) for those arrested for arson under the age of 25. Some 51.7 percent of the

males arrested for arson were juveniles, while some 37 percent of females arrested for arson were juveniles.

Overall, juvenile arrests for arson were down 10.2 percent in 2002 from the previous year. For juveniles under 15, that decrease was even greater, at 10.4 percent. Female juveniles saw the biggest decrease in arson arrests, 15.8 percent, compared to male juveniles, who experienced a 9.4 percent decline. All types of locations witnessed a decline in juvenile arrests for arson, including cities (10.8 percent), suburban counties (5.2 percent), and rural counties (17.7 percent). Between 1998 and 2002, juvenile arson arrests decreased by 11.3 percent; such arrests decreased by nearly a quarter (23.2 percent) between 1993 and 2002.

Although some consider juvenile arsons to be childish pranks, many believe them to be hate crimes. Among the most noted arsons by juveniles since the 1990s are those committed against houses of worship. Between 1990 and 1996 a rash of church arsons occurred, affecting 53 black churches. This wave of crime prompted the

FIGURE 7.1

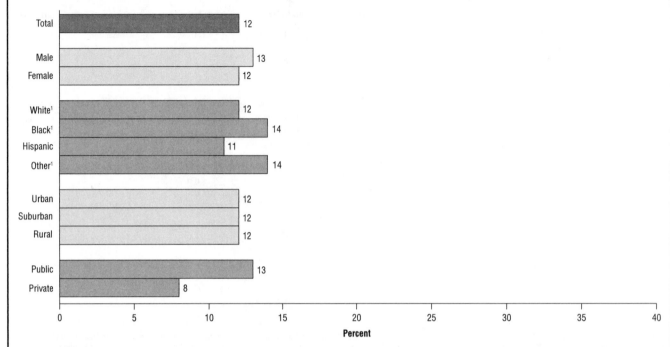

Percentage of students ages 12–18 who reported being targets of hate-related words or who saw hate-related graffiti at school during the previous 6 months, by student and school characteristics, 2001

Hate-related words

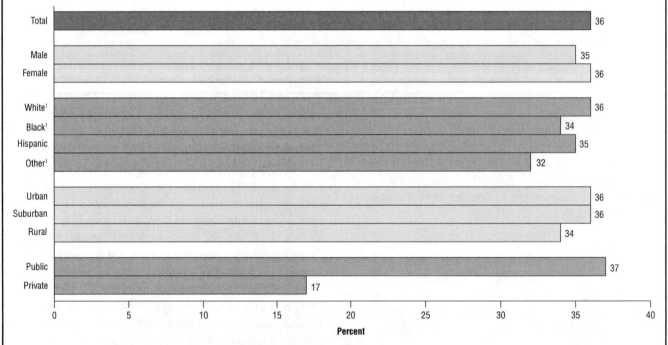

Hate-related graffiti

[1]Other includes Asians, Pacific Islanders, and American Indians (including Alaska Natives). Race categories exclude Hispanic origin.
Note: "At school" means in the school building, on school property, on a school bus, or going to and from school.

SOURCE: Jill F. Devoe, Katharin Peter, Phillip Kaufman, Sally A. Ruddy, Amanda K. Miller, Mike Planty, Thomas D. Snyder, and Michael R. Rand, "Figure 14.1. Percentage of students ages 12–18 who reported being targets of hate-related words or who saw hate-related graffiti at school during the previous 6 months, by student and school characteristics: 2001," in *Indicators of School Crime and Safety: 2003*, U.S. Department of Education, Institute of Education Sciences, National Center for Education Statistics and U.S. Department of Justice, Office of Justice Programs, Bureau of Justice Statistics, Washington, DC, October 2003

FIGURE 7.2

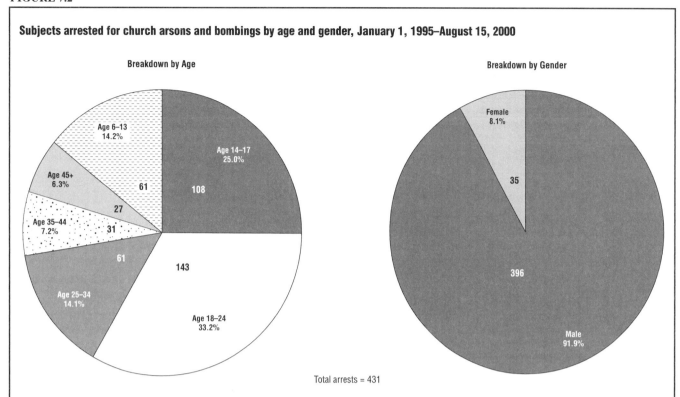

Subjects arrested for church arsons and bombings by age and gender, January 1, 1995–August 15, 2000

Breakdown by Age

Age 6–13
14.2%

Age 14–17
25.0%

Age 45+
6.3%

Age 35–44
7.2%

Age 25–34
14.1%

Age 18–24
33.2%

61

108

27

31

61

143

Breakdown by Gender

Female
8.1%

35

Male
91.9%

396

Total arrests = 431

SOURCE: "Chart D: Demographic Information on Subjects Arrested for Church Arsons/Bombings Nationwide, January 1, 1995–August 15, 2000," *National Church Arson Task Force—Fourth Year Report*, Bureau of Alcohol, Tobacco and Firearms, Washington, DC, 2000 [Online] http://www.atf.treas.gov/pub/gen_pub/report2000/index.htm [accessed April 9, 2002]

federal government to study the situation. As a result, the National Church Arson Task Force (NCATF) was created in June 1996. It is charged with coordinating the efforts of federal, state, and local law enforcement agencies. The Bureau of Alcohol, Tobacco, Firearms and Explosives (ATF) and the FBI work with state and local law officers to investigate such fires. Other federal organizations get involved by helping to rebuild churches, synagogues, and other houses of worship, as well as working with community leaders to ease tensions.

The NCATF investigated 945 arsons and bombings at houses of worship between January 1995 and mid-August 2000. Their findings concluded that nearly 33 percent of the arsons affected black churches (310), with the remaining fires started at other religious facilities. Law enforcement officers made arrests in 36.2 percent of the cases; investigations in 61.8 percent were still pending. Overall, 80 percent of those arrested were white, 15.1 percent were African American, and 3 percent were Hispanic.

More than 58 percent of all church arsons and bombing arrests were among those 14 to 24. A quarter of the arrests involved those aged 14 to 17, while a third were in the 18 to 24 age group. (See Figure 7.2.) Those 6 to 13 and 25 to 34 each represented about 14 percent of arrests, while the rest involved those aged 35 to 44 (7.2 percent)

and 45 and older (6.3 percent). Males were arrested in 91.9 percent of the cases.

The NCATF also maintains detailed records of arsons against houses of worship. Samples of juvenile and youth arrests, culled from task force reports, appears in Table 7.7.

Hate Crimes and Terrorism

Hate crimes and terrorism share many characteristics, both in methodology and the end result. Both types of crime involve the threat or actual implementation of an act against people, property, or society. For example, an arsonist acting out a religious bias may throw an incendiary device into a mosque, church, or synagogue in an attempt to burn it down. A terrorist might use a similar device to destroy a government building. The result in both cases is intimidation, damage, and even injury or death to people. Even if no one is injured, the incident can cause fear and panic among citizens in the community, especially those closely associated with the targeted facility.

Terrorism differs from hate crimes in the motive behind the acts. According to the FBI, terrorism is the unlawful use of violence or force against people or property to intimidate or coerce a government, civilians, or other groups to further political or social agendas. Hate groups, like terrorist organizations, often recruit young, disenchanted males and

TABLE 7.7

Violence committed by juveniles and youths against houses of worship, selected events, 1996–1998

Date	Location	Description of event	Type of congregation
March 25, 1996	St. Andrews Presbyterian Church, Newark, Delaware	Four Caucasian juveniles (12 to 14 years of age) broke in and stole food from the church, then set the building on fire to hide the theft.	Caucasian
May 9, 1996	First United Methodist Church, Hartselle, Alabama	Church damaged by fire when two Caucasian children started a piece of paper on fire. The 12- and 14-year-olds started the fire on a dare.	Caucasian
June 30, 1996	St. James African Methodist Episcopal Zion Church, Maysville, North Carolina	Church damaged by fire; estimated losses were $50,000. Three Caucasian males, two juveniles and one 19-year-old, pled guilty to the crime. The fire occurred after petroleum was poured on the church and seven molotov cocktails were hurled at the building.	African American
July 29, 1996	Pentecostal Holiness Church, Livingston, Kentucky	While services were underway, two Caucasian 13-year-olds tossed a smoke bomb into the church and started a fire. The blaze was put out quickly.	Caucasian
August 6, 1996 – December 9, 1996	Bethel Baptist Church, Faith United Methodist Church, Hunterdale Pentecostal Church, and Southside Church of God, Jacksonville, Florida	Two Caucasian males (16 and 17) pled guilty to a series of arsons at several churches. The 17-year-old also pled guilty to defacing one of the churches, which is considered a "hate crime."	Bethel (African American); Faith (Caucasian); Hunterdale (Caucasian); Southside (African American)
August 14, 1996	New Beginning Baptist Church, Fort Valley, Georgia	A 17-year-old set a fire at the church because he had aspirations to become a volunteer firefighter. He claimed to need practice in extinguishing fires.	Caucasian
October 1, 1996	First Presbyterian Church, Libertyville, Illinois	Church damaged by fire and spray painted with swastikas by four Caucasian juveniles (14 to 16 years old).	Caucasian
December 10, 1996	New Birth Missionary Baptist Church, Lake Charles, Louisiana	Two African American boys started some boxes of clothing on fire at the church. The boys were 12 and 13 at the time of the arson.	African American
April 28, 1997	Brockway Wesleyan Church and Christian Academy, Morley, Michigan	Claiming to be mad at God, a 17-year-old and female student at the academy started a fire at the church.	Caucasian
June 24, 1997	St. Vincent Ferrer, Madison Heights, Michigan	Two juveniles set off a pipe bomb at the church. After reading about the incident, the mother of one of the boys questioned her son and then took him to the authorities.	Interracial
June 30, 1997	Greater Saint Joseph Baptist Church, Baldwin, Alabama	Church totally destroyed by arson. Four 18-year-old Caucasians (three males and one female) were arrested and convicted. Several of the arsonists had gone to a white supremacist rally two days prior to the incident.	African American
October 22, 1997	Trinity Baptist Church, Downey, California	Church damaged by fire started by Caucasian male (18).	Interracial
March 26, 1998	Immanuel Baptist Church, Morgan City, Louisiana	A seven-year-old set eight small fires at the church while services were being conducted.	Caucasian
March 28, 1998	Bethany Lutheran Church, Dallas, Texas	Church burned and vandalized with graffiti. The vandals spray painted racist and anti-gay messages and pentagrams on the church. Two Caucasian males—age 19 and 20—pled guilty; two juveniles were also involved.	Caucasian

SOURCE: Prepared by the staff of Information Plus, based on incident reports issued by National Church Arson Task Force, sponsored by the U.S. Department of the Treasury, U.S. Department of Justice, Bureau of Alcohol, Tobacco and Firearms, and the Federal Bureau of Investigation, 1998.

indoctrinate them in their anger toward specific groups, government entities, and the like. The SPLC reported that as of 2002, 708 hate groups were known to be active in the United States. The ADL notes that hate on the Internet is rampant and many hate-filled Web sites go unchallenged. Various groups do monitor hate speech on the Internet and report their findings to concerned citizens and lawmakers alike. The SPLC counted more than 300 Web sites on the Internet in 2000 that were dedicated to hate. The number of sites, however, can be misleading. Due to the nature of the Internet, a single person can post a Web site and make it appear that a particular group has a large following.

Hate after September 11, 2001

Hate crimes and terrorist attacks by certain groups or individuals can mean a backlash of violence toward others of the same race, ethnicity/national origin, or religion who had no part in the initial event. This was witnessed after the terrorist attacks of September 11, 2001, in the United States. In the months that followed, attacks against people of Arab descent and those of the Muslim religion surged. Many of those incidents were violent, including the fire-bombing of mosques and shootings. Some 33 incidents of anti-Islamic hate crimes were reported in 2000. The number soared to 250 occurrences against Arabs, Muslims, and Southern Asians in the four months after 9/11. At the state and local level, 70 people were charged with hate crimes initiated against Arab or Muslim Americans as a result of the terrorist attacks. The FBI had initiated 318 hate crime investigations as of February 2002. These crimes involved Americans of Arab, Muslim, and Sikh heritage. At that time, charges had been brought against eight people.

Such statistics do not reflect the name calling, harassment, and bullying experienced by Arab and Islamic youth in school. Various news reports focused on what it was like to be one of these students in the aftermath of September 11. Although the hate toward such groups has since subsided to some degree, students representing such minority groups, including those with strong religious affiliations, are often persecuted by their peers for being different.

BULLIES AND BULLYING

Most people can recall certain individuals or a group of children at school being identified as bullies. Every educational facility has its bullies, and such behaviors are not new to schools. Bullies harass certain kids they know will not fight back, including pushing students against lockers and taking their lunch money, CDs, or other personal possessions; pulling gags in attempts to humiliate others and cause extreme embarrassment; shoving others out of their way; threatening others with violence to get their victims to do their homework for them; emailing, instant messaging, or text messaging threats or insults; setting up derogatory Web sites about other students; disrupting class and making threatening stares, even toward teachers; and resorting to threatening acts just to feel they are in charge of a particular situation.

During the late 1990s bullying at schools became a major issue of concern with parents, educators, police, lawmakers, and students as increasing numbers of people perceived that bullying had become more aggressive and hurtful. In addition, a rash of school shootings shocked the nation in the 1990s. Many of the school shooters, mainly middle school and high school white males, complained of being bullied, victimized, and harassed frequently. They had grown tired of being picked on and struck back, they said. Most of the victims of school shootings, however, were not the bullies who had harassed the shooters but average students caught in the crossfire of angry children and teens. The bullied shooters, thus, had become bullies themselves.

In an Alfred University research project (Edward Vaughn, Jay D. Cerrito, and Robert A. Myers, *Lethal Violence in Schools: A National Study,* Alfred University, Alfred, New York, August 2001), 86 percent of the students surveyed said that the biggest motivation in school shootings is "other kids picking on [the shooters], making fun of them or bullying them." And 87 percent believed that the biggest motivation driving school shootings was the need to "get back at those who have hurt them."

Definition and Characteristics of Bullying

One of the world's foremost researchers on bullying is Dan Olweus, who has conducted many studies both in Europe and in the United States. His study of bullying behaviors conducted in Bergen, Norway, in the mid-1980s is frequently cited by other researchers, anti-bullying groups, and behavioral scientists. The creator of the Olweus Bullying Prevention Program, he notes that "[a] student is being bullied or victimized when he or she is exposed, repeatedly and over time, to negative actions on the part of one or more other students."

Bullying can be physical, verbal, and/or emotional. "[Bullying] involves a real or perceived imbalance of power, with the more powerful child or group attacking those who are less powerful," according to Office of Juvenile Justice and Delinquency Prevention (OJJDP) writer Nels Ericson ("Addressing the Problem of Juvenile Bullying," *OJJDP Fact Sheet,* U.S. Department of Justice, Office of Justice Programs, Office of Juvenile Justice and Delinquency Prevention, Washington, DC, June 2001). "Bullying can take three forms: physical (hitting, kicking, spitting, pushing, taking personal belongings); verbal (taunting, malicious teasing, name calling, making threats); and psychological (spreading rumors, manipulating social relationships, or engaging in social exclusion, extortion, or intimidation)."

Some studies divide these bullying behaviors into two categories: direct and indirect. Direct would encompass the physical and verbal attacks and harassment. Indirect would include subtle actions that might be hard for those not directly involved to recognize. These would include psychological activities, such as those listed earlier, as well as obscene gestures, hurtful facial expressions, and turning friends against each other.

BULLY CHARACTERISTICS. In profiles created by various research organizations, bullies are most often identified as males, although girls do engage in bullying behaviors as well. Boys are most likely to use physical and verbal abuse, frequently on a one-on-one basis. Girls typically use verbal and psychological tactics. Female bullies often refrain from one-on-one contact, preferring to work in groups. This might include circulating a "slam book" about another person, which is a notebook containing derogatory remarks about the victim written by the bullying group. Male bullies tend to pick on males, but will also lash out at females as well. Female bullies usually target other girls. In some instances, mixed groups will work together to harass other kids.

Bullies look for situations where they can gain power over someone else through intimidation and threats. Sometimes they work alone; other times they work in groups. Some bullies surround themselves with weaker kids who act as henchmen. Bullies seek out situations to harass others in places like playgrounds and school hallways that are not being supervised by adults. In this way, there are no adult witnesses to either stop the act or report it to school authorities.

Some of the common traits of bullies include, but are not limited to, the following characteristics (though not all of these characteristics apply to all bullies):

- has aggressive behavior, both physically and emotionally
- exhibits anger management issues
- shows controlling tendencies
- has harsh/authoritarian parents
- displays impatience
- acts impulsively
- lacks adult supervision
- lacks attention and warmth from family, or family acts indifferently
- lacks compassion for victim
- lacks imagination
- experiences low school achievement
- behaves in an overconfident way
- has a superiority complex
- has a tendency to pick victims who are younger, smaller, or weaker, including students new to the school or those in cultural/ethnic minorities at the school
- views violence as a legitimate action or reaction
- witnesses violence or verbal aggression at home, either directed at the bully or between parents

VICTIM CHARACTERISTICS. In general, many victims of bullies are male, although girls are subjected to bullying situations as well. Victims are often chosen because they are quiet people, with few friends to step in and help them out of a bullying situation. They have difficulty standing up to people during confrontations, so bullies perceive them to be safe and easy targets.

The common traits of victims include, but are not limited to, the following (though again, not all of these characteristics apply to all victims):

- tends to be ashamed to report bullying for fear of retaliation
- cannot stand up for himself/herself and continues to take the abuse
- has insecurity issues
- lacks assertiveness skills
- lacks confidence in own abilities
- displays loner tendencies—has few friends
- is sensitive
- shows passive tendencies
- may be physically weak, or at least physically weaker than the bully
- has self-esteem issues
- may be timid and shy
- tends to internalize things
- is unable to physically defend himself/herself

- appears vulnerable
- does not believe that violence should be used to solve problems

Some researchers claim that any child can become the victim of bullies—it does not matter who they are. This idea is presented on the British Web site Bully OnLine (http://www.bullyonline.org). According to Bully OnLine in 2004: "Reasons for being picked on include being fat, thin, tall, short, hair or skin colour, being quiet, wearing glasses, having big ears, small ears, sticky-out ears, crooked teeth, being from a different culture, having different likes or dislikes, the 'wrong' clothes, unwillingness to use strength to defend him or herself, or any perceived or fabricated 'excuse.' These excuses have one thing in common: they are all irrelevant."

Effects of Bullying/Being Bullied

In "Addressing the Problem of Juvenile Bullying," OJJDP writer Ericson notes that "researchers [have] estimated that 1.6 million children in grades 6 to 10 in the United States are bullied at least once a week and 1.7 million children bully others as frequently." Research has shown that bullying not only has lasting effects on the victim, but on the bully and bystanders as well. Victims are often described as becoming unhappy, anxious, and feeling distressed. Their feelings of low self-esteem and insecurity may become deeper. They may feel ashamed and afraid and want to avoid going to classes. Victims also might develop a poor body image and experience the inability to concentrate in class. Some fall into periods of depression, and a small percentage have attempted suicide. Such feelings may stay with them into their adult years, and they may continue to experience difficulty making friends.

As bullies commit acts that go unreported, they may come to believe that their actions are legitimate when they go undetected and unpunished. Various studies have shown that bullies have an increased chance of becoming criminals, including seriously violent offenders, upon reaching their late teens and early adult years. In addition, they may continue to bully in the workplace and at home, victimizing their spouses and children.

Bullying situations can have adverse effects on bystanders as well. Bystanders can be those who watch and 1) want to help but do not; 2) want to join in; or 3) feel indifferent toward and/or lack empathy for the victim. For those unable to help, this may lead to feelings of guilt, anxiety, or helplessness. Some become distracted in their studies, while others become fearful of befriending certain types of kids, particularly those being bullied. For those who want to help the bullies, some do join in the harassment and are likely to become bullies themselves if such bullying goes unpunished.

School Surveys

As the prevalence of bullying increases and more parents and educators grow concerned about it, various studies

TABLE 7.8

Percentage of students ages 12–18 who reported being bullied at school during the previous 6 months, by selected student characteristics, 1999 and 2001

Student characteristics	1999	2001
Total	**5.1**	**7.9**
Sex		
Male	5.4	8.6
Female	4.8	7.1
Race/ethnicity[1]		
White	5.3	8.5
Black	5.5	5.9
Hispanic	4.4	7.8
Other	2.5	6.6
Grade		
6th	10.5	14.3
7th	9.0	13.0
8th	5.5	9.2
9th	5.0	8.6
10th	3.2	4.6
11th	2.6	4.3
12th	1.2	2.4
Urbanicity		
Urban	5.0	6.9
Suburban	4.9	8.1
Rural	5.8	8.7
Sector		
Public	5.3	8.0
Private	2.8	7.3

[1]Other includes Asians, Pacific Islanders, and American Indians (including Alaska Natives). Race categories exclude Hispanic origin unless specified.
Note: In the 1999 survey, "at school" was defined as in the school building, on the school grounds, or on a school bus. In the 2001 survey, "at school" was defined as in the school building, on school property, on a school bus, or going to and from school. Population sizes for students ages 12–18 are 24,614,000 in 1999 and 24,315,000 in 2001.

SOURCE: Jill F. Devoe, Katharin Peter, Phillip Kaufman, Sally A. Ruddy, Amanda K. Miller, Mike Planty, Thomas D. Snyder, and Michael R. Rand, "Table 6.1. Percentage of students ages 12–18 who reported being bullied at school during the previous 6 months, by selected student characteristics: 1999 and 2001," in *Indicators of School Crime and Safety: 2003,* U.S. Department of Education, Institute of Education Sciences, National Center for Education Statistics and U.S. Department of Justice, Office of Justice Programs, Bureau of Justice Statistics, Washington, DC, October 2003

are being conducted to learn more about bullies, victims, and the frequency of such occurrences. In *Indicators of School Crime and Safety: 2003* (J.F. DeVoe, K. Peter, P. Kaufman, S.A. Ruddy, A.K. Miller, M. Planty, T.D. Snyder, and M.R. Rand, U.S. Departments of Education and Justice, Washington, DC, 2003), the authors addressed the subject of bullying and how frequently students (12–18) reported being bullied in the past six months. The 2001 survey defined "at school" to mean "in the school building, on school property, on a school bus, or going to and from school." The researchers learned that 7.9 percent of students reported being bullied at school, compared to 5.1 percent in 1999. (See Table 7.8.) The definition "at school" was different in 1999, however. It read "in the school building, on the school grounds, or on a school bus."

Both genders reported increased bullying between 1999 and 2001. Reported male victimization rose from 5.4

percent to 8.6 percent, while female victimization increased from 4.8 percent to 7.1 percent. In 2001 whites reported the most problems with bullies (8.5 percent). Hispanics (7.8 percent) and blacks (5.9 percent) reported slightly less trouble. In 1999 blacks experienced the most problems with bullying (5.5 percent). White students experienced a 3.2 percent growth while Hispanics reported the highest increase at 3.4 percent. Sixth and seventh graders claimed the most trouble with bullies in 2001, which is consistent with 1999 figures. Among school types, bullying also increased most among suburban students (3.2 percent) and at private schools (4.5 percent).

Are America's Schools Safe? Students Speak Out: 1999 School Crime Supplement (Lynn A. Addington, Sally A. Ruddy, Amanda K. Miller, and Jill F. DeVoe, U.S. Department of Education, National Center for Education Statistics, Washington, DC, 2002) presented survey results of students (12–18) who reported being bullied at school. (See Figure 7.3.) The authors note:

> Reports of bullying also varied by certain factors in the school environment. First, students who reported the presence of street gangs at school (8.4 percent) were more likely to have been bullied than were students who did not report street gangs (4.2 percent).... Second, students who reported being afraid of harm or attack at school (26.4 percent) as well as those who were afraid while traveling to and from school (15.1 percent) were more likely to report being bullied than were those who did not have such fears (3.9 percent for those not afraid at school and 4.7 percent for those not afraid while traveling).... Third, students who reported having carried a weapon to school for protection (12.8 percent) were more likely than students who did not carry a weapon (5 percent) to report being bullied.

THE NATIONAL INSTITUTE OF CHILD HEALTH AND HUMAN DEVELOPMENT (NICHD) STUDIES. The National Institute of Child Health and Human Development (NICHD) of the National Institutes of Health has undertaken several studies about bullies and their victims. In a survey of 15,686 students in sixth through tenth grades, the NICHD reported on its Web site that: "Bullying is widespread in American schools, with more than 16 percent of U.S. school children saying they had been bullied by other students during the current term." The study further revealed that 13 percent claimed to be bullies but had not been the victim of bullies themselves; 10 percent said they had been victims but had not bullied others; and 6 percent acknowledged they had been bullies and victims.

The study showed that bullies are often most active in sixth through eighth grades. It also discovered that bullies tended to avoid verbal abuse pertaining to race and religion, perhaps because there is more emphasis in society urging tolerance of these aspects. However, there is less social tolerance, particularly among popular culture, of criticizing the way people look or dress.

FIGURE 7.3

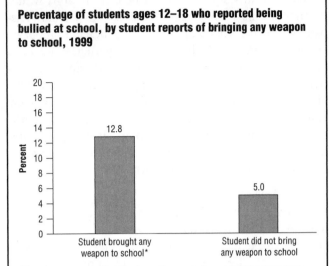

Percentage of students ages 12–18 who reported being bullied at school, by student reports of bringing any weapon to school, 1999

*If students responded that they brought a gun, knife, or some other weapon to school, they are considered having "brought any weapon to school."

SOURCE: Lynn A. Addington, Sally A. Ruddy, Amanda K. Miller, and Jill F. DeVoe, "Figure 40. Percentage of students ages 12–18 who reported being bullied at school, by student reports of bringing any weapon to school: 1999," in *Are America's Schools Safe? Students Speak Out: 1999 School Crime Supplement*, U.S. Department of Education, National Center for Education Statistics, Washington, DC, 2002.

In a second report dated April 14, 2003, the NICHD noted that "both children who bullied and their victims were more likely than youth who had never been involved in bullying to engage in violent behaviors themselves." The survey reported that boys who acknowledged bullying others at school at least once each week had an increased level of carrying a weapon to school in the last month (43.1 percent), carrying a weapon in general (52.2 percent), being involved in frequent physical fighting (38.7 percent), and being injured in fighting (45.7 percent). Male bullies who attacked their victims away from school were even more likely to engage in these behaviors.

REPORT OF THE U.S. SURGEON GENERAL. *Youth Violence: A Report of the Surgeon General* (U.S. Surgeon General's Office, Washington, DC, 2001), which was prompted by the Columbine school shootings, covers a wide range of issues, including bullying. When discussing the issue of violence, as reported in detailed studies like his, the Surgeon General had this to say: "Some situations and conditions that influence the likelihood of violence or the form it takes may not be identified by longitudinal studies as risk factors (predictors) for violence. Situational factors such as bullying, taunting, and demeaning interactions can serve as catalysts for unplanned violence. The social context can influence the seriousness or form of violence—for example, the presence of a gun or a gathering crowd of peers that makes a youth feel he (or she) needs to protect his (or her) reputation. These may not be primary causes of violence, yet they are contributing fac-

tors and are important to understanding how a violent exchange unfolds."

Cyber-bullies

With the advent of the Internet and the increased use of cell phones among students, bullies have found a new way to taunt their victims—Cyber-bullying, also called Digital Bullying or Internet Bullying. Instead of abusing their victims at school, on the playground, or en route to and from schools, bullies are now able to taunt their victims day and night via today's technology. Victims report receiving hateful and hurtful instant messages, emails, and text messages on their cell phones. Use of such technologies allows the perpetrators to be anonymous, if they so choose.

Some students have even become the victims of hate-filled Web sites that discuss why the bullies and his/her friends do not like that certain individual. Visitors to such sites are allowed to add their insults and gossip as well. In some instances, visitors have rallied to the defense of the victim and slammed the bully. Through the use of picture phones, bullies have even taken sensitive photos of students in locker rooms, rest rooms, or being intimidated. Then the bullies pass them around, either via email or on Web sites. Researchers point out that electronic bullying can be done anywhere and does not involve the bully having any personal contact, especially eye contact, with the victim.

Parents have experienced difficulty in getting the Web sites removed by service providers, who suggest that they are not in the business of censorship and that the content is protected under the First Amendment, which guarantees freedom of speech. Some parents have decided to file lawsuits to get the content taken down. Due to their age, bullies often do not realize that they are legally responsible for what they put in print.

Prevention Programs

While some people believe that bullying is fast becoming a serious problem and demands serious intervention, others assert that it's just kids being kids and a regular part of growing up. Duane Alexander, NICHD director, noted his concern in 2001 with the publication of the institute's bullying survey. "Being bullied is not just an unpleasant rite of passage through childhood." He adds: "It's a public health problem that merits attention. People who were bullied as children are more likely to suffer from depression and low self esteem, well into adulthood, and the bullies themselves are more likely to engage in criminal behavior later in life."

Schools throughout the country have implemented anti-bullying programs aimed to bring the subject out in the open. Anti-bullying efforts are not only geared toward bullies but at the students and teachers who do not do enough to stop such aggression from occurring. Some victims have claimed that there are teachers who allow bullying to occur, even encourage it. Others say they are afraid to tell teachers because the educators just ignore it and tell the victims to toughen up. Still other victims are ashamed that they cannot stop the bullies and will retreat into themselves and internalize it.

Some of the techniques used to prevent and stop bullying were developed by Dan Olweus, especially the Olweus Bullying Prevention Program. Through the program, students, parents, and school staff work together to address the issue. By discussing bullying and its effects, people learn the consequences of bullying on people and on the school environment. Rules and plans are developed and enforced. According to the OJJDP, the Olweus program is very successful in elementary and junior high schools. When Olweus implemented his program in Norway, schools achieved a 50 percent reduction in bullying incidents.

Another program gaining popularity in 2004 was developed by singer/songwriter Peter Yarrow in conjunction with the Educators for Social Responsibility. In 2000 Yarrow, part of the folk trio Peter, Paul and Mary, created Operation Respect: Don't Laugh at Me. The group believes that music has the power to educate, including the issues of tolerance, respect, and other elements necessary in building character. The program uses the song "Don't Laugh at Me," recorded by the trio and written by Steve Seskin and Allen Shamblin. The song contains the lines: "Don't laugh at me/Don't call me names/Don't get your pleasure from my pain."

The organization has developed Don't Laugh at Me (DLAM) programs geared to children from second to eighth grades, as well as after-school summer camp programs. Participating members are encouraged to create "Ridicule Free Zones" where children can feel free of harassment and bullying. The group Peter, Paul and Mary are known for their activities promoting civil rights around the world. They have also spoken out against hate crimes and attended the funeral of Matthew Shepard.

HAZING

Like bullying, hazing involves humiliating someone into doing something that he or she would not do normally. In some instances, the hazing act is silly and harmless. However, in the early twenty-first century, parents and educators have become concerned that hazings are getting more and more aggressive and violent. Such hazings, which often occur as initiations to a school or social club, are considered a "rite of passage" to some, just "horseplay" to others, and degrading and devastating to various victims. Some athletic teams claim that hazing is done to toughen up younger players—to help them bond with the team. But unlike bullying, hazing is often done with the consent of its victims. For example, succumbing to peer pressure and wanting to be part of the group or

clique, many students will allow themselves to be subjected to humiliating acts that they do not report.

Hazings, however, can go too far and the victims can be seriously harmed. A few victims have even died. Hazings usually involve older students (veterans) initiating young classmates (newcomers) into the club. The situation can quickly turn violent when the older group gangs up on the younger group, who has no idea what has been planned or what they should expect. Researchers note that students will do things in a mob situation that they would never do on their own.

Several cases of brutal hazings received significant news coverage in 2003, one involving a high school football team and the other concerning senior and junior high school girls. The football incident took place at a training camp over the summer. At camp, several players were allegedly sexually abused with pine cones, golf balls, and broomsticks. Three players were charged in the incident and appeared before a judge, who was to decide if they should stand trial as juveniles or adults. The judge ordered the decision sealed.

The incident involving the teenage school girls occurred in what was supposed to be a "powder puff" football game at a local park. Instead, the younger girls were allegedly beaten, kicked, shoved, and pelted with a variety of objects and liquids, including garbage, mud, paint, animal intestines, feces, and urine. Five girls were taken to the hospital as a result. Fifteen students, who were charged with misdemeanors, were identified through witnesses and a videotape that someone made of the melee. Thirty-two were suspended from school. Although the girls were underage, alcohol was present. Police considered charging some of the girls' parents for providing the alcohol.

Reports of such violent hazings are rare, but nearly half (48 percent) of all students are subjected to some form of hazing, according to a study conducted by Alfred University in 2000 (Nadine C. Hoover and Norman J. Pollard, *Initiation Rites in American High Schools: A National Survey,* Alfred University, Alfred, New York, 2000). The researchers concluded that "more than 1.5 million high school students in the United States are being subjected to some form of hazing each year." The study also attempted to differentiate between hazing that was humiliating rather than just embarrassing. Forty-three percent of students reported humiliating hazing. In addition, 23 percent cited hazing activities involving substance abuse.

Various researchers contend that hazing incidents are underreported. This occurs for several reasons: 1) The victim believes that hazing is an unpleasant, but a necessary part of joining an organization; 2) the victim is threatened into remaining silent; 3) the victim is ashamed and wants to forget the incident occurred; 4) the victim assumes everyone has to endure such acts; or 5) the victim does not want to involve parents, school officials, or police because that would bring more trouble from the hazers. Some school administrators, coaches, and parents also play a role in encouraging students to refrain from reporting the incidents saying that they, too, had to endure such rituals. Many schools, however, are developing anti-hazing programs. Parents of students victimized by hazings have also brought lawsuits against schools and the perpetrators of such events.

GUNS

For many young Americans, schools, neighborhoods, parks, the street, and even the home can be dangerous places. Guns, knives, and other weapons turn up in searches of school lockers on occasion. Newscasts sometimes describe incidents of children being shot on playgrounds or youths firing guns from car windows as they cruise the streets. In "Prevalence of Youth Access to Alcohol or a Gun in the Home" (M.H. Swahn et al., *Injury Prevention,* 2002), the authors note that nearly one-quarter (24.3 percent) of adolescents ages 12 to 18 have easy access to a gun in the home. The use of deadly weapons and force in violent incidents, frequently reported by the news media, has increased fear among citizens of all ages.

By the 1980s guns were readily available to juveniles, according to Stuart Greenbaum, a specialist in public safety. In the publication "Kids and Guns: From Playgrounds to Battlegrounds" (*Juvenile Justice,* vol. 3, no. 2, September 1997), Greenbaum asserts that guns are the weapons of choice for today's youth. The juvenile arrest rate for weapons law violations increased more than 100 percent between 1987 and 1993. Although the rate fell 48 percent between 1993 and 2000, returning to about the same level as 1987, youth use of guns is still a major concern.

The gun as the weapon of choice among youths is backed by statistical data. For example, from 1983 to 1994 gun homicides by juveniles tripled while homicides involving other types of weapons decreased. From 1994 to 1997, however, homicides by youth declined sharply, primarily those involving firearms. Reasons for this are often cited as tougher laws, adult sentencing of youthful offenders, and vigilance by police to prevent violent crime.

Suicides

Other gun violence rose in the 1980s and early 1990s as well, namely suicides. From 1980 to 1994 the suicide rate for persons aged 15 to 19 grew 29 percent. Firearm-related suicides accounted for 96 percent of the increase. Beginning in 1995, the number of firearm-related suicides for those 19 or younger gradually declined, from 1,450 to 1,078 in 1999. Yet, due to the overall decline in all firearm-related deaths during those years (from 5,285 to 3,385), the percentage of firearm-related suicides for persons

under 19 rose from 27 percent of all firearm-related deaths in 1995 to 33 percent in 1998, then dropped off slightly to 32 percent in 1999. According to the Centers for Disease Control and Prevention (CDC), in 2000 more than 1,007 children ages 10 to 19 committed suicide with firearms.

"Protecting Adolescents from Harm: Findings from the National Longitudinal Study on Adolescent Health" (*Journal of the American Medical Association,* vol. 18, no. 10, September 1997) reported that adolescents living in homes where guns were present were more likely to contemplate or attempt suicide. In houses in which guns are present, the risk of suicide is believed to be five times greater than that in houses in which there are no guns.

ATF Tracing Program

When committing crimes, juveniles and youth are more likely than adults to use handguns and semiautomatic weapons, according to the ATF. The ATF's Youth Crime Gun Interdiction Initiative (YCGII), begun in 1996 as a pilot program in 17 cities throughout the country, was aimed at reducing youth violence involving the use of firearms. Under the initiative, participating cities send information on all "crime guns" to the ATF's National Tracing Center (NTC).

The YCGII report of February 1999 presented information about crime guns that were submitted to the NTC for review between August 1, 1997 and July 31, 1998. According to the ATF, crime guns retrieved from juveniles represented 11.3 percent of all such guns retrieved between August 1, 1997 and July 31, 1998. The rate was highest among 18- and 19-year-olds, each totaling more than 1,600. Although the rate for 14-year-olds was about 300, the number quadrupled to about 1,300 for 17-year-olds. The rate took a big drop after age 28. The ATF notes that "crime guns recovered from youth (ages 18 to 24) constitute 32.4 percent of all trace requests. There are more crime guns recovered from this seven-year age grouping than any other seven-year age grouping in the juvenile or adult categories." (The adult category for purposes of this survey is from age 25 to 96 years.) The rate for 15-year-olds is higher than the rate for any age 32 and older.

In the ATF's findings for 2000 (*Crime Gun Trace Reports 2000 National Report,* July 2002), the number of cities participating in the study had grown to 55. The release of the information was delayed due to the terrorist attacks of September 11, 2001. When the findings were published, the ATF reported that more than 18,000 crime guns (33.3 percent) were confiscated from youths aged 18 to 24, and more than 4,000 (7.6 percent) were recovered from juveniles. (See Figure 7.4.) The percentage of juveniles as crime gun possessors decreased more than 3 percent between the 1997–1998 and 2000 tracing periods. Together, however, juveniles and youth accounted for 40.9 percent of the crime guns turned in to the center during 2000.

FIGURE 7.4

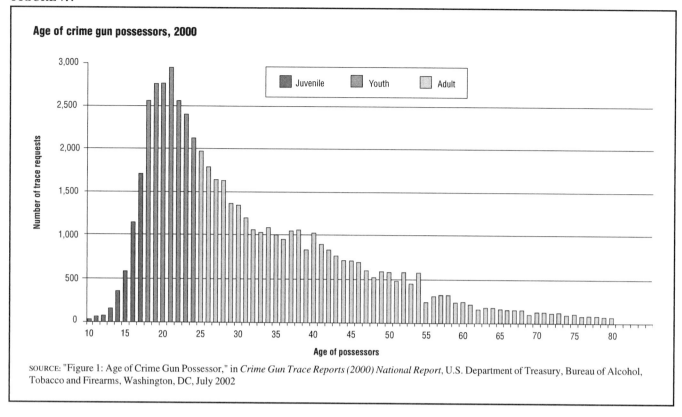

Age of crime gun possessors, 2000

SOURCE: "Figure 1: Age of Crime Gun Possessor," in *Crime Gun Trace Reports (2000) National Report*, U.S. Department of Treasury, Bureau of Alcohol, Tobacco and Firearms, Washington, DC, July 2002

As in the earlier study, the 2002 findings again showed youths as being the largest age group of crime gun possessors. Twenty-one-year-olds topped the chart at 2,930, with 20-year-olds (2,751) and 19-year-olds (2,744) close behind. The age of crime gun possessors surged between age 13 (141 recovered guns) to age 18 (2,569 recovered guns). In 2000 the rate for 16-year-olds was higher than the rate for any age 32 and older, whereas the rate for 15-year-olds was higher than all ages 55 and over. Six of every ten handguns confiscated from youths and juveniles were semiautomatic pistols, slightly higher than the five of every ten confiscated from adults.

The 2002 report also showed that many of the crime guns had been obtained from firearm traffickers, who illegally sell new, used, and/or stolen weapons. "The obliteration of the serial number on a crime gun is a key criminal indicator of trafficking, because it shows that someone in the chain of possession assumes that the gun will be used for a crime, may have to be discarded by a criminal, or may be recovered by the police," according to the ATF. Furthermore, the ATF investigation revealed that nearly 15 percent (6,718) of the crime guns had a time-to-crime duration of a year or less. More than 30 percent had been confiscated three years from purchase. This short "time to crime" indicates the ease with which a criminal can "fence" (or sell a stolen item to a third party) a gun and the pervasiveness of the illegal firearms market.

In the eight cities for which comprehensive serial number data was obtained in 2000 (Baltimore, Chicago,

Detroit, Dallas, Los Angeles, New York City, Philadelphia, and Washington, D.C.), the serial numbers were most often obliterated on semiautomatic pistols. Among crime guns used by juveniles, 119 recovered in the eight cities had obliterated serial numbers. The number was far greater among youth (549) and adults (429).

When tracking major gun types by age during the 2000 study, the ATF reported that firearms retrieved from juveniles were most often semiautomatic pistols/handguns (56.7 percent), followed by revolvers (27.1 percent), shotguns (7.6 percent), then rifles (7.2 percent). Youths had similar gun preferences, as 61 percent of the guns retrieved were semiautomatic pistols, 22.6 percent were revolvers, 8.2 percent shotguns, and 7.1 percent rifles. The number of recovered handguns dropped significantly in the adult category (46.9 percent), followed by revolvers (25.3 percent), rifles (14.1 percent), and shotguns (11.9 percent). Among all age groups, semiautomatic pistols topped the list at 50.1 percent, with revolvers (26.6 percent), rifles (11.3 percent), and shotguns (10.5) being recovered at lesser amounts.

The 2000 YCGII also recorded gun tracings in various cities. According to the ATF: "The age distribution of crime gun possessors can vary considerably from the national averages across cities. In certain cities, firearms were recovered predominately from adults.... In other cities, firearms are most frequently recovered from youth." The participating cities with the highest number of crime guns recovered from youth include: Newark, New Jersey

(58 percent), Washington, D.C. (49 percent), Gary, Indiana (47 percent), and Stockton, California (46 percent). Participating cities with the largest number of crime guns recovered from adults include: San Jose, California (83 percent), Miami, Florida (77 percent), Tampa, Florida (76 percent), and Portland, Oregon (73 percent). Jacksonville, Florida, and Oklahoma City, Oklahoma, tied at 72 percent.

Guns and Homicides

From the late 1980s until 1993 a sharp increase in gun-related juvenile homicides occurred. Most of the homicides of those aged 12 to 17 were male victims killed by males using firearms. Between 1980 and 1997, 3 out of 4 murdered juveniles aged 12 or older were killed with a firearm. According to the Bureau of Statistics, in 1999 some 1,990 persons 19 years of age and younger were the victims of firearm-related homicides. This figure was down from 2,215 firearm-related homicides in 1998, and from 3,274 in 1991. Among teens 15 to 19 years old, 1,708 were victims of firearm-related homicides, while 282 children 14 and under were victims of firearm-related homicides in 1999. The number of homicides did drop in 1999, yet the percentage of those deaths that were firearm related did not. Victims of homicide between 12 and 17 were usually male (81 percent of all victims) in 1999. The murder victims were usually killed by other males (95 percent of all perpetrators) with firearms (86 percent of all deaths).

Weapons Offenses and Offenders

Weapons offenses are violations of local, state, and/or federal statutes or regulations that control deadly weapons. Deadly weapons include firearms and ammunition, silencers, explosives, and certain knives. Juveniles accounted for 16 percent of those arrested for weapon offenses in 1974 and 24 percent in 1996. Between 1985 and 1993 the number of juvenile arrests for weapon offenses more than doubled, climbing from about 30,000 to more than 61,000. According to the OJJDP of the U.S. Department of Justice, from that peak in 1993, however, the rate of arrests declined sharply and steadily. By 2000 the rate was nearly back to 1987 levels.

Bowling for Columbine

In Michael Moore's 2002 Academy Award–winning documentary *Bowling for Columbine,* the filmmaker examines the gun culture of the United States. Noting that the Columbine school shooters had bowling class before they embarked on their shooting spree—killing 12 students, 1 teacher, and ultimately themselves—the film addresses the availability of guns as well as the emphasis placed on guns in American society. In one segment, Moore visits a bank in Michigan that offers customers a free gun when opening a bank account.

As Moore delves into his subject, he visits with militia members, staunch gun ownership advocates, and people affected by violent crimes. To make a point, Moore takes two students who were seriously injured in the Columbine shootings to the headquarters of the department store that sold the bullets used in the Littleton incident. As a result of the shootings, both students have bullet-wound scars and one is in a wheelchair. Ultimately, Moore receives word that the store is planning to stop selling the types of bullets that were used in the shootings.

Throughout his commentary, Moore talks about the various issues pertaining to violence in American culture, including violence on television and gun accessibility. He notes that other countries experience many of the same issues, yet the United States has a larger problem with violence, especially among youth. In conclusion, he discusses the culture of fear that comes from the overemphasis on violence by the media, politicians, and others.

DEATH PENALTY

Much controversy surrounds juveniles and the death penalty. Many advocates believe that if a juvenile commits a capital crime, he/she should receive an adult sentence, including the death penalty. Many opponents feel that a death sentence is not an appropriate punishment for a juvenile. They assert that in many cases, juveniles can be rehabilitated to become productive members of society. In a Gallup Poll conducted in May of 2002, 69 percent of those surveyed said they opposed the death penalty being rendered against juveniles.

In most situations, convicted juvenile killers age 17 or younger do not receive the death penalty. Many receive life sentences, often without the possibility of parole. However, of the 38 states that allow the death sentence for capital crimes, 14 states use age 16 as the minimum age, 5 use age 17, and 19 use age 18. Federal civilian and military jurisdictions also set the minimum age at 18. (See Table 7.9.) South Dakota and Wyoming raised the age to 18 in March of 2004. New Hampshire is considering it as well.

According to Victor L. Streib in *The Juvenile Death Penalty Today: Death Sentences and Executions for Juvenile Crimes, January 1, 1973–March 15, 2004* (available online http://www.law.onu.edu/faculty/streib/JuvDeathMar152004.pdf): "The death penalty for juvenile offenders has become a uniquely American practice, in that it has been abandoned legally by nations everywhere else due to the express provisions of the United Nations Convention on the Rights of the Child and of several other international treaties and agreements." In the United Nations Convention on the Rights of the Child, Article 37a reads: "No child shall be subjected to torture or other cruel, inhuman or degrading treatment or punishment. Neither capital punishment nor life imprisonment without possibility of release shall be imposed for offences committed by persons below eighteen years of age." Streib observes that: "The United States is the only country in the world that has not yet ratified this international agreement, in large

TABLE 7.9

TABLE 7.10

Minimum death penalty ages, by jurisdiction, as of March 15, 2004

Age eighteen		Age seventeen	Age sixteen	
California[1]	New Mexico[1]	Florida[2]	Alabama[1]	Mississippi[2]
Colorado[1]	New York[1]	Georgia[1]	Arizona[2]	Nevada[1]
Connecticut[1]	Ohio[1]	New Hampshire[1]	Arkansas[2]	Oklahoma[2]
Illinois[1]	Oregon[1]	North Carolina[1]	Delaware[2]	Pennsylvania[2]
Indiana[1]	South Dakota[1]	Texas[1]	Idaho[2]	South Carolina[2]
Kansas[1]	Tennessee[1]		Kentucky[1]	Utah[2]
Maryland[1]	Washington[1]	5 states	Louisiana[2]	Virginia[1]
Missouri[2]	Wyoming[1]			
Montana[1]	Federal civilian[1]		14 states	
Nebraska[1]	Federal military[1]			
New Jersey[1]				

19 states and 2 federal jurisdictions

[1]Express minimum age in statute
[2]Minimum age required state or federal court decision.

SOURCE: Victor L. Streib, "Table 2: Minimum Death Penalty Age by Jurisdiction as of March 15, 2004," in *The Juvenile Death Penalty Today: Death Sentences and Executions for Juvenile Crimes, January 1, 1973–March 15, 2004,* Ohio Northern University, The Claude W. Pettit College of Law, Ada, OH, March 16, 2004 [Online] http://www.law.onu.edu/faculty/streib/JuvDeathMar152004.pdf [accessed March 29, 2004]. Reproduced with permission.

Age at time of arrest for capital offense and age of prisoners under sentence of death at yearend 2002

	Prisoners under sentence of death			
	At time of arrest		On December 31, 2002	
Age	Number*	Percent	Number	Percent
Total number under sentence of death on 12/31/02	3,299	100%	3,557	100%
17 or younger	74	2.2	0	
18–19	355	10.8	4	0.1
20–24	894	27.1	153	4.3
25–29	745	22.6	452	12.7
30–34	540	16.4	606	17.0
35–39	355	10.8	619	17.4
40–44	178	5.4	696	19.6
45–49	99	3.0	450	12.7
50–54	40	1.2	304	8.5
55–59	14	0.4	174	4.9
60–64	2	—	59	1.7
65 or older	3	0.1	40	1.1
Mean age	28 yrs.		39 yrs.	
Median age	27 yrs.		39 yrs.	

Note: The youngest person under sentence of death was a white male in Texas, born in April 1984 and sentenced to death in August 2002. The oldest person under sentence of death was a white male in Arizona, born in September 1915 and sentenced to death in June 1983.
—Less than 0.05%.
*Excludes 258 inmates for whom the date of arrest for capital offense was not available.

SOURCE: Thomas P. Bonczar and Tracy L. Snell, "Table 7. Age at time of arrest for capital offense and age of prisoners under sentence of death at yearend 2002," in *Capital Punishment, 2002,* NCJ 201848, U.S. Department of Justice, Bureau of Justice Statistics, Washington, DC, November 2003

part because of [the nation's] desire to remain free to retain the death penalty for juvenile offenders."

However, courts in the United States are often reluctant to sentence juveniles to death for capital crimes. Such was the case of convicted Washington, D.C.-area sniper Lee Boyd Malvo, who was 17 at the time he committed murder. Malvo and his accomplice, John Allen Muhammad, terrorized the area between October 2–22, 2002, with a series of sniper shootings that claimed the lives of 10 people and wounded 3 others. The nature of the shootings appeared random—the victims were people going about their daily routines, such as pumping gas or shopping. A huge manhunt ensued with Malvo and Muhammad finally being captured in a rest area along the highway.

Initially, the federal government had taken custody of the pair, but later turned them over to the state of Virginia, where several of the murders had occurred. Although six of the murders had transpired in Montgomery County, Maryland, U.S. Attorney General John Ashcroft took Virginia's record on the death penalty under consideration. Since 1976 Virginia had executed 89 people, while Maryland had enforced the death penalty only 3 times and was undergoing a moratorium on executions. In addition, Virginia, unlike Maryland, allows juveniles as young as 16 to receive the death penalty.

Malvo was charged with capital murder in the death of Linda Franklin, who was shot outside a Home Depot store in Falls Church, Virginia, on October 14, 2002. He was also charged with an act of terrorism in killing Franklin. When Malvo was sentenced in December 2003 for two counts of capital murder, he was given life without parole. Since Malvo did not receive the death sen-

tence, staunch debate again surfaced whether juveniles should even be eligible for death row. Strong arguments were made by opposing sides. Amid the controversy, the U.S. Supreme Court announced in early 2004 that it would review the constitutionality of using the death penalty on those under age 18.

Some states are reluctant to put juvenile offenders to death, while others are not. Seventeen people were executed for crimes they committed before age 18 between 1973 and mid-year 2000. Sixteen were age 17 at the time of their capital offense; one was 16. Of the 17 put to death, 9 were white, 7 black, and 1 Latino. Nine were executed in Texas. Among the states putting the most juveniles on death row between 1973 and October 31, 1998, were Texas, Florida, Alabama, Mississippi, and Louisiana.

Age When Arrested for Capital Crimes

In *Capital Punishment, 2002* (Thomas P. Bonczar and Tracy L. Snell, U.S. Department of Justice, Bureau of Justice Statistics, Washington, DC, November 2003), the authors present statistics about the men and women on death row. As of yearend 2002, some 3,557 prisoners were under sentence of death. No one on death row at that time was 17 or younger, 4 were 18–19, while 153 were 20–24. (See Table 7.10.) Most prisoners on death row fall into the 30–44 age categories. Yet this can occur because many years pass before someone is sentenced to death and that sentence is carried out. Many prisoners convicted of capital crimes remain on death row for many years so they have enough time to appeal their convictions.

To gain a better understanding of the prisoners who are sentenced to death, Table 7.10 provides statistics on the age when someone on death row committed his/her capital crime. Of the 3,299 prisoners for whom this information is available, 2.2 percent were 17 or less, 13 percent were 19 or less, and 40.1 percent were 24 or less. Nearly half (49.7 percent) fell into the 20 to 29 age group. In contrast, less than 1 percent were 55 or more. The mean age at time of arrest was 28, while the mean age for those on death row was 39. As of 2002, the oldest prisoner on death row was 87, the youngest 18.

Brief History of Juveniles and the Death Penalty

On April 4, 1977, 16-year-old Monty Lee Eddings and several friends were pulled over by a police officer as they traveled in a car. Eddings had several guns in the car, which he had taken from his father. When the police officer approached the car, Eddings shot and killed him. Eddings was tried as an adult even though he was 16 at the time of the murder. He was convicted of first-degree murder for killing a police officer and was sentenced to death.

At the sentencing hearing following the conviction, Eddings' lawyer presented substantial evidence of a turbulent family history, beatings by a harsh father, and serious emotional disturbance. The judge refused, as a matter of law, to consider the mitigating circumstances of Eddings' unhappy upbringing and emotional problems. He ruled that the only mitigating circumstance was the petitioner's youth, which was insufficient to outweigh the aggravating circumstances. (Mitigating circumstances may lessen responsibility for a crime, while aggravating circumstances may add to responsibility for a crime.)

In *Eddings v. Oklahoma* (455 U.S. 104, 1982), the Supreme Court, in a 5–4 opinion, ordered the case remanded (sent back to the lower courts for further proceedings). The justices based their ruling on *Lockett v. Ohio* (438 U.S. 586, 1978), which required the trial court to consider and weigh all of the mitigating evidence concerning the petitioner's family background and personal history.

By implication, since the majority did not reverse the case on the issue of age, the decision let stand Oklahoma's decision to try Eddings as an adult. Meanwhile, Chief Justice Warren Burger, who filed the dissenting opinion in which Justices Byron White, Harry A. Blackmun, and William H. Rehnquist joined, observed,

> The Constitution does not authorize us to determine whether sentences imposed by state courts are sentences we consider "appropriate"; our only authority is to decide whether they are constitutional under the Eighth Amendment. The Court stops far short of suggesting that there is any constitutional proscription [prohibition] against imposition of the death penalty on a person who was under age 18 when the murder was committed.

Hence, while the high court did not directly rule on the question of minors being sentenced to death, the sense of the Court would appear to be that it would uphold such a sentencing.

FIFTEEN IS TOO YOUNG. With three adults, William Thompson brutally murdered a former brother-in-law. Thompson was 15 at the time of the murder, but the state determined that Thompson, who had a long history of violent assault, had "virtually no reasonable prospects for rehabilitation...within the juvenile system and...should be held accountable for his acts as if he were an adult and should be certified to stand trial as an adult." Thompson was tried as an adult and found guilty. As with Eddings, Thompson's age was considered a mitigating circumstance, but the jury still sentenced him to death.

Thompson appealed, and while the Court of Criminal Appeals of Oklahoma upheld the decision, the U.S. Supreme Court, in *Thompson v. Oklahoma* (487 U.S. 815, 1988), did not. In a 5–3 majority vote, with Justice Sandra Day O'Connor agreeing to vacate (annul) the sentence, but not agreeing with the majority reasoning, the case was reversed. (Justice Anthony Kennedy took no part in the decision.)

Writing for the majority (Justices John Stevens, William J. Brennan, Thurgood Marshall, and Blackmun), Justice Stevens observed,

> Inexperience, less education, and less intelligence make the teenager less able to evaluate the consequences of his or her conduct, while at the same time he or she is much more apt to be motivated by mere emotion or peer pressure than is an adult. The reasons why juveniles are not trusted with the privileges and responsibilities of an adult also explain why their irresponsible conduct is not as morally reprehensible (blameworthy) as that of an adult.

Justice Stevens noted that 18 states required the age of at least 16 years before the death penalty could be considered. Counting the 14 states prohibiting capital punishment, a total of 32 states did not execute people under 16.

Justice O'Connor agreed with the judgment of the Court that the appellate court's ruling should be reversed. O'Connor pointed out, however, that, although most 15-year-old criminals are generally less blameworthy than adults who commit the same crimes, some may fully understand the horrible deeds they have done. Individuals, after all, have different characteristics, including their capability to distinguish right from wrong.

Writing for the minority (Justices Antonin Scalia, Rehnquist, and White), Justice Scalia found no national consensus forbidding the execution of a person who was 16 at the commission of the murder. Scalia could not understand the majority's calculations establishing a "contemporary standard" that forbade the execution of young minors. Abolitionist states (states with no death penalty) should not be considered in the issue of executing minors since they did not have executions in the first place. Rather, the 18 states that prohibited the execution of offenders who were younger than 16 when they murdered should be compared to the 19 states that applied the death penalty to young offenders.

AGE 16 OR 17 IS DEEMED ACCEPTABLE. A majority of the Court, with Justice O'Connor straddling the fence, found the death penalty unacceptable for an offender who was less than 16 when he or she committed murder. A majority of the Court, however, found the death sentence acceptable for a minor who was 16 or 17 during the commission of murder. The Supreme Court, in two jointly considered cases, *Stanford v. Kentucky* and *Wilkins v. Missouri* (492 U.S. 361, 1989), ruled that persons who committed their crimes at ages 16 or 17 could be executed for murder.

When he was 17 years old, Kevin Stanford and an accomplice raped Baerbel Poore, an attendant at a gas station they were robbing. They then took the woman to a secluded area near the station, where Stanford shot her in the face and in the back of her head. Stressing the seriousness of the offense and Stanford's long history of criminal behavior, the Court certified him as an adult. He was tried, found guilty, and sentenced to death.

When he was 16 years old, Heath Wilkins stabbed Nancy Allen to death while he was robbing the convenience store where she worked. Wilkins indicated he murdered Allen because "a dead person can't talk." Based on his long history of juvenile delinquency, the Court ordered Wilkins tried as an adult. He was found guilty and sentenced to die.

Writing for the majority (Justices Scalia, Rehnquist, White, and Kennedy), Justice Scalia could find no national consensus that executing minors ages 16 and 17 constituted cruel and unusual punishment. Scalia observed that of the 37 states whose statutes allowed the death penalty, just 12 refused to impose it on 17-year-old offenders and in addition to those 12, only 3 additional states refused to impose it on 16-year-old offenders.

Further, Justice Scalia saw no connection between the defendant's argument that those under 18 were denied the right to drive, drink, or vote because they were not considered mature enough to do so responsibly and whether this standard of maturity should be applied to a minor's understanding that murder is terribly wrong. Scalia added,

> Even if the requisite degrees of maturity were comparable, the age statutes in question would still not be relevant. These laws set the appropriate ages for the

operation of a system that makes its determinations in gross, and that does not conduct individualized maturity tests for each driver, drinker, or voter. The criminal justice system, however, does provide individualized testing. In the realm of capital punishment in particular, "individualized consideration [is] a constitutional requirement," and one of the individualized mitigating factors that sentencers must be permitted to consider is the defendant's age.

Justice O'Connor also concluded that no national consensus prohibited the imposition of the death penalty on Stanford and Wilkins. O'Connor, however, believed that the high court had the constitutional obligation to determine whether the punishment imposed was proportional to the defendants' blameworthiness.

Writing for the minority (Justices Brennan, Marshall, Blackmun, and Stevens), Justice Brennan found a national consensus among 30 states when he added the 12 states forbidding the execution of a person who was 16 years during the commission of the crime to those with no capital punishment, and the states that, in practice if not in law, did not execute minors. Justice Brennan, taking serious exception to the majority's observation that they had to find a national consensus in the laws passed by the state legislatures, stated,

> Our judgment about the constitutionality of a punishment under the Eighth Amendment is informed, though not determined...by an examination of contemporary attitudes toward the punishment, as evidenced in the actions of legislatures and of juries. The views of organizations with expertise in relevant fields and the choices of governments elsewhere in the world also merit our attention as indicators whether a punishment is acceptable in a civilized society.

SUPREME COURT REJECTS STANFORD'S LAST APPEAL. Kevin Stanford has appealed his case several times since the 1989 Supreme Court decision. As a last resort, Stanford filed a *habeas corpus* petition to the high court claiming it would be unconstitutional to execute him because he was under the age of 18 when he committed his crime. This petition required five votes to be heard. On October 21, 2002, a 5–4 majority rejected his appeal, announcing their decision without a written opinion.

Justice Stevens wrote a dissenting opinion, joined by Justices Breyer, Ginsburg, and Souter (*In re Stanford*, 123 S.Ct. 472). Justice Stevens believed that the reasons supporting the *Atkins v. Virginia* decision should apply to the execution of juvenile offenders. In *Atkins v. Virginia* (536 U.S. 304, 2003), the Court held that executing mentally retarded persons violates the Eight Amendment's ban on cruel and unusual punishment. Justice Stevens repeated Justice Brennan's dissent in *Stanford v. Kentucky*, adding that

> In the last 13 years, a national consensus has developed that juvenile offenders should not be executed. No state

has lowered the age of eligibility to either 16 or 17 since our decision in 1989....

The practice of executing [juvenile] offenders is a relic of the past and is inconsistent with evolving standards of decency in a civilized society. We should put an end to this shameful practice.

YOUTH—A MITIGATING CIRCUMSTANCE. Dorsie Lee Johnson Jr., age 19, and an accomplice staked out a convenience store, with the intention of robbing it. They found out that only one employee worked during the predawn hours. Agreeing to leave no witnesses to the crime, Johnson shot and killed the clerk, Jack Huddleston. They then emptied the cash register and stole some cigarettes.

The following month Johnson was arrested and subsequently confessed to the murder and the robbery. During the jury selection the defense attorneys asked potential jurors whether they believed that people were capable of change and whether they, the potential jurors, had ever done things in their youth that they would not now do.

The only witness the defense called was Johnson's father, who told of his son's drug use, grief over the death of his mother two years before the crime, and the murder of his sister the following year. He spoke of his son's youth and the fact that, at age 19, he did not evaluate things the way a person of 30 or 35 would.

Johnson was tried and convicted of capital murder. Under Texas law, the homicide qualified as a capital offense because Johnson intentionally or knowingly caused Huddleston's death. Moreover, the murder was carried out in the course of committing a robbery.

In the sentencing phase of the trial, the judge instructed the jury to answer two questions: (1) whether Johnson's actions were deliberate and intended to kill, and (2) whether there was a possibility that he would continue to commit violent crimes and be a threat to society. If the jury answered "yes" to both questions, Johnson would be sentenced to death. If the jury returned a "no" answer to either question, the defendant would be sentenced to life in prison. The jury was not to consider or discuss the possibility of parole.

Of equal importance was the instruction that the jury could consider all the evidence, both aggravating and mitigating, in either phase of the trial. The jury unanimously answered yes to both questions, and Johnson was sentenced to death.

Five days after the state appellate court denied Johnson's motions for a rehearing, the U.S. Supreme Court issued its opinion in another case, *Penry v. Lynaugh* (492 U.S. 302, 1989). Based on the *Penry* ruling, Johnson claimed that a separate instruction should have been given to the jurors that would have allowed them to consider his youth. (In *Penry,* the Court held that the jury should have been instructed that it could consider mental retardation as a mitigating factor during the penalty phase.) Again, the appellate court rejected Johnson's petition.

Affirming the Texas appellate court decision, Justice Kennedy delivered the opinion of the Supreme Court in *Johnson v. Texas* (509 U.S. 350, 1993). He was joined by Justices Rehnquist, White, Scalia, and Clarence Thomas. Kennedy noted that the Texas special-issues system (two questions asked of the jury and instruction to consider all evidence) allowed for adequate consideration of Johnson's youth. Justice Kennedy stated,

> Even on a cold record, one cannot be unmoved by the testimony of petitioner's father urging that his son's actions were due in large part to his youth. It strains credulity to suppose that the jury would have viewed the evidence of petitioner's youth as outside its effective reach in answering the second special issue. The relevance of youth as a mitigating factor derives from the fact that the signature qualities of youth are transient; as individuals mature, the impetuousness and recklessness that may dominate in younger years can subside.... As long as the mitigating evidence is within "the effective reach of the sentencer," the requirements of the Eighth Amendment are satisfied.

Justice O'Connor, in a dissenting opinion joined by Justices Blackmun, Stevens, and David Souter, stated that the jurors were not allowed to give "full effect to his strongest mitigating circumstance: his youth." Hearing of his less than exemplary youth, a jury might easily conclude, as Johnson's did, that he would continue to be a threat to society.

CHAPTER 8
PREVENTION, INTERVENTION, AND SUPPRESSION

Over the years, politicians, law enforcement officials, teachers, parents, and other concerned citizens have examined countless ideas in an effort to decrease youth violence and crime, from holding parents responsible for their children's crimes to having after-school violence prevention programs. The continuing problem of youth crime has many people devoting significant time and resources to end the cycle of violence. A variety of programs have been implemented in the area of prevention, intervention, and suppression. Efforts are ongoing to determine the effectiveness of such programs.

Prevention and intervention programs have existed since the 1800s. Prevention measures are those aimed at keeping youth, particularly at-risk youth, from beginning a life of crime, joining gangs, and/or otherwise ending up in prison or jail. Intervention programs are those designed to remove youth from gangs, criminal activities, and/or patterns of reckless behavior that would ultimately put the youth in prison or jail. Such programs typically include helping the individual build self-esteem, confidence, and socialization skills while offering education, recreation, and job skills assistance.

Although this chapter examines some of the types of programs available, hundreds of such programs exist throughout the United States, some at the national or state levels, but many at the local/community level. Many involve mentoring—having adults and sometimes other students spend time with at-risk youth to help them explore alternatives to violence and crimes. Mentoring programs take on a variety of activities, including sports, recreation, and education. Mentors help their subjects gain self-esteem, conflict resolution abilities, peer pressure resistance skills, and confidence.

Many prevention and intervention programs have seen some success with delinquent and at-risk youth, as noted by individuals who credit such groups with turning their lives around or keeping them from heading into lives

of crime and violence. Others have proven to be ineffective. Those that succeed provide alternatives to youth and often a safe place to hang out, make new friends, and learn life skills.

Another method aimed at reducing youth crime and violence is called suppression. This tactic is used by law enforcement agencies throughout the country. Suppression usually involves a show of force, such as saturating an area with many uniformed police officers. The idea is meant to show the criminal element that they are being watched and that such activities will not be tolerated. Suppression techniques also include sweeps, where officers sweep through an area rounding up youth and adult offenders. Some suppression programs have proven to be somewhat effective, while others have not.

The remainder of this chapter will focus on a small sampling of the various types of programs tried and tested over the years. It will also discuss some general practices, such as curfews and holding parents responsible, that have been initiated to reduce youth crime and violence.

EXAMPLES OF PREVENTION AND INTERVENTION PROGRAMS

The Chicago Area Project (CAP)

Chicago, like Los Angeles, has been home to many gangs throughout the twentieth century. In an effort to deal with the gang situation on the city's streets, the Chicago Area Project (CAP) was born in 1934. The program, designed by sociologist Clifford R. Shaw (1895–1957), aimed to work with delinquent youth in poverty-stricken areas of Chicago. Project staff sought to prevent youth from joining gangs and ultimately committing crimes.

To achieve this, CAP advocates believed that improvements needed to be made to neighborhoods and communities. According to "Preventing Adolescent Gang Involvement" (Finn-Aage Esbensen, *Juvenile Justice*

Bulletin, U.S. Department of Justice, Office of Justice Programs, Office of Juvenile Justice and Delinquency Prevention, September 2000), "CAP organized community residents through self-help committees based on preexisting community structures such as church groups and labor unions." As noted on the CAP Web site in 2004, "CAP forced people to recognize that juvenile delinquency in low-income/socially disorganized areas is a product of the social experiences children are exposed to[—]not an inherent character flaw or associated with a certain ethnic background."

In the 1940s CAP created a detached worker program aimed at helping youth become more social, find jobs, obtain education, build confidence, and develop other skills. Leaving their offices, CAP staff took to the streets to work with gang members and at-risk youth. They planned activities and represented such individuals when they were in need of legal, job, or other assistance. Similar programs existed in Los Angeles, Boston, and other cities.

CAP and its founder Shaw were unique in their day for several reasons. Shaw asserted that for his program to succeed, staff needed to work from within a neighborhood, rather than from the outside. He also encouraged the participation of community members who were considered to be negative influences. By working with such elements, instead of against them, he was determined to get diverse community members working together to improve and strengthen neighborhoods. For example, ex-convicts were allowed to participate in Shaw's delinquency prevention efforts.

As of 2004, CAP has grown to include more than 40 affiliates and special projects. Continuing to promote self-improvement and self-determination, CAP emphasizes community organizing, advocacy, and direct service. According to its Web site, "CAP has succeeded in arousing in individual citizens a sense of responsibility for the welfare of their children—and a realization that their own united efforts offered the most promising prospect for providing security, protection, and constructive satisfaction of the needs of the children and young people in any community."

Boys and Girls Clubs of America (BGCA)

Offering a variety of programs to help youth, the Boys and Girls Clubs of America (BGCA) works with some 3.6 million children throughout the United States, Puerto Rico, the Virgin Islands, and U.S. military bases in America and abroad. In more than 3,300 club locations, the group uses trained, full-time staff "to inspire and enable all young people, especially those from disadvantaged circumstances, to realize their full potential as productive, responsible and caring citizens," according to the organization's Web site in 2004.

The BGCA offers a specialized program called Gang Prevention/Intervention through Targeted Outreach for those aged 6 to 18. Sponsored by the Office of Juvenile Justice and Delinquency Prevention (OJJDP), the outreach program works with delinquent youth and those "at risk" of becoming delinquent. The goal of the program is to provide educational and fun activities for youth in a safe environment.

Tracing its start to 1860 in Hartford, Connecticut, the BGCA was originally founded to give young boys a chance at making a good life for themselves and their families. Over time, as the organization grew, staff began helping girls as well. Hence, the name was changed in 1990 to reflect the presence of both genders. According to the BGCA Web site in 2004, 44 percent of the group's participants are female and 64 percent are minorities.

BOYS AND GIRLS CLUBS IN INDIAN COUNTRY. Many Native American children grow up in poverty on reservations in the United States. As a result, some of these youth are at-risk to become involved in gangs, attempt suicide, drop out of school, and/or engage in drinking or drugs. To help Native American youth realize their potential, the BGCA began establishing clubs on Indian lands, first on the Pine Ridge Reservation in South Dakota in 1992. As of 2004, the organization serves 70,000 Native American youths in 171 clubs in 22 states.

The goals of the Indian Country groups are similar to the overall BGCA programs. They include gaining new skills, building self-confidence and leadership traits, having a safe place to learn and play, learning more about Native American culture, preparing for careers, working in the arts, and participating in sports and fitness activities.

Jobs for a Future (JFF)

Local community groups also work with gang members and at-risk youth to help them improve their chances of success in the future. One such group is Jobs for a Future (JFF), based in Los Angeles, California. Founded in 1988 by Father Greg Boyle S.J. (a Jesuit priest) to help youth in the Aliso-Pico housing projects, the organization is affiliated with the Dolores Mission. Before the advent of JFF, eight rival gangs roamed the area and caused concern and fear among the community's residents. Fr. Boyle sought to create a safe atmosphere to help youth find alternatives to gang membership and violence.

The goal of the organization, as evidenced in its name, is to help youth secure jobs. Fr. Boyle asserted that most at-risk and gang youth would rather have legitimate jobs than participate in illegal activities. However, such jobs are often scarce for those who have experienced trouble with the law, those who sport visible gang tattoos, those with few skills (if any), those lacking education, and those who are unsure how to act or dress appropriately in a regular job environment. Hence, Fr. Boyle began looking for people who would take a risk and hire such youth. As noted on the group's Web site in 2004: "By giving a gang member a reason to get up in the morning, we provide them with a reason not to gang bang at night." Among JFF's slogans are "Nothing Stops a Bullet Like a Job" and "Jobs Not Jails."

JFF offers a variety of services for at-risk and gang youth as well as those recently released from detention. Among the services provided are: 1) Job referral, which helps youth find jobs and also monitors their progress for 90 days; 2) Job readiness, which offers help with resumes, interview coaching, and information on how to dress and act on the job; 3) Job training, which assists youth in gaining job experience as well as learning proper job etiquette; 4) Tattoo removal, which is performed by doctors who volunteer their time; 5) Counseling services; and 6) Navigation, which is a program that assigns a "navigator" to an individual youth to help him/her enroll in classes, join self-help groups, etc. The group reports assisting some 350 individuals in finding jobs annually.

HOMEBOY INDUSTRIES. Established in 1992 by Fr. Boyle, Homeboy Industries is intended to help those who have difficulty securing employment. Fr. Boyle found that some of the individuals he tried to help find jobs were unable to do so. Sometimes this was due to an individual's lack of job skills, meager education, or prison record. Thus, Fr. Boyle dreamed up the idea of creating his own on-the-job training program. During its years of operation, Homeboy Industries has operated the Homeboy Bakery, which was closed in 1999 after a fire; Homeboy Silkscreen; Homeboy Landscaping; Homeboy Tortillas; Homeboy Graffiti Removal Services; and Homeboy/Homegirl Merchandise. Homeboy Industries counts among its successes the fact that it has employed rival gang members who work together.

Violence-Free Zones (VFZ)

Coordinated by the National Center for Neighborhood Enterprise (NCNE), Violence-Free Zones (VFZ) are aimed at helping gang members and other violent youths turn their lives around through the adoption of a productive and peaceful lifestyle. A community-based program, the project provides various types of assistance, including life-skills training, mentoring, job assistance, substance abuse help, character development, and family services. To establish a VFZ, the NCNE and community leaders seek to end youth violence by working with warring gang factions to call a truce. Such programs have been launched in Washington, D.C.; Dallas, Texas; Houston, Texas; Hartford, Connecticut; Los Angeles, California; and Indianapolis, Indiana.

The first VFZ was launched in 1997 in the Benning Terrace public housing complex in Washington, D.C. At that time, the area was so crime-ridden that people were afraid to leave their homes. The situation became even more desperate after Daryl Hall, 12, was beaten, kidnapped, and later murdered by warring gang members.

Gangs had become so bold they attacked Hall in broad daylight. The NCNE, in conjunction with the Alliance of Concerned Men, stepped in and were able to set up meetings between the leaders of the rival gangs. The groups managed to work out a truce.

When an official at the DC Housing Authority heard about the cease-fire, he joined the cause and offered jobs to some of the youths. Meaningful, legitimate employment proved to be an important asset to the program. Among the jobs available were landscaping, building maintenance, and removing graffiti. Jobs not only provided youth with an income, but with a sense of purpose and belonging as well. The Housing Authority estimates that the program saved the city $13 million. Others have suggested that 15 or more deaths were prevented in the two years following the truce.

LAW ENFORCEMENT STRATEGIES

Gang Resistance Education and Training (GREAT)

Hoping to reach students before they become involved in gangs and crime, uniformed police officers throughout the country visit middle schools to discuss the life consequences associated with such activities. The 13-part curriculum, offered through the Gang Resistance Education and Training (GREAT) program, was initially created by the Phoenix (Arizona) Police Department and the Bureau of Alcohol, Tobacco and Firearms (ATF) in 1991. Since that pilot program, GREAT has expanded to all 50 states and the District of Columbia. Among the topics presented are personal, resiliency, resistance, and social skills. The stated goals of the program are to help youth resist peer pressure, have positive attitudes toward law enforcement, learn ways to avoid violence, develop basic life skills, and set positive goals for the future.

As recorded on the ATF Web site in 2004, the GREAT curriculum includes the following classes:

1) Welcome to GREAT (program introduction; the relationship between gangs, violence, drug abuse, and crime)

2) What's a Real Deal? (message analysis; facts and fiction about gangs and violence)

3) It's about Us (community; student roles and responsibilities; what you can do about gangs)

4) Where Do We Go from Here? (setting realistic and achievable goals)

5) Decisions, Decisions, Decisions (GREAT decision-making model; impact of decisions on goals; decision-making practice)

6) Do You Hear What I'm Saying (effective communication; verbal vs nonverbal communication)

7) Walk in Someone Else's Shoes (active listening; identification of different emotional states; empathy for others)

8) Say It Like You Mean It (body language; tone of voice; refusal skills practice)

9) Getting Along Without Going Along (influences; peer pressure; refusal skills practice)

10) Keeping Your Cool (GREAT anger management tips; practice cooling off)

11) Keeping It Together (recognizing anger in others; tips for calming others)

12) Working It Out (consequences of fighting; GREAT tips for conflict resolution; conflict resolution practice; where to go for help)

13) Looking Back (program review; "Making My School GREAT" project presentations)

Although the GREAT curriculum is targeted at seventh graders, program administrators have also developed a third- and fourth-grade curriculum containing four lessons: "What Is a Gang?"; "Families and Why They Are Special"; "My Future"; and "Do You Know Me?"

The effectiveness of GREAT training became the basis for a study conducted by the National Institute of Justice (NIJ) and the University of Nebraska at Omaha. Program participants were said to have developed more negative opinions about gangs and more positive attitudes about police. They also report experiencing lower rates of victimizations, among other things.

Suppression Programs

In some areas with high gang activity and violent youth crime, law enforcement personnel have tried suppression techniques. To "suppress" such activities, police departments assign extra officers to particular areas to make the presence of the law highly visible. By flooding the area with law enforcement officers, the idea is that criminals will take notice and refrain from crime for fear they will be caught. Suppression programs have been tested out in various cities, including Los Angeles, Chicago, and Houston, among others.

COMMUNITY RESOURCES AGAINST STREET HOODLUMS (CRASH), LOS ANGELES. In 1977 the Los Angeles Police Department (LAPD) created a suppression unit called Community Resources against Street Hoodlums (CRASH). Serving as an elite gang crime unit, CRASH officers took to the streets to learn more about gang members, including their names, addresses, and habits. As they gathered intelligence about gang members, they also tracked their movements. On a regular basis, CRASH officers would have discussions with gang members to learn more about what was happening in the gang and in the community.

In addition to surveillance activities, CRASH officers would study graffiti to learn of potential gang fights and activities. At various times, officers would canvass their jurisdiction areas making arrests of gang members engaged in criminal activities. One of its biggest sweeps occurred in 1988 under the name Operation Hammer. Over the course of two nights (Friday and Saturday), 1,000 officers made more than 1,450 arrests. As the police roamed the South Central area, they picked up suspected gang members on a variety of charges, including curfew and traffic violations as well as other criminal behavior. In some cases, they arrested persons on existing warrants. Although the vast majority of those arrested were let go without any charges filed, the sweep attempted to suppress future crime through the show of force.

The presence of CRASH units in Los Angeles was meant to deter youth and gang-related crime. However, the program itself came under scrutiny in the late 1990s due to allegations that some CRASH officers were acting in a gang-like fashion themselves, making false arrests, and engaging in other forms of corruption. Although the number of officers said to be involved in the wrongdoing was low, CRASH was ultimately disbanded in 2000. In the section of Los Angeles known as Rampart, where much of the police corruption was said to occur, some residents reported increased crime and gang activity once CRASH was canceled. In place of CRASH, smaller gang units were dispatched to work on anti-gang initiatives.

OPERATION CUL DE SAC (OCDS), LOS ANGELES. The LAPD has tried various alternative measures for dealing with its extensive gang problems. One such method was Operation Cul de Sac (OCDS), which was tested in 1990 and 1991. Under the plan, the LAPD chose a hotspot for gang crime, homicide, and drug activity. The 10-block area had experienced the most drive-by shootings (38), homicides (7), and aggravated street assaults (174) in Los Angeles during the year prior to the start of OCDS, according to the NIJ (James Lasley, "'Designing Out' Gang Homicides and Street Assaults," *Research in Brief,* U.S. Department of Justice, Office of Justice Programs, National Institute of Justice, Washington, DC, November 1998).

According to the NIJ report, the operation "involv[ed] the use of traffic barriers to block access by automobiles...as a means to 'design out' crime by reducing the opportunities to commit it.... [T]he traffic barriers were placed in neighborhoods where gangs and accompanying gang violence had spiraled out of control." The goal was to block off certain streets that were often used by criminals when making their getaways. By reducing access to the area, particularly streets connecting to major roadways, the LAPD was able to lessen the mobility of rival gangs who cruised the area performing "hit-and-run" crimes.

Although the operation was controversial, it did succeed in reducing crime in the area, particularly street assaults and homicides. Some people complained that OCDS was infringing on their right to travel as they desired. The operation's success, however, was measured in studies such as that conducted by the NIJ. After the operation concluded, the crime rate in the area again increased.

HOUSTON POLICE DEPARTMENT GANG TASK FORCE/MAYOR'S ANTI-GANG OFFICE. The Houston Police Department Gang Task Force is just one example of the many units of this type operating throughout the United States. Working in conjunction with the Mayor's Anti-Gang Office, the task force focuses on areas with high gang activity and aims to provide a highly visible presence in an effort to lessen gang violence and crime. The Mayor's Anti-Gang Office works with communities and neighborhoods to provide supportive services to at-risk youth, including counseling, job leads, conflict resolution, and recreation programs. As noted on the City of Houston's Web site in 2004, the Mayor's Anti-Gang Office has provided gang awareness training to more than 36,000 individuals, including educators, law enforcement personnel, probation officers, and members of the public since 1994. The group makes use of high-tech devices, such as geomapping and tracking systems. These programs help staff keep track of gang locations as well as youth program assistance sites.

School Resource Officers (SROs)

The implementation of the School Resource Officers (SROs) program is intended to improve relations between youth and police. The project, designed to prevent and intercept the commission of youth crime and violence, also gives students and police officers the chance to get to know one another. In some areas, children grow up with contempt or fear of police. The SRO program works to eliminate those concerns as well as educate students about the law and provide one-on-one mentoring.

Under the program, a police officer is dispatched to a school as an SRO. While at the school, the officer works to prevent crime, violence, and substance abuse; makes arrests if necessary during the commission of crimes; counsels students; and conducts classes about law enforcement and school safety. The program calls this the TRIAD concept (police officer, educator, counselor). To participate as an SRO, candidates must complete a specialized training program. The SRO program is credited with helping reduce youth crime in schools as well as in the community.

NATIONAL ASSOCIATION OF SCHOOL RESOURCE OFFICERS (NASRO). Founded in 1990, the National Association of School Resource Officers (NASRO) has a membership of nearly 10,000 members worldwide. A not-for-profit organization, NASRO holds annual conferences and provides workshops for SROs about various procedures, techniques, and prevention measures. The group also conducts surveys of its members to learn more about current issues affecting SROs and schools today. In its 2003 survey, for example, officers (70.5 percent) expressed concern that elementary school students have become more aggressive during the last five years (Kenneth S. Trump, *School Safety Threats Persist, Funding Decreasing: NASRO 2003 National School-Based Law Enforcement Study,* National Association of School Resource Officers, Osprey, FL, August 19, 2003). The complete results of the NASRO study are available through the group's Web site at http://www.nasro.org.

Police Athletic League

Another way that police try to help juveniles avoid a life of crime, violence, or substance abuse is through organizations like the Police Athletic League (PAL). The association is composed of volunteer officers who work with kids via sports, recreational, or creative arts activities, such as baseball, football, golf, tennis, dance, drama, art, or photography, among others. More than 350 police agencies participate in PAL, helping some 2 million youth (ages 5–18) in more than 700 cities in the United States, Puerto Rico, Virgin Islands, and Canada. PAL works in the inner cities as well as in suburban and rural areas, believing that "[a]ll kids face difficult challenges at school, at home, and on the playing field," according to the group's Web site in 2004. "PAL is dedicated to programs offering kids an opportunity to work with positive role models, learn about success and failure on a playing field without drugs or guns."

PAL operates under the umbrella organization, the National Association of Police Athletic Leagues. The national association's mottoes are "Filling Playgrounds, Not Prisons" and "Cops and Kids Together—Providing Solutions through Sports and Education." In late 2003, PAL teamed with Court TV to develop the "Choices and Consequences" program. An interactive, after-school video and lesson program, it is designed to help youth learn life-skills and understand the lifelong consequences that crime and violence can bring. It is being implemented nationwide in high schools and middle schools.

Gang Summits

Some members of the community work with police to sponsor summits to address the issues of gangs and violence in their neighborhoods. Community leaders and law enforcement meet with local citizens to exchange information, offer ideas, and evaluate current efforts. At some public forums, participants may also urge local gangs to call a truce and thus end violence among rival factions. Gang summits and truces have been successful in some areas. In others, plans have backfired when gangs, feeling that they are under attack, reinforce not only gang loyalty but gang rivalries as well.

SCHOOL PROGRAMS

Students against Violence Everywhere (SAVE)

After student Alex Orange was shot and killed in Charlotte, North Carolina, while trying to stop a fight in

1989, his classmates at West Charlotte High School decided to organize the group Students against Violence Everywhere (SAVE). The organization has grown far beyond Orange's high school to encompass more than 1,100 chapters and nearly 100,000 students as of 2004. The group is active in elementary, middle, and high schools across the United States. Members have their own "colors": orange for Alex Orange and purple for peace and nonviolence.

The group focuses on violence prevention, helping kids gain life skills, knowledge, and an understanding of the consequences of violence and crime. The organization also aims to help members overcome negative peer pressure situations through the development of positive peer interactions. It also plans safe activities, including co-sponsorship of the National Youth Violence Prevention Campaign. During the weeklong campaign, participants spend each day focused on one aspect of violence prevention. Day 1, for example, seeks to "promote respect and tolerance," while other days focus on anger management, conflict resolution, school and community safety, and unity.

Big Brothers Big Sisters (BBBS) in School

Celebrating its 100th year of mentoring youth in 2004, the Big Brothers Big Sisters (BBBS) organization works with young people (ages 5–18) throughout the United States. In 2002 the organization provided assistance to 200,000 juveniles via 470 agencies. The organization, which provides one-on-one mentoring services, seeks to help youth perform better at school, stay clear of drugs and alcohol, improve their relationships with others, and avoid lives of crime and violence. Under the main program, a child is paired with an adult who spends time with him or her several times each month on outings, which can include sports, recreation, visits to museums or parks, etc. Through the experience, the "Bigs" help the "Littles" develop life skills, confidence, and self-esteem.

BBBS has also developed programs for school children. Through the group's outreach program, BBBS volunteers visit schools weekly to provide one-on-one mentoring to students needing help. In addition, high school students also gain experience mentoring elementary school children through the High School Bigs program. While helping older students develop skills working with children, the project helps younger children bond with teens closer to their own age and see that they, too, can grow up to lead productive lives.

Safety Corridors

In some areas, parents and law enforcement officers create safety corridors for students to use when traveling to and from school. Such routes provide a safe area for students who want to avoid conflict with other youth, including gang members. Under such programs, parents and educators supervise the routes, and police patrol the areas to keep kids safe. One such program was devised by the Visalia Unified School District in California. Called Parents and Schools Succeeding in Providing Organized Routes to Travel (PASSPORT), the group recruited people in designated safety corridors to come out of their homes at certain hours and watch for and report signs of trouble.

OTHER ORGANIZATIONS AND PROGRAMS

The Guardian Angels

When it comes to crime and violence on the city streets, most people want to prevent or stop it but feel powerless to do so. They might believe that the actions of just one person would make little, if any, difference. In the late 1970s Curtis Sliwa set out to prove that average citizens could effect such change. As night manager of a McDonald's restaurant in the Bronx section of New York City, he grew tired of violence and crime in the area. He organized a multiracial group of volunteers to monitor streets, subways, and neighborhoods. Without carrying any weapons, 13 volunteers, all sporting red berets, set out to stop crime and violence. As more people joined the cause, the group developed a more formal structure and called themselves the Guardian Angels.

Trained in martial arts, group members went to some of the most high crime areas and made citizen's arrests—detaining those committing crimes until the police could arrive. While many area residents lauded their presence, some called them vigilantes. Over time the Angels won over many of their opponents and have since worked with the National Crime Prevention Council, the Young Men's Christian Association (YMCA), and other groups. Several members have died while trying to protect the streets. Sliwa, himself, was shot and nearly killed in 1992.

As of 2004, the Angels have 25 chapters and hundreds of members throughout the world. In addition to protecting neighborhoods, members also work with schools on safety programs. In 1995 the group expanded its efforts to include the Internet with a program billed as a "cyber-neighborhood watch." Its CyberAngels program, which helps children use the Internet safely, received the President's Service Award in 1998.

In addition to its safety patrols, the group has expanded to include programs geared to children and teens to teach them life skills and show them alternatives to lives of crime and violence. Junior Guardian Angels reaches out to children 7 to 11, while the Urban Guardian Angels is geared to ages 12 to 16. Sliwa is a frequent lecturer and has cohosted radio and television programs. Commenting on the focus of his work with the Angels, according to the group's Web site in 2004, Sliwa states: "Empower people to help themselves, build self-esteem and confidence, arm them with responsibility and you tap into the greatest source of lasting good possible."

Neighborhood Watch Programs

Another crime-fighting strategy involving average citizens is called the Neighborhood Watch. Working with police, citizens involved in such programs monitor areas in their communities and report crimes in progress as well as suspicious activities. The goal is not only to stop crimes currently underway, but to maintain a strong presence in the neighborhood to show would-be robbers, drug dealers, and other criminals that they are not welcome in the community. Begun by the LAPD, the Neighborhood Watch program exists throughout the United States today. Such programs can be implemented in a neighborhood, park, office building, public housing development, or any place where citizens want to reduce crime.

Neighborhood Watch participants receive training on what signs to look for when on their patrols. Such activities include suspicious behavior, including people looking in the windows of parked cars or houses where no lights are on; people carrying large items from houses, such as televisions or stereo equipment; someone in a car or on foot trying to approach a child; people being pushed or shoved; and people shouting or screaming. Those involved in Neighborhood Watches use radios and cell phones to report crimes or suspicious behavior. One of the leading spokesmen for such programs is "McGruff the Crime Dog," an animated dog who sports a trenchcoat and instructs people via television ads that they can "take a bite out of crime." The National Crime Prevention Council's Web site provides documentation for starting Neighborhood Watch programs in communities.

Wilderness Training

Various therapy programs exist for troubled youth, including those who have encountered trouble with the law or those at risk of doing so. Such programs are designed for teens in an effort to help them learn more about themselves, develop life skills, and ultimately turn their lives around. Wilderness training is one example of such therapy programs. It takes teens away from their troubled home environment and puts them into a wilderness setting to give them a chance to see a larger view of the world and what it has to offer. It also provides youth with the opportunity to test themselves in the wilderness and succeed in overcoming the elements, building shelters, and living off the land. Through such programs, counselors and staff seek to educate participants in issues of respect, trust, compassion, and honesty, among others.

OTHER MENTORING PROGRAMS

Juvenile Mentoring Program (JUMP)

Sponsored by the OJJDP, the Juvenile Mentoring Program (JUMP) provides grants to select organizations that aim to provide one-to-one mentoring projects to at-risk youths. According to the JUMP Web site in 2004, the program defines an at-risk youth as someone "who is exposed to high levels of risk in his or her family, home, community, and social environment to a degree that may lead to educational failure, dropping out of school, or involvement in juvenile delinquency, including gang-related delinquent activity." Among the 30 organizations, programs, and schools receiving JUMP grants in 2003 were the Indiana Juvenile Task Force in Indianapolis; the Self-Expression Teen Theater (SETT) in Toledo, Ohio; Utah State University in Logan; the Mountaineer Boys and Girls Club in Morgantown, West Virginia; and Payne County Youth Services in Stillwater, Oklahoma.

The JUMP program, which mandates that mentors be at least 18 years of age, requires a mentor to meet with an at-risk youth for one to two hours each week for one year or more. To assist JUMP participants, the OJJDP sponsors the National Mentoring Center (NMC) and has its programs' successes evaluated by Information Technology International (ITI). Thus far, the ITI has found that JUMP programs have aided those being mentored in significant ways, including reducing aggressive behavior and delinquency. As of 2004, 299 JUMP sites have received funding and helped some 9,200 at-risk youth through one-to-one mentoring.

NATIONAL MENTORING CENTER (NMC). Located in Portland, Oregon, the National Mentoring Center (NMC) was established by the OJJDP and is part of the Northwest Regional Educational Laboratory. The NMC seeks to provide assistance to the more than 5,000 youth mentoring programs that exist in the United States through sharing best practices and implementing standards to help groups create consistent programs that achieve the best results. The NMC provides a variety of resources, including workshops, conferences, publications, and training sessions. Among its publications are *Foundations of Successful Youth Mentoring: A Guidebook for Program Development* and *Training New Mentees: A Manual for Preparing Youth in Mentoring Programs.*

OTHER STRATEGIES

OJJDP Comprehensive Gang Model

The OJJDP advocates the use of a comprehensive gang model developed by I.A. Spergel. The model, which includes five steps to help gang members and their communities, is recorded in "Implementing the OJJDP Comprehensive Gang Model" (Jim Burch and Candice Kane, *OJJDP Fact Sheet,* U.S. Department of Justice, Office of Justice Programs, Office of Juvenile Justice and Delinquency Prevention, July 1999).

These strategies are: (1) mobilizing community leaders and residents to plan, strengthen, or create new opportunities or linkages to existing organizations for gang-involved or at-risk youth; (2) using outreach workers to engage gang-involved youth; (3) providing or facilitating access to academic, economic, and social opportunities; (4) conducting gang suppression activities and holding gang-involved youth accountable; and (5) facilitating organizational change and development to help community agencies better address gang problems through a team "problem-solving" approach that is consistent with the philosophy of community oriented policing.

Holding Parents Responsible

Civil liability laws have held parents at least partly responsible for damages caused by their children for many decades. In addition, child welfare laws included actions against those who contributed to the delinquency of a minor. By the 1990s, in response to rising juvenile crime rates, communities and states passed tougher laws about parental responsibility. According to the National Center for Juvenile Justice, a nonprofit research organization, at the end of the 1998 legislative session, 34 states had statutes that made parents of delinquent children liable to the victim of the crime. Even more states (39) had statutes that either allowed or required parents of delinquents to participate in treatment, counseling, or probation with their children.

For example, a California law mandated that parents could be prosecuted for "gross negligence" (failing to supervise their children in an adequate manner). If convicted, parents would receive a $2,500 fine and a sentence of up to one year in jail. A Louisiana law permitted parents to be fined up to $1,000 and be imprisoned for up to six months if found guilty of "improper supervision of a minor." This could include activities such as a child associating with drug dealers, members of a street gang, or convicted felons. In Idaho, courts could require parents to pay detention costs for their child.

In May 1996 a Michigan jury convicted the parents of a 16-year-old boy of a criminal misdemeanor for failing to control his behavior. The parents claimed that their teenager, who had broken the law more than once, had intimidated them to prevent them from interfering. The judge nonetheless fined them $100 each and ordered them to pay court costs of $1,000. Some punishments have been administered in more unusual ways. In 1995, for instance, Judge Wayne Creech of Family Court in Columbia, South Carolina, ordered a 15-year-old girl to be chained to her mother for an entire month. The juvenile had a history of truancy and shoplifting. In Florida, a mother was convicted of truancy and sentenced to a year's probation because three of her five children refused to go to school.

Critics of parental liability state that victims are just looking for someone to blame. They assert that U.S. law usually holds people responsible for crimes only if they actively participate in the commission of such acts. They believe that if standard rules of American law are practiced, the prosecutor of a case should have to prove that the parents intended to participate in a crime in order to be found guilty.

In many states, parents are required to pay for costs or program fees related to juvenile courts or corrections. For example, in 1995 Idaho, Indiana, and New Hampshire passed laws to force parents to pay for the care of their children confined in juvenile facilities. Parents are responsible for victim restitution in Alaska, Arizona, Idaho, New Hampshire, North Dakota, and Virginia. In Rhode Island and Texas, parents are required to participate with their children in counseling or educational programs and at adjudicatory (court) hearings. Involvement of parents in their child's case-processing can be effective in deterring repeat offenses, according to preliminary reports.

Curfews

To reduce the occurrence of youth violence and crime, lawmakers have enacted curfews in various cities, towns, and rural areas across the country. Curfews for young people have existed off and on since the 1890s when they were enacted to reduce crime among immigrant youth. States and cities often pass curfew ordinances when citizens perceive a need to maintain control over juveniles. Due to the rising rate of juvenile crime in the late 1980s and early 1990s, more than 1,000 jurisdictions in the United States imposed youth curfews. By 1997, according to a U.S. Conference of Mayors survey, 276 of the 347 surveyed cities (80 percent) had some sort of curfew in place. Another 23 cities, or 6 percent, were considering having a curfew law. As a result, juvenile curfew and loitering arrests doubled between 1992 and 1998, according to the OJJDP. In a survey conducted by the National League of Cities in 2000, 490 cities were reviewed. Some 69 percent (337) had nighttime curfews and 14 percent (68) had daytime curfews. Thirty-five of the cities surveyed reported that they were considering adopting a curfew.

Most curfew laws work essentially the same way. They are aimed at restricting juveniles to their homes or property between the hours of 11 P.M. and 6 A.M. weekdays. Such laws usually allow juveniles to stay out a little later on weekends. Exceptions are made for youth who need to travel to and from school, attend church events, or go to work at different times. Other exceptions include family emergencies or situations when juveniles are accompanied by their parents.

To be successful, curfews need sustained enforcement and community support and involvement. In addition, a curfew's success depends on the creation of educational, recreational, and job opportunities for juveniles, the establishment of antidrug and anti-gang programs, and the provision of hotlines for community problems or questions.

Although many people believe that curfews are important in the fight against youth crime, critics of curfew ordinances argue that such laws violate the constitutional rights of children and their parents. They argue that the First, Fourth, Ninth, and Fourteenth Amendment rights of people are endangered by curfew laws, especially the rights of free speech and association, privacy, and equal protection. Opponents also assert that no studies have proven curfew laws to be effective.

THE EFFECTIVENESS OF CURFEWS. Some debate exists over the effectiveness of curfews. However, many cities have reported declines in juvenile crime and victimization rates after enacting curfews. U.S. Conference of Mayors researcher John Pionke noted that a number of cities showed a 30 to 50 percent decline in juvenile crime over a period of one year after instituting curfews.

The 1997 U.S. Conference of Mayors survey asked city officials what they thought about curfew enforcement. Officials in 9 of 10 cities said that curfew enforcement was a good use of police officers' time; 88 percent observed that enforcing a curfew made their city's streets safer; and 83 percent believed that curfews helped curb gang violence. Of the 154 cities that had their curfews in effect for 10 years or less, officials in 53 percent noted a decrease in juvenile crime (attributed by them to the curfew), 11 percent saw no change, and 10 percent saw an increase in juvenile crime (the remaining 26 percent of cities had no data on the curfew's effects available because of its recent implementation).

Various cities have reported a reduction in crime due to curfews. The Dallas Police Department recorded an 18 percent decrease in juvenile victimization and a 15 percent reduction in juvenile arrests during curfew hours. Long Beach, California, and New Orleans, Louisiana, also reported significant decreases. However, Long Beach and several other cities found that, to some extent, the crime rates were "displaced"—that is, more juvenile crime was occurring during the non-curfew hours. Long Beach reported a sizable decrease in gang crimes due to the implementation of its curfew, however.

According to the 2001 National Youth Gang Survey, 62 percent of jurisdictions reporting gang problems used curfews or other ordinances aimed at keeping youth from congregating at night. Of those jurisdictions, 86 percent deemed that such laws "demonstrated at least some degree of effectiveness" (Arlen Egley Jr. and Aline K. Major, "Highlights of the 2001 National Youth Gang Survey," U.S. Department of Justice, Office of Justice Programs, Office of Juvenile Justice and Delinquency Prevention, Washington, DC, April 2003).

Opponents of curfew ordinances assert that such laws have little, if any, measurable effect. Some contend that reports noting reduction figures are politically motivated by city officials to justify the curfew laws or to claim success in fighting crime before elections. They call for more studies to be conducted to determine the true impact of curfews.

In one such study, "An Analysis of Curfew Enforcement and Juvenile Crime in California" (*Western Crimi-*

nology Review, 1999), Mike Males and Dan Macallair concluded that there was "no support for the proposition that stricter curfew enforcement reduces youth crime or risk of violent fatality.... Curfew enforcement generally has no discernible effect on youth crime." The authors added: "In those few instances where a significant effect is identified, it is more likely to be positive (that is, greater curfew enforcement is associated with higher rates of juvenile crime) than negative."

CURFEWS GO TO COURT. In 1994 the U.S. Supreme Court let stand a lower court ruling, *Qutb v. Bartlett* (F.3rd 488, 62 LW 2343, Rev. 1994), that deemed a curfew law was constitutional in Dallas, Texas. In 2003 the Washington State Supreme Court struck down the city of Sumner's curfew law (*Walsh v. City of Sumner* [No. 71451-7]). The court ruled that Sumner's curfew ordinance, which makes it unlawful for juveniles to "remain" in a public place during certain hours, is unconstitutionally vague because "it does not provide 'ascertainable standards for locating the line between innocent and unlawful behavior.'" The court noted that "it may be difficult for a city to draft a curfew ordinance that is not unconstitutionally vague" because "curfew ordinances attempt to make activities that are normally considered innocent, unlawful, i.e., walking, driving, going to the store."

Record-keeping

In an effort to reduce gang activities, some law enforcement jurisdictions maintain detailed files on youth offenders. As noted in the 2001 National Youth Gang Survey, 80 percent of jurisdictions reporting gang problems noted that they kept intelligence records on individuals associated with gangs. Many (72 percent) record the data in computer databases.

School Security Measures

To prevent violence, many schools have added a variety of security features. Such security measures include, but are not limited to, metal detectors to check for weapons possession; security guards to man the hallways and entrances in case fights or violence erupt; other school staff monitoring the hallways; a visitor check-in area so school officials know who visits the school; locker searches for drugs and weapons; and locked doors during schooltime to keep potential violent offenders out.

In its report "Youth Gangs in Schools" (James C. Howell and James P. Lynch, *Juvenile Justice Bulletin,* U.S. Department of Justice, Office of Justice Programs, Office of Juvenile Justice and Delinquency Prevention, August 2000), the OJJDP presented findings comparing the presence of gang members at school to the number of security devices employed at schools. Students were asked about each of these aspects at school. As the number of security measures noted by students increased, the percentage of students acknowledging gangs increased. At schools where no security measures were noted by the students, only 13 percent of the students reported the presence of gangs. This increased to 38 percent of students reporting gangs at school when three security measures were in place. Sixty-three percent of those observing six security devices also indicated gangs were present.

IMPORTANT NAMES AND ADDRESSES

Administration for Children and Families
U.S. Department of Health and Human Services
370 L'Enfant Promenade SW
Washington, DC 20447
(202) 619-0257
Toll-free: (877) 696-6775
E-mail: hhsmail@os.dhhs.gov
URL: http://www.acf.dhhs.gov/

Amnesty International U.S.A.
National Office
322 Eighth Ave.
New York, NY 10001
(212) 807-8400
FAX: (212) 627-1451
E-mail: admin-us@aiusa.org
URL: http://www.amnestyusa.org

Anti-Defamation League
823 United Nations Plaza
New York, NY 10017
(212) 885-7700
FAX (212) 867-0779
E-mail: webmaster@adl.org
URL: http://www.adl.org

Bureau of Alcohol, Tobacco, Firearms and Explosives
650 Massachusetts Ave. NW, Rm. 8290
Washington, DC 20226
(202) 927-7970
E-mail: ATFMail@atf.gov
URL: http://www.atf.gov/

Bureau of Justice Statistics
U.S. Department of Justice
810 Seventh St. NW
Washington, DC 20531
(202) 307-0765
Toll-free: (800) 732-3277
E-mail: askbjs@ojp.usdoj.gov
URL: http://www.ojp.usdoj.gov/bjs

Centers for Disease Control and Prevention
1600 Clifton Rd.
Atlanta, GA 30333
(404) 639-3311
Toll-free: (800) 311-3435
E-mail: http://www.cdc.gov/netinfo.htm
URL: http://www.cdc.gov

Children's Defense Fund
25 E St. NW
Washington, DC 20001
(202) 628-8787
E-mail: cdfinfo@childrensdefense.org
URL: http://www.childrensdefense.org

Child Trends, Inc.
4301 Connecticut Ave. NW, Suite 100
Washington, DC 20008
(202) 572-6000
FAX: (202) 362-5533
E-mail: webmaster@childtrends.org
URL: http://www.childtrends.org

Executive Office of the President
Office of National Drug Control Policy (ONDCP)
P.O. Box 6000
Rockville, MD 20849-6000
(800) 666-3332
FAX: (301) 519-5212
E-mail: ondcp@ncjrs.org
URL: http://www.whitehousedrugpolicy.gov/

Federal Bureau of Investigation
J. Edgar Hoover Building
935 Pennsylvania Ave. NW
Washington, DC 20535-0001
(202) 324-3000
URL: http://www.fbi.gov

Federal Bureau of Prisons
Office of Public Affairs
320 First St. NW
Washington, DC 20534

(202) 307-3198
E-mail: webmaster@bop.gov
URL: http://www.bop.gov

Federal Interagency Forum on Child and Family Statistics
E-mail: childstats@ed.gov
URL: http://www.childstats.gov/
Gallup Organization
901 F St. NW
Washington, DC 20004
(202) 715-3030
FAX: (202) 715-3041
Toll-free: (888) 274-5447
E-mail: GallupHelp@gallup.com
URL: http://www.gallup.com

National Center for Victims of Crime
2000 M St. NW
Suite 480
Washington, DC 20036-3398
(202) 467-8700
FAX: (202) 467-8701
Toll-free: (800) 394-2255
URL: http://www.ncvc.org

National Crime Prevention Council
1000 Connecticut Ave., NW, 13th Fl.
Washington, DC 20036
(202) 466-6272
FAX (202) 296-1356
E-mail: webmaster@ncpc.org
URL: http://www.ncpc.org

National Institute of Justice
810 7th St. NW
Washington, DC 20531
(202) 307-2942
FAX (202) 307-6394
URL: http://www.ojp.usdoj.gov/nij

National Institute on Drug Abuse
National Institutes of Health (NIH)
6001 Executive Blvd., Rm. 5213
Bethesda MD 20892-9561

(301) 443-1124
E-mail: Information@lists.nida.nih.gov
URL: http://www.nida.nih.gov/

National Youth Gang Center
P.O. Box 12729
Tallahassee, FL 32317
(850) 385-0600
FAX: (850) 386-5356
E-mail: nygc@iir.com
URL: http://www.iir.com/nygc

Office for Victims of Crime
U.S. Department of Justice
810 7th St. NW, 8th Floor
Washington, DC 20531
(202) 307-5983
FAX (202) 514-6383
E-mail: askovc@ojp.usdoj.gov
URL: http://www.ojp.usdoj.gov/ovc

Office of Juvenile Justice and
Delinquency Prevention
810 7th St. NW
Washington, DC 20531

(202) 307-5911
FAX (202) 307-2093
Juvenile Justice Clearinghouse (800) 851-3420
E-mail: askjj@ncjrs.org
URL: http://www.ojjdp.ncjrs.org

Office of the U.S. Surgeon General
U.S. Department of Health and
Human Services
5600 Fishers Ln., Rm. 18-66
Rockville MD 20857
URL: http://www.surgeongeneral.gov/
sgoffice.htm

Southern Poverty Law Center
400 Washington Ave.
Montgomery, AL 36104
(334) 956-8200
URL: http://www.splcenter.org

United Nations
Department of Economic and
Social Affairs
United Nations Plaza

New York NY 10017
E-mail: esa@un.org
URL: http://www.un.org/esa/

U.S. Census Bureau
Washington, DC 20233
(301) 457-4608
FAX: (301) 457-4714
E-mail: webmaster@census.gov
URL: http://www.census.gov

U.S. Department of Education
Institute of Education Sciences
National Center for Education Statistics
1990 K St. NW
Washington, DC 20006
(202) 502-7300
E-mail: NCESWebMaster@ed.gov
URL: http://www.nces.ed.gov

U.S. Department of Justice
950 Pennsylvania Ave. NW
Washington, DC 20530-0001
E-mail: askdoj@usdoj.gov
URL: http://www.usdoj.gov

RESOURCES

The Office of Juvenile Justice and Delinquency Prevention (OJJDP) of the U.S. Department of Justice (Washington, D.C.) is a valuable resource of information about youth violence, crime, and gangs in the United States. Various sources of the OJJDP provided important data that helped in the compilation of this book. These include: *2000 Survey of Youth Gangs in Indian Country* (June 2002); "Addressing the Problem of Juvenile Bullying," *OJJDP Fact Sheet* (June 2001); "Census of Juveniles in Residential Placement" (CJRP, 1999); "Detention in Delinquency Cases, 1989–1998," *OJJDP Fact Sheet* (January 2002); "Early Precursors of Gang Membership: A Study of Seattle Youth," *Juvenile Justice Bulletin* (December 2001); "Female Gangs: A Focus on Research," *Juvenile Justice Bulletin* (March 2001); "Hybrid and Other Modern Gangs," *Juvenile Justice Bulletin* (December 2001); "Implementing the OJJDP Comprehensive Gang Model," *OJJDP Fact Sheet* (July 1999); "Juvenile Arrests 2000," *Juvenile Justice Bulletin* (November 2002); *Juvenile Court Statistics 1999: Celebrating 100 Years of the Juvenile Court, 1988–1999* (July 2003); "Juvenile Justice: A Century of Change," *1999 National Report Series*; *Juvenile Offenders and Victims: 1999 National Report* (September 1999); "Juvenile Offenders in Residential Placement: 1997–1999, *OJJDP Fact Sheet* (March 2002); "Juvenile Residential Facility Census, 2000: Selected Findings" *OJJDP Bulletin* (December 2002); "Mentoring Makes a Difference," *OJJDP News @ a Glance* (November/December 2003); *National Youth Gang Survey* (1998, 1999, 2000, 2001, 2002); "National Youth Gang Survey Trends From 1996 to 2000," *OJJDP Fact Sheet* (February 2002); "Preventing Adolescent Gang Involvement" *Juvenile Justice Bulletin* (September 2000); "Short- and Long-Term Consequences of Adolescent Victimization," *Youth Violence Research Bulletin* (February 2002); "Youth Gangs," *OJJDP Fact Sheet* (December 1997); "Youth Gangs in Schools," *Juvenile Justice Bulletin* (August 2000); and *Youth Gang Programs and Strategies* (August 2000).

Other offices in the U.S. Justice Department—including the Bureau of Justice Assistance, the Bureau of Justice Statistics, the National Institute of Justice, the Office of Justice Programs, and the Office for Victims of Crime—routinely issue publications pertaining to youth crime and punishment. Publications from these divisions consulted for this book were: *Capital Punishment, 2002* (November 2003); *Criminal Victimization, 2002* (August 2003); "'Designing Out' Gang Homicides and Street Assaults," *Research in Brief* (November 1998); *Hate Crimes Reported in NIBRS, 1997–1999* (September 2001); *High School Youths, Weapons, and Violence: A National Survey* (1998); *Homicide Trends in the United States* (2001); *Juveniles in Adult Prisons and Jails: A National Assessment* (October 2000); *National Crime Victimization Survey* (NCVS, multiple years); *National Crime Victimization Survey, 1995–2000: Violent Victimization of College Students* (December 2003); *National Victim Assistance Academy Textbook* (June 2002); *Prison and Jail Inmates at Midyear, 2002* (2003); and *Prisoners in 2002* (July 2003).

Other publications that were valuable in the preparation of this book were created jointly by the U.S. Department of Education and the U.S. Department of Justice: *Indicators of School Crime and Safety* (2003); *Investigating Hate Crimes on the Internet*; and *Safeguarding Our Children: An Action Guide* (2000). The Department of Education also issued the following helpful reports: *Are America's Schools Safe? Students Speak Out: 1999 School Crime Supplement* (2002); *Coming of Age in the 1990s: The Eighth-Grade Class of 1988 12 years later* (2002); *The Condition of Education in Brief* (2003); *Digest of Education Statistics* (2002); *Dropout Rates in the United States* (various years); *Report on State/Territory Implementation of the Gun-Free Schools Act: School Year 1999–2000*; *Schools and Staffing Survey* (SASS; various years); and *School Survey on Crime and Safety* (SSOCS; various years). In addition, the Georgia Department of ducation Web site provided insight into the application of the No Child Left Behind Act in schools.

The Federal Bureau of Investigation (FBI) produces a wide range of reports that detail various aspects of crime. Of particular help were: *Hate Crime Statistics, 1990: A Resource Book*; *Hate Crime Statistics, 2002*; *The School Shooter: A Threat Assessment Perspective* (1999); the Uniform Crime Reports (UCR; multiple years); and *Crime in the United States 2002: Uniform Crime Reports* (2003). Reports issued by the Centers for Disease Control and Prevention (CDC) provided information on a variety of subjects, including youth risk behaviors and school violence. CDC reports included: *Federal Activities Addressing Violence in Schools* (April 2000); *HIV/AIDS Surveillance Report* (vol. 13, no. 2, 2001); *Morbidity and Mortality Weekly Report: Youth Risk Behavior Surveillance, United States, 2001* (June 28, 2002); *National Vital Statistics Reports* (September 18, 2003; November 7, 2003; and December 17, 2003); *Sexually Transmitted Disease Surveillance, 2002* (September 2003); and *Youth Risk Behavior Surveillance—United States, 1999* (June 28, 2002). Two U.S. Census Bureau reports provided general statistics on the number of children in the United States and their living arrangements: *Fertility of American Women: June 2002* (October 2003) and *Grandparents Living with Grandchildren: 2001* (October 2003).

Other reports provided by government entities or sponsored by the government that were consulted include the U.S. Department of Health and Human Services' *2000 National Household Survey on Drug Abuse* (2001) and *Child Maltreatment 2001* (2003); the Executive Office of the President's *Drug Policy Information Clearinghouse Fact Sheet*; the U.S. Department of Agriculture's *Expenditures on Children by Families, 2002*; and the National Institute on Drug Abuse's *Monitoring the Future* studies (various years). Additional studies included the Federal Interagency Forum on Child and Family Statistics' *America's Children: Key National Indicators of Well-Being 2003* and its ChildStats database; the Jefferson County Sheriff's Department's *The Columbine High School Shootings: Jefferson County Sheriff Department's Investigation Report* (May 15, 2000); the U.S. Bureau of Alcohol, Tobacco, Firearms and Explosives' *Crime Gun Trace Reports 2000 National Report* (July 2002) and the National Church Arson Task Force findings (various years); and the U.S. Surgeon General's *Youth Violence: A Report of the Surgeon General* (2001).

Alfred University published two reports of particular interest to youth crime and violence in schools, including one on deadly violence and another on hazing. The hazing report, one of the only such studies in existence, is called *Initiation Rites in American High Schools: A National Survey* (2000). The university's school violence report, issued in 2001, is titled *Lethal Violence in Schools: A*

National Study. Also of help were reports by the National Association of School Resource Officers (*School Safety Threats Persist, Funding Decreasing: NASRO 2003 National School-Based Law Enforcement Study*, August 19, 2003); the Southern Poverty Law Center (*Discounting Hate*, available via the SPLC's Web site, accessed February 2004); and Victor L. Streib (*The Juvenile Death Penalty Today: Death Sentences and Executions for Juvenile Crimes, January 1, 1973–March 15, 2004*, also available online, accessed in March 2004).

Other reports consulted include Amnesty International's *Betraying the Young: Human Rights Violations Against Children in the US Justice System* (available online, accessed February 2004); the Carnegie Council on Adolescent Development's *Great Transitions: Preparing Adolescents for a New Century* (1995); Child Trends' *CTS Facts at a Glance* (2002); the Children's Defense Fund's *The State of Children in America's Union: A 2002 Action Guide to Leave No Children Behind* (2002); the Hamilton Fish Institute's "School-Based Surveillance of Violence, Injury, and Disciplinary Actions" (January 2001); the Justice Policy Institute's *School House Hype: School Shootings and the Real Risks Kids Face in America* (1998); and the Koch Crime Institute's *Juvenile Boot Camps: Cost and Effectiveness vs. Residential Facilities* (1998).

Additional sources used in the compilation of this book include: the "National Longitudinal Study of Adolescent Health" and "Protecting Adolescents from Harm," *Journal of the American Medical Association* (vol. 278, no. 10, September 10, 1997); "The Transfer of Juveniles to Criminal Court: Does It Make a Difference?," *Crime and Delinquency* (April 1996); "Prevalence of Youth Access to Alcohol or a Gun in the Home," *Injury Prevention* (2002); "Kids and Guns: From Playgrounds to Battlegrounds," *Juvenile Justice* (vol. 3, no. 2, September 1997); and "An Analysis of Curfew Enforcement and Juvenile Crime in California," *Western Criminology Review* (1999).

The United Nations' Department of Economic and Social Affairs also provided statistics pertaining to youth as did the Evan B. Donaldson Adoption Institute's *Adoption by Lesbians and Gays: A National Survey of Adoption Agency Policies, Practices, and Attitudes* (October 29, 2003) and *Youth on Trial: A Developmental Perspective of Juvenile Justice* (2000).

Other Web sites consulted include: American Medical Association (AMA); American School Board Journal (ASBJ); Anti-Defamation League (ADL); Big Brothers Big Sisters (BBBS); Boys & Girls Clubs of America (BGCA); Center on Juvenile and Criminal Justice; Center for the Study and Prevention of Violence; Centre for Children and Families in the Justice System; Chicago Area Project (CAP); Crimes Against Children Research Center; Gang Resistance Education and Training (GREAT); Guardian

Angels; Institute for Intergovernmental Research; Jobs For a Future (JFF); Mayor's Office of the City of Houston; Juvenile Mentoring Program (JUMP); Mothers Against School Hazing (MASH); National Association of School Resource Officers (NASRO); National Center for Neighborhood Enterprise (NCNE); National Clearinghouse on Child Abuse and Neglect Information; National Crime Prevention Council (NCPC); National Institute of Child Health & Human Development (NICHD); National Mentoring Center (NMC); National Youth Gang Center (NYGC); National Youth Violence Prevention Campaign; No Child Left Behind; NYU Child Study Center; Operation Respect: Don't Laugh at Me; PBS' *Frontline*; Police Athletic League (PAL); Southern California Center of Excellence on Youth Violence Prevention; Southern Poverty Law Center (SPLC); Students Against Violence Everywhere (SAVE); Violence Policy Center; www.bowlingforcolumbine.com; www.bullyonline.org; www.keystosaferschools.com; www.lapdonline.org; and www.matthewsplace.com. Several opinion polls on youth violence and crime topics were also helpful, particularly those prepared by the Gallup Organization, the *New York Times*/CBS News, and Public Agenda Online.

INDEX

various criteria, from Youth Risk
Criteria Survey, 2001, 38*t*
students in grades 9–12 who reported
using alcohol during the previous 30
days, by sex, selected years 1999 and
2001, 34 (*f*2.4)
Alexander, Duane, 140
Alfred University
*Initiation Rites in American High
Schools: A National Survey*, 141
*Lethal Violence in Schools: A National
Study*, 85, 137
Allen, Nancy, 147
Alliance of Concerned Men, 151
Alternative correctional facilities, 126
American Association of Single People, 13
American Bar Association, 13
American Civil Liberties Union (ACLU), 13
American Indians and Alaska Natives
AIDS cases, by demographic
characteristics, reported through
December 2001, 42*t*
arrest statistics, 114
arrests by race, 2002, 115*t*–116*t*
birthrates, 10, 11
Boys and Girls Clubs of America and,
150
child abuse/neglect, 18
child care and, 14, 15*t*
child population, 10, 10 (*t*2.3)
drugs at school and, 75
foster care and, 14
gang-related victimization, 104
hate crimes and, 130
hate crimes, race of known offenders,
2002, 131*t*
homicide rates, 47
incarceration of juveniles, 119
juveniles in residential placement, 126
physical fights and, 69
sniper-attack murder offenders by age,
sex, and race, 1982–2001, 60*t*
sniper-attack murder victims by age, sex,
and race, 1982–2001, 59 (*t*3.14)
students in grades 9–12 who reported
drugs were made available to them on
school property during the previous 12
months, by race/ethnicity, 1999 and
2001, 34 (*f*2.3)
suicide and, 53
youth gang members, 99
youth violence of, 78
Amnesty International, 122
"An Analysis of Curfew Enforcement and
Juvenile Crime in California" (Males and
Macallair), 157
Anti-bullying programs, 140–141
Anti-Defamation League (ADL), 128
Arabs, hate crimes against, 136–137
*Are America's Schools Safe? Students Speak
Out: 1999 School Crime Supplement*
(Addington, Ruddy, Miller, and DeVoe)
bullying, 139
gangs in schools, 100–101
percentage of students ages 12 through
18 who reported experiencing criminal
victimization at school, by student

reports of knowing or seeing another
student with a gun at school, 1999, 81*f*
student attitudes about school violence,
83–84
victimizations and weapons, 78
Arrest trends, juvenile
among specific age groups, 110–112
arrests in geographic locations, 114–115
arrests of persons under 15, 18, 21, and
25 years of age, 2002, 111*t*
in cities, suburbs, and rural areas,
115–117
by gender, 112–114
prosecuting minors as adults and, 117
by race, 2002, 115*t*–116*t*
by race/ethnicity, 114
by sex, ten-year, 1993–2002, 113*t*
statistics, 109–110
ten-year, 1993–2002, 110*t*
Arrests
arson, 111, 133, 135*f*
death penalty, age at time of arrest for
capital offense and age of prisoners
under sentence of death at yearend
2002, 145 (*t*7.10)
weapons law violations, 142
weapons offenses, 144
of youths, percent of arrests, 1
Arson
as hate crime, 133, 135
juvenile arrests for, 111
subjects arrested for church arsons and
bombings by age and gender, January 1,
1995-August 15, 2000, 135*f*
violence committed by juveniles and
youths against houses of worship,
selected events, 1996–1998, 136*t*
Ashcroft, John, 145
Asian and Pacific Islander Americans
AIDS cases, by demographic
characteristics, reported through
December 2001, 42*t*
arrest statistics, 114
arrests by race, 2002, 115*t*–116*t*
birthrates, 10, 11
child abuse/neglect, 18
child care and, 14, 15*t*
child population, 10, 10 (*t*2.3)
drugs at school and, 75
foster care and, 14
hate crimes and, 130
hate crimes, race of known offenders,
2002, 131*t*
homicide rates, 47
incarceration of juveniles, 119
juveniles in residential placement, 126
physical fights and, 69
sniper-attack murder offenders by age,
sex, and race, 1982–2001, 60*t*
sniper-attack murder victims by age, sex,
and race, 1982–2001, 59 (*t*3.14)
students in grades 9–12 who reported
drugs were made available to them on
school property during the previous 12
months, by race/ethnicity, 1999 and
2001, 34 (*f*2.3)
suicide and, 53

youth gang members, 99
youth gangs, 98
At-risk youth, 155
ATF. *See* Bureau of Alcohol, Tobacco,
Firearms, and Explosives
Atkins v. Virginia, 147
Attitudes, school violence, 83–84

B

Babcock, Lewis, 81
"Baby boom"
birthrate during, 9
school enrollment and, 19
Bachman, Jerald G., 29
Badlands (film), 3
Bank robberies
bank robberies by age and gender of
offender, 1996–2000, 59 (*t*3.13)
statistics, 58
Bartlett, Qutb v., 157
Batzig, Edward, Jr., 5–6
BBBS (Big Brothers Big Sisters) program,
154
Beatles, 6
Beatty, David, 55
Beck, Allen J., 119–120
Beds, 124
Bell, Mary Flora, 6
*Betraying the Young: Human Rights
Violations Against Children in the US
Justice System* (Amnesty International),
122
BGCA (Boys and Girls Clubs of America),
150
Bi-Partisan Working Group on Youth
Violence of the 106th Congress, 78
Bias
hate crime reporting and, 128
hate crimes based on, 129
incidents, offenses, victims, and known
offenders by bias motivation, 2002, 130
(*t*7.3)
Big Brothers Big Sisters (BBBS) program,
154
"Billy the Kid" (a.k.a William H. Bonney
Jr.), 2
Birthrates
births to unmarried women, selected
years, 1980–2001, 11*t*
child population and, 9
of children, 10–11
marital and nonmarital birth rates (births
per 1,000 females), selected years
1960–2000, 40 (*t*2.23)
school enrollment and, 19
statistics, 10–11
teen birth rate (births per 1,000 females)
selected years, 1940–2001, 40 (*t*2.22)
teen birth rate by race/ethnicity
1990–2001, 41*f*
of teenagers, 32
unmarried parents, 11–12
Births
to unmarried parents, 11–12
to unmarried women, selected years,
1980–2001, 11*t*
BJS. *See* Bureau of Justice Statistics

Black/African Americans
aggravated assault rates among, 57
AIDS cases, by demographic characteristics, reported through December 2001, 42t
arrest statistics, 114
arrests by race, 2002, 115t–116t
arsons at churches and, 133, 135
birthrates, 10, 11
bullying and, 139
child abuse/neglect, 18
child care and, 14, 15t
child population, 10, 10 (t2.3)
child population, persons in selected age groups as a percentage of the total population, and children under age 18 as a percentage of the dependent population, selected years 1950–2001 and projected 2002–20, 10(t2.2)
death rates for firearm injuries, 50
detached youth, 27
drugs/alcohol/tobacco and, 30–31
drugs at school and, 75
fear/avoidance of school, 73–74
foster care and, 14
hate at school and, 131
hate crimes against, 130
hate crimes, race of known offenders, 2002, 131t
high school dropout rates, 23
high school dropouts among persons 16 to 24 years old, percent of, by sex and race/ethnicity, April 1960 to October 2001, 28t
homicide rates, 46, 47
incarceration of juveniles, 119
juveniles in residential placement, 126
living arrangements for children, 12, 12t
median earnings (in current dollars) for persons 25 years old and over, by selected characteristics, 2000, 30t
murder offenders by age, sex, and race, 2002, 50t
murder statistics, 49
murder victims, by age, sex, and race, 2002, 51 (t3.5)
murderers, number of, 45
percentage of high school students who drank alcohol and used marijuana, by various criteria, from Youth Risk Criteria Survey, 2001, 38t
percentage of high school students who engaged in sexual behaviors, by sex, race/ethnicity, and grade, from Youth Risk Behavior Survey, 2001, 40 (t2.21)
percentage of high school students who felt too unsafe to go to school, by sex, race/ethnicity, and grade, 2001, 76t
percentage of high school students who used tobacco by sex, race/ethnicity, and grade, from Youth Risk Behavior Survey, 2001, 39t
physical fights and, 69
poverty, percent of related children under age 18 living below selected poverty levels by age, family structure, race,

and Hispanic origin selected years 1980–2001, 18t
rape, 54–55, 70
rates of violent crime and personal theft, by gender, age, race and Hispanic origin, 2002, 55t
robbery and, 57
school desegregation, 6
school enrollment, percent of population 3–34 years old enrolled in school, by race/ethnicity, sex, and age, October 1980-October 2001, 20t–21t
sentenced prisoners under state or federal jurisdiction per 100,000 residents, by gender, race, Hispanic origin, and age, 2002, 121 (t6.9), 121 (t6.10)
sentenced youth under state or federal jurisdiction, 120–121
simple assaults and, 57
sniper-attack murder offenders by age, sex, and race, 1982–2001, 60t
sniper-attack murder victims by age, sex, and race, 1982–2001, 59 (t3.14)
students in grades 9–12 who reported drugs were made available to them on school property during the previous 12 months, by race/ethnicity, 1999 and 2001, 34 (f2.3)
suicide and, 53
teachers, crimes against, 72
teen pregnancy rates, 32
unemployment rate by demographic characteristics, 1999, 2000, and 2001, 29t
unmarried parents, 11
victimization rates for persons age 12 and over, by gender and age of victims and type of crime, 2002, 56 (t3.11)
youth gangs, 97, 99
Blackmun, Harry, death penalty cases, 146, 147, 148
Bloods gangs, 96, 98
"bombing" (graffiti), 96
Bombings
houses of worship, 135
juvenile bombing incidents, 1992–1996, 61 (t3.17)
statistics, 59–60
subjects arrested for church arsons and bombings by age and gender, January 1, 1995-August 15, 2000, 135f
Bonney, William H., Jr. (a.k.a "Billy the Kid"), 2
The Boomtown Rats, 4
Boot camps, 126
Bosket, William, 3
"The Boston Boy-fiend" (a.k.a Jesse Pomeroy), 2
Bowling for Columbine (documentary), 144
Boyle, Greg S.J., 150–151
Boys and Girls Clubs of America (BGCA), 150
Brennan, William J., 146, 147
Breyer, Stephen, 147
Bridges, Ruby, 6
Brodzinsky, David M., 13
Brown, Randy, 80

Bully OnLine Web site, 138
Bullying/bullies
definition/characteristics of, 137–138
effects of bullying/being bullied, 138
percentage of students ages 12–18 who reported being bullied at school, by student reports of bringing any weapon to school, 1999, 140f
percentage of students ages 12–18 who reported being bullied at school during the previous 6 months, by selected student characteristics, 1999 and 2001, 139t
prevention programs, 140–141
rate of, 85
school surveys, 138–140
Burch, Jim, 155–156
Bureau of Alcohol, Tobacco, Firearms, and Explosives (ATF)
arson investigation by, 135
GREAT program and, 151
gun tracing program, 142–144
Bureau of Justice Statistics (BJS)
Correctional Surveys, 121–122
gang definition of, 94
hate crime definition of, 128
homicide report of, 46
National Crime Victimization Survey by, 43–44
Burger, Warren, 146
Burglary
by gangs, 104
statistics, 58
Bush, George W., 86

C

California
gang-related homicides in Los Angeles, 103
juveniles in residential placement, 124
youth gangs in, 93
See also Los Angeles (CA)
CAP (Chicago Area Project), 149–150
Carneal, Michael, 7
Carnegie Council on Adolescent Development, 31
CDC. *See* Centers for Disease Control and Prevention
CDF (Children's Defense Fund), 16
Census 2000, 13
Center on Juvenile and Criminal Justice, 122
Centers for Disease Control and Prevention (CDC)
birthrates, 10–11
STDs, 32, 34
unmarried parents, 11–12
Youth Risk Behavior Surveillance System, 27
Youth Risk Behavior Surveillance-United States, 1999, 29–30
Cerio, Jay D., 85, 137
Chicago (IL)
gang loitering in, 105
gang-related homicides in, 103
youth gangs in, 93
Chicago Area Project (CAP), 149–150
Chicago v. Morales, 105

Fertility of American Women: June 2002
(Downs), 15
Firearms
firearm-related homicide/suicide, 53
firearm-related homicides and suicide
rates per 100,000 children under age 15
in 16 industrialized countries, selected
years, 1990–95, 54*f*
gang members and, 105
gun issues, 142–144
murders with, 50–51
rates of homicide, suicide, and firearm-
related death among children 0–14
years old: United States and 25 other
industrialized countries, 1996, 53*t*
at school, 75–78
Fishtown murder, 5–6
Florida
death penalty in, 145
gangs in, 104–105
Foster care, 14
Foster parents, 14
Franklin, Linda, 145
Franks, Bobby, 2–3
Fugate, Caril Ann, 3
Furman, Mark, 4

G

Gang Congregation Ordinance, 105
Gang Prevention/Intervention through
Targeted Outreach program, 150
Gang Resistance Education and Training
(GREAT), 151–152
Gang summits, 153
Gangs. *See* Youth gangs
Garrett, Pat, 2
Gaughan, Edward, 85, 137
Gay parents, 13
Gays. *See* Homosexuals
GDOE (Georgia Department of Education),
87–88
GED (General Educational Development)
diplomas, 23
Gender
AIDS cases, by demographic
characteristics, reported through
December 2001, 42*t*
arrest trends by sex, ten-year, 1993–2002,
113*t*
arrests by, 112–114
arson arrests and, 133
bank robberies by age and gender of
offender, 1996–2000, 59 (*t*3.13)
bully characteristics, 137
bullying and, 139
causes of death and, 45–46
fear/avoidance of school, 73
hate at school and, 131
homicide rates and, 46–47
inmates under age 18 held in state and
federal prisons, number of, by gender,
1990, 1995, and 1999–2002, 120 (*t*6.6)
juvenile detention cases and, 123
of juveniles in residential placement,
125–126

murder offenders by age, sex, and race,
2002, 50*t*
murder statistics by, 48–49
murder victims, by age, sex, and race,
2002, 51 (*t*3.5)
nonfatal crimes at school and, 68
percent of high school dropouts among
persons 16 to 24 years old, by sex and
race/ethnicity, April 1960 to October
2001, 28*t*
percent of population 3–34 years old
enrolled in school, by race/ethnicity,
sex, and age, October 1980-October
2001, 20*t*–21*t*
percentage of high school students who
engaged in sexual behaviors, by sex,
race/ethnicity, and grade, from Youth
Risk Behavior Survey, 2001, 40 (*t*2.21)
percentage of high school students who
felt too unsafe to go to school, by sex,
race/ethnicity, and grade, 2001, 76*t*
rates of violent crime and personal theft,
by gender, age, race and Hispanic
origin, 2002, 55*t*
sentenced prisoners, number of, under
state or federal jurisdiction by gender,
race, Hispanic origin, and age, 2002,
121 (*t*6.9)
sentenced prisoners, number of, under
state or federal jurisdiction per 100,000
residents, by gender, race, Hispanic
origin, and age, 2002, 121 (*t*6.10)
sentenced youth under state or federal
jurisdiction, 120–121
sniper-attack murder offenders by age,
sex, and race, 1982–2001, 60*t*
sniper-attack murder victims by age, sex,
and race, 1982–2001, 59 (*t*3.14)
sniper attacks and, 58–59
students in grades 9–12 who reported
using alcohol during the previous 30
days, by sex, selected years 1993–2001,
34 (*f*2.4)
subjects arrested for church arsons and
bombings by age and gender, January 1,
1995-August 15, 2000, 135*f*
suicide and, 53
unemployment rate by demographic
characteristics, 1999, 2000, and 2001, 29*t*
victimization rates for persons age 12 and
over, by gender and age of victims and
type of crime, 2002, 56 (*t*3.10)
weapons at school and, 76
of youth gang members, 98, 99–100
General Educational Development (GED)
diplomas, 23
Geographic locations, arrests in, 114–115
Georgia Department of Education (GDOE),
87–88
Gergen, David, 3
Ginsburg, Ruth Bader, 147
Girls, violence by, 4–6
See also Females
Gist, Nancy E., 108
Gonorrhea
cases of, 34
risk of, 32

Grade
drug use and, 74
hate at school and, 131
percentage of high school students who
felt too unsafe to go to school, by sex,
race/ethnicity, and grade, 2001, 76*t*
weapons at school and, 76
See also Age
Graduation, high school
graduates compared with population 17
years of age, by sex and control of
school, 1869–70 to 2001–02, 26*t*–27*t*
statistics, 22–23
Graffiti
gang, 95–96
hate crimes, percentage of students ages
12–18 who reported being targets of
hate-related words or who saw hate-
related graffiti at school during the
previous 6 months, by student and
school characteristics, 2001, 134*f*
hate-related, at school, 131
removal of, 151
Grandparents, 13
Grandparents Living with Grandchildren
(Centers for Disease Control and
Prevention), 13
GREAT (Gang Resistance Education and
Training), 151–152
*Great Transitions: Preparing Adolescents
for a New Century* (Carnegie Council on
Adolescent Development), 31
Greenbaum, Stuart, 142
Grisso, Thomas, 117
Grunbaum, Jo Anne, 29
Guardian Angels, 154
Gun-Free Schools Act of 1994, 75
Guns
access to, 142
age of crime gun possessors, 2000, 143*f*
ATF tracing program, 142–144
homicides and, 144
suicides and, 142
weapons offenses/offenders, 144
See also Firearms

H

Hacking. *See* Computer hacking
Hall, Daryl, 151
Hand signs, gang, 96
Harris, Eric David, 79–81, 127
Harrison, Paige M., 119–120, 122
*Hate Crime Statistics, 1990: A Resource
Book* (Federal Bureau of Investigation),
128
Hate Crime Statistics, 2002 (Federal Bureau
of Investigation), 128–130
Hate Crime Statistics Act of 1990, 128
Hate crimes
age estimates, 131–132
agency hate crime reporting by state,
2002, 129*t*
church arsons and bombings, subjects
arrested for, by age and gender, January
1, 1995-August 15, 2000, 135*f*
definition of, 128
hate at school, 130–131

HIV (human immunodeficiency virus), 32, 34
Holtmeyer, Jessica, 5
Homeboy Industries, 151
Homicide
    as cause of death, 45–46
    death penalty and, 144–148
    firearm-related homicide and suicide rates per 100,000 children under age 15 in 16 industrialized countries, selected years, 1990–95, 54f
    firearm-related, rise in, 142
    gang homicides, 103–104
    gun-related juvenile homicides, 144
    homicide rates, by age, 1976–2000, 47 (f3.5)
    homicides, suicides of youth ages 5–19 at school and away from school, number of, 1999–2000, 68f
    juvenile homicide offenders' victims, by age, 1980–97, 45 (f3.2)
    juvenile homicide trends, 44
    of Matthew Shepard, 127–128
    murder offenders by age, sex, and race, 2002, 50t
    murder victims by age and weapon, 2002, 52t
    murder victims by age, sex, and race, 2002, 51 (t3.5)
    number of homicides/suicides of youth age 5–19 at school/away from school, 1999–2000, 68f
    offender relationship to juvenile homicide victims, by age and gender of victims, 1980–97, 51 (t3.5.6)
    prosecuting minors as adults and, 117
    rate of homicide, suicide, and firearm-related death among children 0–14 years old: United States and 25 other industrialized countries, 1996, 53t
    rates, 46–47
    rates for juveniles worldwide, 51, 53
    at school, 67
    school-associated, number of, 78
    single- and multiple-offender murders of juveniles, 1980–97, 45 (f3.1)
    Uniform Crime Reports on, 47–50
    victim-offender relationship, 50
    weapons used in, 50–51
    by youth in U.S. history, 2–6
Homosexuals
    hate crimes against, 130
    Matthew Shepard, 127–128
    suicide rate among teenagers, 53
Hoover, Nadine C., 141
Households, living arrangements for children, 12–13, 12t
Houses of worship
    juvenile arsons against, 133, 135
    subjects arrested for church arsons and bombings by age and gender, January 1, 1995-August 15, 2000, 135f
    violence committed by juveniles and youths against houses of worship, selected events, 1996–1998, 136t
Houston Police Department Gang Task Force, 153

Howell, James C., 101, 157–158
Huddleston, Jack, 148
Huff, C. Ronald, 104–105
Human immunodeficiency virus (HIV), 32, 34
"Hybrid and Other Modern Gangs" (Starbuck et al.), 93–94

I

"I Don't Like Mondays" (song by The Boomtown Rats), 4
Illinois
    Chicago Area Project, 149–150
    gang-related homicides in Chicago, 103
    Juvenile Court Act of 1899, 107
    youth gangs in, 93
"Implementing the OJJDP Comprehensive Gang Model" (Burch and Kane), 155–156
Incarceration. See Crime and punishment
Income
    children and family income, 14
    event dropout rates of 15- through 24-years-olds who dropped out of grades 10–12, by family income, October 1972-October 2000, 31f
    gang membership and, 101
    median earnings (in current dollars) for persons 25 years old and over, by selected characteristics, 2000, 30t
    percent of related children under age 18 by family income relative to the poverty line, selected years 1980–2001, 16t
Indicators of School Crime and Safety: 2003 (DeVoe, Peter, Kaufman, Ruddy, Miller, Planty, Snyder, and Rand)
    bullying, 139
    disciplinary action, 85
    fear/avoidance of school, 73–74
    gangs in schools, 100
    hate crimes at school, 130–131
    homicide/suicide, 67
    violent crimes, 68
Individual gang members, 98–100
Infant mortality, 17
Infanticide, 4–5
Information Technology International (ITI), 155
Inhalants, 30
Initiation
    gang, 97
    hazing, 141–142
Initiation Rites in American High Schools: A National Survey (Hoover and Pollard), 141
Institute for Social Research at the University of Michigan, 28–29
Internet Bullying, 140
Intervention programs, 149
    See also Prevention/intervention programs
Islam, hate crimes against, 130, 136–137
ITI (Information Technology International), 155

J

Jails
    average daily population and the number of men, women, and juveniles in local jails, midyear 1995 and 2000–02, 122 (t6.12)
    imprisoning juveniles and adults together, 122
    juveniles in, 121–122
    juveniles in, statistics, 118–119
    juveniles in adult jails, 1983–2000, 122 (t6.11)
    juveniles removed from adult jails, 108
    juveniles under confinement in jails and prisons, 1983–2002, 120f
"Jeremy" (song by Pearl Jam), 4
Jews, hate crimes against, 130
JFF (Jobs for a Future), 150–151
Jobs
    Chicago Area Project, 150
    Jobs for a Future, 150–151
    Violence-Free Zones and, 151
Jobs for a Future (JFF), 150–151
Johnson, Dorsie Lee, Jr., 148
Johnson, Lloyd D., 29
Johnson v. Texas, 148
Journal of the American Medical Association, 28
JPI (Justice Policy Institute), 84–85
JUMP (Juvenile Mentoring Program), 155
Junior Guardian Angels, 154
Jurisdictions
    average number of youth gangs and gang members per jurisdiction, by population size, 1996–98, 93t
    death penalty ages, minimum, by jurisdiction, as of March 15, 2004, 145 (t7.9)
    gang crime in, 104
    percentage of jurisdictions reporting active youth gangs, by division, 1998, 92f
    youth gang statistics, 92–93
Justice. See Juvenile justice
Justice Policy Institute (JPI), 84–85
"Juvenile Arrests in 2000" (Snyder), 109, 112
Juvenile Boot Camps: Cost and Effectiveness vs. Residential Facilities (Zaehringer), 126
Juvenile Court Act of 1899, 107
Juvenile court system
    advent of, 107–108
    changes to, 108
    juvenile jurisdiction, 108–109
The Juvenile Death Penalty Today: Death Sentences and Executions for Juvenile Crimes, January 1, 1973-March 15, 2004 (Streib), 144–145
Juvenile Delinquency Prevention and Control Act of 1968, 108
Juvenile justice, 107–108
"Juvenile Justice: A Century of Change" (Office of Juvenile Justice and Delinquency Prevention), 108
Juvenile Justice and Delinquency Prevention Act, 108
Juvenile Mentoring Program (JUMP), 155
Juvenile Offenders and Victims: 1999 National Report (Snyder and Sickmund)

percentage of high school students who engaged in sexual behaviors, by sex, race/ethnicity, and grade, from Youth Risk Behavior Survey, 2001, 40 (*t*2.21)

percentage of high school students who felt too unsafe to go to school, by sex, race/ethnicity, and grade, 2001, 76*t*

percentage of high school students who used tobacco, by sex, race/ethnicity, and grade, from Youth Risk Behavior Survey, 2001, 39*t*

physical fights and, 69

poverty, percent of related children under age 18 living below selected poverty levels by age, family structure, race, and Hispanic origin selected years 1980–2001, 18*t*

rape and, 54–55, 70

rates of violent crime and personal theft, by gender, age, race and Hispanic origin, 2002, 55*t*

robbery and, 57

school enrollment, percent of population 3–34 years old enrolled in school, by race/ethnicity, sex, and age, October 1980-October 2001, 20*t*–21*t*

sentenced prisoners under state or federal jurisdiction per 100,000 residents, by gender, race, Hispanic origin, and age, 2002, 121 (*t*6.9), 121 (*t*6.10)

sentenced youth under state or federal jurisdiction, 120–121

simple assaults and, 57

sniper-attack murder offenders by age, sex, and race, 1982–2001, 60*t*

sniper-attack murder victims by age, sex, and race, 1982–2001, 59 (*t*3.14)

suicide and, 53

teachers, crimes against, 72

teen birth rate by race/ethnicity 1990–2001, 41*f*

teen pregnancy rates, 32

unemployment rate by demographic characteristics, 1999, 2000, and 2001, 29*t*

unmarried parents, 11–12

victimization rates for persons age 12 and over, by gender and age of victims and type of crime, 2002, 56 (*t*3.11)

weapons at school and, 77

youth gangs and, 93, 94, 99, 100

Rape

juveniles imprisoned with adults and, 122

statistics, 54–55

of students, rates of, 70

Reactive offenders, 132

Recidivism, 126

Record-keeping, 157

Recruitment, gang, 97, 105

Rehabilitation, 107–108

Rehnquist, William H., 146–147, 148

Religion

arson as hate crime, 133, 135, 135*f*, 136*f*

hate crimes based on, 130

incidents, offenses, victims, and known offenders by bias motivation, 2002, 130 (*t*7.3)

Rennison, Callie Marie, 44

Reporting

agency hate crime reporting by state, 2002, 129*t*

hate crimes, 128, 129

hazing incidents, 141–142

percent of victimizations reported to police by types of crime and age of victims, 2002, 57*t*

percentage of public schools with various types of crime and percentage of public schools that reported various types of crime to the police, by school level, 1999–2000, 89*f*

percentage of public schools with various types of crime and percentage of public schools that reported various types of crime to the police, by urbanicity, 1999–2000, 90*f*

rape, 55

violence/crime at school, 88

Residential placement

demographics, 125–126

juvenile offenders in, by offense, 1999, 124*t*

overcrowding, 124

placement status, 124–125

residential facilities by state, juvenile, 2000, 125*t*

statistics, 123–124

Resnick, Michael D., 28

Rights, Miranda, 117

Rights, victims', 108

Robbery

bank robberies by age and gender of offender, 1996–2000, 59 (*t*3.13)

bank robberies, statistics, 58

statistics, 57

Rockwell, Norman, 6

Ross, James G., 29

Ruddy, Sally A.

Are America's Schools Safe? Students Speak Out: 1999 School Crime Supplement, 78, 81*f*

bullying, 139

gangs in schools, 100–101

hate crimes at school, 130–131

Indicators of School Crime and Safety: 2003, 67

student attitudes about school violence, 83–84

Runaway Gang, 5

Rural areas, 116–117

S

Safeguarding Our Children: An Action Guide (Dwyer and Osher), 63–64

Safety corridors, 154

Sanders, Dave, 81

Sanford, Robert Russell, 8

SASS (Schools and Staffing Survey) (U.S. Department of Education), 72

SAVE (Students Against Violence Everywhere), 153–154

Scalia, Antonin, 146–147, 148

Scavenger gangs, 98

School

attendance statistics, 22

avoidance/fear, 73–74

avoidance/fear, percentage of high school students who felt too unsafe to go to school, by sex, race/ethnicity, and grade, 2001, 76*t*

avoidance/fear, percentage of students ages 12–18 who reported being afraid at school or on the way to/from school and away from school during the previous 6 months, by selected student characteristics, 1995, 1999, and 2001, 77 (*t*4.7)

avoidance/fear, percentage of students ages 12–18 who reported that they avoided one or more places in school during the previous 6 months, by selected student characteristics, 1995, 1999, and 2001, 77 (*t*4.8)

bullying at, 137–141

bullying, percentage of students ages 12–18 who reported being bullied at school, by student reports of bringing any weapon to school, 1999, 140*f*

bullying, percentage of students ages 12–18 who reported being bullied at school during the previous 6 months, by selected student characteristics, 1999 and 2001, 139*t*

disciplinary action, percentage of public schools that took a serious disciplinary action for selected offenses, by type of offense, 1999–2000, 87*f*

discipline problems, percentage of public schools that reported selected, by school level: 1999–2000, 86*f*

drug use, past-year illicit drug use among 8th, 10th, and 12th graders, 1991–2002, 78*t*

drugs at, 74–75

gangs in, 100–101

gangs, percentage of students ages 12–18 who reported that street gangs were present at school during the previous 6 months, by urbanicity and school sector, 2001, 101*f*

gangs, percentage of students ages 12–18 who reported the presence of street gangs at school, by selected characteristics and perceptions of conditions at school, 1995 and 1999, 102*t*–103*t*

hate crimes at, 130–131

hate crimes, percentage of students ages 12–18 who reported being targets of hate-related words or who saw hate-related graffiti at school during the previous 6 months, by student and school characteristics, 2001, 133*t*, 134*f*

hazing, 141–142

homicides, suicides of youth ages 5–19 at school and away from school, number of, 1999–2000, 68*f*

No Child Left Behind Act, 86–88

nonfatal crimes against students ages 12–18 occurring at school or on the way to/from school, number of, by type